Medieval Arthurian
Epic and Romance

Medieval Arthurian Epic and Romance

Eight New Translations

Edited by William W. Kibler *and*
R. Barton Palmer

McFarland & Company, Inc., Publishers
Jefferson, North Carolina

LIBRARY OF CONGRESS CATALOGUING-IN-PUBLICATION DATA

Medieval Arthurian Epic and Romance : Eight New
Translations / edited by William W. Kibler and R. Barton Palmer.
p. cm.
Includes bibliographical references and index.

ISBN 978-0-7864-4779-4 (softcover : acid free paper) ∞
ISBN 978-1-4766-1466-3 (ebook)

1. Arthurian romances. 2. English literature—Middle English,
1100–1500. 3. Epic literature, English. 4. Chivalry in literature.
I. Kibler, William W., 1942– editor. II. Palmer, R. Barton, 1946– editor.
PN6071.A84M43 2014   808.8'0351—dc23   2014019605

BRITISH LIBRARY CATALOGUING DATA ARE AVAILABLE

© 2014 William W. Kibler and R. Barton Palmer. All rights reserved

*No part of this book may be reproduced or transmitted in any form
or by any means, electronic or mechanical, including photocopying
or recording, or by any information storage and retrieval system,
without permission in writing from the publisher.*

On the cover: Illuminations from a late medieval manuscript
of the Vulgate Cycle of Arthurian prose romances, Yale 229
(courtesy Beinecke Library, Yale University)

Printed in the United States of America

*McFarland & Company, Inc., Publishers
Box 611, Jefferson, North Carolina 28640
www.mcfarlandpub.com*

Table of Contents

Preface 1

Part I: Arthurian Epic

Geoffrey of Monmouth. *Historia Regum Britanniae* (*History of the Kings of Britain*): A Selection
  Translated by DOUGLAS MCFARLAND 4

Wace. *Roman de Brut* (The Romance of Brutus): A Selection
  Translated by R. BARTON PALMER 30

Lawman. *Brut*: A Selection
  Translated by R. BARTON PALMER 50

Part II: Arthurian Romance

Arthur in Early Wales/*Culhwch and Owen*
  Translated by CRAIG DAVIS 70

Chrétien de Troyes. *Perceval* (The Story of the Grail)
  Translated by WILLIAM W. KIBLER 99

Perlesvaus (Le Haut Livre du Graal): Selections
  Translated by WILLIAM W. KIBLER 194

La Queste del Saint Graal (The Quest of the Holy Grail): Selections
  Translated by R. BARTON PALMER 235

La Mule sans Frein (The Girl with the Mule)
  Translated by WILLIAM W. KIBLER 272

Selected Bibliography 285
About the Contributors 289
Index 291

Preface

The twelfth century French poet Jean Bodel famously observed that the literature of his age, impressive in its vastness, could most properly be divided according to subject. There were, Bodel observed, three great groupings of texts: the so-called "matters" of Britain, France, and Rome, the common currency of poets composing in every medieval language, including Latin. The matter of Rome (meaning of the classical world more generally) treats the legends of such figures as Alexander the Great and Julius Caesar, and its works include as well vernacular versions of Virgil's *Aeneid* and Statius's *Thebaid*. The matter of France found its origins in the legend-centered epic poetry of the early Middle Ages and its principal genre, the *chanson de geste*. Its main characters are the emperor Charlemagne, and other warrior figures associated with the Carolingian era such as Doon de Mayence who enjoyed a popularity that endured long after the end of the Middle Ages, providing themes and narratives for such Renaissance works as Ariosto's *Orlando Furioso*.

Beyond doubt, however, it is the matter of Britain, centered on the legendary, and perhaps marginally historical, figure of King Arthur, that dominates medieval literature. Arthurian story crossed every political and linguistic border, and its popularity continues unabated, as the steady number of well-received recent popular treatments, including films, attests. *Pendragon: Sword of His Father* (2008), for example, re-imagines Arthur as a warrior, chosen by God, whose mission it is to re–Christianize a Roman world overrun by pagan, barbarian hordes. It would be no exaggeration to say that modern understandings of the Middle Ages can hardly exclude the figure of Arthur, the legend of the Round Table more generally, as well as the complex webs of stories featuring his principal knights, including Perceval and Gawain, the adulterous love that binds his best knight, Lancelot, and queen, Guenevere, as well as the tragic tale of the king's death and the subsequent passing of his world.

Essential to the study of medieval literature and the preoccupations of the era, the matter of Britain, however, thus presents quite a challenge to the student of medieval literature, including as it does hundreds of texts, many of considerable length. With a selection of important Arthurian works, some complete, others excerpted, the present volume provides a ready entry to the field, exemplifying the two larger strands of Arthurian story: an epic tradition in which Arthur is the principal character and whose main subject is the building, and then defense, of a considerable empire through constant war against a variety of enemies; and a romance tradition, whose themes are courtly love and spiritual questing, in which Arthur recedes into the background and various knights of the Round Table instead take center stage.

Part I of this volume is devoted to the epic tradition, which was put into definitive shape by Geoffrey of Monmouth, a Welsh cleric who, in the 1130s, wrote in Latin verse the *Historia Regum Britanniae*, a history of the kings of Britain based in part on material of often dubious historical value from earlier writers, but including much of his own fabrication. This pseudo-historical book features a lively, if at times scarcely credible, account of Arthur's reign; it is included here in a lively new translation that emphasizes the epic features of the tale, aspects of style and theme then picked up by Geoffrey's two most important popularizers, who are also represented here in excerpts: the Anglo-Norman poet Wace, in his *Roman de Brut*, and Wace's English adaptor, Lawman, in a version, also known as the *Brut*, that looks back in formal terms to Old English poetry.

After an initial section of Welsh texts that trace the beginnings of Arthurian story, Part II offers an introduction to Arthurian romance through works that treat one of its most enigmatic and important characters, Perceval, and the adventure that occupies him, the search for the Grail (at first a miraculous object of pagan origin, its meaning is thoroughly Christianized as the succession of stories unfolds over more than a century). Included is the full text of Chrétien de Troyes's *Perceval* (The Story of the Grail), left unfinished at the poet's death; selections from *La Queste del Saint Graal* (Quest of the Holy Grail), a prose expansion of Chrétien's original tale; and selections from one of the tale's principal continuations, the *Perlesvaus*. The volume concludes on a contrasting note, with the complete text of one of the most charming and humorous of medieval short romances, *La Mule sans Frein* (The Girl with the Mule).

Part I
Arthurian Epic

Geoffrey of Monmouth. *Historia Regum Britanniae* (History of the Kings of Britain): A Selection

Translated by DOUGLAS MCFARLAND

The first extended narrative of the life and exploits of King Arthur appears in the *Historia Regum Britanniae* written by Geoffrey of Monmouth in the twelfth century. We know little of the life and career of Geoffrey. He was born near the beginning of the twelfth century and died sometime near its midpoint. In the Dedication to the *Historia* and on two other occasions within the text itself, he refers to himself as Geoffrey of Monmouth, and so we can assume that he came from that area of Wales in which the relatively small city of Monmouth is located. This would suggest a Welsh origin, but one cannot be certain since at the time of Geoffrey's birth many Normanized Celts had returned to the region from Brittany. Geoffrey might easily, therefore, have come from Breton rather than Welsh stock. We do know that in 1129 Geoffrey began his tenure as a resident member of the clergy at Oxford and that he held the position until 1151 when he became Bishop of St. Asaph in northeast Wales, an office which did not require residency. His first work of any note was the *Prophetiae Merlini* or the *Prophecies of Merlin*, written in Latin verse and purported to be the prophetic utterances of Merlin as spoken to King Vortigern. They were eventually incorporated into his major prose work, the aforesaid *Historia Regum Britanniae*, completed by 1139 and covering the period of English history from its legendary founding in the twelfth century BCE, through the reign of Arthur and the Saxon invasions of the seventh century CE.

The Arthurian materials occupy the climactic position in Geoffrey's narrative of British history. That narrative begins with the arrival of the Trojan Brutus in the twelfth century BCE, thereby providing for Britain a founding myth comparable to the one provided by Aeneas, his grandfather, for Rome. After an extended odyssey in the aftermath of the destruction of Troy, Brutus reaches the island of what was then called Albion. Once he had cleared the landscape of a race of uncivilized giants, he renamed the island Britain and claimed it a "second Troy." Geoffrey follows this with a chronological narrative of British Kings from the time of Brutus until the invasion of the island in the first century by Caesar. He then expands and fills out the narratives of the English Kings who rule under the auspices of Rome. Arthur comes at the end of this series of monarchs, and he is credited with uniting Britain, driving out the Saxons, and freeing the kingdom from Roman control. His reign represents the pinnacle of British achievement, both internally and externally. His achievement, however, is short lived; upon Arthur's death Britain collapses, succumbing to civil war, plague, and Saxon domination. Geoffrey concludes his history with the undoing of Arthur's success, eschewing a teleological conclusion to the linear narrative of British history.

Although he claims in the dedication that his work is the translation of an ancient manuscript written in English, Geoffrey, in fact, borrowed from multiple sources, both written and oral, and shaped those borrowings into a connected prose narrative. The histories of Gildas and Nennius stand out in importance, and it is useful to consider how Geoffrey refashioned these materials. In the sixth century Gildas wrote a history of Britain entitled the *De Excidio Britanniae* or Fall of Britain, which begins in the first century CE and ends in the author's own time. The work is informed by the moral condemnation of Britain's leaders and clerics. Basing his understanding of the past upon biblical historiography, Gildas portrays the Saxon invasions of the sixth century as the result of political and moral decay. In the Book of Judges, the rise and fall of Israel's political fortunes are the direct result of the rise and fall of its moral character. When Israel turns away from God, it is handed over to its enemies. Similarly the political collapse of Britain in the sixth century represents for Gildas the triumph of divine justice.

Writing in the ninth century, Nennius draws upon multiple sources to shape, although at times it is an awkward and disjointed shaping, his own national history of Britain. Nennius significantly expands the narrative scope of Gildas and incorporates two important additions: the legendary founding of Britain by Brutus and the reign of King Arthur, who, although treated briefly in a single chapter, begins to take on the character of a national hero. In what amounts to little more than a short catalogue of achievements, twelve separate victories in battles against the Saxons are attributed to Arthur. Nennius places Arthur's epic exploits within the context of Christian typology. Arthur is not simply a hero in his own right who is able to slay 960 men in a single attack, but is also the instrument of God's justice, a deliverer who draws his strength from the virtue of Christ and of Mary.

This relatively short panegyric in honor of Arthur is expanded into a full scale narrative in Geoffrey's *Historia*. Although Arthur is still a teenager, the impending Saxon invasions demand that he be quickly crowned King after the death of Utherpendragon. From the very beginning of the narrative, therefore, Arthur is characterized as a political leader whose task is to unite a nation against a common enemy. Although there may be echoes here of Old Testament historiography—the notion that God fills a charismatic warrior with his own strength to lead Israel against its enemy—Arthur is primarily portrayed as a national political leader, one chosen not by God but by the interested parties. Grafting Livy's narrative design onto Christian chronicle, Geoffrey places Arthur at the end of a parade of national icons, providing what was no doubt his largely Norman audience with a historical tradition which they might deem worthy. Arthur represents the fulfillment of British political history and functions as a secular typology modeled on the role of Caesar Augustus in Livy's *Annales*. Arthur will not only drive out the Saxons but also acquire new territories on the continent and end Roman domination of the region.

Geoffrey's narrative differs, however, from Livy's in one important and obvious aspect. As mentioned, Arthur's reign disintegrates just at the point of achieving its greatest success. Geoffrey ends the *Historia* with the death of Arthur and the ensuing Saxon invasions. How Arthur, and England along with him, fell is instructive. When Arthur begins his march on Rome, he appoints his nephew Mordred as the surrogate King. But Mordred almost immediately betrays his uncle, claiming royal kingship for himself and taking Gwenivere as his Queen. When news of this reaches Arthur, he returns to Britain, and the civil war which then commences leads to the collapse of political stability and provides in its aftermath the opportunity for the Saxons to return and eventually dominate Britain.

One might have expected Geoffrey to characterize Arthur in this case as an overreacher, a leader whose ambition for power caused his own and his country's downfall. His march to Rome might very well suggest an aggressive hubris and as such would shift Geoffrey's narrative from the pattern of typological fulfillment to one of Satanic ambition followed by political collapse, God's punishment for disobedience. But although this final episode is indeed informed by sin, it is Mordred's and Gwenivere's sin, not Arthur's. The fall of the monarchy occurs because Arthur makes a poor political decision, one which is doomed because of the duplicitous ambition within his own family. In short, a family drama intrudes into a narrative of national history. Robert Hanning has astutely recognized the implications of this scenario: "the individual begins to emerge as a person from the pattern of history, a person moreover whose extrapolitical relationships, especially kindred ones, determine his actions, even if the result is national chaos" (Hanning 143). Geoffrey's narrative representation of the British monarchy marks a shift, therefore, from an understanding of history as driven by the relationship between God and mankind to one driven by individuals caught up in social, political, and familial contexts. Perhaps it is not coincidental that Shakespeare found in Geoffrey the source material for the story of King Lear and his daughters. The dramatist extends and deepens Geoffrey's foregrounding of the individual in national history, not only creating an individual character enmeshed in family embroilments, but exploring in the most intimate of ways his inwardness.

Geoffrey's seminal contribution to western historiography begs a question, one particularly important for this anthology. How does the *Historia* contribute to the genre of Arthurian romance? At first glance the romances of Chrétien and others would seem to have little to do with Geoffrey's Arthur. As one might expect of a historical narrative of a national hero, Arthur's exploits are frequently cast in an epic mold. Battle scenes, speeches, and even diction are indebted to classical epic, little of which would seem ostensibly to contribute to the emergence of chivalric romance. If, however, we look carefully at Geoffrey's narrative, we can detect motifs of courtly literature and the ethos of Arthurian romance.

Although the formation of Arthur's court comes in response to the need for political stability and cohesion in face of the Saxon threat, it is also the prototype for what will become the courtly center of Arthurian romance. When he is crowned king, Arthur is an unproven youth, but he immediately displays values which inform courtly literature. The new King bestows gifts on the members of his court until he has exhausted his supply. The imminent campaign against the Saxons is undertaken not only to protect Britain but also to replenish his store of spoils so that he might continue to bestow wealth onto his court. Largesse will become of central importance in romance literature, eventually finding its way into the set of values essential to courtly love literature. Moreover, Geoffrey depicts Arthur's court as a center of cultural values, attracting knights and ladies who wish to emulate its fashions and styles. The model for one of the more important motifs of courtly literature appears at the Pentecostal celebration of Arthur's kingship. The gathering is abruptly interrupted by a messenger from Rome conveying the Emperor's demand that Britain pay its customary tribute to the Empire. While in this instance, the intrusion signals a political crisis that requires immediate attention, the convention will appear in the works of Chrétien and the *Gawain* poet as a device to test courtly values. A stranger suddenly appears with a challenge to the courtly ethos. This challenge is taken up by an individual knight who sets out to undergo trial and testing. In Geoffrey, we can detect the beginnings of this generic set piece in the response of one of Arthur's knights to the Roman messenger. He asserts that the court has become complacent and that the skills of individual knights have ossified. He welcomes, therefore, the chance to renew the values of Arthur's court in combat.

This convention raises the possibility that the aforementioned emergence of the individual in Geoffrey's historical narrative foreshadows the emergence of the individual in courtly literature. The knight who responds to the challenge of the stranger and sets out from the court does represent the values of that court, but those values have been internalized. As R.W. Southern has pointed out, in a chivalric epic like *Roland*, the knight fights a communal action, but "in Chrétien the enemy is dispersed; he is everywhere and may be found everywhere. The knights of Chrétien seek the enemy in solitude" (Southern, 244). The courtly love component of the genre, the testing of the knight as lover whose exploits are undertaken for the sake of a lady dear to his heart, is even more to the point. The lover necessarily turns inward, cultivating the memory of his lady in his heart as he sets out to prove his worth. The testing of the knight is conducted not only in the physical solitude of the landscape beyond the borders of the court, but also in the psychological solitude within the confines of his own soul. It may very well be that the removal by Geoffrey of the hero from the context of a providential design and the curtailing of his role as an actor in God's drama looks ahead to the new sense of individuality in courtly literature.

Geoffrey's influence can be seen throughout courtly literature, but it is Edmund Spenser in his sixteenth century chivalric epic, *The Faerie Queene*, who seems to recognize the tension between the historical and personal in Geoffrey. His poem is, in fact, informed by that tension. Spenser translates, in a very compact form, the linear narrative of the *Historia* into English verse, inserting it into two distinct sections of his narrative poem. In each instance, the historical and the individual quests stand in uneasy juxtaposition to one another. Arthur seeks to fulfill his passionate desire for the lady whose image has appeared to him in a dream but also seeks to fulfill his obligation to the linear narrative of English history. These collapse into the figure of the Faerie Queene, who concurrently represents the telos of erotic desire and that of national history. The implicit tension between romance and epic, between the personal and the corporate, implicit in Geoffrey's *Historia*, becomes explicit in *The Faerie Queene*.

The Reign of Arthur, King of Britain (Books IX.i through XI.ii)

After the death of Utherpendragon, the nobles convened from different shires of Britain in the Cathedral city of Silchester to urge Dubricius, Archbishop of the City of Legions, to consecrate Arthur, the son of Utherpendragon, as monarch of the realm. Necessity compelled them. For upon hearing of the death of King Uther, the Saxons had summoned their own peoples from Germany, and under the command of Colgrin, were now making every effort to drive the Britons from their land. The Saxons had already subjugated that portion of the island stretching from the Humber River to the sea of Caithness.

Dubricius, grieving over his country's calamity, gathered the Bishops around him and adorned the head of Arthur with the royal diadem. The new king was a youth of fifteen years and possessed unrivaled courage and generosity. His innate worthiness provided evidence of such God-given talent that he was loved by all the people. Once fitted with the outward emblems of kingship, Arthur followed custom and took pleasure in a display of royal generosity. But because such a multitude of knights flocked around him, the new King soon depleted his assets and found himself without any more to give. Although a man of innate magnanimity and nobility might for a time lack resources, by no means will he be afflicted by a continual shortage. And so, because in Arthur goodness attended generosity, the new King was determined to press hard upon the Saxons in order to seize their wealth and enrich those who served his own court. Arthur also recognized the justice in driving out the Saxons since he himself bore the hereditary right to rule the entire island. Thus he set out for York with an army of young men gathered under his command.

Once Colgrin became aware of the British advance, he gathered Saxons, Scots and Picts into a very great army and intercepted Arthur alongside the Douglas River. The greater parts of each side were put to the test, but the day belonged to Arthur, and Colgrin was forced to flee and take refuge at York. Arthur pursued him and upon his arrival at York immediately laid siege to the city.

When the Saxons were making their initial assault against the British, Baldulf, the brother of Colgrin, was at the coast awaiting the arrival of Cheldric, who was bringing aid from Germany. Once aware, however, of his brother's flight, Baldulf could delay no longer and immediately made for York with six thousand men in order to break the siege and free his entrapped brother. Having arrived within ten milestones of the city, Baldulf decided to march under cover of night and mount a covert attack. When Arthur learned of his plan, he ordered Cador, Duke of Cornwall, to intercept Baldulf with six hundred knights and three thousand foot soldiers. Cador met the enemy on its way to York and attacked without warning. Those Saxons not cut to pieces or killed by Cador's men were forced to flee.

Deeply troubled over his failure, Baldulf pondered how he might enter York and contrive with his brother to gain safe passage from the city. When Baldulf could find no other way to enter the besieged city, he cut his hair and beard and in the manner of a jester ambled into the enemy camp, singing and playing the lyre. Disguised in such a manner, Baldulf was able to avoid suspicion and gradually work his way toward the walls of the city. When the besieged Saxons recognized him, they lowered ropes and drew him up over the wall. At the sight of his brother Colgrin rushed forward and revived himself with long sought kisses and embraces. It was as if Baldulf had been returned from the dead. After much deliberation, however, the impossibility of escape cast them into despair. But at last couriers returned from Germany to announce that under the command of Cheldric a fleet of six hundred ships had arrived at Albany, ready to discharge a powerful army.

When the counselors of the King learned of the arrival of Cheldric, they argued against continuing the siege at York, fearing an uncertain outcome of a battle against such a large enemy force. Arthur heeded their advice and went to London where he gathered the bishops and priests together from every corner of the realm to solicit the best and most effective strategy for confronting the pagan invasion. By common consent, it was eventually decided to send messengers to King Hoel in Brittany notifying him of the impending disaster to Britain. Hoel was the son of the sister of Arthur and was fathered by Budicius, King of the Armorican Britons. Upon learning of the dire situation facing his uncle, Hoel ordered his fleet to be made ready and at the next favorable wind made port at Southampton with fifteen thousand armed men. Arthur received him with all proper honors, and the two embraced repeatedly.

After a few days, Arthur led this combined force toward Kaerluideoit which as I recalled earlier was then besieged by the pagans. This city, also known as Lincoln, was located in the region of Lindsey atop a hill between two rivers. Arthur arrived with a legion of battle ready troops and inflicted unheard of slaughter upon the Saxons. On that bloody day six thousand men fell, some drowning in the rivers, others impaled on spears. Those not killed were shaken and took flight rather than continue the siege. Arthur did not cease his pursuit of the enemy until they drew near the Caledon forest. Gathering themselves together from all sides, the Saxons decided to make a final stand in the forest. In the fighting which ensued, they heaped devastation on the Britons and defended themselves courageously, using the trees to avoid enemy spears. As soon as Arthur recognized the situation, he ordered the trees in that part of the forest to be cut down and the trunks placed in a ring around the enemy in order to deny any possibility of escape, thereby starving them into submission. Surrounded in the forest for three days by a host of British troops, the Saxons found themselves with nothing to eat. In order to prevent starvation and win release, they offered to leave behind their gold and silver, asking only that they be allowed to return to Germany with their ships. They also promised to send back tribute from Germany and to hand over hostages to secure their pledge. After consultation, Arthur agreed to their terms. He accepted their wealth and hostages and granted from his side only their unimpeded departure. But as they churned the waters and made their way across the sea, the pact annoyed the Saxons more and more until they reversed their sails and came back around to Briton, eventually landing on the shore at Totnes. They immediately began to ravage the countryside all the way to the Severn Sea. After attacking and killing the British settlers, they eagerly set out for Bath and upon their arrival laid seige to the city.

When this was reported to Arthur, he was astounded by the lawlessness of the Saxons. He ordered that judgment be passed and that the hostages be hanged without delay. The campaign which he had begun against the Scots and Picts was put aside, and although it caused Arthur great distress to leave behind the ailing Hoel at Alclud, he nevertheless hastily set out to break the Saxon blockade of Bath. As they were approaching the siege in the province of Somerset, Arthur paused and addressed his troops with these words:

"Now that these creatures of a most ungodly and hated name, these Saxons, have scorned to hold faith with me, I will on this day preserve faith to my own God and will labor to exact payment for the spilling of my countrymen's blood. Arm yourselves ... I say arm yourselves, and like men smite down those who breed treachery. With Christ at our side and free from doubt, we will triumph over them."

After Arthur spoke, the saintly Dubricius, archbishop of the City of Legions, mounted a hill top and proclaimed in a ringing voice these words:

"You men who bear the mark of those professing the Christian faith, let devotion to your country and to your people remain in your hearts. Unless you undertake to repel the invader, the deceitful slaughter by the pagans of your fellow countrymen will forever shame you. Fight for your fatherland, and if it comes to it, suffer death as well. Death is itself a victory, for death will redeem your souls. Each one of you who dies for his brothers will offer himself up as a living sacrifice. In so doing you will be following Christ himself, who thought it worthy to give his life for his brothers. If, therefore, anyone of you should meet death in this war, death will prove a penance and will absolve all sins, provided you do not hesitate to embrace it."

Without delay each man followed the bidding of the sainted Archbishop and hastened to arm himself. Arthur donned a breastplate worthy of a so great king and placed atop his head a helmet engraved with the likeness of a dragon. On his shoulder he bore the shield named Pridwen, on which was depicted Mary, the mother of Christ, whose saintly image continually recalled her to the memory of the King. Next he girded Caliburn about his waist, a wondrous sword forged on the island of Avalon; in his powerful right hand he held Ron, whose long and broad lance was ready to deal out death.

Thus equipped, Arthur drew up his men and boldly attacked the Saxons, who had been positioned in their customary wedge formation. The Saxons were cut down on every side and yet were able to offer resistance throughout the day until withdrawing at sunset and setting up camp on a nearby hill. Still confident because of the size of their army, the Saxons believed the hilltop would afford ample protection. At dawn of the following day, Arthur led his army up the side of the hill. The Saxons held the initial advantage since they were attacking with downward momentum, enabling them to inflict deadly wounds on their enemy ascending up the slope of the hill. Although many Britons fell that day, Arthur's men fought courageously and eventually were able to reach the hilltop. At once the two sides fell into hand to hand combat. With their chests pressed forward, the Saxons struggled with every effort to hold off the British troops. The fighting continued in this way for most of the day, and Arthur grew indignant that the Saxons were still resisting his troops, indignant that his army had not yet attained victory. So with his sword drawn and proclaiming the name of Holy Mary, the English King hurled himself with a sudden charge into the densely packed line of the enemy. Arthur called upon God as he cut down in single strokes each man he met. Nor did he cease until his sword had slain four hundred and seventy men. When they beheld their King's exploits, Arthur's men quickly followed in close formation and inflicted devastation all around. On that day Colgrin and his brother Baldulf were slain, along with many thousand others. But Cheldric, when he recognized the peril to his men, fled with the remaining survivors.

With victory in hand, the King ordered Cador, Duke of Cornwall, to pursue the fleeing Saxons, while he hastened toward Albany. It had been reported to him that the Scots and Picts were besieging his nephew Hoel at Alclud where, as I mentioned earlier, Arthur had left behind his nephew plagued with illness. He now hastened to bring Hoel aid lest the barbarians take him prisoner.

Cador, accompanied by ten thousand men, broke off immediate pursuit of the Saxons and raced ahead to the enemy ships in order to block an escape across the sea. He soon took possession of the fleet and fortified the ships with his best soldiers in order to prevent the Saxons from boarding if they should reach the shore. Cador then hastened back to resume his pursuit of the enemy. In accordance with the orders of Arthur, Cador's men pitilessly cut down whomever they encountered. Those who had been fulminating with savagery in their cheeks were now driven by faint hearts to take flight. Some attempted to conceal themselves in the forest, others in the mountains and mountain caves. They used any means to prolong their lives. Finally when no refuge could be found, they made their way in a broken column to the island of Thanet. Cador, however, hunted them down, inflicting slaughter as he went. Nor did the killing stop until Cheldric had been slain, hostages taken, and any of those still remaining forced to surrender.

With peace thus secured, Cador set off for Alclud. Arthur had already freed the town from the barbarian assault and was leading his army to Moray where the Scots and Picts were under siege. They had earlier struggled three times against the King and his nephew before finally being forced to flee to the region of Moray where they sought safe haven on the islands at Loch Lomond. The lake holds sixty islands, and although sixty rivers flow into it, only one flows out. Sixty cliffs can be seen on the islands, and each contains an eagle's nest. Here the eagles flock together each year and in high pitched clamor give portents of the future fate of the kingdom. To these islands the aforementioned enemies had fled in order to take advantage of the lake's natural protection. But this strategy gained them little. For Arthur gathered his ships and sailed around the rivers. In this way the British King beseiged the enemy for fifteen days, reducing them to such hunger that they perished in the thousands.

While Arthur was thus afflicting the enemy at Moray, Gilmour, the Hibernian King, arrived with a great contingent of men and ships hoping to break the British siege. Arthur was forced to divert his attention from the immediate task and to direct his troops against the Hibernians. After he had pitilessly cut them down and forced those remaining to sail back home, he was once again free to indulge in the relentless slaughter of the Scots and Picts. When it became clear that Arthur would spare no one, all the Bishops and Clergy of this woeful region, on naked feet and bearing the relics of the saints and sacred objects of the church, congregated to implore the King to take pity on their people and to see to their well being. They bent their knees before Arthur and begged him to show mercy to a contrite people. They argued that he had punished them enough and that no need compelled him to slay down to a single man those few who had survived. Seeing that they were about to bear the yoke of perpetual servitude, the holy men beseeched Arthur to grant them possession of but one portion of their country. Their piety moved the King to tears, and so he acquiesced to their pleas, granting favor to their petition.

After these events had transpired, King Hoel of Brittany began exploring the region of the lake and marveled how so many rivers, so many islands, so many ridges, and so many eagles' nests should all be of the same number. Arthur drew near his nephew and told him of another lake not far off even more marvelous. Its length was twenty feet, its width the same, and had a depth of five feet. Each of its four corners produced its own type of fish. One could not say if its square shape had been fashioned by the art of man or of nature. Arthur then described another lake in Wales near Sabrina, called Lincoln by the local people. This lake took in the sea as if it were an open abyss. Although the turbulent waters would pour into its basin, never would they fill the lake and spill over its banks. And when the sea receded, the lake would spew up the swallowed waters, taking on the shape of a mountain before cascading over the banks. Moreover, if anyone in that entire region were to stand near and face this lake and the splash of the wave were to touch his garment, he would hardly ever, or perhaps not at all, escape being engulfed by its waters. With one's back turned, however, even if standing near the bank, the splashing is not to be feared.

After granting pardon to the people of Scotland, the King set off for York to celebrate the season of our Lord's birth. Upon his arrival in the city, however, the sight of the desolate churches filled him with grief. With the saintly Archbishop Samson and other religious men driven away, the half burnt churches had ceased to stand in service to God. Such was the magnitude of the triumphant madness of the pagans. Arthur called the clergy together and appointed his own chaplain, Piramus, as the Bishop of the Metropolitan See. The King rebuilt the churches which had been razed to the ground and supplied them with holy orders of men and women. Arthur then restored to those nobles who had been driven out by the Saxon upheaval the honors of their fatherland. Three brothers of royal lineage, Loth, Urian, and Auguselus, held lordships over this region before the Saxon assault. And so as he had restored to others what their paternal rights had guaranteed, Arthur now returned the royal power of Scotland to Auguselus; handed back the scepter of Moray to Urian; and to Loth, who in the time of Ambrose had married the sister of Arthur himself and had fathered Gawain and Mordred, he reinstated the earldom of Lothian and other regions which pertained to it. After he had restored order and dignity to the countryside, the King married Guinevere, born of Roman blood and raised in the household of Duke Cador, whose beauty surpassed that of all other women of the isle.

In the following summer, Arthur sailed with his fleet to Hibernia in order to place that kingdom under his power. The aforementioned King Gilmaurius met Arthur head on with a mighty host of men. The Irishmen, however, were quickly dispatched. Bare and unarmed, they fled to wherever they might find safe haven. Gilmaurius was immediately captured and forced to submit. The remaining nobles of the country were dumbstruck and following the example of their king, surrendered themselves to the Britons.

Once Hibernia was made secure, Arthur directed his fleet to Iceland and subdued its peoples. After the news of his conquests had spread to the other islands, no region could muster a defense. And so Kings Doldavius of Gotland and Gunhpuar of the Orkneys surrendered without resistance and pledged to pay Arthur tribute. In the spring, Arthur returned to Britain and solidified the peace in his kingdom and here he remained for twelve years.

After these victories, Arthur resolved to increase the size of the court and so invited the best men from the furthest kingdoms to join him. So great refinement did his court exemplify that peoples far away wished to emulate it. Every noble considered himself of no value unless he dressed and bore arms and generally conducted himself in the manner of Arthur's royal household. Arthur's reputation for largess and chivalry spread throughout the furthest reaches of the earth, and Kings across the seas feared lest they be subjugated by him and lose dominion over those they themselves had conquered. They anxiously reinforced their cities with towers and built castles in strategic locations so they would have refuge if Arthur were to mount an attack against them.

When this was reported to Arthur, the King praised himself for generating fear in others and decided to subjugate all of Europe. And so he prepared his fleet and first set sail for Norway where he intended to raise up his brother-in-law, Loth, to the kingship of the realm. Loth was the nephew of Sichelm, the former King, who just before his death had named him as heir to the crown. The Norwegians, however, deemed Loth unworthy and instead advanced a certain Riculf to royal power, trusting that from their fortified cities they could repel Arthur's army. Loth had a son named Gawain, a young man of twelve years. He had been placed by Arthur into the service of Pope Sulpicius, who had conferred knighthood upon him. When Arthur arrived on the shore of Norway, King Riculf and the entire population of the country met him. The battle began immediately. After the spilling of much blood and the death of Riculf himself, the British army at last prevailed. As soon as victory had been attained in the field, the Britons rained fire down upon the cities and scattered the rural inhabitants, not holding back their savagery until all Norway and all Denmark had been forced to submit to the lordship of Arthur.

With these peoples now subdued and having advanced Loth to the kingship of Norway, Arthur sailed to Gaul. He drew his troops into formation and began to lay waste to the surrounding countryside. Gaul was then considered a province of Rome and was ruled by Frollo, a tribune under the authority of Leo. Frollo led forth his entire army to thwart the invasion of Arthur but was able to mount only minimal resistance. The youth of the islands which

Arthur had already subdued now came to the side of the British King. Consequently Arthur was said to have amassed an army of such great size so as to be invincible. Moreover, the generosity of Arthur had won over to his side the better part of the Gallic army. When Frollo recognized his weakened position, he immediately fled to Paris with a handful of men. Here he reassembled his broken troops, fortified the city, and began planning a counterattack against Arthur with the support of those living nearby. But Arthur arrived without warning and besieged the city. After a month had passed, Frollo so grieved over the starvation and death of his people that he proposed to Arthur that they meet in single combat with the victor taking possession of the kingdom. Exceedingly confident of his great stature, his boldness, and his fortitude, Frollo sent his message with the belief that he would secure his safety. The proposal pleased Arthur greatly and he replied that he would indeed meet Frollo in single combat. After each side had pledged to abide by the terms of the proposal, the two leaders met on an island outside the city. Awaiting their respective fates, both armies stood nearby.

The combatants sat properly armed atop horses of wondrous speed, and it could not easily be ascertained which of the two would triumph over the other. With raised lances they faced off and without delay dug their spurs into the flanks of their horses. Although they struck one another with powerful blows, it was Arthur who bore his lance with the greater care. Avoiding his opponent's weapon, he struck Frollo high up on the chest and drove him to the ground. Thereupon he unsheathed his sword and rushed to strike his enemy dead. But Frollo quickly regained his feet, bolted forward and buried his lance in the chest of Arthur's horse. Mortally wounded, the horse fell to the ground taking Arthur along with him. When the Britons saw their King topple to the ground, they feared lest he had been slain. They were scarcely able to restrain themselves from breaking their pledge and rushing forward to attack the Gauls with a single will. But while they were still considering whether to cross the boundary and enter the fray, Arthur quickly arose and with uplifted shield sought out Frollo. Now the combatants redoubled their blows, each striving to deal death to the other. Frollo was first to find an opening and struck Arthur on the forehead. The blow would have been lethal if it had not been blunted by Arthur's helmet. When Arthur saw that his breastplate and shield were growing red from the blood which flowed downward from his head, he grew hot with anger. Lifting up Caliburn with all his strength, he thrust that wondrous sword through the helmet of Frollo and split his head into two parts. Frollo toppled to the ground, striking the earth with his heels just as his final life breath escaped into the wind.

Once news of Frollo's fate had spread throughout the army, the Gauls opened the gates and handed their city over to Arthur. With victory secured, the King divided his army into two parts. He placed Hoel in command of one contingent and instructed him to attack Guitard, the leader of the Picts. Arthur himself led forth the remaining squadron, intending to subjugate other rebel provinces. Soon Hoel had entered Aquitania where he attacked the cities and forced the war weary Guitard to surrender. He also laid waste to the countryside of Gascony with sword and flame and forced its leaders into submission.

Meanwhile nine years passed. After all the regions of Gaul had been subjugated, Arthur returned to Paris to hold court. Once he had confirmed to the assemblage of clergy and people that peace and legitimacy filled the realm, he bestowed Neustria, now called Normandy, to Bedevere, his cup bearer. To Kay, his seneschal, he entrusted Anjou and to other nobles in his service, other provinces. In the spring, with these cities and peoples pacified, he returned to Britain.

When the celebration of Pentecost drew near, Arthur was filled with happiness over his great victory and decided to hold court so that the crown of the kingdom might be placed upon his head and that he, along with all his Earls, might respectfully celebrate the season and renew an abiding peace amongst themselves. Having announced his intentions to the court, he accepted their advice to carry out his plans in the City of Legions. Such solemnities were well suited to Glamorganshire since it was situated in a pleasing locale above the river Usk not far from the Sabrina Sea, a region surpassing all others in its abundance of wealth. On one side of the city flowed the Usk, the river on which the kings and nobles from across the seas would be conveyed to the celebration; on the other side, bordered by meadows and woods, the splendor of the golden gables of the regal palaces rivaled that of Rome herself. Striking, however, were the two churches of the city. One was built in honor of Julian the Martyr and was graced by a most beautiful virgin chorus of nuns; the other church was founded in the name of blessed Aaron, the companion of Julian, and was maintained by a religious house of canons. The later church held in tenancy the third Metropolitan See of Britain. In addition, the city housed a university of two hundred scholars, who were learned in astronomy and other arts and who would diligently observe the course of the stars and foretell to Arthur with clear proofs the wondrous events of the future. It was, in short, a city famed for a profusion of charms. Envoys were now sent out to different kingdoms to summon from Gaul and neighboring isles those who owed their allegiance to Arthur's court. Thereupon a host of nobles came:

Auguselus, King of Albany, now called Scotland; Urian, King of the men of Moray; Cadwallo Laurh, King of the Venedoti, now called the North Welsh; Stater, King of the Demetiae, now called the South Welsh; Cador, King of Cornwall. Also the Archbishops of three Metropolitan Sees: namely, of London, of York, and Dubricius from the City of Legions. The piety of this last man, the Primate of Britain and the Legate of the Apostolic See, was so great that he could by his own prayers restore the health to one gravely ill. There came the noble earls of noble cities: Mordvid, Earl of Gloucester; Mauron of Worcester; Anarauth of Salisbury; Artgualchar of Guerensis, now called Warwick; Jugein from Leicester; Cursalem from Caistor; Kynniare, Duke of Durobernia; Urbgennius from Bath; Jonathal of Dorchester; Boso of Rydychen, that is Oxford. In addition to these Earls came noblemen of no lesser worth: Donaut map Papo, Cheneus map Coil, Peredur map Eridur, Grifud map Nogord, Regin map Claut, Eddelivi map Oledauc, Kyncar map Bangan, Kynmaroc, Gorbonian map Goit, Worloit, Run map Neton, Kymbelin, Edelnauth map Trunat, Cathleus map Kathel, Kynlit map Tieton, and many others whose name would take too long to number. From the neighboring islands came Gilmaurus, King of Ireland; Malvasius, King of Iceland; Doldavius, King of Gotland; Gunvasius, King of the Orkneys; Loth, King of Norway; Aschil, King of the Danes. From regions across the sea came Holdin, leader of the Ruteni; Loeodegarius, Earl of Hoiland; Bedevere the cup bearer, Duke of Normandy; Borellus of Cenomania; Kay the Seneschal, Duke of Anjou; Guitard of Poitou; also twelve Peers of the Gauls, led by Gerin of Chartres; and Hoel, Duke of Armorcorian Britons, with the princes subject to him, who entered with such magnificence of trappings and mules and horses that it is difficult to describe. In addition to these, no prince of any renown on this side of Spain ignored the royal edict. There is little wonder. The largess of Arthur was known throughout the world and caused every man to love him.

After all had congregated in the city and the rites of coronation were ready to begin, the archbishops were led to the palace to crown Arthur with the royal diadem. Since the court was being held in his own diocese, Dubricius was ready to fulfill his obligation to celebrate the divine service. Once having been crowned, Arthur was conducted to the Metropolitan See with splendor. On each side an archbishop attended him, and the Kings of Albany, Cornwall, Demetia, and Venedotia, as was their privilege, bore gold sabers before him. A convent of clerics, each of priestly rank, sang marvelous melodies. In another of the day's festivities, archbishops and Bishops led the laurel crowned Queen to the church of the Virgins dedicated to Christ. The four queens of the aforementioned kings fulfilled custom and carried before them four doves.

Finally, with the procession complete, the music of organs and the voices of choirs filled each church with such sweet tones that the attending knights did not know which church to seek out first. Bunched in crowds, they hurried now to one, now to another setting. Not even if the entire day had been spent in celebration, would any tedium have set in. At length, with divine services fully celebrated in each church, the King and Queen removed their crowns and donned lighter regalia. They then proceeded to the feast. The King went to his own palace with the men while the Queen went to hers with the women. Preserving the ancient practices of Troy, the British were accustomed to celebrate such feasts separately, the men with their kind, the women with theirs. After all had been seated at the table as honor and rank required, Kay, the seneschal, clad in ermine and accompanied by a thousand others also in ermine, served the dishes. From another side, the same number variously dressed and led by Bedevere, the cup-bearer, served many kinds of drink in goblets of varying design. In the palace of the Queen, innumerable stewards, also adorned in a variety of dress, were discharging their duties. It would take too many words and a narrative too long if I were to describe it all. Britain had been restored to so great a stature that it excelled all other kingdoms in the copious wealth of its splendor and in the courtly wit of its denizens. Every knight who was known for his worth wore the trappings and arms of one color. Women, elegant and sophisticated and clad in the same color, thought no knight worthy of love unless he had been tested three times in battle. Such courtly love taught ladies chastity and knights virtue.

At length, after banqueting had refreshed everyone, all adjourned outside the city walls in order to attend games in different parts of the field. Emulating the conditions of battle, the knights competed on horses while their ladies looked down from parapets and aroused fierce flames of love in the knights with their playful mirth. They competed in an array of games: some with arrows, others with spears, still others with the tossing of heavy stones and rocks, and others with dice. These were games only, for all animosity had been put aside. Each knight who was victorious in his own competition was awarded a gift by Arthur. The games consumed three days. On the fourth and final day Arthur awarded to each knight who excelled in duty and reverence to the King a particular holding: a city, castle, archbishopric, bishopric, or other honor. Holy Dubricius, yearning for the life of an anchorite, retired from the office of Archbishop. David, the uncle of the King, was consecrated in his place, a man whose life exemplified goodness to those whom he had taught holy doctrine. In the place of Samson, archbishop of Dolensis, Tebaus, the distinguished priest of Laudavia, was approved by Hoel, King of Armorica, whose life and good character had recommended him. The bishopric of Silchester was settled on Maugannius; Guintonie on Divvanio; the bishopric of Alclud on Eledenio. While Arthur was meting out these offices, twelve men of wise and reverent bearing, carrying olive branches in their right hands, the sign of envoys, discretly entered and with a salute to the King, delivered these words from Lucius Hiberius:

"Lucius, Procurator of the Republic, desires that Arthur, King of Britain, receive his just deserts. I am in awe of your tyrannical insolence. I am beset by amazement when I recall the injury which you have inflicted on Rome. I am indignant that you have overstepped yourself and disdained to acknowledge your transgression. Indeed, it is clear that you are loath to consider the significance of your wrongful offense to the Senate. It is at your peril that you ignore the power which Rome wields over the entire world. Oblivious to her august power and ignoring the decree of the Senate, you have withheld from Rome the tribute due to her. This practice has been in place since the time of Gaius Julius and other Romans of dignity, and yet you brush it aside. Moreover, you have seized Gaul, the Allobroges' province, and all the islands of the ocean, whose kings, as long as Roman power has prevailed, paid tribute to my ancestors. Because of this great multitude of transgressions, the Roman Senate has decreed that justice be done. I, therefore, setting a date in the middle of August, order you to come to Rome to satisfy your masters, to acquiesce to the sentence which justice dictates. But if I must come to your country, I will take up the sword and will restore to the Republic whatever of value which your madness has compelled you to steal."

After the letter had been read in the presence of the kings and lords, Arthur retreated with his nobles into a huge turret at the entrance to the castle in order to fashion a fitting response to the Roman mandate. As they were climbing the steps, Cador, Duke of Cornwall, a man of mirth, dissolved into laughter. He faced the King and spoke these words:

"Up until now I have been in fear lest the lengthy period of peaceful inactivity which has occupied our time might turn us into cowards and deface our once widely esteemed renown for battle. When the chance to raise weapons grows scarce, replaced by dice and women and other attractions, it must not be doubted that courage, honor, bravery and fame will be defiled by sloth. Already five years have elapsed during which we have given ourselves over to delights and deprived ourselves of soldierly exercise. God, therefore, in order to release us from this lethargy, has prompted the Romans to take this course of action. The enemy itself will restore us to our original perfection."

After Cador had spoken and all had taken their seats, Arthur addressed the assemblage with these words:

"Men of my court, whose worthiness in giving counsel in whatever time of prosperity or adversity I duly recognize, summon now your collective thoughts and wisely advise how we should respond to these commands. With the future thus diligently and shrewdly asessed, when the time comes for action, we will be able to withstand more easily the onslaught of Lucius. If with common cause we consider beforehand the ways by which we ought to resist, I judge there is little we need fear from the Romans. How irrational is the charge which compels this greedy Roman to demand tribute from Britain! Lucius argues that tribute must be now rendered simply because it was rendered in the past to Julius Caesar and his successors. Thinking to take advantage of the splintering discord of Britain's civil unrest, long ago the Romans in full arms landed in Britain and brought our already wavering fatherland to its knees by force and violence. And so I deem that because they took this country unjustly, they have taken tribute unjustly as well. Nothing taken by force and violence is rightfully held and since Rome took Britain by means of arms, Lucius irrationally tries to justify Britain's tributary status. Since he presumes to collect revenue from us unjustly, let us by a similar rationale demand tribute from Rome. And whoever emerges the stronger, let them plunder what they will. If Rome determines that tribute now ought to be paid because Julius Caesar and other Roman kings once subjugated Britain, then by the same reasoning I think Rome ought to pay tribute to us since my ancestors long ago held mastery over Rome. Bellinus, that most exalted King of Britain, along with his brother Brennius, Duke of Allobroges, seized Rome and in the middle of the forum hanged twenty Roman nobles. And after once having captured Rome, they held it for a goodly long time. Moreover, Constantine, the son of Helen, and Maximianus, each my relative, wearing the crown of Britain in succession, themselves once seized the throne of Roman power. Do you not think, therefore, that tribute ought to be exacted from the Romans? With respect to the other charge, that we unjustly seized Gaul and the nearby islands, there should be no response. While we were freeing them from Roman domination, Rome disdained to mount a defense."

After Arthur had spoken these words, Hoel, King of British Armorica, was the first to speak:

"Even if each one of us were able to ponder all possibilities and to reexamine all courses of action, I do not believe that anyone would discover a plan superior to that which your discrimination and shrewd discernment have taught us. The foresight of your words, spoken with Ciceronian eloquence, have anticipated our needs. We ought to praise as much as possible the disposition of this unwavering man, the effect of so wise a mind, and the profit rendered up by the best strategy. If in accord with your plan you wish to set off for Rome, I do not doubt but that we will triumph and in so doing we will safeguard our liberty and exact justice from our enemies, that same justice which they have wrongly sought to exact from us. Whoever tries to seize the belongings of another deservedly loses his own property to those whom he has attacked. Because, therefore, the Romans have set out to strip us of our possessions, undoubtedly once we have met them on the field of battle, their goods will be our own. Britain must relish such a meeting. Recall that the prophetic Sibyl foretold in verse that one born from the British race would possess three times the Roman *imperium*. The first two of these oracular predictions has been fulfilled, for it is clear that the famed princes, Belinus and Constantine, seized the insignia of Roman power. Now truly we have a third to whom is promised this pinnacle of honor. Hasten, therefore, to receive what God wishes to bestow. Hasten to subjugate that which asks to be subjugated. Hasten to exalt us all, who, in order that you yourself might be exalted, will neither shirk wounds nor fear death. To support you in this task, I pledge ten thousand armed troops."

After Hoel had finished speaking, Auguselus, King of Albany, proceeded to make clear his judgment:

"From the moment when I first recognized the intentions of my lord, such great joy entered my mind that I am now unable to express it. We would seem to have accomplished nothing in the victorious wars which we have previously fought with so many great kings and their people, as long as the Romans and Germans remain untouched ... as long as we have not courageously vindicated the slaughter which they once carried out against our people. Now since the opportunity is here to confront them, I fully rejoice and seethe for that long desired day when a meeting will take place. I thirst for their blood as I would the water from a fountain if I had been denied drink for three days. If only I might see the light of that day. How sweet will be the wounds whether received or inflicted once we have join hands in combat. Death itself will taste sugared if it comes while revenging our fathers, safeguarding our liberty, and exalting our King. Let us attack these womanly men and let us stand firm in our attack so that once we have defeated them, we might strip them of honor and achieve our joyful victory. I will add to the contingent two thousand armed knights and an untold number of foot soldiers."

After Hoel had finished, the other nobles in attendance responded in turn. One by one they pledged as many men as service to their King warranted. In addition to those promised by the Duke of Armorica, sixty thousand armed troops from the island of Britain alone were assembled. The kings of the other islands, since it was not their practice to command knights of this kind, promised as many foot soldiers as their obligation required. One hundred and twenty thousand men were drawn up from the six islands: Hibernia, Iceland, Gotland, the Orkneys, Norway, and Denmark. From the Dukedoms of the Ruteni, the Portivenses, Neuitrians, the Cenomanni, Andegauensii, and Pictavensii, eighty thousand more were assembled. And from the twelve shires of those accompanying Gerin of Chartres, one thousand two hundred men were gathered. Excluding the foot soldiers, whose number is not easily counted, the army totaled one hundred eighty three thousand and three hundred men.

As soon as King Arthur saw that all were of one mind to serve him, he instructed them to return quickly to their homes and set aside the promised number of men and then in the Kalends of August to hasten to the port of Barfleur so their armies might accompany him to the border of the Allobroges where they would engage the Romans. He ordered that it be made known to the Emperor through those same Roman envoys that the King of Britain would not return tribute and would not acquiesce to journey to Rome to face judgment over his refusal to pay. On the contrary, he sought from them what they by their own decree sought from him. Thereupon the messengers departed. The British Kings and Princes also departed and did not delay in carrying out their King's instructions.

Once Arthur's response had been made known to him, Lucius Hiberius, by the decree of the Senate, ordered the eastern kings to prepare their armies to accompany him in bringing the British people to their knees. The following quickly assembled: Epistrofus, King of Greece; Mustensar, King of the Africans; Alifatima, King of Spain; Hirtacius, King of the Parthians; Boccus of the Medes; Sertorius of Libya; Serses, King of the Iturei; Pandrasus, King of Egypt; Micipsa, King of Babylon; Politetes, Duke of Bithynia; Teucer, Duke of Phrygia; Evander of Syria; Echion of Boethia; Ypolitus of Crete; with the leaders and princes bound to them. From the Senatorial Order came Marius Lepidus, Gaius Metellus Cocta, Quintus Milvius Catullus, Quintus Carucius, and so many others that amongst them all were tallied some four hundred thousand one hundred and sixty men.

And thus with the necessary preparations made, the Romans set out for Britain at the beginning of the Kalends of August. As soon as Arthur had confirmed their advance, he entrusted the safekeeping of Britain to his nephew Mordred and Queen Guinevere. He then proceeded to Southampton and from here set sail with a favoring wind. With innumerable ships surrounding him, Arthur joyfully cut through the waves on his intended course. In the middle of the night a most heavy sleep fell upon Arthur and he dreamed that he saw a bear flying through the air. The growling of the beast caused the shoreline itself to tremble. He also saw a dreadful dragon soaring in from the west, casting a glow on the countryside with its flashing eyes. When these two creatures met, a wondrous battle ensued. The dragon repeatedly rushed at the bear until it had scorched its foe with fiery breaths and laid out his burnt carcass on the ground. When he awoke, Arthur described the dream to those standing around him. They explained that the dragon signified Arthur himself and that the bear was some giant whom he would meet in battle. The victory of the dragon foretold the same victory for Arthur. The British King, however, rejected their interpretation, believing instead that the dragon and the bear represented himself and Lucius.

At last with the night yielding to the crimson glow of dawn, they made port at Barfleur.

After pitching their tents, they awaited the arrival of the island kings and leaders of the nearby provinces. Meanwhile it was announced to Arthur that a giant of wondrous size had arrived from the regions of Spain and that it had snatched Helena, the niece of Hoel, away from her guardians and fled to the top of the mountain now called Saint Michel. The knights of the region had met with little success in their pursuit of the bear. It made no difference whether they attacked by sea or by land. The bear either sank their ships with huge rocks or impaled them on spears of various kinds. He devoured half-alive all those whom he snatched. And so at the second hour of the following night, Arthur arose and secretly set out from his tent to the side of the mountain, accompanied only by Kay, his seneschal, and Bedevere, his cupbearer. So great was the courage of Arthur that he disdained leading an army against this monster. He believed he might inspire his own men by slaying the beast himself.

When they came near the mountain, they sighted a funeral pyre burning near the peak and another on a lesser mount. Arthur ordered Bedevere to sail around to that second mountain. It was situated on the sea and hence could only be approached from the water. As Bedevere began his ascent, Arthur started climbing up the side of the other mountain. Before Bedevere had reached the summit, the sudden shriek of a woman caused him to bristle since he had not expected to encounter the monster. But he quickly recalled his courage and drew out his sword. When he arrived at the top of the mountain, however, he saw nothing other than the fire he had spotted earlier. A moment later he beheld a newly formed funeral mound and a woman weeping and wailing alongside it. When the woman saw Bedevere, she broke off her mourning and arose to address him:

"Oh unlucky man, what curse has led you to this place? I take pity on you who are about to suffer the indescribable tortures of death. On this night a terrible monster will consume the flower of your youth. A most wicked giant, called by a hateful name, will arrive here on this very spot. He carried off the niece of Duke Hoel along with me, her nurse, to this mountain top. Only just now have I buried the dear girl. Without the least hesitation he will inflict upon you the same unspeakable death. Oh what sad fates! O dear foster-child, once so serene. When that evil monster snatched her, fear seized her delicate heart and so ended a life worthy to have lasted many more days. Since he was unable to defile the body of the girl, who was like another breath to me, another life, my own sweet joy, he violently brought down all his burning lust upon my unwilling body. By God I swear it's true. Oh flee dear friend, flee lest when he returns to rape me, he should discover you here and rip your body into pieces, making pitiful slaughter of you."

Bedevere was moved as much as human nature might allow and immediately calmed her with tender words. After he had given his solemn promise to bring help quickly, he hurried off to report his discovery to Arthur. The King bemoaned the ruin of the girl and ordered that he alone be given the chance to slay the monster. Only if necessity demanded it, should they forcefully rush forward with aid. Entrusting their mounts to the squires, Arthur and his two men turned to the taller of the mountains and with the King leading the way began their ascent.

The inhuman beast was sitting near a fire, befouling his mouth with the putrid flesh of a half eaten pig which he had roasted on a spit over live coals. When he caught sight of his unexpected guests, he quickly turned to grip a club so heavy that two young men might scarcely lift it off the ground. Arthur drew his sword, held his shield before him, and rushed forward as fast as possible in order to reach the brute before he could seize its club. But the giant recognized Arthur's bloody intent and had already gripped his weapon. He struck the King's shield with such force that the sound of the blow reverberated along the shoreline and deafened beyond human measure the ears of Arthur. The anger of the British King was now set ablaze. He brought down his raised sword and inflicted a wound, which although not lethal, penetrated so deeply that blood flowed down across the face of the beast and blinded his eyes. Only by deflecting the blow at the last moment had the giant staved off death. Now the beast rose up literally in a blind rage, and just as a boar rushes past the huntsman's spear to assault the huntsman himself, so did this monster sweep past Caliburn to attack his attacker. The giant took hold of Arthur about the midsection and drove him to his knees. But Arthur quickly regained his manly strength and broke free from his grasp. Now on this side, now on that, the King used his sword to thrash at his ungodly foe. Nor did he rest until he had dealt a lethal wound forcing down the sharp point of his sword into the head of the beast where the skull covered the brain. The monster screamed out and then collapsed in a heap just as an oak ravaged by the force of the wind lets out a groan and falls to the earth. Now free from the burden of combat, Arthur fell into laughter. He ordered Bedevere to sever the monster's head from its body and carry it to the camp so that it might serve as an emblem for all to see.

Arthur avowed that he had never encountered a foe of such strength since that time on Mount Arvaius when he slew Retho, another giant who had challenged him to do battle. That creature had fashioned a pelt from the beards of slain kings and had ordered Arthur to shear his own beard and add it to his collection. Since Arthur was preeminent over all other kings, the giant promised to place his beard atop the other hairy trophies. If, however, Arthur chose combat, whoever prevailed would carry off the pelt itself, as well as the beard of his victim. Hardly had the contest begun when Arthur triumphed and seized his shaggy prize. In the days that followed, he boasted that he had never encountered an adversary stronger than Retho.

Now with victory in hand, Arthur and his men returned to their camp at dawn of the following day, bearing the severed head with them. Crowds rushed forward to wonder at the spoil and praised Arthur for having freed the country of such a gluttonous beast. But Hoel, saddened by the death of his niece, ordered a basilica to be built above her burial mound on the mountain top where she was lying. To this day that mountain is called Helen in honor of her grave site.

At last, after all of those expected had assembled, Arthur set out for Autun where he believed he would encounter the Roman Emperor. When Arthur reached the Aube River, it was reported that the Emperor had made camp not far off and was marching with an army of such size as to be invincible. Arthur, however, was unimpressed and had no intention of abandoning his undertaking. Above the bank of the river the King made his own camp, selecting a site from which he could easily lead forth his army or if necessity demanded, withdraw from battle.

Arthur sent two envoys, Boso of Oxford and Guerin of Chartres, along with his nephew Gawain, to demand that Lucius Hiberius leave Gaul or on the next day meet the Britons in combat to determine who had the greater right to possess the region. The young men of the court shook with pleasure at the prospect of fighting and took it upon themselves to convince Gawain to provoke an incident in the Emperor's camp so that the battle with the Romans might begin immediately. The envoys approached Lucius and ordered him to withdraw or prepare for battle on the following day. The Emperor shot back that he had no thought of leaving and that he intended to rule the entire territory. Amongst the throng of Romans was Gaius Quintillianus, who proclaimed that the British had a greater supply of boasts and threats than they had of courage or battle tested valor. The insult enraged Gawain, and he immediately drew his sword from its scabbard and loped off the head of Gaius. Gawain and the other envoys then raced for their horses with the Romans in hot pursuit, some mounted and others on foot, all seeking revenge for their slain comrade. When one of the Romans had almost reached him, Gerin of Chartres suddenly turned and with his upturned lance laid out his pursuer on the ground, piercing through the armor into his midsection with as much force as he could muster. Full of envy over the exploit of his comrade, Boso of Oxford turned his own horse and thrust his lance into the throat of the first Roman he met, driving him to ground and inflicting a mortal wound. Meanwhile, Marcellus Mutius, hot to revenge the death of Quintillianus, had nearly reached Gawain and was about to lay hold of him when Gawain suddenly turned, cutting downward with his sword straight through the Roman's helmet and skull. Gawain ordered his victim to announce to the already Hell-bound Quintillianus that the British held in great abundance such boasts as had been fulfilled on this day.

Gawain now grouped his company together and urged each one to turn about and in like manner choose his own victim for slaughter. Following his command, each British soldier turned and dealt death to his pursuer. The Romans, however, pressed on, striking at the British with swords and lances, yet failing to seize or slay any of their enemy.

When the two sides finally reached the edge of a wooded area, six thousand British soldiers rushed forth from their hiding places without any warning. When they learned of the plight of their comrades, they decided to conceal themselves amongst the trees in order at the right moment to burst forth with aid. Now they dug their spurs into their horses and filled the air with shouting. With shields held high to protect their chests, they attacked the Romans and immediately forced the enemy to flee. Pressing on with a single intent, they used their lances to knock some from their horses; others they took as prisoners; still others they killed.

When news of the British counterattack reached the Roman Senator Petreius, he rushed forth with ten thousand soldiers to provide support for his troops now under assault. Although not without suffering their own losses, the Romans forced the British to retreat back into the woods from which they had come. Yet when they reached narrow passageways in the forest, Arthur's men turned on their attackers and inflicted the greatest carnage possible. Hyder, the son of Nu, charged forward with his soldiery to aid his comrades who were yielding ground to the Romans. Mounting heavy resistance, the British faced their chests to the enemy and labored to bring powerful blows down on those to whom a short while ago they had shown their backs. So now it was the turn of the Romans to offer resistance. Some Romans were knocked to the ground but others were leveling their enemy. The British lusted for battle and no care, not even of death, slackened their passion for killing. The Romans, however, fought more wisely. In the manner of an experienced leader, Petreius instructed his men in when to attack and when to fall back. As a result, the Romans were threatening to rain down on Arthur's men the greatest devastation. When Boso recognized the imminent peril, he took aside those whom he knew were the boldest and spoke these words:

"Since we began this battle with Arthur as yet unaware, we must take care lest we fall into the worst of it on this day. If we fail, we will incur a very great loss of men and be cursed by our King as well. So find your courage and follow me through this throng of Romans, and if fortune so favors, let us either kill or capture Petreius himself."

At once they put spurs to their horses' flanks and in tight formation pushed through the wedge shaped ranks of the enemy. Having reached the site where Petreius was directing his men, Boso quickly darted forward, grabbed the Senator by the neck, and just as he had planned, pulled him to the ground. The Romans rushed up to rescue Petreius while the British pushed forward to aid Boso. One side struggled to free their leader, the other to hold him fast. All this happened amidst the confusion of wild shouting and the clamor of the greatest slaughter. Men on both sides were being wounded. Some were inflicting death, others suffering it. One could look out and see at any one moment who was prevailing with spear, with sword or with lance. Finally, the closely packed formation of the British was able to fend off the Romans and reach their own fortified lines with Petreius in tow. They then immediately launched a counterattack against the enemy. Bereaved of their leader and debilitated by the fighting, the Romans turned their backs to the British. Pressing forward, Arthur's men brought down any that had slowed, striped spoils from those already on the ground, and trampled over plundered bodies in pursuit of those whom they still might take as prisoners for their King. Finally satiated with battle, the British withdrew with spoils and captives to their camp. Along with a gladsome victory, they presented Petreius and other Roman prisoners to Arthur.

Arthur congratulated his men and promised them honors, indeed, an abundance of honors, since in his absence they had displayed such worthiness. Arthur ordered the confinement of the Roman prisoners and called forth a company to convey them to Paris where they would be handed over to the guards of the city and retained until further notice. He ordered Duke Cador, Bedevere the cup bearer, and his two counsels, Borellus and Richerius, along with their retinue of men, to lead the prisoners along the route where they least feared an enemy attack.

The Romans learned by chance of Arthur's preparations, and at their leader's command, selected fifteen thousand men to intercept the British during the night and steadfastly fight to free the prisoners. The Romans placed two Senators, Vulteius Catellus and Quintus Carucius, along with Evander, King of Syria, and Sertorius, King of Libya, at the head of their troops. That night they set out as ordered with the aforementioned troops and having reached a position suitable for ambush, the Romans concealed themselves where they determined the enemy would pass.

On the following morning, the British set out with their prisoners, unaware of the treachery their enemy had planned. When Arthur's men had advanced to the point of ambush, the Romans unexpectedly rushed out, attacking and penetrating the ranks of their unsuspecting enemy. Although they had been set upon without warning, Arthur's men managed to regroup and to offer fierce resistance. While Richerius and Bedevere stationed men to guard the prisoners, Cador, the Duke of Cornwall, and Borellus drew into formation those remaining troops to hold off the enemy. The Romans, however, refused to be organized into ranks and attacked in disorder. While the British were still coming into formation and deciding upon a strategy of defense, the Romans attacked making every effort to bring slaughter down onto their enemies.

Crippled beyond measure, Arthur's men would have given up their prisoners to the Romans if fortune had not quickly delivered them much needed help. After news of the ambush had reached the camp, the Duke of Poitevins, Guitard, rushed forth with three thousand men. Buttressed with these reinforcements, the British prevailed in turning the slaughter back onto the impudent and insidious Romans. Nevertheless, they lost Borellus, the famous Lord of Cenomanni, who while battling Evander, King of Syria, felt a lance pierce through his body and along with his blood spewed forth his life. The British also lost four noble princes: Hyrelgas of Periron, Maurice Cador of Cahors, Aliduc of Tintagel, and Her, the son of Hyder. Men more daring than these cannot easily be found. Despite their initial losses, the courage and spirit of the British did not wane, fighting to the utmost to hold their prisoners and kill the enemy. At last, the Romans could no longer bear the onslaught of the British and hastily retreated to their camps. Arthur's men gave chase, slaughtering some of the Romans and taking others prisoner. Nor did they let up until Vulteius Catellus and Evander, King of Syria, had been killed. Those Romans still remaining were dispersed and scattered across the battlefield. Once having achieved victory, the British sent the aforementioned prisoners ahead to Paris and delivered those newly captured to Arthur. Since a few had overcome so many, this engagement promised victory for the British in the war against Rome.

Lucius Hiberius suffered the defeat badly. His tortured mind flew about from one thought to another, uncertain whether he should immediately do battle with Arthur or withdraw to Autun and await reinforcements from Emperor Leo. Surrendering to his fears, Lucius set out for Autun and on the following night led his army into the city of Langres. When Arthur learned of the Roman withdrawal, he decided to position himself ahead of Lucius. And so on that same night, Arthur marched past Langres and entered a valley called Siesia through which the Romans would necessarily pass. Arthur decided to divide his troops into squadrons. He placed one of these under the command of Morvid and ordered him to stay in place. If the need arose, Arthur would then have a place to which he might withdraw, reform his troops and mount a counterattack against the enemy. He divided the remaining troops into seven squadrons and to each assigned five thousand five hundred and fifty armed men of which cavalry made up one part, foot soldiers the other. Arthur ordered the cavalry to wait until the infantry was advancing to meet the enemy head on and then to draw itself into formation and be ready to strike from an oblique angle and scatter the unsuspecting enemy. In the British custom, the foot soldiers were formed into a square with left and right wings. Auguselus, King of Albany, commanded the right wing, Cador, Duke of Cornwall, the left. Two distinguished leaders, Gerin of Chartres and Boso of Rydychen, which the Saxons call Oxford, were placed in charge of the second squadron. The third command went to Aschil, King of Denmark, and Loth, King of Norway; the fourth to Hoel, Duke of Armorica, and Gawain, nephew of Arthur. Four other squadrons were stationed at the rear. Kay, the Seneschal, and Bedevere, the cup bearer, commanded one; another Holdin, Duke of the Ruteni, and Guitard, Duke of Poitevens; the third, Jugenis of Leicester, Jonathel of Dorchester, and Cursalem of Caichester; the fourth, Urbgennius of Bath. Arthur stationed one squadron of his own behind these troops. Here he planted his standard, marked with a golden dragon, to designate a place, as if it were a garrison, where if necessary the weary and wounded could withdraw. In Arthur's squadron there were six thousand six hundred and sixty six men. After these arrangements had been completed, the British King addressed his men with the following words:

"My fellow countrymen, you who have made Britain master of thirty kingdoms, I praise your excellence which I see does not slacken but grows greater and greater. Although for five years you have not trained for acts of war, devoted more to delights of court than to military exercises, in no way has your native worth deteriorated. Persevering with that integrity, you have forced the Romans to flee. Spurred by their own pride, they came here to strip you of your freedom. And although they struck in greater numbers, they were unable to withstand your own advance. In lock step did they shamefully retreat to that city from which they are about to begin their march to Autun. They will pass through this very valley, and here you will be able to trap them and slaughter their troops like unsuspecting sheep. They believed you were tainted with the lethargy of eastern peoples, and so they sought to make Britain a tributary nation and yourselves a slavish people. Did they not know that you carried war to the Danes, the Norwegians, and the Gauls and that you released those peoples from the shameful mastery of the Romans and brought them instead under the auspices of my own authority? We, therefore, who have prevailed in weightier battles, if with the same resolve we strive to trample these effeminate Romans, so too in this lesser contest will we prevail. Great is the honor each one of you will possess, if by my will and command you persist in being faithful soldiers! Once we have trampled on these Romans, we will immediately set off for Rome. Having sought it out, we will seize it; having seized it, we will own it. Gold, silver, palaces, towers, towns, and along with all the other spoils of the conquered, these will be yours."

All replied with a single shout, each man eager to embrace death rather than flee the scene of battle and shamefully hold onto their lives.

When Lucius Hiberius learned of the trap which the British had prepared for him, his initial impulse was to flee. But he summoned his previous courage and decided to meet the enemy head on in the valley rather than to retreat. He called together his leaders and uttered these words:

"Venerable fathers, by whose power the kingdoms of east and west are compelled to submit, remember our ancestors who in order to subdue the enemies of the Republic did not shrink from spilling their own blood and by so doing bequeathed to their descendants a model of worthiness and soldiery. They fought as if God had foreordained that not one of them should die in battle. Repeatedly did they triumph, and in their triumphs they cheated death, believing that such a fate would come to no man unless decreed by God. Thus the Republic did grow and so too the eminence of these men. The repute, the respect, and the largesse which is expected of men of noble stock, flourished in these men for a long time. These qualities provided our ancestors with the strength needed to hold dominion over the entire world. I wish to ignite that same strength in you and so I beseech you to call up into yourselves that same ancestral valor. I beseech you to maintain that valor and to seek out your enemies in this valley where treachery festers. Take from them what by right you may call your own. Do not think that I entered this city because I abhorred meeting the British in battle but rather that I reckoned they would stupidly pursue us and that we would be able turn and scatter them headlong before striking them dead. Now since they have done otherwise, let us do otherwise as well. Let us seek them out and audaciously bring the fury of war down onto them. If they at first should prove stronger, let us together resist them and hold off their first wave of attack. In this way we will triumph, for those who are able to persist in the first sortie most often leave the field as victors."

Having uttered these words and many others, Lucius put an end to speaking. With all approving by common assent and all swearing allegiance by the pledge of hands, the Romans hastened to arm themselves. Once armed, they left Langres and entered the valley where Arthur had stationed his troops. In accordance with Roman practice, the troops were divided into twelve wedged shaped squadrons each containing six thousand six hundred and sixty six men and each under its own commander with the authority to signal when to attack and when to hold firm against those attacking. Lucius Catellus and Ali Fatima, King of Spain, commanded one cohort; another, Hirtacius, King of the Parthians, and the Senator, Marius Lepidus; the third, Boccus, King of the Medes, and the Senator, Gaius Metellus; the fourth, Sertorius, King of Libya, and the Senator, Quintus Milvius. These four legions were stationed on the front line. Behind these were another four. At the head of the first, Serses, King of the Iturei; the second, Pandrasus, King of Egypt; the third, Politetes, Duke of Bithynia; and the fourth, Teucer, Duke of Phrygia. Behind these were the final four legions. The Senator, Quintus Carucius, commanded the first; the second, Lelius Hostiensis; the third, Sulpicius Subuculus; and the fourth, Mauricius Silvanus. Lucius himself went here and there amongst the men to advise and instruct how they should conduct themselves. He ordered that the golden eagle, which he brought as his standard, be firmly fixed in the center where anyone separated in battle could fall back.

Finally, with lances raised, the two armies faced one another, the British on one side, the Romans on the other. At the sound of the battle horns, the Roman legion commanded by the King of Spain and Lucius Catellus immediately and boldly charged the British contingent headed by the King of Scotland and the Duke of Cornwall. The Romans, however, were unable to scatter the tight formation of the British. At this point the cavalry commanded by Gerin and Boso raced up to meet the fierce Roman attack. With the aforementioned British squadron holding off the frontal attack, suddenly the cavalry charged the Romans, breeching the enemy line and encountering the legion which the King of the Parthians was leading against the troops of Aschil, King of the Danes. Without delay, the sides rushed together in a scattered melée. In every part of the battlefield a frenetic clamor arose amidst the pitiful slaughter. Men struck the ground with their heads and heels and disgorged their souls along with their life blood.

The misfortunes of battle first fell upon the British. Bedevere, the cup bearer, was killed and Kay, the seneschal, mortally wounded. The former was run through with the lance of Boccus, King of the Medes, and fell dead amidst the enemy. Kay tried to avenge his comrade's death, but surrounded by a crowd of Medes, received what would prove a lethal wound. Nevertheless, in the manner of a fine warrior, Kay led his men forward and opened a path through the fallen and disbanded Medes. He would have carried his squadron of men unbroken back to his own camp if he had not encountered the cohort of the King of Libya which now broke through and scattered his troops. Falling back with only a handful of men, Kay fled to the standard of the Golden Dragon carrying the body of Bedevere with him. How great was the lamentation of the Neustrians when they saw the corpse of their leader torn to pieces with so many wounds. How great was the wailing of the Angevins as they attended to the many wounds of Kay.

But it was not yet time to indulge in mourning. The bloody lines of battle would not permit it; the British were forced instead to defend themselves. Hyrelgas, the nephew of Bedevere, moved beyond measure by his uncle's death, gathered together three hundred of his own men. Just as a boar drives through a pack of dogs, so did his cavalry charge through the enemy legions, setting its sights on the standard of the King of the Medes. Oblivious to danger, Hyrelgas reached his goal and slew the King. He bore the body back to camp, laid it alongside that of Bedevere and then proceeded to rip it to shreds. Hyrelgas urged his comrades to rush the enemy, to rain upon them repeated blows while they were still filled with fresh rage, while the chests of their enemies were trembling with fright, while men of fearsome violence were wisely positioned through their ranks, and while they were able to inflict repeatedly cruel destruction on their enemy. Aroused by the urgency in his voice, the British attacked. The greatest slaughter fell on each side. Innumerable Romans were killed: Ali Fatima, King of Spain; Micipsa of Babylon; the Senators, Quintus Milvius and Marius Lepidus. On the British side: Holdin, Duke of the Ruteni; Leodegarius of Boulogne; and three other British leaders: Crusalem of Caichester; Guallauc of Salisbury; and Urbgennius of Bath. Finally, the British troops, crippled beyond measure, pulled back all the way to the line of the Armoricans which was under the command of Hoel and Gawain. And just as a flame might ignite without warning, the battalion suddenly turned and attacked the enemy. With those restored who a moment before had taken flight, the British forced their former pursuers to flee, knocking them to the ground as they went. Nor did they back away from the bloody slaughter until they had reached the Roman leader's own troops. Lucius witnessed the disaster to his men and hastened to shore up his defensive lines.

In the initial clash of arms, the British suffered great losses. Chinmarchocus, Duke of Treguier, along with two thousand others, fell to the ground. Then three more went down, each a famous prince: Riddomarcus, Bloctonius, and Iaginvius of Bodloan. So eminent was their native virtue that if they had lived to be kings, these men would have been celebrated in ages to come. When the British launched their attack, led by Hoel and Gawain, these three encountered no one who could escape their deadly weapons. But after they had reached the battle line of Lucius, they found themselves hemmed in on every side and so along with the aforementioned Chinmarchocus and his men, they too were struck down.

No previous age had given birth to men more noble than Hoel and Gawain. Thus when they learned of the butchery done to their men, they girded themselves and charged ahead, attacking the wedge of the Emperor's legion from every side. Gawain, always bursting with fierce energy, did his utmost to reach Lucius himself. Boldly advancing he knocked to the ground and stripped of life anyone that came in his path. Hoel, hardly inferior to Gawain, flashed like lightning from the other side, pressing his men forward as he cut down the enemy. He was undaunted by enemy blows and at each instance he was either attacking or being attacked. It is not an easy task to say which of these two exceeded the other on the battlefield that day.

Gawain continued to work his way through the enemy troops until he finally had achieved the long sought encounter with Lucius. He rushed at the Roman commander and so began the combat between them. Lucius possessed the daring, vigor, and worth of a young man and yearned for the meeting. Against a warrior such as Gawain he would be forced to prove on the battlefield his strength and worthiness. And so he gloried to enter the fray against one of such great fame as Gawain. They fought for a long while and dealt each other powerful blows, each fending off the other with his shield.

While they fought so fiercely with one another, the Romans suddenly gathered themselves. Determined to bring aid to their leader, they charged the Armoricans and steadily pushing forward forced Hoel, Gawain, and their cohort to pull back. But then they suddenly crossed the path of Arthur. Having heard the sounds of the enemy onslaught against his men, the British King had moved a legion forward. He now raised Caliburn aloft and in a booming and turbulent voice sought to inspire his men with these words:

"What are you doing? Will you permit these women to escape? Oh, let not one of them escape alive. Remember your powerful right hands which in the past have added to my kingdom thirty more. Remember that in the past when the Romans were strong, they reduced your forefathers to tributary status. Remember your liberty which these effeminate half men, weaker than yourselves, dare to snatch from you. Let not one of our enemy escape alive ... I say not one. Now answer me ... what will you do?"

After he had shouted out these words and others, Arthur immediately charged the enemy. The British King tossed Romans to the ground, hacked at them, slaughtered whoever came in his path, either killing the rider or the horse with a single blow. Just as sheep flee a fierce lion driven by savage hunger to devour whatever victim chance might offer up, so the Romans fled from Arthur. Their armor afforded them no protection. That mighty sword Caliburn vibrated in Arthur's powerful right hand as he forced his enemies to spew forth blood along with their souls. Two kings, Sertorius of Libya and Politetes of Bithynia, had the misfortune to step in his way. Arthur dispatched them to Hell, separating their heads from their bodies.

The sight of their King delivering death to the Romans filled the British troops with greater daring. In a closely packed formation and with a single intention, they charged the Romans. While from one side the foot soldiers repeatedly attacked, from the other the cavalry knocked the enemy to the ground and impaled their bodies. The Romans offered fierce resistance. With Lucius shouting encouragement, they struggled to heap onto their enemy the same slaughter which King Arthur had bestowed. The two sides fought with the ferocity one would expect on the first day of battle. On this side, Arthur repeatedly struck down the enemy and urged his men to stand firm. On the other side, Lucius Hiberius exhorted his men and led them on in noble deeds. Nor did he himself shrink from the sword. He went amongst his troops and struck down with blade or lance whatever enemy chance offered up. Horrid slaughter fell on each side. At one moment the British prevailed, at another the Romans. With the bloody contest proceeding in this manner, Morvid, Lord of Gloucester, with a legion stationed on a hill above the battlefield, charged at the back of the unsuspecting enemy. He broke through their ranks, scattering the enemy and delivering death as he went. By the thousands the Romans fell, and at length Lucius himself, the leader of these men, fighting amidst his troops, was pierced full of holes by some soldier's lance and toppled dead to the ground. The British pressed them on every side, and although it took the greatest effort, finally seized victory.

Disorganized and goaded on by fear, some Romans fled along hidden pathways into the forest; others ran to cities and towns. Regardless, each Roman sought asylum from the carnage. The British, however, pressed on in pursuit and inflicted pitiless slaughter. They took prisoners and stripped them of spoils. The greatest part of the captured Romans stretched forth their hands and like women begged to be bound so that they might live a short while longer rather than be killed on the spot. The conclusion of this fierce battle came about through the agency of Divine Providence. The Romans of earlier times had hounded the ancestors of the British with hateful abuse, and now the British were striving to safeguard the freedom which the Romans were attempting to seize and to deny the tribute which the Romans unjustly demanded.

Having achieved victory, Arthur ordered that the bodies of his fallen nobles be separated out from the enemy carcasses and prepared in royal fashion to be conveyed to their provincial abbeys where they would be buried with honor. Bedevere, the cup bearer, was carried to Bayeux, the city founded by his grandfather, the first Bedevere. Amidst the greatest lamentations of the Normans, his body was born away. There is a certain cemetery in the southern part of the city, and it was here alongside the wall where Bedevere was interred with honor. The gravely wounded Kay was taken to Chinon, a city he himself had founded. Here, a short while later, he died. Within a monastery of hermits in a wooded area not far from the town, as was befitting the Duke of Angevins, Kay was placed in the ground. Holdin, Duke of the Ruteni, was conveyed to Flanders and buried in his own city of Therouanne. The remaining princes and retainers were carried to nearby abbeys. Taking pity on the enemy, the King instructed that the fallen be buried by the local inhabitants. But he ordered the body of Lucius to be sent to Rome with the message that the British were no longer obliged to pay tribute.

Arthur remained in this region through the following winter where he was granted the time to subjugate the cities of the Allobroges. When summer came, Arthur set out for Rome. But just as he was about to ascend the mountains, news came that Mordred, the King's nephew, to whom he had entrusted the safekeeping of his kingdom, in the manner of a tyrant and thief had crowned himself with the royal diadem and that Guinevere, Arthur's own queen, violating her nuptial pledge, had joined herself to Mordred in foul lust.

Concerning this matter, O August Lord, Geoffrey of Monmouth will hold his tongue. Instead, he will disclose, albeit in a low style, the battles which King Arthur fought with his nephew once he had returned to Britain with victory in hand. These events Geoffrey discovered in the aforementioned book in the British language and from Walter of Oxford, a man most skilled in the many histories he has heard.

When the traitorous impiety of the aforementioned crime touched his ears, the King decided to put off his planned attack against Leo, Emperor of the Romans. Arthur sent Hoel, Duke of Armorica, along with an army of Gauls, to pacify the region. He then immediately returned to Britain accompanied only by the island kings and their troops. The wicked traitor Mordred sent Cheldric, a Saxon duke, to Germany to gather together whatever allies he could muster and return with them as quickly as possible. He had pledged that he would give the Saxons that part of the island which stretched from the Humber all the way to Scotland and those parts of Kent which Horsus and Hengist had held in the time of Vortigern. Cheldric carried out the order and landed in Britain with eight hundred ships filled with armed pagans. He pledged to obey the traitorous Mordred as if the usurper were truly King. In addition, Mordred formed an alliance with the Scots, Picts, Hibernians, and whomever else he understood to hold a grudge against his uncle. All told, he amassed around eighty thousand men, some pagans and others Christians.

Accompanied by this multitude and confident of his strength, Mordred met Arthur as he arrived on the British coast and in the battle which ensued, inflicted the greatest slaughter on those attempting to leap ashore. Auguselus, King of Albany and Gawain, nephew of the King, and countless others died that day. Ywain, son of Urian, the brother of Auguselus, succeeded his uncle in holding the kingdom and in many later wars proved his worth and attained great fame. Nevertheless, with great effort Arthur's men finally took the shore, dealing out death and forcing Mordred and his army to retreat. Arthur's men were well experienced in battle and had stationed themselves wisely. The cavalry was so positioned that when the foot soldiers were either attacking or holding off an attack, the horsemen could ride up quickly from an oblique angle and break through the enemy line, forcing the enemy to take flight. Having regrouped what was left of his army, the oath breaker Mordred entered Winchester on the following night. When these events were reported to Guinevere, she immediately fell into despair and fled from York to the City of Legions. In the church of Julius the Martyr she adopted the ways of the nuns, choosing to live a chaste life.

Arthur was filled with rage over losing so many hundreds of men. And so on the third day, after the dead had been given proper burial, he proceeded to Winchester and laid siege to the city where the foul traitor Mordred had taken refuge. But the King's nephew was not deterred from his undertaking. He urged on those troops which had remained loyal to him and with these and his own men marched out of the city and put his army in position to do battle with Arthur. Once the battle began, great slaughter fell on each side. So great, however, was the carnage to Mordred's army that he was forced shamefully to abandon the battlefield. With little concern over the burial of the dead, he was swiftly conveyed by oarmen toward Cornwall. Arthur grieved that his nephew had again eluded him. At once he pursued the traitor all the way to the River Camblam. Here Mordred awaited the King's arrival. Always the boldest of men and most ready to attack, Mordred divided his men into squadrons, resolved to conquer or to die before again taking flight. There remained to him from the earlier number of allies sixty thousand men, and from these he drew up six battalions, placing in each six thousand six hundred and sixty six men. After appointing commanders to these cohorts, he formed from those remaining one additional battalion which he entrusted to himself. He urged them on and promised them the spoils of the enemy if they stood firm and triumphed.

Arthur divided his own army into nine battalions of foot soldiers and positioned them directly facing Mordred's troops. He drew the battalions into a square with a right and left wing and to each he assigned a commander. He exhorted his men to slay those perjurers and thieves who had been brought by a traitor from foreign lands in order to strip them of their honor. He called the enemy a mongrel pack of barbarians assembled from different lands, untested in war and ignorant of the techniques of battle. He told his troops that if they boldly attacked and fought like men, the enemy would not be able to hold off troops of such strength and so well practiced in war. And thus with each side exhorted to do battle, they met in a sudden surge of energy and strained to rain showers of blows onto one another. So great was the slaughter on each side, so great the groans of the dying, so great the furor of those attacking, that it is painful to describe. There was wounding and being wounded, killing and being killed. After much of the day had been spent in this way, Arthur rushed forward with his battalion of six thousand six hundred and sixty six men. They blasted through the enemy in the direction of Mordred, cutting a path with their swords and inflicting horrific slaughter on all around them until they finally reached the false King himself. The foul traitor was cut down and with him many thousand more. Although their leader had fallen, those remaining did not flee. Instead, they came together from every part of the battlefield and tried to hold their ground with as much valor as possible. The fiercest of battles ensued. Nearly every leader who was present on each side charged forward with their troops into the melée. On the side of Mordred these Saxons fell: Chelric, Elaf, Egbrict and Bruning; these Irish: Gillapatric, Gillamor, and Gillasel; and all the other Scots and Picts under the traitor's command. On the side of Arthur fell Odbrict, King of Norway; Aschil, King of Denmark; Cador Limenich, Cassibellaunus; and others, both British and foreign troops. The renowned King of Britain, Arthur himself, was mortally wounded on that day and was carried to the Island of Avalon for the tending of his wounds. He yielded the crown of Britain to his cousin Constantine, son of Cador, the Duke of Cornwall. In the year 542 from the Lord's incarnation.

Wace. *Roman de Brut* (The Romance of Brutus): A Selection

Translated by R. Barton Palmer

After defeating the English army under Harold at the Battle of Hastings (14 October 1066), William, duke of Normandy, quickly consolidated his rule over the rest of the country. Once resistance to his rule had been crushed, William had himself crowned king at Westminster Abbey (25 December 1066). Within a short time, the English aristocracy was displaced in favor of a new class of local and regional rulers, mostly but not exclusively Norman. Continental in outlook and language, these men, and the courts over which they presided, were naturally interested in the culture of a land they had previously little reason or opportunity to come to know. England's French aristocracy thus constituted an audience interested in treatments, especially in the pleasing form of poetry, of the history and legends of their new possession. The fascination with an Arthur conceived as a major figure in that history quickly translated itself into a series of Latin and then French and English works that came to constitute a kind of epic tradition, at the center of which looms the impressive figure of this remarkable king. Arthur dominates this tradition in much the same way that Charlemagne figures in the various *chansons de geste*, most notably the *Chanson de Roland*, that treat his accomplishments as a warrior king, as well as the considerable exploits of the figures associated with him.

During the century or so after the conquest, writers were attracted by the prospect of finding support or patrons to England's courts, especially that of the magnificent royal court William and his successors established in London, who constituted the Angevin dynasty. The dialect in which they composed, Anglo-Norman, became one of Europe's most important literary languages, even as the English nobility, now part of the French-speaking world, became indispensable patrons of a vernacular literature that was fast becoming a potent rival to narratives written in Latin for a narrowed, less secular readership. This literary efflorescence constituted an important part of a more general cultural awakening, perhaps renaissance, that was a central feature of the High Middle Ages (c. 1125–1300).

One would-be writer attracted to this vibrant court culture was a man named Wace, born around 1100 on the Channel Island of Jersey, then attached to the duchy of Normandy. Wace eventually made his way to England and established himself as an important figure at the court of Henry II during his long and illustrious reign (1154–1189). Wace was the poet's Christian, not family, name, and it is the only one he provides us in a series of autobiographical passages in the *Roman de Rou*, one of his two major vernacular poetic works, a history of the duke of Normandy, who traced their line back to a ninth-century Viking chieftain, Hrolfr, Rollo or Rou in its Latinized and French vernacular forms. As a young man, Wace was brought to the abbey-dominated Norman city of Caen for an education that was intended to prepare him for a career in the church. He proved an apt enough pupil to secure further schooling in the Île de France, likely at a cathedral school such as the one established at Notre Dame on the Île de la Cité, but by his early twenties Wace had returned to Caen, where, as he says, he found employment as a *clerc lisant*, by which he perhaps means as a secretary, one of whose duties was to read aloud.

But it seems that he was much too ambitious to be satisfied working as only one of the numerous clerics preoccupied with the details of ducal administration. A path for preferment lay open to educated men like him who could produce entertaining and edifying works for lay readers and listeners, and during his twenties Wace transformed himself into an impressively productive writer of religious narratives. Most of these texts are now lost, but the three that have been preserved, lives of St. Nicholas and St. Margaret, as well as a treatment of the Virgin Mary's immaculate conception, demonstrate considerable poetic gifts. In them, he displays a knack for writing free-flowing octosyllabic lines with verve and style, even as he manages narratives of some complexity, qualities he would further develop when he later turned his hand to secular subjects. Whether providentially or by design, Wace arrived in England at about the same time that Henry, duke of Anjou and Normandy, was able to press successfully his claim to the throne, ending a period of unrest, uncertainty, and civil war. He was crowned Henry II, king of England, in 1154 and, along with one of the most eminent figures of lay literary culture in the Middle Ages, his queen, Eleanor of Aquitaine, he made the royal court the age's leading literary center. The literature of the age was in large part a literature of translation and adaptation, with Latin texts of various kinds (including ancient ones like Virgil's *Aeneid*) furnishing materials for vernacular treatment. English history had already established itself as a popular subject with Geffrei Gaimar's *Estoire des Engles*, finished in the late 1130s for a regional noble patron. Wace soon devoted himself to composing a narrative of much bigger scope, translating into French octosyllabic couplets the *Historia Regum Anglorum* of Geoffrey of Monmouth, written about 1138 or perhaps two decades before Wace turned his hand to translating it for a French-speaking lay audience. Wace was not the first French writer to produce a vernacular version of the *Historia*; the work furnished Geffrei Gaimar with some of his materials (he also drew on a vernacular source, the *Anglo-Saxon Chronicle*). But Wace was the first to produce a full version of Geffrei in French, which he titled the *Roman de Brut* after the Roman Brutus, the legendary progenitor of the British people. His *Brut* is much more than a straightforward translation of its Latin exemplar. Wace infuses his story with many reminiscences of vernacular epic, the *chanson de geste*, such as intermittent addresses to the reader or listener, who is called upon to imagine what it would have been like to "see" or "hear" the events then being recounted by the narrator. The descriptions of knightly combat are convincingly detailed, with careful accounts of physical action enlivening the otherwise inevitably repetitive nature of the subject matter. Wace's attention to psychology, though hardly producing the round characters desired in modern fiction, makes his characters stand out as individuals, even when they are evoked only momentarily on their way to a death in battle that swiftly follows. It is altogether a virtuoso performance, and Wace stands comparison with other master storytellers of the period, including Chrétien de Troyes, Marie de France, and Wace's own rival for the favor of Henry and Eleanor, Benoît de Sainte-Maure, author of the celebrated *Roman de Troie* (Romance of Troy). Wace's contribution to the continuing popularity of Arthurian story in the Middle Ages is incalculable.

Because of its suspenseful narrative and effective management of a complex story involving numerous focus characters, we have decided to include the section of Wace dealing with Arthur's defeat of the Roman emperor Lucius. This English version follows Judith Weiss's careful edition of the text (based on Ivor Arnold's 1938 edition, which was based on two of the extant thirty-two manuscripts of the poem that Arnold, for numerous good reasons, used as base texts). Her translation was consulted on several difficult points. Arnold's approach has been criticized, but no scholar has suggested how it might in practice be improved and has undertaken to do so. We can be certain, I think, Weiss-Arnold offers a reliable, authentic version of the poem, one of the real gems of the twelfth-century efflorescence of vernacular writing. An additional virtue of Weiss's re-edition of the text is her inclusion of lengthy notes referring to the not inconsiderable body of scholarly discussion of the text's various historical and, especially, geographical references. See Judith Weiss, *Wace's Roman de Brut: A History of the British, Text and Translation*, rev. ed. (Exeter: University of Exeter Press, 2010).

Arthur Defends His French Holdings Against the Roman Emperor

After the men from Ireland arrived,
11610 Along with the others appointed to join them,
Arthur made his way, day
After day, through Normandy,
Bypassing castles and villages
While his host grew in numbers and strength.
All these men were eager to take part.
Beyond France they passed, came to Burgundy,
Making straight for Autun, his destination,
For he had heard how those from Rome
Were heading for that city
11620 And intended to occupy the country.
At the head of this army was
Lucius Hiber, then the emperor of Rome.
As Arthur was about to ford
The river you hear called the Aube,
Peasants crowded forward to bring him news,
And the information came from his spies as well
That not far from this spot he could,
If he so wished, find the emperor.
There his men had pitched their tents
11630 And erected shelters close by.
His host was so huge, he led so many kings there,
And so great was the number of those on horse

That Arthur would be a fool to oppose them.
Never could he measure his force against theirs
Since for every one of his men, the Romans had four.
He should make peace, forswear battle.
Arthur was not dismayed in the least.
He was a brave man and trusted in God.
Many a threat had he heard in his time.
11640 By the Aube, at a very defensible position,
Within a fortress that he had built
And quickly fortified, he lodged his numerous host.
In this strong point he found the room
To store the wargear he required
So that if great need compelled him,
To this fort he could repair.
Then he called to his side two counts,
Men of wisdom who were well-spoken,
And each was of fine lineage.
11650 One of them was Gerins of Chartres,
The other Bos of Oxford,
A man who could well distinguish right from wrong.
To these two barons Arthur added Gawain,
Who had spent a long time in Rome
It was because these three men were held worthy

By those there, were well known and of good repute
That Arthur constituted them as an embassy,
And then dispatched them to the emperor.
They were to order him to turn back,
11660 France belonged to Arthur, he was not to enter it.
And if he did not choose retreat,
He should advance to do battle
On the first day possible, and thus prove
Which of them had greater right to the place.
For Arthur, as long as he lived,
Would defend France against the Romans.
In war had he conquered it,
In war had he taken it,
Just as in times gone by Rome had
11670 Acquired that same land in battle.
Now a battle again could prove
Who had the greater right to France.
The messengers departed from Arthur,
Mounted on their best chargers,
Their hauberks laced on, their helmets as well,
Shields hung around their necks, lances in their hands,
And then you'd have seen some knights, young men
Among the most inexperienced, who went
To Gawain to offer their counsel,
11680 And begged him to follow a certain course
When he made his way to that court,
Namely that before he departed from the Romans
He should do something to start the hostilities
That had long been threatened.
It would be an unfortunate development
After the two armies had closed with one another
That a battle should not be fought between them,
And that they should depart instead too quickly.
The embassy passed over a mountain,
11690 Then a wood and open fields.
They spied the lodgings of their enemies,
Making their way there as quickly as they could.
Then you should have seen the Roman knights
Coming out of their tents to catch
A glimpse of the three messengers
And learn what news they brought.
Who it was these men sought, they asked,
And had they come to make peace?
But the messengers said nothing, making no reply
11700 Until coming up to the emperor.
At his tent they dismounted,
Had their horses tied up in front.
To the emperor they made their way,
Telling him what Arthur commanded.
Each man said what pleased him,
And what he thought was good to say.
The emperor listened to it all,
And when he saw fit gave this answer:
"From Arthur," said Gawain, "we have come,
11710 And from Arthur we bear this message.
We are his men, he is our lord,
So we must repeat all he wants you to know.
Through us he issues this command, forbidding you
(So it might be known by one and all)
From putting a single foot in France
Or interfering in the affairs of this land.
He holds France, and he will hold France,
Defending it as his very own.
And he orders you to take nothing from the country.
11720 And if you are determined to defy him,
Your challenge must be battle,
And this battle will decide the issue.
In war the Romans seized this land,
Were the victors after making a fight,
And Arthur in turn seized this land in war,
And through battle has retained his rights thereto.
A battle once again will determine
Who should wield power here.
Tomorrow, with no further delay,
11730 Advance if you intend to contest France.
You should either attack or return home.

Go back then—there is nothing for you
   to accomplish here.
We have conquered, you have lost."
The emperor answered
That he need not beat a retreat.
France was his, he would proceed.
He would be troubled to lose the land
Which he would conquer since the
   power was his.
For he trusted in his expectation
11740 That he would win France and possess
   all of it.
Quintilian was seated by the emperor's
   side
And began to speak as soon as the other
   finished.
He was his nephew, a man of great
   arrogance,
A knight who loved trouble.
"The Britons," he said, "are boasters,
And are very artful in making threats,
Bragging and threats are what they've
   got;
They make a brave show and do but
   little."
He would have gone on this way, I
   think,
11750 Continuing to insult the messengers,
But Gawain, who grew quite angry,
Drew his sword and moved toward him,
Making the man's head fly off his
   shoulders.
To his companions he shouted: "On
   your horses!"
And the two counts mounted at once,
Gawain with them, and those two by his
   side.
All the men seized their horses
And at speed made off,
Shields on their necks, lances in their
   hands,
11760 Not asking leave of the Romans.
You would have seen the court in
   turmoil then!
The emperor cried out loudly:
"What are you doing? They have
   shamed us.
Get them for me, bad for us if they
   escape!"
You should have then heard his vassals
   shout:
"Arms, arms, horses, horses!
Fast, fast now, get up, get up,
Make for them, get at them, get going,
   get going!"
You should have seen his great army on
   the move,
11770 Saddles laced on, horses made ready,
Lances taken in hand, swords strapped
   on,
Everyone spurring to catch up with the
   three
Britons fleeing that place in haste,
Looking back at the others from time to
   time.
The Romans mounted a ragged pursuit,
Some on the road, others on the soggy
   ground,
Here two, here three, here five, here six
   of them,
Here seven, here eight, here nine, here
   ten.
One Roman spurred to the front,
11780 His horse was good and fast;
He passed his companions as he rode
   on,
And, as he went, he kept shouting:
"You knights, stand fast, stand fast!
Only a varlet would fail to turn
   around!"
Gerins de Chartres turned his mount,
Grasped his shield, lowered his lance,
Used it to thrust that man right off his
   good horse
A good spear's length.
Then he said to the man: "All the worse
   for you
11790 That your horse sped ahead at so
   impressive a pace.
Better for you to have turned around
Than to be lying on the ground where
   you now are."
Bos saw well what Gerins did,
And he heard the rough rejoinder he
   uttered.
Feeling the urge to do much the same,
He turned the head of his horse,
Charging at one of the Roman knights,
As that man did likewise, fearing
   nothing.
Bos struck him in the throat, the lance
11800 Passed through his neck into the
   spine,
And he fell dead, his mouth gaping
   open,
For the lance had pierced him there.

And the count cried out: "You there, honored sir,
My intention is to feed you morsels like this one.
May you find peace where you lie dead,
Waiting for those following you.
Tell the men who come to this spot
That the messengers went this way."
One among them was a man born in Rome,
11810 Connected to one of the better families there,
Called Marcellus by his fellow Romans.
He rode a horse that was very swift.
And though he was among the last to mount,
He soon passed all those ahead of him.
His hands grasped no lance, for he
Had forgotten it in his haste to get going.
This man made for Gawain,
Spurring his horse, lashing with the reins,
And soon coming up beside him.
11820 So that Gawain could not move ahead,
The man reached out to grab hold of him,
Having promised to take Gawain alive.
Gawain saw he was moving quite fast
And able to ride at great speed.
So he pulled on the reins and stopped dead in his tracks,
While Marcellus, being close, rode right by him.
As the man passed, Gawain drew his sword,
Delivering a mighty blow to his head,
Cleaving into him as far as the shoulders.
11830 The helmet offered no protection at all.
The man tumbled down, his life at an end.
And Gawain with all due courtesy said this:
"Marcellus, in Hell where you will be going,
Tell Quintillian this,
Make this announcement,
That the Britons are brave and eager enough
To defend what is theirs by right.
And they do more than issue threats,"
Then Gawain turned to his companions,
11840 Gerins and Bos, calling them by name,
Saying they should each turn around
And ride down one of those pursuing them.
Gawain said this, and they did what he said,
Striking down three Romans together.
The messengers then rode their way,
As their chargers bore them along in fine fashion,
While the Romans continued the pursuit,
Not disposed at all to spare them.
The Romans rode on and reached the three,
11850 Often thrusting with their lances,
Delivering many a hard blow
With their lances or swords.
But they could never strike fiercely enough
To make any of them stand his ground,
Or wound him, or push him from his horse,
Or do them any harm whatsoever.
One among the Romans, kin to Marcellus,
Was on a horse that was very swift;
He grieved deeply for his kinsman,
11860 Whom he glimpsed lying on the path,
And he spurred his horse across the fields,
Reaching the three messengers
And thinking to strike while moving across their front.
But Gawain saw well what he was about,
And turned his way to deliver a blow.
Now the man could not turn his horse,
And so let his lance fall to the ground,
For he had no need of it;
He drew his sword, thinking to strike with it,
11870 Raised his arm, turned the point of the blade,
And Gawain cut off the arm
As he raised it to strike,
Which, with the hand still holding the blade,
Flew off some distance into the field.
Gawain would have delivered another blow,
But the other Romans were closing fast.
They continued their pursuit
Until the messengers hastened into a wood

That was between them and the castle
Arthur had just recently constructed.
Six thousand knights had Arthur selected,
And these he sent after the messengers
To scout through the woods and valleys
And report what was happening there.
Following the path of the messengers,
They should come to their aid if need be.
They had crossed a wooded area
And halted at its margins,
Sitting, still armed, on their horses
When they caught sight of the messengers,
And saw too these great companies
Of armed men covering the plains.
In this crowd, they picked out the messengers
And noticed who was pursuing them.
Seeing this, they sprang into action,
Raising with one voice a single war cry.
The Romans immediately recoiled,
Scattering across the fields.
Some were quite chagrined
To have ridden so far in pursuit
Now that the Britons launched a strong attack,
Striking down many as they turned tail,
Capturing a multitude of others and taking them prisoner,
Cutting them down even as they killed a multitude.
Petreïus, a powerful baron,
A man unequaled in arms among the Romans,
Had ten thousand knights under his command,
A great many together in one battalion.
This man heard tell of the skirmish
That the Britons had begun,
And at once with ten thousand shields
Rode off to aid those from Rome.
Through force and might,
With the armed men he was leading,
He forced the Britons into the woods,
As they could not hold out against them.
And the pursuit lasted until the edge of the forest,
For they could not make a stand.
In the woods the fight continued, and among the trees
The Britons defended themselves.
Petreïus moved to attack them,
But lost many of his men in the attempt.
For the Britons cut them down,
Battling hard in the woods.
The fighting ranged far and wide
Between the woods and the plains.
When Arthur learned
That his messengers were delayed,
While the others had not returned
Who had gone off after them,
He summoned Yder, the son of Nu,
And provided him with a thousand knights,
Sending them to go after the others,
And seek them out, for this is what he asked.
Gawain and Bors took part in the battle,
And the others delivered many a hard blow.
A great uproar arose, a huge tumult
When Yder, son of Nu, arrived,
For this cheered the Britons.
And they took back the field to their front.
Yder attacked, shouted out his war cry,
As did those he had led there with him,
All put their lances to good use
And many a saddle was emptied as a result,
Many a horse captured and won,
And many a knight sent sprawling.
Petreïus continued the fight,
Held back his men, gave ground,
He knew how to retreat, and then turn around.
He knew how to give chase and to stand firm,
And often you could have seen magnificent pursuits
And single combats in many a place.
Those who were brave found others just the same,
Those who wished to joust found others to challenge,
Those who wished to strike, struck many a blow,
Those who could not stand fast, fell dead.
The Britons moved forward impetuously,
Not wanting to stay in formation.
They were eager instead to joust,

11960	Interested in performing feats of arms.		And had seen and scouted out
	It was chivalry they pursued there,		Where Petreïus then was,
	And so they often fought as individuals.		Taking charge of all the others,
	How the battle was going did not concern them,		He set off at a quite fierce gallop
	Only that the war had now begun.		In that direction, along with all the others.
	Petreïus fought like a madman,		They never stopped, never halted
	With his best vassals right by his side,		Until they entered the melée
	He knew about combat, he was experienced in war,		Where Petreïus was riding to and fro,
	He knew how to bide his time and then press the attack.	12010	Directing the others as they battled.
	Often he turned away, often he charged ahead,		Recognizing him, Bos rode toward him,
11970	Rescuing those fallen from their horses.		And the two horses crashed together.
	Bos of Oxford saw this,		Bos threw his arms around the man
	A man well-versed in battle strategy,		And dragged him toward his companions,
	Realized that they could not disengage without loss		Then threw himself to the ground!
	If they did not first kill Petreïus,		You would have seen something quite remarkable!
	Either kill the man or take him prisoner,		Clasped to him, the man fell to earth.
	For the Romans closed ranks around him,		His arms around Petreïus.
	While the Britons quite foolishly		Bos held on as Petraeus struggled,
	Pressed the assault, abandoning their formation.	12020	Doing what he could to escape.
	Bos drew to his side the best and bravest,		To his rescue hastened the Romans,
11980	And with several of his men took counsel:		And those with lances soon broke them,
	"Barons," he said, "Let us discuss this,		And when their lances failed them,
	You who faithfully love Arthur.		They fought on with their gleaming swords.
	This war has been begun by us		Rescuing Petreïus was what they intended,
	Without the knowledge of our lord.		While the Bretons were eager to aid Bos.
	If we do well, good and fine,		There you would have witnessed a fierce struggle,
	If things go amiss, the king will hate us.		Hand to hand, a bitter contest.
	If it so happens that our knights		Helmets crushed, shields pierced,
	Are not the ones to rule this battlefield,	12030	Hauberks sliced through, spear shafts shattered,
	Shame and spite will be our reward,		Saddles were emptied, saddles slipped off,
11990	And we will earn Arthur's disregard.		Men fell dead, others suffered wounds.
	And so we must do our best		The Britons shouted their war cry,
	If we're going to overcome Petreïus,		And the Romans raised up their own.
	Take him prisoner or kill the man,		One side struggled to drag that man off,
	Dead or alive, we'll bring him to Arthur.		While the other was intent on pulling him back.
	Otherwise, we'll never break off the fight		And this made it hard to distinguish
	Without losing too many of our men.		Who was Roman, who a Briton,
	Do everything that I do,		If not by their war cries and the words they spoke,
	And charge in the same direction."	12040	So thick then was the press of battle.
	They said that they would do their utmost,		Gawain made his way through the press of men,
12000	Would rush forward wherever Bos did.		Making a path for himself with his sword.
	When Bos had the men he wanted,		

He struck and thrust, delivering blows
   as he fought on,
Striking down many, crushing others.
No Roman who saw the blows he struck
Did not yield place him if he could
   manage it.
On the other side Ider moved forward,
Making a great slaughter of the Romans.
Gerin of Chartres fought by this man's
   side,
12050 And each struggled fiercely for the
   other.
They overtook Petreïus, toppling
That man and Bos together,
Then helping Bos to his feet
And mounting him on a charger.
They kept Petreïus their prisoner,
And he had suffered many blows.
Through the mass of men, they led him
To the safety of their own ranks.
There they left the man under careful
   guard
12060 And resumed their struggle against the
   Romans,
Who were without a leader,
Just like a boat lacking a helmsman
That the wind drives wherever it will,
When there is no one to steer it,
So was this band of men
Who had lost their commander.
They could hardly defend themselves,
Having no one to take charge.
The Britons drove them back on every
   side,
12070 Felling a great multitude.
Over the bodies of the slain they moved
   quickly,
Intent on reaching those who fled them.
Some were captured, others they killed,
Some stripped of arms, some bound
   with ropes.
Then along with their companions they
   made for
The woods with those they had captured.
They took Petreïus with them,
Presented him to their lord,
And many others prisoners as well.
12080 Arthur thanked them,
Promising to increase the lands held
By every man should he prove
   victorious.
Arthur arranged for them to be
   watched,

And after giving them over to the
   guards
And discussing the matter with his
   council,
He decided to send them to Paris.
There he'd hold them in prison
Until he did with them whatever he
   determined,
For he feared that if they were kept
12090 With his army he would somehow lose
   them.
He then decided who would constitute
   their escort,
And who would be in charge:
Cador, Borel, Richier,
And Bedoer the cupbearer,
Four counts of quite exalted lineage.
These men, so he asked, were to rise up
   early in the morning
And ride along with the prisoners
Far enough and convey them
Until the escorts would be safe,
12100 Having passed through the area of
   danger.
Through his spies that he had
The emperor learned
Very quickly the news that those con-
   veying
The prisoners would be departing quite
   early.
Ten thousand men he had take to horse,
And they were to ride all night long
In order to get in front of the prisoners
So that his own might then be rescued.
Sextorius, the king of Libya,
12110 And Evander, the king of Syria,
Caricius, Catellus Vulteïus,
Both of whom were from Rome.
All four possessed large fiefs.
Quite skilled in warfare were they all.
These men were chosen and charged
   with
Effecting the rescue of the prisoners
Since they were the leaders of all the
   others.
Ten thousand men set out that night.
Peasants from the countryside were
   their guides,
12120 Men who knew the right paths to take.
All night long they rode, moving
At great speed and going far enough
To enter the city of Paris,
Where they found a place that was ideal

For springing their ambush.
There, observing silence, they waited.
Look then at Arthur's men that next morning,
Riding along quite confidently
And fearing no ambush.
12130 In two squadrons they moved ahead.
Chador and Borel, with their men as well,
Rode in the vanguard.
Counts Richier and Bedoer,
Appointed to guard the prisoners,
Followed them with five hundred men at arms,
And the prisoners were led along,
Hands tied behind their backs,
And their feet roped together under their horses.
Watch as those in front come upon the ambush
12140 The Romans had laid for them,
With the men from Rome rushing out all at once,
As the whole earth trembled and shook!
They were brave in the assault they launched,
And the others defended themselves stoutly.
Bedoer and Richier heard
The great tumult, saw blows being struck.
They had the prisoners halt
And then moved to a safe spot,
Entrusting them to their squires,
12150 Who were to act as guards.
The horses were given the reins
And the knights never stopped spurring them on
Until they matched lances with the enemy,
Fiercely offering battle.
The Romans attacked at different points,
For their intention was not
To defeat the Britons,
But to rescue their men held prisoner.
And the Britons advanced together,
12160 Holding their formation quite well,
In a squadron they rode back and forth,
Carefully defending themselves,
While the Romans probed here and there
In their search for the prisoners.
So intent were they rescuing the captives,
That they lost many of their men in the process.
Into four groups the Britons
Divided their forces:
Chador with the men from Cornwall,
12170 Bedoer with the Neustrians,
Richier and all his own men in a group,
And Borel along with the knights from Maine.
King Evander saw clearly
How his force was diminishing, as he was losing men.
He ordered them all to form a single formation
Since were proving unable to reach the prisoners.
They should keep together
And attack in one group.
Then the Romans began to get the better of it,
12180 And the Britons found themselves in a bad spot.
Their forces were pressed very hard, many were taken,
And four of their best men killed:
Er, the son of Ider, was struck dead,
A knight who was valiant and strong,
And Hyreglas of Periron,
There was no one braver than him,
And Aliduc of Tintagel
(This caused his kin much grief),
As well as Mauric from Cahors.
12190 I know not if he was British or Welsh.
Borel of Le Mans, a noble count
Who was invaluable to his own company,
Conducted himself with great bravery,
Encouraging his soldiers.
Then Evander charged furiously at him,
Passing the iron tip of his lance
Right through the man's throat.
Borel fell down, could stand no longer,
And the Britons were dismayed
12200 At having lost so many of their men.
The Romans outnumbered them seven to one,
So soon, at the least, they would be taken,
Captured, killed, or brought low,
And their prisoners taken from them,

But Guitart, the count of Poitiers,
Who that day was escorting the foragers,
Suddenly discovered how
A company of Romans
Was making to rescue the prisoners.
12210 He turned his horse in their direction,
As did the three thousand knights with him,
Along with the foragers and archers.
Their goal was to launch an attack on the Romans
Who were pressing the Britons hard,
And so Guitart made haste, spurring on
His men, whose lances were lowered.
They unhorsed more than a hundred Romans,
And not a one among them ever remounted.
Look now at the Romans thrown into disarray,
12220 All thinking they had been put to shame.
They thought Arthur would be in pursuit,
And that the rest of his army would follow.
Seeing how many of theirs had fallen,
They gave up hope of any rescue.
The men of Poitou attacked with fierceness,
And the Britons did not fail to follow close behind.
The two squadrons drew strength from one another,
As they strove to cut down the Romans,
Who then began to turn their backs, exposing
12230 And leaving themselves completely defenseless.
They wanted to return to their encampment,
Not knowing where else to find safety.
For some distance the Britons gave pursuit,
Taking revenge through killing many of them,
Riding them down fiercely,
Not failing at all to cut them to pieces.
The kings Evander and Catellus,
Along with five hundred or more others,
Were engaged there and brought low,
12240 Some were killed, others taken prisoner.
The Britons seized as many as they liked
And could take along with them,
Then returning by the path
That led to where the battle had taken place.
They looked for Borel, the good count
From Mans, and their other dead through the fields.
They found the count all bloody,
And he was breathing his last.
The wounded were conveyed away
12250 And the dead buried on the spot.
To those who had been so charged
And commanded by Arthur,
They turned over the first group of prisoners,
Sending them off to Paris.
The second group, just captured recently,
They had tightly bound.
To the fortress they escorted them,
Presenting them to the king.
They told him about the ambush and what had happened,
12260 And with one voice they made this vow,
That if they would do battle against the Romans
Without doubt the Britons would be the victors.
The emperor learned about the course of events,
Heard the news of the great defeat,
Learned that Evander had been killed,
Found out that others had been taken prisoner,
Saw that his people had grown downcast,
For war had indeed broken out,
And he saw that much had not gone his way,
12270 And that he had gained nothing.
He was filled with hate, found himself distraught
Obsessed by thoughts and doubt as well.
What to do next he did not know,
Whether to offer Arthur further battle
Or wait for the arrival of his rear guard,
Then expected to be making its way to him.
If he agreed to further battle, he feared
That he would gain nothing.
So he determined to march his army to Autun,

12280	Passing through Langres along the way.
	The men were summoned and put en route.
	Late that night they arrived in Langres,
	Making camp right in the city
	And pitching tents in the valleys nearby.
	Langres sits on a mountain top,
	With dales on all sides of the city.
	Arthur knew immediately what to do
	And where he would move the army.
	The emperor, he thought, would not fight
12290	Until his army reached greater strength.
	He did not want those forces on the move to rest
	Or get close enough to reinforce the emperor.
	As quietly as he could manage, he had his troops
	Sent for so they could concentrate.
	He left Langres on his left,
	Passed beyond it to the right,
	And his plan was to move his men between the emperor
	And Autun, seizing the road that led to that place
	That whole night, until morning came,
12300	He moved on with his army, through woods,
	Across plains, until they came to a valley
	That is called Soeïsse.
	All who make the journey to Autun
	From Langres must pass through the place.
	Arthur had his men arm themselves
	And then put their squadrons in order
	So that no matter when the Romans arrived
	They would be ready to oppose them.
	All the equipment, as well as the servants
12310	Who are of no use in a fight,
	He had positioned above a rise
	So they seemed a huge host of armed men,
	While the Romans, should they catch sight of them,
	Would fear such a multitude.
	Six thousand, six hundred, and sixty-six
	Formed one group, every one a brave man,
	Which took cover in the woods atop a hill,
	Whether on the right or the left I do not know.
	Morvid, the count of Gloucester,
12320	Took command of this company.
	And the king urged them: "Hold this position!
	Abandon it for no reason!
	If need be, I will move my troop to this spot,
	Dispatching others this way as well,
	And if it happens that the Romans
	Feel that the battle is lost and take flight,
	Spur on your horses to catch up to them.
	These men you should kill, not spare."
	And the soldiers answered: "This we will surely do."
12330	Then Arthur selected another squadron
	Of noble warriors and vassals,
	Their helmets laced on, mounted their horses,
	And stationed them where they would be spotted.
	Save for him, these men had no leader,
	For this was his household company,
	Men he had supported and helped raise.
	In their midst, he had his dragon raised up,
	From the top of which flew his standard.
	The remainder of his force made eight companies,
12340	To each of which he appointed two leaders.
	Half were on horseback,
	While the others remained on foot.
	To these men all together he gave this order,
	Speaking to them directly as he told
	The horsemen to stay in ranks
	Until the infantry were engaged,
	At which point they should attack the Romans
	From the flanks and engage them in that fashion.
	Five thousand, five hundred, and fifty-five
12350	Men selected for their valor,
	Such were the numbers for each division,
	And every one was armed from head to toe.
	In groups of four were they drawn up,

Each of which consisted of eight units,
With four in front and four to their rear,
And in their midst were a number of others,
Each man armed in his own fashion.
Auguissel of Scotland was in the van
Of the first division, which he led,
12360 As Cador of Cornwall did the next.
Bos and count Gerin of Chartres
Were in charge of the second,
The third, with men well armed and equipped,
Was given to Aschil,
Who was king of the Danes,
And to Loth, king of Norway.
Hoel took charge of the fourth,
As did Gawain, who was no coward.
Beyond these, there were four others,
12370 Ready to do battle.
Kay and Bedoer the cupbearer
Were the leaders of one,
With Bedoer commanding the Herupeïs,
And Kay the men from Anjou and Chinon.
The other squadron was commanded
By Holdin, count of Flanders,
And Guitart of Poitou,
Who quite willingly assumed that role.
Count Jugein of Leicester,
12380 And Count Jonathas of Dorchester
Assumed charge of the seventh,
And they were its lords and commanders.
Cursal, count of Chester, and count
Urgen of Bath took charge
Of the eighth battalion,
And Arthur put much faith in them.
He put good foot soldiers and archers,
As well as intrepid crossbowmen
In two squadrons at the very front
12390 So they could shoot into the enemy's flanks.
All these men were stationed to the front of the king.
He positioned himself a bit to their rear with his household knights.
Once Arthur had positioned his men,
Dividing them up into squadrons,
Hear what he said to his retainers,
To his barons and their sons:
"Barons," he said, "I take great comfort
As I remember your many virtues,
Your great strengths, your impressive conquests.
12400 I have always found you valiant and brave.
In your prowess I have always placed my trust,
At all times, no matter who might be displeased.
When I remember and consider
That Britain in your own time,
Through what you and your companions have done,
Has become mistress of thirty regions,
I am quite pleased, it gives me great satisfaction,
And I trust to God, and to you as well,
That you will conquer additional lands,
12410 Seize more that you will come to possess.
Your bravery, your strong hands
Have now twice brought the Romans to defeat.
Know that in my heart it is very clear
That destiny has been shaped in such a fashion
That this day you will prove victorious,
And then you will have beaten them three times.
You have vanquished the Norwegians,
You have vanquished the Danes,
You have vanquished the French,
12420 And you rule France as if it were your own land.
You should certainly defeat those who do not measure up
To the greater foes you have already defeated.
They wish to turn you into vassals,
Force you to make peace
Since their intention is to reclaim France.
Here they expect to find the same kind
Of men they are leading here from the East.
But one of our own is worth ten of theirs.
Don't fear them in the least,
12430 For they are worth no more than women.
And you should certainly put your faith in God,
So let us not despair,
For with just a little bit of valor

We will easily defeat them.
Never because of any man will you fail
  me.
Never because of any man will you flee
  my side.
I will see clearly what every man does,
And those who accomplish the most I
  will notice.
I will ride everywhere and see everything
  that happens.
12440 And on every side I will lend a hand."
With the speech at an end,
The one the king had delivered,
The men answered as if with one voice
And all together, those who had
  listened,
That they would rather die where they
  stood
On that field than retreat with no
  victory in hand.
You would, to be sure, have heard them
  swear oaths,
Make pledges, and proclaim their
  bravery,
How, save in death, they would not fail
  him,
12450 Would share whatever end the king
  might come to.
Lucius had been born in Spain,
Into a family highly placed from Rome.
He was still young enough,
Not quite forty but more than thirty.
An audacious man, and brave as well,
He had accomplished many worthy
  deeds.
His strength and fortitude
Had made him emperor.
In that morning he set out from
  Langres,
12460 Thinking to march straight to Autun.
His whole army was put on route,
Its mass impressive, its columns
  crowded with men.
When he saw and considered the
  position
Arthur had occupied to his front,
He knew that he must either fight at
  that spot,
Or beat a retreat from that place.
In no way would he endure backing
  down,
For this seemed cowardly to him,
And if the enemy chased them down,

12470 On his host they could inflict great
  damage,
Because to fight and retreat at the same
  time
Can be managed well by no one.
He summoned his kings, his princes,
And his dukes, of whom there were
  more
Than a hundred, as well as the older men
Among them, and this is what he said:
"My peers," he said, "Noble lords,
Worthy vassals, able conquerors,
Sons you are of honored ancestors
12480 Who won great reputation in war.
Through them Rome was made leader
  of the world,
And so it will remain, as long as
  Romans live on.
These men conquered a great empire;
In our own time, we'd be shamed to let
  it slip away.
Our forebears were worthy men, and so
  are you,
Valiant sons of valiant fathers,
The father of every one of you was a
  brave man,
And that courage, I have heard, makes
  itself known in you.
Every man among you should be
  resolved
12490 To do just what his father did.
Shamed will be the man who merits
Forfeiting the inheritance of his father,
And who in his wickedness tosses aside
What his father managed to conquer.
I do not think—know this for a fact—
That you are lesser men.
They were valiant, and you are too,
And I think every man here is brave.
Lords, I see it, and so do you,
12500 You know, and so do I,
That our way ahead is blocked,
The road that leads straight to Autun.
We cannot march down it
Unless we do so by first giving battle.
I don't know what upstart thief,
What robber or scoundrel
Has blocked the road in front of us
Down which my intention is to lead
  you.
They thought I should turn tail,
12510 And let them take possession of this
  land,

But I have changed direction
So that they would be to our front.
Now they have attacked us.
Take up your arms, prepare yourselves!
If they wait for us, we will strike them.
If they flee, we will give chase
Pull up on the reins of their arrogance
And reduce their power to nothing."
Then they made haste to take up arms.
12520 No one intended to delay further.
Their formation was assembled,
Divided into squadrons, and their men were put in line,
With many a pagan duke and king
Among those who were Christian,
And these men held fiefs from Rome
And so to the Romans offered military service.
Their knights moved off in groups of thirty,
Groups of forty, sixty, and one hundred,
In their legions and in their thousands
12530 They set out on the path,
Many on foot and numerous others on horseback,
Some on the rise, others in the valley,
In this fashion they made off, holding
To their ranks, toward Arthur's army.
The Roman army moved down one side
Of the valley, and, as they witnessed
On the other side of the valley,
The Britons took to the field.
Then you would have heard trumpets ring out,
12540 And other brass, making a great tumult.
Holding their ranks, moving at a walk,
They both forward to close the distance,
And as they came together you would have seen
Arrows let fly and lances hurled.
No man could open his eyes
Or uncover his face.
Arrows flew like hail through the air,
They darkened and turned black the sky itself!
Then they set to breaking lances,
12550 Shattering shields, and piercing them through.
A terrible din of splintering shafts arose,
The pieces spinning off high into the air.
Next came play with swords,
Dealing great blows with shining blades.
The battle was a marvel to gaze upon,
No one had ever seen one more fraught with peril,
No greater press of men or melée.
The man intending to strike could do so there.
Fools or the easily cowed had no place,
12560 No coward could have made a stand.
The crowded mass, the thick press
Made it hard for one man to strike another.
You would have witnessed the earth itself tremble,
As squadrons attacked each other,
With soldiers in their ranks colliding,
Some striking blows, others shoving,
Some advancing, others stepping back,
Some men falling, others standing their ground,
Shafts breaking, splinters sent flying,
12570 Swords unsheathed, shields raised on high
As the strong terrified the weak.
The feet of the living trampled the dead,
Girths snapped, and breastplates were cracked,
Saddles emptied, horses put to flight.
For a long time they fought,
For a long time they struck blows,
As the Romans did not retreat,
Nor did they force the Britons from their position.
It was then no easy thing to divine
12580 Who might claim the victory
Until the division led by Kay and Bedoer came onto line.
They saw well the Britons were only barely winning
And that the Romans held well to their ranks.
With furor and such aggressiveness as was fitting,
They fell upon the Romans
At once, along with their troops,
Just where the melée was thickest.
Bedoer struck hard, and so did Kay.
12590 God, what fighters the king had at his court!
What a chamberlain, what a cupbearer!
They made put their steel blades to good use.

What good vassals, if only they had
    lived!
They accomplished much and would
    have done more.
Into the press they moved, dealing
    blows,
And many a man there did they lay low.
Their huge companies followed after,
Fighting fiercely, striking with their
    swords.
Many a blow they delivered and gave,
12600 Killing many, wounding many others
    there.
Bedoer moved into the mass of soldiers,
Never stopping, never halting.
On the other side, Kay was not reluctant.
He beat down many, laid low a multitude.
Then they held back a little,
Restraining their troops
Until the Britons positioned themselves
    on the flanks,
And the other troops arrived on the
    scene.
They would have won great fame and
    renown,
12610 And saved themselves from death,
But they proved too reckless
Too intent on striking blows.
They trusted to their abilities,
And to the many troops they led.
They were not careful of themselves,
But too intent on pressing the fight.
However they met up with a squadron
Led by the king of the Medes.
Boccus was his name, and he was a
    pagan.
12620 Yet very brave, and his company
    numbered many.
With them the counts joined battle,
Having no fear of such a huge force.
Battle quickly raged between them,
And the melée went was one, on the
    one side,
Between the pagans and the Saracens,
And the Herupeis and the Angevins, on
    the other.
King Boccus wielded his sword.
Whoever encountered him met a
    miserable destiny.
He laid low the two counts,
12630 As he stabbed Bedoer through the chest
With a lance that went right through
    his body,

As the iron point came out his back.
Bedoer fell, his heart failed,
His soul fled, and Jesus took charge of it.
Kay found Bedoer dead,
And he wished to bear away the body,
For he loved the man fiercely, held him
    dear.
With all the men under his command,
He made the Medes retreat
12640 And cede the field to him.
But because he stopped and attended
To claim the corpse of Bedoer,
The king of Libya drew near him,
Sertorius by name, a quite worthy
    knight.
He led a strong troop of pagan men
That he had brought from his native
    land.
These fighters dealt Kay a mortal
    wound,
Killing many of his men as well.
Several wounds they gave Kay, the result
    of many blows,
12650 But he kept hold of the body.
What remained of his troop circled
    round
To act in his defense.
To the golden dragon standard they
    brought him,
No matter if it displeased the Romans.
Hyrelgas was the nephew of Bedoer,
And he had long loved his uncle.
From among his friends and kinsmen
He chose many, three hundred in all,
Men in helmets and hauberks who
    wielded swords,
12660 And were mounted on horses spirited
    and swift.
He formed these men into a squadron,
Then said to them: "Follow me.
I intend to avenge the killing of my
    uncle."
At once he advanced close to the
    Romans,
Caught sight of the king of the Medes,
Recognized his banner.
At this man's company he launched his
    assault,
Often shouting out Arthur's war cry
Like a man who had gone insane
12670 And has left behind all moderation.
He fears nothing, fears no soldier he
    comes upon,

Thinks only about revenge for his
   uncle.
His companions push forward with
   him,
Hefting their shields, lowering their
   lances.
They killed many, laid low numerous
   others,
Treading the bodies of the slain.
They reached the company of household
   Knights belonging to the man who
   killed Bedoer.
With the strength of their fine horses,
12680 And the spirit of these good men,
They wheeled right and left,
As Hyrgelas led them on.
Never halting until coming to the
   standard
Where they found King Boccus.
Hyrgelas took good notice of him,
Turned his horse in the man's direction,
Moved swiftly through the press of
   men,
Dealing Boccus a blow on the head.
The man was strong, the stroke mighty,
12690 And the sword hard and sharp.
The helmet was split and crushed,
And he cut through his hauberk,
Slicing into the man's shoulders.
His heart shattered, his soul fled,
While Hyrgelas reached out with his
   arms,
Catching the body before it fell
And pulling it up across him,
Laying it across his saddle,
As he pulled it up and before him.
12700 No cry or whimper did he utter.
The knight was impetuous,
And the horse eager in his swiftness.
To his army he made his way back
And so no pagan or Roman could strike
   him.
Through the press he drove and
   struggled,
While his companions made way for him.
Beside his uncle he set down the corpse,
Which he then hacked into pieces,
Saying this to his companions:
12710 "Come," he said, "you barons' sons!
Let's go and kill these Romans,
These bastards, all sons of whores.
Here to this country they have led
A people who confess

No faith in God so that they might
Kill us and our friends.
Let us advance to destroy these pagans,
And the Christians too
Who fight by their side
12720 In order to destroy Christianity.
Come and match strength with them!"
See them return to the battlefield!
And you'd have heard the cries and the
   terrible noise
As you looked upon a mighty struggle,
Helmets and swords shining,
Sparks flying off from the steel.
Guitart, the good duke of Poitou,
Did not conduct himself in the least
   like a coward,
But held his own in the fight.
12730 He rushed against the King of Africa,
And they struck hard at one another.
But the King of Africa fell dead,
And the count rushed ahead,
Killing Africans and Moors as he went.
Holdin, who was duke of the Flemings,
Who held Bruges and Lens as his fiefs,
Turned his horse to attack the division
Of Alifatin, a Spanish king.
For a long time they fought,
12740 For a long time they exchanged blows
Until Alifatin was killed,
And Holdin was as well.
Ligier, count of Boulogne,
Matched lances with the king of
   Babylon,
And who struck the better blow, I do
   not know,
But each unhorsed the other,
Dead was the count, dead the king as
   well.
Three others counts met their deaths:
Baluc and Cursal and Urgent.
12750 Each of them led a huge company.
Urgent was the lord of Bath,
Baluc the count of Wiltshire,
And Cursal the count of Chester,
Which borders on Wales.
These men fell in but a brief time,
As they were attacked from both sides.
The soldiers these men were appointed
   to lead,
And who followed their banners there,
Rode over to join the squadron
12760 Gawain had conducted there,
Along with his companion Hoel.

Never were there two such vassals!
Never in ages past or days gone by
Lived any barons who were their like
In virtue, courtesy, and chivalric
Audacity had ever lived.
The knights from Brittany
Obeyed Hoel as their lord.
This company was so fearless
12770 And intrepid that they shrunk
Not in the least from melée or battle.
They rode all over the field, delivering blows.
Those who were pursuing them
And felling them in heaps,
They made these men turn tail,
Striking down many as they retreated.
Delivering staggering blows,
Leading their knights,
They reached the banner
12780 That bore on its top the eagle.
There they found the emperor
And those of his household guard,
With him were the nobles
And the finest knights of Rome.
You'd have seen a deadly fight at that spot.
Never did you witness the like, I think.
Kimar, count of Tintagel,
Was among Hoel's company.
He was a man of great valor,
12790 And he wrought havoc among the Romans,
But a Roman footsoldier
Killed him with a sword.
Two thousand Bretons died by his side,
Including three noble companions.
One of these three was named Jaguz,
Who had come there from Bodloan;
The second was Richomarus,
And the third man named Boclovius.
There were not six others in that company
12800 Who possessed the same valor and worthiness.
Had they been either kings or counts,
They would have been, so I think,
Forever afterward praised for their prowess.
These men were quite fearless,
And they made a slaughter of the Romans.
They came upon no man
Whose life they did not bring to its end,
Either with the lance or sword.
They fought their way into
12810 The company of the emperor,
And those from Rome stopped them there,
Killing all three together.
This filled Gawain and Hoel
With anger and rage,
As they saw their men slaughtered,
In the fight with the Romans.
To do hurt to these enemies
And take revenge for their friends,
They threw themselves like lions
12820 Upon them, like ravening beasts.
They killed and brought low the enemy soldiers,
Raining blows and strokes upon them.
Those from Rome defended themselves well,
Receiving, but also giving many a blow,
They were fiercely attacked even as they attacked fiercely,
They struck well and were struck well in return,
They pushed with vigor and were vigorously pushed,
Did great damage and suffered great damage in turn.
Gawain's warlike spirit was indomitable,
12830 As he never tired of delivering blows.
His strength always seemed fresh,
And he never appeared to tire.
He advanced, pursuing the Romans
And forcefully made his way forward
In order to get at the emperor
And engage him in combat.
Then he had come far enough, fought
Hard enough, as he moved forward and back,
To meet up with the emperor.
12840 They looked each other over carefully.
The emperor caught sight of Gawain,
While Gawain recognized him.
With great energy, they exchanged blows,
Very strong they were and neither was unhorsed.
The emperor was a big man, and strong,
Young, brave, and quite vigorous,
Cunning, and possessed of much prowess.
He felt great joy and pleasure
In fighting against Gawain,

12850   Who was a knight of great renown.
If he could survive the encounter,
He would boast of it back in Rome.
They raised their arms and hefted their shields,
Harassing one another with great blows.
They delivered punishment, striking fiercely,
Delivering blows of different kinds.
In their audacity, each man pursued the other,
And struck the other hard.
Splinters flew from their shields,
12860   And sparks from their blades.
They struck high, they struck low.
The two were such valiant knights
That, had they the field to themselves,
One would have made an end of the other.
But the Roman forces recovered,
Rallying to the golden eagle,
And rescuing the emperor,
Whom they had nearly lost.
The Breton were driven back,
12870   While the Romans held the field.
Arthur saw his men falling back,
And those from Rome taking heart,
And gaining ground again to his front.
No longer, no more could he delay.
Throughout his host he rode, crying out:
"What are you doing? Move forward!
Come with me. I will protect you.
Leave none of them alive,
I, Arthur, will be your leader,
12880   And I flee no man on the field.
Follow me! I'll cut us a path,
Make sure no one holds back.
Consider the virtues you possess,
The many realms you have conquered.
Not while I live will I leave this place.
Here I will conquer, or here I will die."
Then you would have seen Arthur do battle,
Killing men, felling others,
Cleaving through mailshirts, crushing helmets,
12890   Severing fists, and arms, and heads.
He wielded Caliburn, splattered with blood,
Every man he struck fell dead.
I cannot write down the number of his blows.
With every one, he killed a man.
Like the lion, made desperate by hunger,
That slays whatever beast he chances upon.
The good king did just the same,
Leaving alive no man or horse.
Whoever he struck or wounded
12900   Had no use for a physician.
No man survived a blow from Arthur
Even if the wound seemed slight.
All fled from Arthur's path,
Just like sheep put to flight by a wolf.
The king of Libya, whose name was Sertorius,
A powerful man, became his quarry.
Arthur severed the head from his body.
Then he spoke these words to him: "You
Were unlucky to have borne your arms to this place,
12910   Only to smear Caliburn with your blood."
The man made no response as he fell dead.
Polidetes was by his side,
A wealthy king, from Bithynia,
A pagan country.
Arthur found the man to his front,
And he dealt him a powerful blow.
From his shoulders he cut off the head,
Which tumbled down, while the trunk remained upright.
With Arthur's blows, and the words he spoke,
12920   The Britons launched themselves at the Romans,
And the Romans received them eagerly,
Drawing their swords, splintering their lances,
Doing great hurt to the Britons,
Meeting their force with force of their own.
Arthur saw them doing so—it made his valor increase,
As he delivered mighty blows with Caliburn.
The emperor did not hold back,
But killed many of Arthur's men in turn.
These two could not meet,
12930   Could find no space to fight one another,
So great was the press of men between them,

And the melée so hard fought.
Arthur struck hard, as did his opponent,
You would have seen a thousand fall dead there.
The battle raged between the two armies,
And they killed one another with great fierceness.
It was not apparent who would prove the victor,
Nor who would lose and meet death
At the moment Morvid arrived, with his men,
12940 Who had been on the heights, in the woods,
Where Arthur was to have rallied his forces
If things went badly with the army.
Sixty-six hundred knights,
And sixty-six more, all mounted on chargers,
Their helmets gleaming, their mailshirts sparkling,
Lances lowered, spearheads menacing,
Down from the mountain they rode,
But the Romans did not see them coming.
From behind they fell upon them,
12950 Splitting their formation in two,
Separating one squadron from another,
And bringing low so many,
Trampling them with their horses,
Cutting into them with their swords.
The Romans could not withstand them,
Nor recover from the onslaught,
But in a press took to flight,
Knocking one another down.
The emperor was unhorsed,
12960 Struck through the body with a lance,
But by whom, this I do not know,
Nor do I know who struck at him.
In the melée, they set upon him,
And there he was killed.
Among the other dead, he was found lifeless,
Pierced by a spear.
Those from Rome and those from the East,
Along with all the others of their army,
Fled the field as best they could.
12970 The Britons chased them down and slew them.
Killing so many they grew tired of killing,
Riding over the bodies with their horses.
There you'd have seen blood flow in rivers,
Dead men lying in heaps,
Fine chargers and horses wandering
Free through the open fields.
Arthur felt joy and happiness at the sight,
For the arrogance of Rome had been beaten down.
To God Almighty he rendered thanks,
12980 For it was from Him that victory came.
He had all the dead searched out,
And the corpses of his men and friends taken up.
Some he had buried on the spot,
While the bodies of others he sent to their homeland.
Throughout the countryside, in abbeys
He had many a man buried.
The body of the emperor he ordered
Taken up and guarded with great honor.
To Rome he dispatched it on a bier,
12990 And to those in that city he sent this message:
That he owed them no other tribute
From Britain, which was his to govern.
Whoever requested tribute from him
Would be sent back to them in the same condition.
Kay, mortally wounded, he had
Taken to Chinon, which was his stronghold,
A fortress that man had laid out and built,
And Chinon had taken its name from him.
Not much longer did he live,
13000 But died soon afterward.
He was laid to rest in a woodland
Close to a hermitage near Chinon.
At Bayeux in Normandy,
A fief whose lord he was
Bedoer was buried,
By the gate, at the hour of noon.
Holdin was taken to Flanders
And buried in Thérouanne.
Ligier's body was borne to Boulogne.

Lawman. *Brut*: A Selection

Translated by R. Barton Palmer

Most medieval texts are anonymous and give little direct indication about where and when they were composed, or why. Only a few, most notably the *Lais* of Marie de France, are associated with the name of an author and offer some information about the process, literary or personal, that brought them into being. One of the most important witnesses to the development of an epic tradition in which Arthur plays a central role, the Middle English *Brut* is exceptionally self-revelatory. The poem begins with a remarkably detailed prologue in which the author, a priest named Laʒamon, son of Leovenath, discusses where and how he came to compose what is beyond doubt in literary terms the most impressive (perhaps the only impressive) large-scale poem of the early Middle English period (1066–1300). He provides no title, but the work has come to be called the *Brut* since its principal source, much modified and somewhat expanded, is the *Roman de Brut* of the Anglo-Norman poet Wace. Laʒamon (whose name, ultimately of Scandinavian origin, is usually modernized to Lawman) served the village church of Arsley Kings in the closing decades of the twelfth century, or perhaps the early years of the thirteenth. The village, still inhabited today, is located on the River Severn about ten miles from Worcester in the West Midlands.

At that church, Lawman says he spent his time "reading books," something worth remarking in an age of almost universal illiteracy and the scarcity of written materials, especially in an out of the way parish. But what exactly does Lawman mean? Is he saying that this was one of the functions he served in a parish where perhaps his fellow priests were unlettered and he was called upon to conduct those parts of the service in which reading was called for? Or, more likely since the plural form *boek* does not specify sacred texts but seems tantalizingly indefinite, is Lawman in essence bragging that he has spent a good deal of his time in Arsley reading books of various kinds, perhaps because he was interested in literary matters and the parish, surprisingly enough, possessed a library of sorts. We can certainly say that the style of the *Brut* demonstrates that he had mastered the formal features of Old English alliterative poetry, perhaps through his reading, but more likely, as generations had before him, through listening to oral performances of this traditional art and absorbing its techniques. The stylistic finesse of the *Brut* strongly suggests that this was not his maiden effort at producing such verse himself. In any case, Lawman's work was the last alliterative work to survive until the middle of the fourteenth century when a revival of such poetry (or, perhaps, a re-establishment of written texts in this tradition), which simply generated no surviving textual legacy for more than a hundred years.

In Lawman's time, five generations or so after William's conquest, Arsley Kings was a cultural backwater, not sustained by either a notable religious foundation or a nearby court. There were few places in England further removed from the French culture then quite firmly established in southern England. And yet, as it turned out, Arlsey Kings was in sufficient contact with Anglo-Norman literary traditions that a priest from that parish who could read French as well as his native English and who entertained literary ambitions could learn of the existence of Wace's national epic, which at the time was perhaps the most popular work in the burgeoning tradition of Anglo-Norman literature, and then obtain a copy he used as a source text during the long period it took for him to compose a version in English. Wace wrote for the Angevin court of Henry II where a grande dame, Eleanor of Aquitaine, was a famed patroness of writers. The culture of that court, and its not surprising interests in the rich kingdom with a long and complex history that this Norman dynasty was now ruling, explains the language of Wace's text, as well as its subject matter and impressive scope (about 14,000 lines). What is more remarkable is that Lawman's version of the origin and history of civilization on the island of Britain is substantially longer than its French source (at about 16,000 long lines that are about double the length of those of Wace), of which it is more a creative adaptation than a translation.

Fortunately for scholars, Lawman's *Brut* survives in what must be close to its original form in the British Library manuscript Cotton Caligula A.ix, a largely error-free copy upon which the partial translation printed here is based. Lawman discusses the origin of the project in exclusively personal terms, and it is a rather remarkable story. The desire came to him, he says, to relate the noble history of the English (he does not say British), and the land they inhabit, from the time of the first settlement of the island of Britain after the flood recounted in the book of Genesis. More interesting, perhaps, once he had formed the intention to tell this story he says he embarked on a series of travels "around the people" collecting materials, which he then identifies as Bede's *History of the English Church* (evidently in the original Latin since he misreads its opening section, thinking it consisted of two separate works) and Wace's *Roman de Brut*.

In an age when a text of this length required a substantial supply of very expensive "bookskin" or parchment, an immediate question arises. Who could have underwritten the enterprise upon which Lawman embarked, including the "sabbatical travel" and the purchasing of source materials? And, perhaps more to the point, why? Wace's purpose was to entertain those at court who had the interest to listen to such a text being read and the leisure to spend many pleasurable hours so doing. And so it is unlikely in the extreme that the project was simply personal and individual in the way that Lawman describes it, emphasizing simply his desire to compose such a narrative. Certainly he was not supported simply by the local parish, which, if its financial situation was typical, struggled sufficiently in maintaining its priests, facilities, and various missions, while at times sponsoring needed construction. Arsley Kings enjoyed no unusual endowment, nor can any wealthy patron be identified who might have been encouraged by Lawman's obvious talents to support what must have been a time-consuming project, one that surely took him away from his regular duties. In any case, a wealthy patron, that is, a churchman with funds or a member of the nobility, would most likely be Francophone; those interested in books written in English would have constituted a very limited group of an already small cultural minority of the literate. Why an English version then of Wace's work, which was destined to become one of the era's most popular, as the extensive survival of manuscripts eloquently testifies? And why a version of the work in English that radically transforms its poetry, refusing to adopt something like the easy narrational flow of rhymed octosyllabic couplets, then already established as a standard form for this kind of poetic text in French? Why in particular a version of a French work about the English/British nation that utilizes the conventions of Old English poetry, which employed alliteration rather than end rhyme as well as a repertoire of set metrical patterns dominated by a strong caesura? Literary history, unfortunately, provides no answers to these compelling questions. Despite what Lawman tells us about his work and the circumstances under which it was composed, his *Brut* remains something of an inexplicable mystery.

The *Brut*, it should be emphasized, is not simply a translation of Wace's Anglo-Norman text, making available to those who read English a work that would otherwise be inaccessible to them. As Lawman himself exemplifies, the small literate minority of the age—a cultural elite, if you will—was likely, at least if English-born, to be multi-lingual, not requiring a translation. Lawman's poem is perhaps more accurately thought of as a transculturation. It is an adaptation of an existing literary text that involved not only a change in language, but a radical shift in cultural context, as a work in the French tradition was transformed into one that fit readily into a pre-existing form of exclusively English poetry. The thorough-going change in verse form eliminates the Frenchness of Wace's version (there are virtually no French loanwords, for example), producing a different kind of literary experience, one that Lawman thought worth his time and effort, one that others lost to history thought worth supporting and promoting. At a time when the English language, as a result of radical social change, was losing the social status and prestige it had once exclusively enjoyed, at least as a vehicle for writing in the vernacular, Lawman's text seems an important intervention.

Lawman's work continued to enjoy a certain prestige even when the enthusiasm for Old English culture it exemplifies had begun to wane and French literary culture was more universal among the elite. Later in the thirteenth century, an abridged version of Lawman's work was produced (Cotton Otho C.xiii) in which Old English poetic diction is less in evidence and there are many more French loanwords, testifying to a change in taste and also reading/listening public for the work. The passage offered here deals with materials already present in Geoffrey's *Historia* and passed along through both Geffrey Gaimar and Wace to Lawman. Vortigern has enlisted the aid of the Saxons Hengest and Horsa against the incursions of the Picts, but they have turned against him, massacring many Britons and forcing Vortigern himself into exile in Snowdonia. The Britons turn to the prophet Merlin in their distress, and he predicts the return of the royal line under Maximian that Vortigern had displaced. Two sons of the Roman Constantine II, named Aurelius and Uther, return from Brittany (where many followers of Maximian had settled). The two brothers manage to kill Hengest, but Aurelius is poisoned by the Saxons. Uther will suffer the same fate, but not before he fathers Arthur in a strange sequence of events recalled at the beginning of this section of Lawman's *Brut*. Seized by an irresistible passion for Ygerne, wife of Gorlois, the duke of Cornwall, Uther attacks the man's kingdom and, transformed by Merlin's magic into a likeness of Gorlois, enters his castle at Tintagel and the bed of his wife, where he sires Arthur. Gorlois is killed in battle by Arthur's men at that very moment (thus insuring Arthur's legitimacy), and Uther eventually marries Ygerne, who then gives birth to Arthur, several of whose early successes against the Saxons constitute the subject matter of this passage. Through alliteration and the use (though not rigorous) of Lawman's metrical patterns, the translation attempts to produce something of the style of the original. It is based on lines 9589–10704 of the *Brut* (text from W.R.J. Barron and S.C. Weinberg, *Laʒamon's Arthur: The Arthurian Section of Laʒamon's Brut* [Austin: University of Texas Press, 1989]).

Three days the king delayed in that land,
And then to Tintagel, on the fourth, took the path.
To that fortress his finest soldiers he sent,
Knights to inform Ygerne, noblest of women,
Bring her signs of what in bed she'd said before,
Constrain her to surrender the stronghold at once,
No other course deemed for her, her king was now dead.
Ygerne trusted the truth then lay elsewhere,
That her earl had escaped to seek his soldiers,
And the lady held it strongly to be lies
That Uther had been where only that other belonged.
Her knights met in council, considered the case,
Decided she could defend the fortress no further,
Let drop the drawbridge, deemed the donjon was Uther's,
Once more the realm was that man's to rule.
Uther made Ygerne at once his consort.
With child was Ygerne, and the child was king Uther's,
Because of Merlin's magic before the marriage.
Arrived the term for the birth, and Arthur was born.
Into the world forth he came, and fairies then fetched him,
With charms of great strength they strove to enchant him.
Wondrous might would be his, worthiest of warriors.
And, more, he'd reign as the richest of rulers.
The gift they gave last, his life to be long.
From them he got great virtue and goodness,
And was the mildest of men who draw breath.
Such were the gifts they gave, with them the child thrived.
After Arthur, a glorious girl made her way to this world,
Anna by name, none could equal this lady,
She'd have as her husband royal Lot who ruled Lothian,
Of that kingdom was she queen, over those he called kin.
Many years Uther reigned, these pleased him in passing
In peace with no riot, ruled the realm at his ease.
But old in years, an evil befell him.
Dark luck was his doom, as disease undid Uther,
And this illness endured, seven years, never ending.
Emboldened the Britons, who at this point began
To war on the warrant that was his to wield.
In London's tower was Octa, offspring of Hengest,
Complaining in chains, at York he'd been captured
Along with two thanes, Ebissa and Ossa.
Watched day and night, by warders a dozen,
Weary of keeping this watch there in London.
To Octa, the king's illness was announced,
And these words he spoke to his warders:
"Hear what I say! What I wish you to know!
In London we rot, locked up in this room,
And to your duty as guardians no end yet determined.
Better we all should settle in Saxland,
In wondrous wealth, than remaining here wretched.
And were you moved to do what I wish
Estates would I give, and gold, lots of silver,
There you would live, all your lives, men of wealth,
In whatever way you think to be worthy.
From Uther the king do not expect this,
Not long and he'll die, leave leaderless his house;
Not this reward or another yours to receive.
Ponder this, men of power, and take pity upon us,
Figure what you'd wish, were you in this fix,
But could be in your country, and live there contented."
Often did Octa utter such words to the soldiers.
These knights reconsidered, these knights in their council.
And to Octa allowed: "As you have advised,"
Swearing they'd not betray this bond they had sworn.
One night the wind blew, a breeze that was best.
At midnight the men departed the tower,
And Octa was with them, Ebissa and Ossa.
The river they reached, rowed out to the sea,
And sailed on that ship to the land of the Saxons.
Great crowds of kinsmen gathered to greet them.
Through that country they went wherever they wished.
Estates given to keep, coins of gold and of silver.
Octa considered what his course might then be:
To England to avenge the injury done his elder.
A host they assembled, armed men in huge masses,

On the sea they set out, their strength was stupendous,
To Scotland's shore their ships sailed before stopping.
Some sought dry land, set the country alight.
No Saxons showed pity, but pillaged the Scots,
Put the torch to their towns, three hundred in total,
Felled Scottish folk, in numbers none could figure.
This news came to Uther, the man who was king;
Much anguish he felt, much aggrieved he was then,
Sent messengers to Lothian, to men that he loved there,
Greeted son-in-law Lot, wishing him well,
Commanding him to control the country whose king he then was,
Knights and freemen he should nourish with friendship,
Form them as a force, such was the country's custom.
Advised his men-at-arms to accept Lot for their lord,
To revere and respect him as that realm's ruler.
Since Lot was quite worthy, a warrior war-proven,
Who held out to every man what honor was his,
To him Uther entrusted rule of the realm.
Octa offered battle, and Lot often fought him,
Gaining land in this war, then giving it up.
The British were bold, bravery filled them,
But the ruler was old, no respect due to him,
They did not obey Lot, though he was their earl,
Heeded his commands only half-heartedly,
Of two minds they were, so much the worse!
To the king in his sickbed this then was acknowledged,
That unloyal to Lot were men of rich rank.
Now in this book I'm writing I intend to inform you
How Uther the king endured this crisis.
He would, he said, make his way to the army,
There to determine those doing their duty.
So he commanded a litter to carry him,
Summoned the host from their homes to assemble.
All soldiers to stand up or suffer death,
Forfeit life and limb, to right wrongs done to Uther:
"And if some man at arms is unwilling to speed here,
Soon shall he die, be struck down or hung."
Pressing, they pushed on to his presence.
No one failed to follow his law, not the fat nor the lean.
At once the king put in order his army
Ventured with them to the city of Verolam.
Around the circling walls Uther encamped.
With all his men Octa occupied the place.
Verolam was a burgh whose fame then was burnished,
St. Alban endured death there, saw the end of his days.
The city then destroyed, and some of them slain.
Uther encircled Octa's army inside.
Uther's men in haste advanced to the walls,
These noble fighters with fierceness fought hard,
From those walls worked free not one single stone.
Nothing they attempted could there undermine them.
Quite happy was Octa, son of Hengest,
Observing Uther's men abandon the wall,
Returning dismayed, in retreat to their tents.
Octa then uttered to Ebissa his comrade:
"In Verolam has come Uther the cripple,
Bent on bidding us battle from his bier.
With his crutch he'd crush us, such his intention.
When dawn comes with day, our men will depart
To open the gates of the castle; we'll capture their nobles.
For this one sovereign, we'll not stay behind walls.
On fine steeds in force soon will we stream out,
Set out then toward Uther, strike down all his soldiers,
For doomed to death are those who drew here.
That cripple we'll capture, cast irons upon him,
Keep that wretch captive till he's wasting away.
His legs we will straighten, align all his limbs,
Healing his bones with the blade that bites hard!"
Octa confided all this to Ebissa his comrade.
But what happened was not then what they had hoped.
Day came and dawn broke, the gates were unbolted,
Octa, Ebissa, and Ossa arose from their beds,
Bade their men bear arms for the battle,
Then open the doors and unlock the town.
Octa hurried out, a great host in his trail.

These daring men to their doom then departed.
Uther saw this, saw Octa oppose him,
And these men make ready to hew down his host.
With a shout Uther showed his stoutness:
"Where are you, Britons, bold men of this band?
The day has dawned when God can deliver us,
As Octa shall acknowledge, a bold man who'd bind me.
Think on your fathers, who were fierce in the fight!
Recall I respected and carefully sustained you!
Let not these heathens destroy the houses we dwell in,
Dogs who are rabid rule over our realm.
And I seek from the Lord, who shaped this day's light,
And all the saints, there in heaven's heights seated,
That I on this field might find their assistance.
Now step toward the foe, the Lord fights at your side,
And I pray God Almighty my army protects!"
Knights spurred their horses, spears filled the air.
The shafts shattered with the clashing of shields,
And helmets were hewn as men dropped down dead.
The Britons were brash and brave in the battle,
Hurled to the ground these heathenish hounds.
Octa, Ebissa, and Octa were slain in that slaughter.
Seventeen thousand thrown down Satan's pit.
Flight took many toward the north of that field.
As long as light lasted the knights of lord Uther
Slew and took captive all those they could catch.
When evening arrived, theirs to own was the victory.
The spearmen of his house, their spirits high,
Sang out these words in many a song:
"Uther Pendragon ventured to Verolam,
Where he abased Octa, Ebissa and Ossa as well,
And they paid a penalty here to our people,
And their kin in Saxland can learn of this loss
From songs to be sung in Saxony land."
Uther exulted in the fight they had fought,
And said to the soldiers, the men he much loved.
These words uttered Uther, a man of some age:
"The Saxons showed me their scorn,
Of my sickness it was slander they spoke
Because to this battle was I borne in a bed.
They deemed I was dead, that my fighters were feckless.
But now in this kingdom a miracle has come,
This dead king dealt death to men then still living.
And like a fierce wind forced others to flee.
May God's will be done in days yet to dawn!"

The fighters from Saxony sought safety like fiends,
Those who in fear took flight from the field.
Hastened to harbor in Scotland, there escaping,
And making their new king a man named Colgrim.
Loyal kin to Hengest, the man he loved most,
And Octa, while living, loved Colgrim as well.
Horribly humbled, the Saxon host disheartened
Assembled in Scotland, the one and the all,
Making royal Colgrim their sovereign and ruler.
Around their kingdom they called men to come,
Said their plan was to slay Uther Pendragon
With what wiles they might muster, in Winchester town.
What a calamity this was, for it then came to pass!
Now in council the Saxons set this accord:
"Six soldiers we'll select, men smart and skillful,
Spies who are crafty, dispatch them to court.
As beggars bedraggled then they'll depart,
Homes to inhabit quite near the king's house,
Among the wretched in rags who beg for their bread,
Accept the king's alms as though they're unwell,
And among the desperate, take care to discover
How through some deception, by day or by night,
They might wend to Winchester, close with the king,
And with some plot that's perfect slay that sovereign.
And it was their wish that so would it be.
Once Constantine's kin was killed, no need for concern.
These men set off by the light of the sun,
As the poorest of poor, men armed with great evil,
To the king's house in haste, there to do harm.
As if they were sick they sought out that place,
Eagerly hearkening to hear what might hurt him,
How to the end of his days they might then deliver him.
They happened on a knight in haste from the king,

A kinsman of Uther, and quite close to his heart.
These caitifs called to him, stretched out on the street,
Spoke to that soldier words worthy and kind,
"Sir, of this realm we here are the wretched,
Yet once thought loyal men in this land,
Until Saxons showered shame upon us,
Robbing what was ours, grabbing our goods.
Now for Uther's soul psalms we all sing,
But every day no food do we find,
No man puts meat or fish in our pots.
No drink is donated, only water, not wine,
Just water alone, which is why we are wasted."
The knight heard their words, and hastened away,
Went to the ruler, reclined in his room,
Said this to his liege: "Lord, be in good health,
Outside sit six men, all in the same fix,
Companions they call themselves, now clad in rags,
Once lords in this land, and fighters of force,
God-fearing thanes, possessed of great goods.
Now the Saxon host such men has humbled,
Reduced them to wretches, or so the folk feel,
For food they've but bread, no more do they find,
And for their drink, only water—they are wasting away.
In this fashion they live in the midst of our folk,
They pass time praying God permits you long life."
Uther then uttered these words: "Let them enter,
Garments I'll give them, feed them my food
Out of love for our Lord, as long as I live."
These wicked men went to his chamber.
The king gave them a meal and garments to wear,
And at night provided palettes for sleeping,
Yet each, for his part, would lead him to perish,
Mulled over how to murder the sovereign.
But could conceive no way to bring this king low,
No plan could they plot to put him to death.
Then one day dawned with a drenching rain,
A physician in the fortress said to fetch water,
Bid a boy to do this, to go in great haste
To the fountain that flowed hard by the hall,
And there post a picket to protect it from pollution:
"For the king cares not for any drink for his men
Than the water from this fountain, which he finds welcome,
Which for his disease he deems best to drink."
To this speech that he uttered, the six knights attended.
Eager to assault him, at night they went out,
Straight to the well, where they did what caused harm.
They took out glass phials, which gleamed in that gloom,
Filled these with poison, most bitter of potions,
Which this brook brimmed with, with all that deals death.
These traitors rejoiced, joyful to remain living,
And went their way, wary of waiting any more.
Two servants stood up, strolled to the stream,
Bore in their grip two bowls made of gold.
To the well they went, filled them with water,
Then rushed to the king in his room,
To Uther ill on his pallet, full prone.
"Be well, Uther! For we have arrived here
To bear you, as you lie in your bed,
Cold water from the well, may it provide comfort!"
The king, feeling sick, sat up in his couch.
Wolfed down the water, sank into a sweat;
Felt weak in his heart, his face turning white,
His belly was bloated; that baron was dying.
The die was cast; King Uther lay dead.
Death would destroy all who drank from this water.
His thanes grasping this, grieved then for the king
And their fellows as well, all felled by that foulness,
Made off to the spring, men moving with speed,
Put their backs into blocking that stream,
With dirt and with stones built a steep dam.
Then the household, a host of some size,
Fetched the king's body, forth as they bustled,
Men quite stouthearted bore him to Stonehenge,
Buried him there, not far from his brother;
Body to body, to the grave they were then given.
Then they held court, in that country the highest,
The earls and the soldiers, the scholars as well;
To London they came, made there a great council.
And soon it was decided, by these dominant thanes,
That over the sea, messengers would be sent
To Brittany, who'd seek the best of brave warriors,
In all the earth, the only one of this age,
Arthur son of Uther, the ablest of knights,

Who should come at speed to his kin in that kingdom.
For Uther had died, like Aurelius before him,
And no other heir had Uther Pendragon,
None for the realm, to rule Britons by right,
Reign with righteousness, keep safe the kingdom.
For living in this land were soldiers from Saxony,
Contemptuous Colgrim, with a company of thousands,
Who again and again beleaguered the Britons.
At once the Britons elected three bishops,
Seven knights too, soldiers of wisdom;
These men made haste, hurried to Brittany,
And soon with speed arrived before Arthur:
"King Arthur; we come to you, ablest of warriors,
As he lay dying, on this errand Uther dispatched us,
Requested that you'd reign over and rule
The Britons by law, look out for that people,
Protect this realm, perform like a ruler,
Put the foe to flight, dislodge them from London,
Praying Lord God that he'd take your part,
So you might gain much, get the land from God.
For Uther has passed, and you are Arthur, his heir,
And dead is that other, Aurilius his brother."
This the speech they made, as Arthur sat still.
First he turned pale, seemed sick with that shade,
Then reddened as rage struck him hard.
He burst with words, blurted out what was best;
At once he avowed, this Arthur, of knights the most noble:
"Lord Christ, son of God, send us your love,
So I keep God's commands, as long as I live."
Fifteen years old was Arthur, when so informed;
That time passed with profit, it had made him a man.
His speech at an end, Arthur summoned his soldiers,
Announced that all the men should order their arms,
Saddle their steeds with such speed as they could,
To the Britons he'd betake himself in haste.
His fighters, so favored, sought out the sea,
At Michael's Mount, their host was quite huge.
To the shore at Southampton, the sea brought them soon.
Arthur spurred on his steed, a hero in haste,
Straight to Silchester, where it seemed best.
And the British in bold bands assembled.
That host was quite happy when Arthur arrived;
Trumpets sounded high, the soldiers took heart.
Then to be ruler, young Arthur they raised up.
Now when Arthur was king (an amazing event),
To all the folk, he made known his free hand,
Bestowed much on his knights, this man in his bounty,
To the children a father, to the aged a comfort,
And the unruly found him exceptionally stern.
Injustice he loathed, but loved men of loyalty.
The staff of his servants, helpers of his household,
Good men in his chambers, all these got gold coin,
Were clad in fine cloth, dear drapes for their couches,
No cook did he keep who could not bear arms,
No squire not proven bold in the battle,
In high esteem holding his household knights,
And with such soldiers ruined other rulers,
With his fierceness of force, and the gifts that he gave.
He proclaimed his nobility, all came to know him.
A good king was this Arthur, admired by knights,
The renown of his realm reached every ear.
In London the king counseled his countrymen,
His soldiers and earls sought out the city,
Men of power, paupers too, came to their prince.
Once all arrived, it was the hugest of hosts,
Arthur got to his feet, of rulers the finest,
Had brought to the throne relics quite rare.
Three times he kneeled down, this knight who was king,
His thanes not knowing what course he would chart.
His right arm shot up, as he swore them an oath:
No matter who allowed, as long as he lived
These Saxons would not settle among them,
No realm would they rule, no honors they'd have,
But put to flight all these foes, men who would fight him,
Killers of Uther Pendragon, Constantine's offspring,
Who had brought low Aurilius his brother,
Most loathsome were they of all in the land.

Arthur assembled the knights with most knowledge;
If so was their will, or not, all then swore him oaths,
Avowed they'd stay ever loyal to this Arthur,
Uther they'd avenge, a victim of the Saxons.
To all in the realm Arthur rushed off his writs,
Seeking all soldiers who then could assemble,
Men who might come at once to the king,
And rewards in this realm thus would they win,
Estates they would get, and silver and gold.
The king advanced with the most awesome of armies,
A force of fine splendor, to the city of York,
Remained there one night, at dawn made his way
To where Colgrim lay camped, his lords at his side.
After Octa was brought down, bereft of his life,
(Who was Hengest's son, a hero from Saxony).
Colgrim was highest in rank of those from that country
After Hengest, and Horsa his brother,
And Octa, Ossa, and their companion Ebissa.
For the Saxons Colgrim set down the statutes,
Ruled over and managed them, judged them with rigor.
An army immense, the warriors that went with Colgrim.
To Colgrim's ears came news of King Arthur,
Then coming his way, who could do him much harm.
What course to take, Colgrim carefully considered,
Sent to the north for soldiers to assemble.
Soon all Scotland to that summons submitted,
Picts and Scots pushed off together,
Fighters from many a clan followed Colgrim.
Then this man set out, with his masses of soldiers,
To oppose Arthur, noblest of knights.
Meant to slay this man in the midst of his soldiers,
Deal death to his warriors, wear down their strength,
And retake the realm, every region of Britain
By overcoming Arthur, then still not of age.
Colgrim moved forth, his fighters among him,
Rushed off with his troops, came to a river;
Douglas its name—deadly to warriors!
Arthur fought him there, his men in formation.
At a ford that was broad, he offered him battle.
Men struck at each other, speeding their strokes,
The doomed falling dead, right down to the dirt.
Gore gushing everywhere, corpses in clumps.
Spears clashed together, sparing few of the troops.
Arthur gazed on this, his heart hot with anguish.
Arthur considered, how now he should act
And to a broad field, ordering troops to fall back.
His fighters retreating, so it seemed to his foes,
Colgrim's spirit soared, as did those of his soldiers.
Their conclusion: Arthur had become a coward.
Across the stream they marched, minds bent on madness.
When Arthur observed this, that Colgrim was closing,
With both hosts on the bank, foe close to foe,
This is what Arthur avowed, most noble of knights:
"Look now, my Britons, how they bring themselves near,
Our most bitter enemies, may Christ beat them down,
And Colgrim from Saxony, a soldier keen and strong.
In this country, his kinsmen killed those kin to us.
But the day has now dawned that the Lord determined,
For he is to lose his life, and his friends shall fall dead;
If not, we must die, we cannot, still living, look on him.
The Saxons are doomed, soldiers destined for death,
We shall wreak revenge on our foes, as it is fitting."
High to his head, Arthur hefted his shield,
At their warriors he rushed, like a ravenous wolf,
When, bristling with snow, he bursts from the woods,
Bent on mangling every man whom he meets.
He summoned his soldiers, this Arthur their sovereign:
"Make fast for those men, my fighters most keen.
All massed as they are, they shall be mowed down.
And to the earth they'll tumble, like trees in the forest,

When the wind in its wildness strikes with great
   strength."
Over the hills hastened this host in their
   thousands,
Slew Colgrim's soldiers, the doomed sought the
   dirt.
Broad spears were broken, shields shaken and
   shivered.
Saxons sank to the ground, covering the grass.
Colgrim witnessed all, and thought it great woe,
This high-born hero, who'd sailed there from
   Saxony.
As fast as a fiend, Colgrim then took flight,
With brute strength, his steed bore him off
Over that deep-running stream, saved him from
   death.
To the sand sank the Saxons, fated at the ford,
Arthur's spear showed they would not be
   spared,
Seven thousand Saxons drank death at that
   shore.
Some wandered off, just like the wild crane
In the marshy moors, when in that fen his flock
   scatters,
With hawks to harry them, who hunt in their
   swiftness,
When raging hounds through the reeds
   ruthlessly pursue,
But no safety to seek, neither the shore nor the
   stream.
Hawks swoop with talons, dogs tear with their
   teeth.
Regal but wretched, these birds destined for
   death.
Through the fields Colgrim fled, fleet in his
   flight,
To York he rode hard, this man on his horse.
Into the fortress he fled, secure in that safety.
In that town, he counted ten thousands of
   troops,
His worthiest warriors, the bravest of his band.
With his host, thirty thousand, hastened on
   Arthur.
To the fortress of York, the folk with him
   splendid,
Set his men to lay siege, surrounding the Saxons.
Seven days before had bustled from the south
Badolf, a baron, brother to Colgrim,
By the shore set his tents, searching for Childric.
Childric ruled then all the realm of the Germans,
Respected for royalty, a lord who made laws.
To Badolf the news came, as he camped on the
   beach,
Arthur surrounding the city, where Colgrim
   then sat.
Seven thousand all armed had Badolf for battle,
A band of bold fighters, troops at the ready.
Their council concluded, to Colgrim they'd
   come,
Ride to York, rush to his aid, not waiting for
   Childric,
Do battle with Arthur, bring low all his men.
Burning with anger, Badolf said he'd rob him of
   realm,
Kill king Arthur, be king then with Colgrim, his
   kin.
Badolf would not bide his time and be there for
   Childric,
Set out from that place, sought out the north
   path,
Drove his men hard, that band of bold fighters,
Who reached then a wood in that wilderness,
Seven leagues from where Arthur lay encamped.
He would come upon Arthur before the king
   was aware,
Fell all his folk, and himself slay their sovereign.
All other it befell, not as Badolf believed,
A British fighter in his band, a man who was
   family
To Arthur, Maurin was the name of his man.
With stealth Maurin moved, marched through
   the woods,
Took his way through that fastness, to Arthur's
   tents he did go,
Said this to the king, spoke then these words:
"Most regal of rulers, it's well that I wish you,
I'm a kinsman of yours, which is why I have
   come.
Baldolf has brought here a host of the hardy,
And he seeks this night to slay all your soldiers,
In revenge for his brother, the man you brought
   down;
But God in his glory, strong in his might, will
   say no.
Now send out Cador, who is of Cornwall the
   earl,
With his fighters, fine men, knights who are
   keen,
Seven hundred in all, the boldest of bold,
I'll show them the path, show them the place
They might bring down Badolf, this wolf in the
   wild.
With all of his fighters, Cador hastened toward
   the foe,
Came then to Badolf, where he'd built his
   billets,

From both flanks upon him in their fierceness they fell,
Slew the fighters they found, or in bonds made them fast,
Nine hundred and more were numbered as killed,
Badolf fled through the fields, sought safety in flight,
Through the forest he hurried, fast as a fiend,
Abandoned them all, the battlers in his army,
Northward he went, until he was near
The army of Arthur, in tents by the town,
Near the city of York, a most splendid ruler.
In that city lay Colgrim, and the Saxons that served him.
Then he considered, what course he should take,
This Badolf, what trick he might then try,
To make his way to the town, where he wanted to be,
To be with his kin, Colgrim his brother,
Most beloved to him of men who then lived.
To the bare skin, Badolf had his beard shaven,
Cleaning his chin and his cheeks, a fool then he'd seem,
Half the hair on his head was soon gone, as he hefted a harp,
For music he had mastered, while not yet a man,
And he took up the harp, made his way to the host,
Played for their pleasure, and made the men merry.
Many a time they struck him with sticks,
Thought him for a fool, what fighters were there,
Beat him for a beggar, scorned him as scum.
A madman he was, men said, who'd come to the camp.
That this was Badolf the bold, no man there believed,
Who it was who'd made his way to the court.
But he walked by the walls until they became aware,
The soldiers in the city, this man to Colgrim was kin.
Down they reached him a long rope, Badolf took it,
And up they hauled the man until he was in.
This was the trick Badolf turned, a wile of much worth.
Colgrim and his knights, mark well now their mirth,
As they showed Arthur their anger and enmity.

He saw all their doings, this dastardly trick,
At once was enraged, in the blink of an eye,
Asked his men to seize arms, and set out for the city,
The town would they take, with strength would they strive.
The wall they approached, to start their assault,
But up rode a knight, a man rich and mighty,
A soldier from Scotland, a knight from that nation,
At once he advanced, addressing king Arthur:
"Arthur, be well, best of the Britons.
Heed now my news, hear this of the emperor, Childric by name,
Fierce in the fight, well known for his strength.
Proud of his power, in Scotland his ships shoved ashore.
Buildings he burns there, strongholds set blazing,
Now he rules there, a rich man in the realm.
His boasts are bold after draining his beer,
Wine-drunk he derides you, it's coward he calls you,
Not in field, in forest, have you taste for the fight.
And should you beard him, with bonds he will bind you,
Slay your soldiers, seize the land that is yours."
Often had Arthur been pressed hard, but this was awful,
Some distance from the town he drew back,
Called his knights to counsel, the need to consider was great,
The nobles and clergy, knights of all ranks
Asked them all how he was then to uphold
His lordship among those loyal to him in the land,
Strike mighty Childric, a man with great strength,
Then hastening to Colgrim, bringing him help,
And the Britons said this, men on both sides:
"Lead us straight to London, let him seek after us,
And if he pursues, it will be at his peril,
We will destroy him, his army to death will be doomed."
Arthur approved, their advice was accepted,
The soldiers took the lead, to London they set out.
In York Colgrim waited, Childric was on his way.
Through the north he marched, he and his men,
There laid waste to much of the king's land.

To one of his captains, Childric gave Scotland
Northumberland to his brother then bestowed,
Orkney and Galloway to one of his earls.
For himself he took land from the Humber to London.
No mercy did he mean to offer Arthur,
Save the Briton, Uther's kin, could become his man.
In London was Arthur, with all of his army.
Orders went out, every man should now march
To London, not lingering, not allowing delay.
All England was afflicted, mired in misery.
Men wept and wailed, lost in lamenting,
A people famine pained and want wore down.
Across the ocean Arthur sent two from his army,
To Howel, who held Brittany, a man he much loved,
Worthiest of warriors, kin to this king,
Bade him sail the sea to bring him help,
For huge was the host Childric had chosen,
Of his land his allies were Badolf and Colgrim,
All eager to expel Arthur from that country,
Rob him of the realm that was his to rule,
Kill his kinsmen, drive them to destruction,
Dishonor them all, torture and trouble them.
Better for Arthur had he never been born!
Howel heard this, who was highest in Brittany,
Summoned his soldiers, said be ready for battle,
Saddle their horses and hurry to Arthur,
To France should they fare, call on their kin,
Muster these men for war, they should march fast
To St. Michael's Mount, with many men,
Gold and silver would be given them,
To win their loyalty with this world's riches.
To Poitiers he dispatched the best of his people,
A few to Flanders, fighters there to find,
And two to Touraine wended their way,
Good knights to Gascony he ordered,
All soldiers should speed to St. Michael's.
They should stock their ships with gifts for giving,
Richly rewarded were the soldiers there assembled,
Happy were those who hurried with Howel,
There to aid Arthur, noblest of kings in his country.
Thirteen days dawned since the messengers hurried,
Like hail from the heavens, soldiers stream to the ships.
Two hundred boats, finely fitted and filled to the brim,
Men crowded on board, the ropes were cast off.
Wind and weather favored these fighters.
At Hampton they hauled up their anchors, all safe.
Fierce in the fight, these soldiers set feet on the land,
Wearing their wargear, shields and spears shone bright.
These Britons were bold, made many a boast,
Swore on their souls to punish powerful Childric,
And if he would not go to Germany, flee this fight,
But stand by his banner, stay to do battle,
Bid his soldiers to withstand that storm,
In Britain they'd leave behind what they loved,
Their heads and hands, their helmets bright burnished,
In this fight their friends would fall dead,
Their heroes sent to Hell, those heathen hounds!
In London was Arthur, the noblest knight,
The news, no lies, came to the ear of the king,
How Howel had arrived, with the most awesome of armies,
Tramped to Hampton, his troops thirty thousand,
A host beyond numbering, knights following Howel.
Spirits high, Arthur advanced, his soldiers would seek him,
He'd encounter his kinsman, his army a multitude.
They both came together, in bliss they embraced,
Kissed as they clinched, uttered encouragement,
Then ordered their soldiers, squadrons to assemble.
Then two armies had Arthur, men bold and brash.
Forty thousand fighters, ready for battle's rush.
Toward the north, these knights then went their way,
Men in battalions to Lincoln, then besieged by Childric,
But the town was not taken, not worthily won,
Seven thousand soldiers within, manning the walls,
Fearless fighters, and fearsome, day after day.
With his huge host, Arthur hastened toward the town.
Enjoined his army to advance in secret, trumpets silenced,

Like thieves they should step forth with stealth.
Arthur selected a soldier who was brave and bold,
Sent him to Lincoln, to the ones he loved there,
The man brought a message "Arthur's advancing,"
The most regal of rulers, in haste with his host,
At midnight his men would arrive, knights enough,
"Then warriors at the wall, aware of our army,
Should open the gates, put your men on the march,
Do battle with the besiegers, break out of the burgh,
Hew down the heathen, and Childric, their hero,
The songs we sing with be British, bright with triumph."
The moon at midnight, shone from the south.
With his host Arthur advanced, in haste for the fight,
The soldiers still as stone, like thieves bent on theft.
In sight was the city, Lincoln where the foe lay.
Arthur addressed them, bade them to battle:
"Aware what city you now see, soldiers mine?
These lodgings belong to your foe, Childric lies there,
And Colgrim and Badolf, keen for the battle,
Their host is huge, German heathens who harmed us,
And soldiers from Saxland, whose hatred is hotter,
Of my kin they have killed the most noble of knights,
Constance and Constantine, and Uther my father,
Aurelius Ambrosius, who was that man's brother,
Thousands thrown dead, those I held dear.
Let's close with them quickly, cut them down now,
Revenge wrongs done to us, do right for our realm,
All at once we'll advance, every man should move forward."
Arthur rode swift, others rode after,
The soldiers surged forward, the earth was ablaze,
They tore into the tents, pitched there on the plain,
Arthur the first to find words, with courage cried out,
And with a roar that befit a ruler so brave:

"Mary have mercy, mother of God, do help us!
Say to your son he should be at our side!"
No more to say, the sword used for stabbing,
Hewed down the heathen, and soldiers in haste
Emerged from the city, men bent on striking.
The Saxons were stuck, could not flee for the forest,
Doomed to die there, no safety to seek, slaughter found them.
In no book of the British is another such battle recorded,
So many cut down, killed in their multitudes,
No army fated so ill, its fighters felled to the earth.
Blood blotted the field, bodies bloated with gore.
Death roamed wide, a din from woe welled up.
Childric the king had constructed a castle,
A fort in the field, close to Lincoln it lay,
Built to withstand what battle might bring it,
There the king camped, with Colgrim and Badolf,
Witnessed the war then wasting their army.
Arrayed themselves in arms, and with a coward's courage
Abandoned the fort, no fight would they offer,
Fled the field for the forest men called Calidon,
Soldiers, seven thousand, streamed to their side,
On the field lay the others, forty thousand there felled,
Warriors wearied by battle, beaten down in that fight,
Saxon soldiers were slaughtered, the slain held the field.
Arthur, of knights the noblest, soon knew of all this,
Saw the soldiers of Childric stream from the site,
That king make for Calidon, with Colgrim and Badolf.
They went for the wood, thought the high ground to hold,
Arthur advanced, his army sixty thousand in all.
His fighters surrounded the forest, felled many trees,
Seven miles to that circuit, one side of the woods,
On the other his army arrayed in earnest,
Three days they did so, not moving for three nights as well.
Colgrim saw clearly, as he lay in the forest,
No water in that woods, no food for a feast,
No hay for their horses, no help for this host.

Colgrim called to Childric, the man who was king,
"My lord, tell me truly, I would learn the reason.
Might we not move from this place, make haste
And do battle against Arthur and his Britons?
It were better, I deem, that we die bravely
Than have hunger hunt us down, waste us away,
Such an end will abase us, dishonor will damn us.
Or send messengers, beg mercy from his soldiers,
Ask Arthur for freedom, offer friendship and peace."
These words heard Childric, in the midst of the host,
He responded with sadness, sorrowful his speech:
"If Badolf agrees, should your brother accord,
And others in the army, that we pursue peace,
Then a truce we should ask for, if Arthur accepts.
What my warriors wish, this is what I want too.
Many a knight knows Arthur is honorable,
Loved by his liegemen, his lineage the highest,
Only from kings does he come, kinsman of Uther.
It often occurs, among many a people,
When men bold and brave do battle,
They first hold the field, but are then forced to flee,
Such a fate must be faced by our folk in this fight,
But better we will abide if now we can escape."
Not waiting a whit, his warriors answered:
"This plan pleases, your speech now was splendid."
Twelve soldiers selected as able ambassadors,
Sent swiftly to Arthur, this errand to argue.
Found the king in his tent at the edge of the forest,
One among them called out clear and loud:
"Lord Arthur allow us your mercy, let us affirm
That Childric the emperor had us embark here,
Colgrim and Badolf were in accord with his bidding.
To honor you, they agree evermore to this.
Homage they'll offer, as their liege they accept you,
Hostages will hasten from them, this bargain to bind,
As their lord will they love you, as the highest of high,
So they depart now defeated, but allowed to live longer,
From hence to their homesteads, bring the bad news.
Here our destiny has been dark, grief has gripped us,
Our kinsmen killed, lying lifeless at Lincoln,
Sixty thousand sent from this world, slain in that slaughter.
And if you would want, if your heart wished it,
We'd embark on our boats, sail that salty sea,
Never come to this country, where our kinsmen will stay
Until kingdom come, to return we'll refuse."
A loud laugh Arthur let out, hearing this offer.
"God's grace has granted, all destiny He deems,
Childric is now weary of warfare, tired of trying
This realm to recover, lands to allow his highmen to have,
Rob me of my right, the fealty of my folk.
He counted me a coward, would steal my kingdom.
He'd kill all my kinsmen, slay all my subjects.
Now his is the fate of the fox, a destiny dim,
In the forest he's fierce, far from the plain,
Plays as he pleases, bolts down many birds.
Then greediness grips him, the hills he ascends,
Digs a den in the wasteland, holes he can hide in,
Wanders where he wants, worry does not move him,
He believes that his boldness, his bravery are best.
The hunters blow horns, come for him in his hole,
Hounds hotly pursue, shouts raised on high.
A din undiminishing, dogs bark, beaters yell.
Down the dunes the fox flees, across valleys,
Hastens toward home, dives down in his den,
Wriggles within, as soon as he sees it.
Of his pleasure he's deprived, his happiness halts,
Men dig down deep, pull him out by his paws.
The boldest of beasts, to wretchedness reduced.
Such a destiny, dark and dreary, is for Childric now deemed.
Recklessly would he have robbed me of this realm.
Like the fox he has been forced to flee, must now fight to live,
And I choose for Childric: him I can hang or hack down.
But mercy I'll show him, let him say what is meet,
No noose for him, no axe, his asking is accepted,

Hostages I'll have, chosen from your chieftains,
And your horses I'll have, the soldiers' swords in a heap.
As outcasts they'll come, from the forest to board boats,
Then sail across the salty sea, shove to on your shores,
With honor at home will they live all their lives,
Tell tales of king Arthur, talk of his deeds,
How I set them all free, to honor the soul of my father,
And, generous, gave the wretches this undeserved gift."
But Arthur was wrong, and in accepting this he erred.
No man there so bold, was brave enough to say "but"
Yet soon he would sorrow over what he here decided.
From his camp Childric came, to Arthur the king,
Swore loyalty as his liege, as did all his soldiers.
Hostages—twenty-four—he then handed over,
Warriors of some worth, knights nobly born.
Swords and steeds were sent on to Arthur,
Spears spared as well, all the arms they then owned.
The men then set out and marched on to the ocean,
By the shore they sought, ships on their anchors.
The breeze favored these fighters, blew the boats out to sea,
Left the land behind them, over the ocean,
Quite soon their country no longer could see.
The waves waxed calm, in accord with their wishes,
The excellent ships, of great size, sailed together,
Hull on hull, soldiers huddled side by side,
Boasted they would be back, come to Britain again,
Wrest this land from Arthur, rob him of this realm,
Kill his kinsmen, and capture castles, work what they willed.
The Saxons sailed onward, as far on this sea
Until they arrived between England and Normandy,
Then set sail for the west, turned toward Dartmouth,
Delighted were they, beached their boats on the land.
Coming ashore, they killed the folk they found there,

They felled the farmers plowing the plains,
Strung up the soldiers that sought to defend them.
With knives they wounded all the women of worth,
Murdered the maidens, killed every one among them.
Laid low the learned, roasted them at the stake,
Beat out the brains of the serving boys.
The castles they captured, burning barns as they came on,
Set fire to churches, put fear into the folk.
Infants at the breast were drowned in a brook
All the cows were killed, the ones they could catch,
Took the meat to their men, fed their fighters,
Carried to their ships whatever they came upon.
All day long they sang songs of King Arthur,
Boasted they now held his homesteads,
As their realm they'd retain them, own them as theirs,
And if Arthur were so bold to face them in battle,
To contest with king Childric, a man of power and might,
From his spine they'd make a bridge, span the river with it,
Bind fast the bones of that British king,
Tie them together with twine made from gold,
Stick them on the floor for all then to step on,
And so increase the great glory of Childric the king.
This sham was a sport meant to shame king Arthur,
But it would not happen as they then did hope.
What they devised was destined to damn them,
As ever it occurs when men mean such madness.
Childric the king took the land that he looked on,
Somerset, Dorset, and Devonshire as well,
Did to death all who dwelled there,
Then went to launch an attack on Wiltshire,
Took all the counties as far as the coast.
He announced with horns his host to assemble,
Intending in his boldness the invasion of Bath,
And with his boats block the harbor to Bristol,
This before his men to Bath should make their march.
To Bath came this king, laid siege to its castle,
The warriors within mounted up on the walls,
Well-armed they were, with hauberks and helmets,
Defended the city against Childric, dealing out death.

With Colgrim his companion, Childric encamped,
With his brother Badolf, and other brave men.
In the north was Arthur with his army, knowing nothing,
Marching through Scotland, conquering that country,
Making his own Orkney, Galloway, Man, and Moray,
And all of the lands that lay close around them.
King Childric by then had come to his country,
But, so believed Arthur, never again in Britain would he be.
To Arthur the king, the news was announced,
That Childric has chosen to come there once more,
In the south he was making the people suffer.
Most regal of rulers, Arthur admitted:
"Alas, my foes I should not have unfettered,
In that deep woods hunger would have undone them,
Or out in the open my men could have massacred his.
With rapine and pillage they have repaid my pity.
My the Lord now aid me, who illumines us with his light,
So that this monster meets with the darkest of destinies,
Unkindest of outcomes, for no I'll undo him,
His soldiers we'll slay, the hugest of slaughters.
Colgrim will I kill, and I'll bring Badolf low,
And all who follow them will be felled in this fight.
If the Lord of the Heavens allows this to happen,
I'll revenge myself for the wrongs they have done me.
While breath lasts in my breast, giving me life,
And if He who wields power over the world so wills it,
No further chance for Childric to deceive me."
Then Arthur, most awesome of rulers, roared out:
"Where are you, warriors mine, brave and bold,
Hasten to your horses, you finest of fighters,
To Bath we will go, to that burgh we will ride.
Hang high the noose, the hostages shall swing,
On beams we will dangle them until they are dead."
Four and twenty found death there, yielding up their youth.
Arthur then learned news that alarmed him,
His kinsman Howel was sick, for that he was sorry,
In Dumbarton he lay, and there he left him,
Hurried onward, making great haste while advancing.
To Bath he beat a path, in a nearby plain dismounting,
His fearless fighters accoutered in their coats of mail.
Into five squadrons he separated these soldiers.
All things were in order, his army set as Arthur said,
He donned his hauberk, of the strongest steel,
With cunning assembled by an elvish craftsman,
Wygar was the armor, Witege its maker elf.
His calves with steel plate then he covered.
Strapped to his side his sword Caliburn,
Forged in Avalon by fairy art, with magic manufactured.
The helmet on his head was fashioned of hard steel,
Worked with gold, studded with wondrous gems,
Once it was Uther's, owned by that sovereign.
Goswhit it was named, no other as good!
On his shoulder he slung a magnificent shield,
The Britons called it Pridwen, a brave man's protector.
Imaged within in lines of gold, craftily made,
Was the Mother of God, a good likeness.
The spear he hefted in his hand was called Ron.
All now in armor he stepped up on his steed.
Whoever was there would have seen quite a wonder,
The most magnificent knight who ever led men.
No warrior in this world was ever more worthy
Than this Arthur, who alone enjoyed such honor.
Then this king called out so all there could hear:
"Look here at the heathen dogs lurking,
Who killed our kinsmen, made war with wickedness,
And are in any land the most loathsome to us.
Now we'll attack them, advance and oppress them,
Find revenge for our fathers, and for our realm,
Diminish the dishonor done by these demons,
Who have driven their ships to Dartmouth.
They forswore the oath they accepted,
God grant us the mercy to undo them.
Close now your ranks and keep facing to your front,
No noise now, as if no harm we're intending.

When we come close, the battle will begin with me,
Your horses at the walk, as we work our way toward them,
You soldiers should stay silent, but be quick to the kill,
And may the Lord allow us success in this skirmish.
Arthur, most noble of knights, advanced on his horse,
Forth over the fields, bent on riding to Bath,
And the news made known to Childric at last,
That Arthur and his men moved to attack, fit for the fight,
Then Childric and his men made for their horses,
Wielding their weapons, knew well what would happen.
Arthur, most regal of rulers, was aware of all this,
Saw this pagan people, seven hundred strong,
Make for his men, emboldened for battle.
The earl himself attacked at the front of his army,
And Arthur rode, first in the ranks, as head of his host.
The bold Briton reached for Ron, hefted it in his hand,
Strong-minded and resolute, stretched out the stiff shaft,
Gave the reins to his horse, galloped hard, the ground groaned,
Hefted the shield to his head, a ruler enraged.
Stuck his spear in earl Borel, pieced his heart with the blow,
Through his breast went the blade, the king called out loud:
"Killed is their captain, God gives us his aid."

Britons battled the Saxons, wailed blows on the wicked,
With axe blades and swords they beat down those slayers,
To the earth threw two thousand, their lives at an end,
But not one of Arthur's, not one soldier fell slain.
Then the folk of the Saxons was the most fraught by sorrow,
In great misery then these Germans were mired.
With his sword Arthur struck brutally, blow after blow,
Each man his blade bit, to death soon was doomed.

Wracked with rage, battle-minded as the boar,
When wild in the woods he spies huge herds of swine.
Childric soon saw this, fled the field in his fright,
Across the Avon he went, in search of some safety.
Arthur sped after, angry lion on the loose
Drove them down into the river, doomed there to drown,
Sank to the bottom, soldiers in battle gear, twenty-five hundred,
Brimming with steel, a strange bridge on the Avon,
Fifteen hundred were fleeing, Childric chief among them,
Sought out the sea, wished to set sail on their ships.
The Saxon king climbed up the hillside, as saw Arthur,
Hastened to high ground there, bordering Bath,
And Badolf behind him, with soldiers seven thousand,
Would defend that dune, hold fast on that height,
There wield their weapons, keep Arthur away.
Arthur saw this, that most regal of rulers,
Colgrim at bay, emboldened for battle,
And the king called out, his voice raised up high.
"Be brave now and bold, head for those hills.
Colgrim was yesterday quite keen on killing,
But now a goat who stands guard on a mound,
High up on that hill, would fight with its horns,
Though the wolf stands alone, on his own for the hunt,
And sees goats in their hundreds behind a locked gate,
In his ruthlessness he rushes them, rips them to pieces.
This day I'm determined to destroy Colgrim utterly,
I am the wolf, he the goat—I will grind him down.
Arthur, most regal of rulers, continued to call out:
"Badolf was yesterday the bravest of battlers,
Holds forth now on this height, on the Avon looks down,
Sees the steel fish that float in that stream,
Put to sleep with the sword, their swimming has stopped,
Scales shining like shields worked with silver and gold,
Their fins look like spears, fit for the fight.

Such a marvel in this land for men to look on,
Such beasts on this bluff, such fish in that flood.
The emperor yesterday was the most courageous of kings,
Now a hunter who's harried, by those who wear horns,
Fleeing over the broad fields, the hounds barking at him.
His bold depredations were undone at Bath.
No chase for this Childric, his prey now pursues him,
His ravages find their finale, beaten down is his boasting,
And we will regain for our realm what has been our right."
All spoken his speech, to his head his shield hefted,
Before his breast the king brandished it,
Shook his stout spear, stepped up on his steed,
Almost as fast as some bird could have flown there,
Fighters—twenty-five thousand—followed after,
Men bold in battle, maddened for massacre,
Started up the hill, a force huge in strength,
Collided with Colgrim, beat his men with bitter blows.
Their king these Britons encountered, their sword bites killed many.
Five hundred with felled in the first of these onslaughts,
King Arthur saw his soldiers cut down there,
Anger overcame him, a rage beyond reason,
This finest of sovereigns called out to his fighters:
"Britons, where are you, bred for boldness in battle?
Our enemies stand there, the stoutest of opponents.
To the ground let us grind them, most worthy of warriors!
Arthur stepped forward, struck a Saxon with his sword,
In the man's mouth the blade lodged, stuck tight in his teeth.
Then brought it down on that man's brother,
Hewed into the man's helmet, to the dirt threw him down.
Yet another came upon him, with his blade cut him in half.
Such deeds, done with courage, emboldened the Britons,
Who struck at the Saxons, with sword strokes they slew them,
Spiked them on their spears, pierced them with sword points.
Their foes fell down to earth, these enemies fated to die.
In their hundreds they were hewed down, the dead were in heaps.
A massacre that mounted to thousands and thousands,
Toward Colgrim Arthur advanced, and that king caught sight of him,
Encompassed by corpses, Colgrim could not escape,
But Badolf his brother bravely stood there beside him.
With a brash cry, Arthur bravely called out:
"Here I come, Colgrim, contest now the kingdom.
This land we'll divide, but the deal won't delight you."
Speaking this speech, Arthur raised up his sword arm,
Down went the blade for a blow, it cut Colgrim through,
His helmet was hewn, the sword split him in half,
Did not halt in his hauberk, but broke into his breast.
Then at Badolf he struck, the stroke beheading the man.
Arthur, a knight most noble, then loudly laughed,
Addressing the dead men with words that mocked them:
"Rest there a while, Colgrim, you reached so high,
As beside you your brother Badolf abides.
Into your keeping I entrust now this kingdom,
Its downs and its dales, and the subjects there resident.
This hill you scaled, as to heaven you'd ascend,
Instead you now sink to Satan, in Hell have your home.
In that country you'll encounter many a kinsman,
Hengest will hail you, most noble of knights,
Ebissa and Ossa, Octa, and the others,
For ever and ever you'll find there your future.
But we'll live on in the land, content in this country,
Your souls to never enjoy salvation, this we'll pray,
But your bones to remain buried on this hill beside Bath."

Part II
Arthurian Romance

Arthur in Early Wales/*Culhwch and Owen*

Translated by CRAIG DAVIS

The story of Arthur begins among the Brittonic-speaking Celts of post–Roman Britain, many of whom had converted to Christianity, along with the rest of the Roman Empire, during the fourth century AD. When the Romans withdrew their armies and government from the island around the year 410, the Romanized Britons were eventually conquered or driven back from the lower-lying parts of Britain by various Germanic-speaking groups who moved inland up the river systems from the east and south. In the more rugged west and north of the island, British chieftains and petty kings maintained a beleaguered, though often mutually hostile, independence against these newcomers. A religious writer of the mid-sixth century, Gildas, wrote an account in Latin, *De Excidio et Conquestu Britanniae* (On the Ruin and Conquest of Britain), in which he describes these events in vivid language. Gildas saw his people as *praesens Israel* (the present-day Israel), a chosen nation whom God had indeed punished for their manifold sins, but whom he had also led to victory against the pagans at the *obsessio Badonici montis* (siege of Mount Badon) around the turn of the sixth century (ca. 500). The site of this battle is unknown, but Gildas attributes the success of the Britons there to a *dux* (leader) named Ambrosius Aurelianus, who won a significant respite for his people, lasting perhaps a generation or two, from the advance of the Anglo-Saxons into Britain. Gildas was the first writer to conceive of the various British chiefdoms as a single nation and to see in their affairs the hand of the Christian God. He explicitly interpreted their collective experience according to the pattern of national sin, chastisement but ultimate redemption he found in the Bible. Over the course of the next millennium, the legend of Arthurian Britain would echo ever more deeply these biblical resonances, even as it drew upon an equally rich tradition of archaic Celtic motifs and story-patterns: the quest for marvelous adventures; passionate but destructive loves; encounters with a preternatural realm of magic, beauty and danger; potent vessels of plenty or rebirth; wise enchanters or mysterious "sovereignty maidens" who offer their chosen leaders the symbols of charismatic authority—swords, rings, vessels of gold and silver.

The Celtic Britons were proud of their Christian faith and their Roman names and ways. In fact, Venedotia, the later kingdom of Gwynedd in northwest Wales, was the very last province of the western Roman Empire to fall to the "barbarians," when the Anglo-Norman king Edward I finally completed his conquest of Wales in 1282. Yet, there is evidence that the Romans first, and then the Britons themselves later, had invited some of these Germanic groups to live among them as auxiliary troops to help keep out other invaders. One tradition names such a mercenary captain *Hengist* (the Stallion), who turned on his British overlord *Vortigern* (Great Tyrant) to set himself up as king of Kent. The names *Wales* and *Welsh* are from the Old English words *Wealas* (Romans) and *Wielsc* (Romanish), referring at first to all the occupants of the former Roman Empire, whatever their local language or ethnicity. The Welsh called themselves *Brython* (Britons), including speakers of Britonnic in Wales, Cornwall, Cumbria, southern Scotland, and Brittany, and then eventually *Cymry* (Fellow Countrymen), referring to those living in Wales proper.

It was not until 829–30, nearly three centuries after Gildas wrote *De Excidio*, that we find our first unambiguous reference to a Christian leader in the post–Roman period named Arthur. The Latin *Historia Brittonum* (History of the Britons), attributed to Nennius, was compiled in northern Wales from various historical and legendary sources as part of a new genre of national ethnic origins. Here the British nation is said to descend from a certain Britto or Brutus (the grandson or great-grandson of the Trojan founder of Rome, Aeneas), who gave his name to the island after his arrival from Italy. Aeneas himself is made to descend through nine generations from Noah in the Book of Genesis. The *Historia Brittonum* thus links the founding of Britain with the two most authoritative traditions of the past known in early medieval Europe, that of classical Greece and Rome on the one hand and that of the Bible on the other.

Even here, Arthur is not specifically identified as a king, but rather as a *dux bellorum* (leader of battles), twelve of which are named and seem to have been obtained from a battle- or praise-poem in which such lists of victories were common: we can even discern the rhyme scheme of the Old Welsh verses in the various river- and other place-names listed. These battles are said to have culminated in the decisive engagement at Mount Badon, where leadership of the Britons, once attributed by Gildas to Ambrosius, has been transferred to Arthur. In fact, *Arthur* may simply be the Brittonic form of *Artorius*, the family name of a Roman military officer serving in Britain, though the first element *arth* (bear) also chimes with that of an animal hero of Celtic folklore. In any case, the presence of a *dux bellorum* named Arthur in the post–Roman period is unproven, unless this figure should be seen as a legendary permutation of the historically attested *dux* Ambrosius Aurelianus or of some similar Romano-British war-leader, perhaps a captain of cavalry, to whom the victory at Badon was later assigned in popular memory. The heroic figure of Arthur, as last great defender of his people, was known in all Brittonic-speaking territories from Scotland in the north to Brittany across the Channel in the south where his name appears in local traditions, usually place-names, whenever records first become available.

The earliest such toponymic record is appended to the *Historia Brittonum* in a list of amazing phenomena, natural and otherwise, called the *Mirabilia Britanniae* (Marvels of Britain). Two of these refer to Arthur *miles* (the warrior), one to his famous hunting of the boar Twrch Trwyth (later retold in *Culhwch ac Olwen*), the other to the tragedy in which Arthur killed his own son, here called Amr. The *Annales Cambriae* (Welsh Annals) of the tenth century include a brief notice of the Battle of Mount Badon, here dated 516, and another of the Battle of Camlann dated 537, where both Arthur and his son Medraut (later Latinized as Modredus or, in English, Mordred) are said to have fallen together. Although it is not explicitly stated that father and son were antagonists in this last battle, later traditions of their deadly rivalry came to epitomize why the Britons lost so much of their country to the Anglo-Saxons in the Welsh popular imagination. It was the very failing which Gildas had castigated so vehemently in *De Excidio*: their inability to unite against the invaders, the treacherous in-fighting among themselves. Writers in other languages over the next few centuries would elaborate both the glorious and the darker sides of the legend of Arthurian Britain, but the Welsh themselves were the first to use his story as a way to reflect upon their national character and contemporary situation as a people.

Some of the tensions within the Arthurian world, its glorious ideals and tragic fate, may be seen in what is probably the first complete poem about Arthur to survive. *Preiddeu Annwn* (The Spoils of Annwn) is preserved in the early fourteenth-century *Book of Taliesin*, though it seems first to have been composed much earlier, sometime between the mid-ninth and the mid-eleventh centuries, on account of the archaic form of its language and poetic style. It describes Arthur's voyage over the sea in his ship Prydwen to a mysterious fortress of glass in order to rescue one of his men and make off with a treasure, the magical pearl-rimmed cauldron of the Lord of Annwn, who rules the (Unworld) or (Otherworld) of ancient Celtic tradition. The attempt is a brave but terrible disaster from which only seven of Arthur's men survive, including Taliesin his chief bard, who is recounting the adventure. Many scholars have seen in this fateful search for a miraculous vessel, elsewhere called the Cauldron of Renewal, a precursor of the later quest of the Holy Grail, the chalice of the Last Supper that caught the blood of Christ on the Cross.

Pa Gwr yw y Porthawr? (What Man Guards the Gate?) is an incomplete poem in its present form, composed during the same pre–Norman period as *Preiddeu Annwn*. It is preserved in *The Black Book of Carmarthen* of the mid-thirteenth century. In it, Arthur is challenged on his return home by his own gatekeeper Glewlwyd Great-Grip to identify himself and the men with him, so that the poem attempts a kind of inventory of Arthur's warriors and their bona fides. As with *Preiddeu Annwn*, the antiquity of *Pa Gwr* is indicated by its old-fashioned language and the deep obscurity of its allusions. Fortunately, some of these can be clarified by the earliest extant Arthurian prose tale, *Culhwch ac Olwen*, which contains a similar, though much longer list of Arthur's followers, who are invoked to aid Culhwch in his quest.

The story of how Culhwch won Olwen was composed from popular tales circulating during the last decades of the eleventh century and is preserved in two later manuscripts, *The White Book of Rhydderch* (ca. 1325–50) and *The Red Book of Hergest* (ca. 1400). Here Arthur is depicted as chief of the kings of the island of Britain, but with Roman imperial flavor to his conquests abroad, "as far as Greece to the east." There is no mention of invading Angles or Saxons, though there are allusions to a terrible battle yet to come at Camlann. Instead, Arthur and his warriors have the leisure to drink and feast and go on a wild hunt after various *anoethau* (difficult tasks) set for Arthur's cousin Culhwch by Ysbaddaden Pencawr (Chief of Giants), before this fierce old man will consent to Culhwch's request for the hand of his beautiful daughter Olwen. These marvelous adventures inspired by the love of a woman anticipate the romantic quests of later Arthurian romance, but Arthur's court here at Celliwig in Cornwall is not the refined Camelot of French and English tradition. Instead, it is a great timber feasting-hall of barbaric proportions where warriors with various super-talents—a mighty hand-grip, super-sight, super-hearing, super-heat, magical weapons—down horns of honey-sweetened beer and eat their fill of smoking pork chops. And while Arthur delegates most of the stipulated tasks to his men, he must finally take charge of the hunt himself as the huge boar Twrch Trwyth, a wicked king under enchantment, defies all their efforts to snatch the symbols of a chieftain's authority—razor, scissors and comb—from between its ears. As Arthur says, "The boar Twrch Trwyth has killed many of my men. By the courage of my men, he will not go into Cornwall while I am still alive. I will not chase him further, but will go against him myself, life for life. Do what you can." Despite a fierce encounter in the Severn River, however, Twrch Trwyth does indeed escape into Cornwall just the same. In the end, for the very last task, Arthur forgoes all pretense to royal dignity when he is forced to face a dire witch alone with his knife, after she has ravaged his bravest men and sent them howling from her cave. The king gets this dirty, dangerous job done himself—the witch's scalding blood is needed to soften the giant father-in-law's stiff beard—and Arthur finally fulfills his promise to help Culhwch win Olwen, but only after much pain, humiliation and loss of life. Even so, the king's staunch "loyalty down" to his young kinsman means that a prince of his blood may now marry the springtime maiden who, freed from the power of her grim father, will bring the blessings of peace and prosperity to Arthur's realm.

As often is the case with Celtic narratives, the episodic tale surges forward in three larger movements: (1) the account of Culhwch's unusual birth and his coming to the court of Arthur, ending with the long list of Arthur's followers charged to help him win Olwen (over 270 names, not counting some repetitions and patronyms); (2) the search for Olwen herself, culminating with the list of 40 difficult tasks set by Ysbaddaden before he will grant consent to her marriage; and (3) the achievement of the tasks themselves, only a dozen of which are described in detail, including a few never stipulated in the first place. In fact, subsequent copyists of the original eleventh-century text seem to have expanded these lists even further, but exaggerated catalogues of this kind were a popular feature of Celtic oral tradition in both Wales and Ireland. So in spite of its rough, over-the-top panache and often comic hyperbole, *Culhwch ac Olwen* reveals that many of the forms and preoccupations of incipient Arthurian romance long flourished in native Welsh storytelling before the coming of the Normans to Britain in 1066, after which this obscure folk-hero was introduced to the wider world of medieval Europe and proved an extraordinarily compelling figure of the literary imagination for centuries to come.

Pronunciation of Early Welsh Names

Consonants are pronounced roughly the same as in English, except that c is always hard as in "cat," g is always hard as in "go," ch is guttural as in "Bach," dd is a voiced th as in "the," th is a voiceless th as in "thing," f is a v as in "vine," ff is an f as in "fine," s is always voiceless as in "assess" (never voiced as in "busy"), si is sh as in "shop," and ll is a voiceless sound similar to tlh.

Vowels are similar to those in Spanish or Italian, except that w can be pronounced as a long or short u like the oo in "goon" or "good"; u is pronounced either long or short like the ee in "see" or the i in "pin"; y is pronounced like the ee in "see" or the i in "pin" in the last syllable of a word or in a monosyllabic word, but like the u of "uh" in all syllables of a word but the last. The diphthongs ae, ai, au, ei, ey, eu are all pronounced like English "aye"; aw as ou in "ouch"; wy is often disyllabic as in "gooey."

Accent is almost always on the second-to-last syllable, except in certain compounds. Examples: Annwn = "AHN-noon"; Cafall = "KAH-vahtlh"; Celliwig [Forest-Grove] = "KEH-tlee-WEEG"; Culhwch = "KILL-(h)ooch," with the ch as in "Bach"; Glewlwyd = "GLE-oo-LOO-id"; Goleuddydd = "go-LAYE-theeth," with both th's as in "the"; Twrch Trwyth = "TOORCH TROO-ith," with the ch as in "Bach," th as in "thing"; Ysbaddaden = "UHSS-ba-THA-den," with the th as in "the."

From Gildas, *On the Ruin of Britain* (sixth century AD):

25.3–26.1 Our men rallied and challenged the victors to battle under a leader named Ambrosius Aurelianus, a nobleman who virtually alone of the Roman people escaped the crash of the storm that killed his parents, a family that had once worn the imperial purple, but whose offspring have now in our day sadly declined from their grandfather's excellence. What a victory was granted by God's assent! After that, sometimes our citizens, sometimes the enemy, were victorious, so that the Lord as usual could test this nation, his present-day Israel, to see whether we loved him or not: right up to the year of the siege of Mount Badon, which was almost the last, but not the least, slaughter of those criminals. It is now one month into the forty-fourth year after that battle: I should know, since it was also the year of my birth.

From *The Marvels of Britain* (ninth century):

73. There is another marvel in the region called Buellt, where a pile of stones, with one particular stone set on top, is imprinted with the footstep of a dog. When the boar Porcus Troynt [Twrch Trwyth] was being hunted, Cabal [Cafall], the warrior Arthur's dog, pressed his footprint into the stone, and Arthur later gathered a pile of stones under the one in which the footprint of his dog had been pressed. It is now called Cabal's Cairn. And men come and carry away that stone by hand for a whole day and night, but the next day it is found back on its pile.

There is another marvel in the region that is called Ercing [Ergyng]. A sepulcher is there next to a spring called Licat Amr and the name of the man who is buried in the tomb is said to be Amr; he was the son of the warrior Arthur, and Arthur himself killed him and buried him there. And when men come to measure the tomb, it is sometimes six feet long, sometimes nine, sometimes twelve, sometimes fifteen. At whatever length you measure it on one occasion, you will not find it to be the same length a second time. And I myself have tested this.

From *The Welsh Annals* (tenth century):

The year 516: Battle of Badon, during which Arthur carried the cross of our Lord Jesus Christ three days and three nights on his shoulders and the Britons were the victors.

The year 537: Gueith [Battle] of Camlann, during which Arthur and Medraut fell, and there was death from plague in Britain and Ireland.

The Spoils of Annwn (ninth century)

I

I honor the Lord, chieftain of a royal domain
who has stretched his rule over the strand of the world.
Perfect was the imprisonment of Gwaer in Caer Siddi,
as told in the tale of Pwyll and Pryderi.
No one had gone in there before him,
into those heavy, blue chains: they held a brave lad!
And for the spoils of Annwn mournfully he sang.
And until Doomsday my own song of his longing will live.
Three shiploads in Prydwen we went into it:
save seven, none returned from Caer Siddi.

II

I am of great renown. My song is heard
in the four-square, steep-sided fortress,
where I first told of the cauldron,
one kindled by the breath of nine maidens.
The cauldron of the chief of Annwn, what is its nature?
Black around its rim, set with pearls,
it will not cook the food of a coward: that cannot happen!

A deadly bright sword was pulled from
   it
and in the destined hand it stayed.
In the entrance to Hell's gate lamps were
   burning,
and when we entered with Arthur, a
   brilliant disaster:
save seven, none returned from Caer
   Feddwid.

III

I am of great renown. My song is heard
in the four-square stronghold, bulwark
   of this island.
Noonday and jet-dark become one
as they drink bright wine with their
   war-band.
Three shiploads in Prydwen we went by
   sea:
save seven, none returned from Caer
   Rigor.

IV

I, lord of knowledge, do not deserve
   mean men:
in the Fortress of Glass they did not
   know the courage of Arthur.
Six thousand men were standing on the
   wall:
it was hard to speak with their watchman.
Three shiploads in Prydwen we went
   with Arthur:
save seven, none returned from Caer
   Goludd.

V

I do not deserve mean men, dragging
   their round shields.
They do not know who makes the day,
what hour the Creator was born,
who made it so they did not return to
   Dolau Defwy.
They do not know about the speckled
   ox with its thick neck-rings:
there were seven score links in that jew-
   eled chain.
So when we went with Arthur, it was a
   terrible journey:
save seven, none returned from Caer
   Fanddwy.

VI

I do not deserve mean men: slack their
   attack.
They do not know what makes the day
   break,
what hour of the day the Ruler of all
   was born,
what animal they keep with a head of
   silver.
When we went with Arthur, a hideous
   struggle:
save seven, none returned from Caer
   Ochren.

VII

Monks in their choirs squeal like pup-
   pies
at the tale of lords and witches.
Does the wind have one path? Is the sea
   one water?
Is fire, that unquenchable roar, only one
   spark?

VIII

Monks howl like wolves
at the tale of lords and witches.
They do not know the moment dawn
   leaves night,
nor of the wind, where it goes, where it
   gusts,
what place it ravages, what land it
   strikes,
destroying how many shrines and how
   many altars.
I adore the Lord, the great chieftain.
I will not be sad: Christ is my treasure.

What Man Guards the Gate? (tenth century):

"What man guards the gate?"
"Glewlwyd Great-Grip.
   Who wants to know?"
"Arthur and Cei the Fair."
5   "Who goes with you?"
"The best men in the world."
"You will not come into my house,
   unless you vouch for them."
"I will name them,
10   and you shall know them.

Gwythneint of Elei
and three wise men:
Mabon son of Modron,
servant of Uthir Pendragon;
15   Cysteint son of Panon;
and Gwyn Godyfrion—
my servants have been fierce
in defending their rights.
Manawydan son of Llyr,
20   whose counsel has been deep:

```
        Manawyd escaped                              He was a stern captain of the host
        with broken shields from Tryfrwyd.           in the defense of his land.
        And Mabon son of Mellt [Lightning],          Bedwyr son of Bridlaw:
        who stained with blood the grass.            nine hundred in defense,
   25   And Anwas the Winged,                  60    six hundred in attack
        and Llwch Smite-Hand,                        was his leading the fight worth.
        who were defending                           I had some fine young men:
        Eidyn in the borderlands.                    it went better when they were there.
        A lord would assuage them,                   Before the kings of Emrys,
   30   my nephew offer amends;                65    I saw Cei charge:
        Cei would beseech them,                      the taker of spoils,
        while killing three by three.                the tall man was angry.
        At the loss of Celli,                        Heavy was his vengeance,
        a fierce defense was gotten;                 bitter was his fury.
   35   Cei would plead with them,              70   When he drank from a horn,
        while he cut them down.                      he would drink for four;
        Though Arthur was laughing,                  when he came into battle,
        blood was flowing                            he would kill like a hundred.
        in the hall of Afarnach,                     Unless God himself should perform it,
   40   fighting with the witch-hag.            75   Cei could not be killed.
        He pieced Penn Palach                        Cei the Fair and Llacheu
        in the dwellings of Dissethach.              used to start the battles,
        On the mountain of Eidyn                     rushing against the pain of blue-tipped
        he fought the were-dogs.                       spears.
   45   By the hundred they fell,                    On the summit of Ystafngwn
        they fell by the hundred,              80    Cei pierced nine witches.
        before Bedwyr Bedrydant:                     Cei the Fair went to Mon [Anglesey]
        on the sandbanks of Tryfrwyd,                to kill lions:
        fighting with Garwlwyd                       his shield was shattered
        [Rough-Grey]—                                against the Cat Palug.
   50   fierce was his spirit                   85   People ask who
        with sword and shield.                       pierced the Cat Palug:
        An army was worthless                        nine score warriors
        against Cei in battle:                       would fall as its food;
        he was a sword in battle;                    nine score chieftains
   55   his hand took hostages.                 90   and ...
```

Culhwch and Olwen

A FATE IS SWORN UPON CULHWCH BY HIS STEPMOTHER

Cilydd son of Prince Celyddon wanted a wife as well born as he was himself. The wife he chose was Goleuddydd daughter of Prince Anlawdd. After he had slept with her, the whole country took to prayer that they might have children. And they got a son through the prayers of that land. But from the moment she conceived, Goleuddydd went mad and would not seek shelter indoors. When her time came, reason returned to her. It happened in a place where a swineherd was keeping a herd of pigs. And it was from fear of the pigs that the queen gave birth. The swineherd took the boy and brought him to the court. And the boy was baptized and given the name Culhwch [Pig-run] since he was found in a place where pigs were kept. Yet, the boy was of noble birth; he was Arthur's own cousin. So they put the boy out to fosterage.

But after that, Goleuddydd daughter of Prince Anlawdd fell ill and called her husband to her, telling him, "This illness will be my death and you will want another wife. Women these days expect to possess much wealth, but it would be wrong for you to disinherit your son. So I ask you not to take a wife until you see upon my grave a thorn branch with two heads." He made her this promise. She called a wise man to her and charged him to clear the grave every year so that nothing would ever grow on it.

The queen died. The king would send a boy every morning to see if anything was growing on the grave. At the beginning of the seventh year the wise man forgot what he had promised the queen. One day, while the king was hunting, he went to the graveyard; he wanted to see the grave that would let him seek a wife. He saw the branch of thorn. And when he saw it, he called his council to decide where he might get a wife. One of his counselors said, "I know a woman who would suit you well. She is the wife of King Doged." They decided to seek her out. They killed the king and brought his wife back home with them, and she had a daughter with her. And they took over that king's country.

One day the lady went out walking. She came to the house of an old wise woman in the town without a tooth in her head. The queen asked, "O wise woman, will you answer me what I ask you, in God's name? Where are the children of the man who abducted me by force?" The wise woman answered, "He has no children." The queen exclaimed, "Woe is me to have come to a childless man!" The wise woman said, "Your grief is needless. It is prophesied that he will have offspring; from you will he get what he has not gotten from another. And do not be sad: he does have a son."

The lady went home rejoicing and asked her husband, "Why did you hide your children from me?" The king answered, "But I am not hiding him." The boy was sent for and he came to the court. His stepmother said to him, "It would be good for you to marry, son. I have a daughter well-born enough for any nobleman in the world." The boy answered, "It is not time for me to marry yet." She replied, "I swear this fate upon you that your loins shall not strike against a woman until you take Olwen daughter of Ysbaddaden Chief of Giants. The boy blushed, and love for the girl pierced every limb in his body, even though he had never seen her. His father asked him, "Son, why are you blushing? What is wrong with you?" "My stepmother has sworn that I shall never get a wife until I get Olwen daughter of Ysbaddaden Chief of Giants." "That is easy for you to achieve, son," said his father to him. "Arthur is your cousin. Go to Arthur to trim your hair, and ask him for this as a gift."

Culhwch Comes to Arthur's Court

The boy went on a horse that was four winters old, muscular, shell-hoofed, with a bridle of gold tubes on its silver grey head. A rich gold saddle sat under him, and he had two sharpened silver spears in one hand. In his other hand was a battle-axe, as broad from shaft to edge as the length of a grown man's forearm. It would draw blood from the wind quicker than the quickest dew drop falls from stem to ground in June when the dew falls heaviest. A gold-hilted sword lay on his thigh, with a golden blade, and a gold-adorned shield with a flash of heaven's lightning around its ivory boss. And two brindled, white-breasted greyhounds ran in front of him with a collar of red gold from shoulder-swell to ear around the neck of each one. The one on the left would be on the right, and the one on the right would be on the left, like two sea swallows darting around him. The four hooves of his horse cut four clumps of earth like four swallows in the air over his head, sometimes in front of him, sometimes behind. He wore a purple cloak with an apple of red gold at each one of the four corners. Each apple was worth a hundred cows. On his leggings and stirrups, from the top of his thigh to the tip of his toes, there was gold the worth of three hundred cows. Not a wisp of hair stirred on him, so light was the canter of that horse, riding up to the gate of Arthur's court.

The boy asked, "Well, is there a gatekeeper here?" "There is. And you, beware your head for asking it. I am Arthur's gatekeeper every first day of January, but for the rest of the year my task is done by Huandaw and Gogigwr and Llaesgymyn and Penpingion who walks on his head to spare his feet, neither toward the sky nor toward the earth, but like a stone rolling on the floor of the court." "Open the gate." "I will not." "Why will you not open it?" "Knife has gone into meat, and drink into horn, and a crowd has gathered in Arthur's hall. Only the rightful king of a country or a craftsman bringing his skill may enter. There is meat for your dogs, and grain for your horse, and hot peppered chops for you, plus wine overflowing and songs for your pleasure. Food for fifty men awaits you in the guesthouse. Travelers stay there and sons of foreign lands, those who offer no craft at the court of Arthur. In no way will it be worse for you there than in the court of Arthur. A woman will sleep with you and there will be pleasing songs before your knees. Tomorrow, at the third hour [9 a.m.], when the gate is opened for the crowd that has arrived here today, it will open first for you. And then you may take a seat wherever you wish in Arthur's hall from high end to low."

The boy replied, "I will do nothing of the sort. If you open the gate, that's well and good. If you do not open it, I will bring shame on your lord and disgrace to you. And I will raise three shouts at the entrance to this gate that will be no harder to hear on the peak of Pengwaedd in Cornwall than at the bottom of Dinsol in the North Country or on Esgeir Oerfel in Ireland. And every woman in this court will miscarry, those who are with child; and those without child, their wombs will become such a burden within them that they will never conceive from this day on." Glewlwyd Great-Grip answered, "Whatever you may shout about the laws of Arthur's court, you will not be allowed to enter until I first go to speak with Arthur."

So Glewlwyd went into the hall. Arthur asked him, "Do you have news from the gate?" "I do. Two thirds of my life have come and gone, as have two thirds of yours. I have been in Caers Se and Asse, in Sach and Salach, in Lotor and Ffotor. I have been in India the Great and India the Lesser. I was once in the fight between the two Ynyrs when the twelve hostages were taken from Norway. And I have been in Europe, and I was in Africa, and in the isles of Corsica, and in Caers Brythwch and Brythach and Nerthach. And I was there when you destroyed the war-band of Gleis son of Merin, when you killed the Black Creature son of Dugum. I was there when you conquered Greece to the east. I have been in Caers Oeth and Anoeth, and in Caer Nefenhyr of the Nine Streams: kingly warriors we saw there. But never in my life have I seen a man like the one who stands in front of your gate right now." Arthur said, "If you came in walking, go out running. To open one's eyes to the light only to close them again is a shame. And let some of you serve him with golden drinking horns and others with hot peppered chops, so that there is plenty of food and drink for him. It is a disgrace to leave out in the wind and the rain a man like the one you describe." Cei said, "By my friend's hand, if my advice were followed, the laws of the court would not be broken for this one man." "Not so, fair Cei. We are noble men as long as people seek us out. The greater our generosity, the greater will grow our own nobility and good faith and esteem."

So Glewlwyd went to the gate, and opened it for him. And what everyone else did—dismount onto the horseblock by the gate—Culhwch did not do. Instead, he rode inside on the horse. He said, "Hail, chief of the rulers of this island. May it be no worse for the lower end of your house than for the upper. May this greeting extend with equal good will to your noblemen and to your host and to your leaders in battle. May there be no one without a share in it. As my greeting to you is full, let full be your grace and good faith and esteem in this island." "Let that be God's truth, chieftain. Hail to you. Take a seat between two of my warriors, with songs for your pleasure and the rank of a royal prince, one who expects the throne, for as long as you are here. And when I share my wealth with guests and visitors from afar, I will begin at your hand in this court." The boy said, "I have not come here to beg for food and drink. But if I get a gift, I will repay it and I will praise it. If I do not get it, I will make you lose face as far as your fame extends unto the farthest four corners of the world." Arthur replied, "Even if you do not stay here, chieftain, you shall get whatever gift your head and tongue may name, as far as wind dries, as far as rain wets, as far as sun shines, as far as sea extends, as far as earth is, except for my ship and my cloak, and Caledfwlch my sword, and Rhongomyniad my spear, and Wyneb Gwrthucher my shield, and Carnwennan my knife, and Gwenhwyfar my wife." "God's truth on that?" "You shall have it gladly. Ask what you will." "I will. I want my hair trimmed." "You shall have that." Taking a golden comb and silver-looped scissors, Arthur combed his hair. He asked who he was. Arthur said, "My heart is softening towards you. I know that you come of my blood. Tell us who you are." "I will: Culhwch son of Cilydd son of Prince Celyddon by Goleuddydd daughter of Prince Anlawdd, my mother." Arthur said, "This is true. You are my own cousin. Ask what you will, and you shall have it, whatever your head and tongue may name." "God's truth to me on that and the truth of your kingdom?" "You shall have it gladly." "I ask then to get as my wife Olwen daughter of Ysbaddaden Chief of Giants; and I hereby charge it upon your warriors."

ARTHUR'S FOLLOWERS

He charged his request upon Cei and Bedwyr, and Greidawl Gallddofydd, and Gwythyr son of Greidawl, and Greid son of Eri, and Cynddylig the Guide, and Tathal Plain-Deceit, and Maelwys son of Baeddan, and Cnychwr son of Nes, and Cubert son of Daere, and Fercos son of Poch, and Lluber Beuthach, and Conul Bernach.

And Gwyn son of Esni, and Gwyn son of Nwyfre, and Gwyn son of Nudd, and Edern son of Nudd, and Cadwy son of Gereint, and Prince Fflewdwr the Flame, and Ruawn the Bright son of Dorath, and Bradwen son of Lord Moren, and Lord Moren himself, and Dalldaf offspring of Cimin Cof, and the son of Alun of Dyfed, and the son of Saidi, and the son of Gwryon, and Uchdryd Defender of the Host, and Cynwas Staff-Point, and Gwrhyr of the Fat Cattle, and Isberyr Cat's Claw, and Gallgoid the Suppliant, and Duach and Bratach and Nerthach, sons of Gwawrddur the Twisted—men from the uplands of Hell.

And Cilydd Hundred-Snatches, and Canhastyr Hundred-Hands, and Cors Hundred-Claws, and Esgeir Gulhwch Gofyn Cawn, and Drustwrn Iron-Fist, and Glewlwyd Great-Grip, and Llwch Smite-Hand, and Anwas the Winged, and Sinnoch son of Seithfed, and Wadu son of Seithfed, and Naw son of Seithfed, and Gwenwynwyn son of Naw son of Seithfed, and Bedyw son of Seithfed, and Gobrwy son of Echel Great-Thigh, and Echel Great-

Thigh himself, and Mael son of Roycol, and Dadweir Blind-Head, and Garwyli offspring of Gwyddawg Gwyr, and Gwyddawg Gwyr himself, and Gormant son of Ricca, and Menw son of Teirgwaedd, and Digon son of Alar, and Selyf son of Sinoid, and Gusg son of Achen, and Nerth son of Cadarn, and Drudwas son of Tryffin, and Twrch [Boar] son of Perif, and Twrch [Boar] son of Anwas, and Iona King of France, and Sel [Watch] son of Selgi [Watchdog], and Teregud son of Iaen, and Sulyen son of Iaen, and Bradwen son of Iaen, and Moren son of Iaen, and Siawn son of Iaen, and Cradawg son of Iaen—these men are from Caer Dathal, kinsmen of Arthur on his father's side. Dirmyg son of Caw, and Iustig son Caw, and Edmig son Caw, and Angawdd son of Caw, and Gofan son of Caw, and Celin son of Caw, and Conyn son of Caw, and Mabsant son of Caw, and Gwyngad son of Caw, and Llwybyr son of Caw, and Coch son of Caw, and Meilig son of Caw, and Cynwal son of Caw, and Ardwyad son of Caw, and Ergyriad son of Caw, and Neb son of Caw, and Gildas son of Caw, and Calcas son of Caw, and Hueil son of Caw—he never submitted to a lord's hand.

And Samson Dry-Lip, and Taliesin Chief of Bards, and Manawydan son of Llyr, and Llary son of Prince Casnar, and Sberin son of Fflergant King of Brittany, and Saranhon son of Glythfyr, and Llawr offspring of Erw, and Anynnawg son of Menw son of Teirgwaedd, and Gwyn son of Nwyfre, and Fflam son of Nwyfre, and Gereint son of Erbin, and Ermid son of Erbin, and Dywel son of Erbin, and Gwyn son of Ermid, and Cyndrwyn son of Ermid, and Hyfeidd One-Cloak, and Eiddon the Magnanimous, and Rheiddwn Arwy, and Gormant son of Ricca—brother to Arthur on his mother's side; his father was overlord of Cornwall.

And Llawfrodedd the Bearded, and Nodawl Cut-Beard, and Berth son of Cado, and Rheiddwn son of Beli, and Isgofan the Generous, and Ysgafn son of Panon, and Morfran offspring of Tegid. No man laid a weapon on him at Camlann because he was so ugly: they thought he was a devil helping. There was hair on him like the hair of a stag. And Sandde Angel-Form. No one put a spear in him at Camlann because he was so fair: they thought he was an angel helping. And Saint Cynwyl, one of the three men who survived Camlann: he was the last to leave Arthur, on his horse Hengroen [Old-Skin].

And Uchdryd son of Erim, and Eus son of Erim, and Henwas the Winged son of Erim, and Henbeddestyr [Old Walker] son of Erim, and Sgilti Lightfoot son of Erim. These last three men had three strange things about them: Henbeddestyr never found anyone who could keep up with him, either on horse or on foot; Henwas the Winged—no four-footed creature could keep up with him across a single acre of land, much less a distance further than that; Sgilti Lightfoot—when the urge was on him to run a message for his lord, he never used a road if he knew where he was going; but wherever there were woods, he would run along the tops of the trees, and whenever there were mountains, he would run along the tufts of heather, and in his whole life not a reed would bend under his feet, much less break, since he was so light.

Teithi the Old son of Gwynnan, whose country the sea inundated so that he barely escaped and came to Arthur. There was a strange thing about his knife: from the time he came here, a haft would never stay on it, and because of this an illness grew within him and a lethargy as long as he lived, and from this he died. And Carnedyr son of Gofynion the Old, and Gwenwynwyn son of Naf, Arthur's first warrior, and Llygatrudd the Stallion, and Gwrbothu the Old—these were Arthur's uncles, brothers of his mother.

Culfanawyd son of Goryon, and Llenlleawg the Irishman from the promontory at Gamon, and Dyfnwal the Bald, and Dynart King of the North Country. Teyrnon Tide-Roar, and Tegfan the Lame, and Tegyr Talgellawg. Gwrddyfal son of Efrei, and Morgant the Generous, Gwystyl son of Nwython, and Rhun son of Nwython, and Llwydeu son of Nwython, and Gwydre son of Llwydeu by Gwenabwy daughter of Caw, his mother—his uncle Hueil stabbed him, and from this there was bad blood between Arthur and Hueil, on account of that wound.

Drem son of Dremidydd [Sight son of Seer], who could see from Celliwig in Cornwall all the way to Penn Blathaon in Pictland, even a gnat rising in the morning with the sun. And Eiddoel son of Ner, and Glwyddyn the Builder who made Arthur's hall Ehangwen [Beautifully Spacious]. Cynyr Fair-Bearded—Cei was said to be his son. Cynyr said to his wife: "If there is anything of me in your son, girl, his heart will always be cold, and there will be no warmth in his two hands. There will be another strange thing about him: if he is a son of mine, he will be stubborn. There will be another strange thing about him: when he carries a load, however large or small it may be, it will never be seen either from the front or from behind. There will be another strange thing about him: no one will endure water and fire like he will. There will be another strange thing about him: there will be no servant or steward like him."

Henwas, and Hen Wyneb, and Hengedymddeith. Another one, Gallgoig: whenever he came to a town, even if there were three hundred houses in it, if he was in need of anything, he would never leave sleep in a man's eye while he was there. Berwyn son of Cerenyr, and Fferis King of France, and from his name the city there is called Paris. Osla Big-Knife, who carried Bronllafyn [Breast-Blade] Short-Broad. When Arthur and his armies came to the brink of some rapids, a narrow place in the river would be found and he would put the knife in its sheath across the rapids—that would be bridge enough for the armies of the three islands of Britain and their three adjacent islands with their all their spoils of war. Gwyddawg son of Menestyr, who killed Cei, and Arthur killed him and his brothers to avenge Cei. Garanwyn son of Cei, and Amren son of Bedwyr, and Ely, and Myr, and Rheu Rhwyddyrys, and Rhun Red Alder, and Eli, and Trachmyr—Arthur's chief huntsmen. And Llwydeu son of Celcoed, and Hunabwy son of Gwryon, and Gwyn Godyfron, and Gweir Bird-Servant, and Gweir son of Cadellin Silver-Brow, and Gweir of False Courage, and Gweir White-Spear—uncles of Arthur, brothers of his mother, sons of Llwch Smite-Hand from beyond the Tyrrhenian Sea.

Llenlleawg the Irishman, and Ardderchawg [Excellent One] of Britain, Cas son of Saidi, Gwrfan Bridle-Hair, Gwilenhen King of France, Gwitar son of Aedd King of Ireland, Garselid the Irishman, Panawr Chief of the Army, Atlewdwr son of Naf, Gwyn the Irascible overseer of Cornwall and Devon—one of the nine who plotted the Battle of Camlann. Celli, and Cuel, and Gilla Stag-Leg—he could leap three hundred acres in a single bound, the chief leaper of Ireland. Sol [Heel], and Gwaddyn Heel, and Gwaddyn Bonfire: Sol could stand all day on one foot; Gwaddyn Heel—if he stood on top of the highest mountain in the world, it would flatten out to a level plain beneath his foot; Gwaddyn Bonfire—the bright fire of his foot-soles was just like hot metal drawn from a forge when something hard strikes against it; he would clear a path for Arthur's armies on the march. Tall Erwm and Tall Atrwm—the day they came to a feast, they would seize three counties for their needs: feasting till noon, drinking till night. When they went to sleep they would snap up bug-heads from hunger as if they had never eaten a bite. When they went to a feast they left neither fat nor lean, hot nor cold, sour nor sweet, fresh nor salt.

Huarwar son of Halwn, who asked his fill from Arthur as a gift: it was one of the three great plagues of Cornwall and Devon before that fill was gotten for him. Not the trace of a smile was ever to be seen on his face, except when he was full. Gwarae Golden-Hair, the two pups of the bitch Rhymhi, Gwyddrud, and Gwydden the Enigmatic, Sugyn son of Sugnedudd [Suck son of Sucker], who would suck up a sea on which there were three hundred ships until nothing was left but dry sand—a red-hot fever was in his breast. Cacamwri servant of Arthur—shown a barn, even if there were room for thirty plows in it, he would beat it with an iron flail until it would be no better for the planks and the rafters and the side-beams than for the sifted oats in the bottom of the barn. Llwng, and Dygyflwng, and Anoeth the Bold, and Tall Eiddyl, and Tall Amren—they were two servants of Arthur—and Gwefyl [Lip] son of Gwastad [Level]—on a day he was sad, he would loosen one lip as far down as his navel, and the other would become a hood over his head.

Uchdryd Cross-Beard, who could throw his bristling red beard over the fifty rafters in Arthur's hall. Elidyr the Guide, Ysgyrdaf, and Ysgudydd—they were two servants of Gwenhwyfar: their feet were as swift on their business as their thoughts.

Brys son of Bryssethach from the bottom of the Black Ferns of Britain, and Gruddlwyn the Dwarf. Bwlch and Cyfwlch and Sefwlch, sons of Cleddyf Cyfwlch [Perfect Sword], grandsons of Cleddyf Difwlch [Unnotched Sword]: three bright flashes their three shields, three piercing points their three spears, three keen carvers their three swords. Glas [Grey], Glesig, Gleisad [Salmon]—their three dogs. Call [Clever], Cuall [Quick], Cafall [Steed]—their three horses. Hwyr Dydwg [Late-Bearer] and Drwg Dydwg [Bad-Bearer] and Llwyr Dydwg [Full-Bearer]—their three wives. Och [Alas] and Garym [Scream] and Diaspad [Shriek]—their three grandsons. Lluched and Neued and Eisywed—their three daughters. Drwg [Bad] and Gwaeth [Worse] and Gwaethaf Oll [Worst of All]—their three maidservants.

Eheubryd son of Cyfwlch, Gorasgwrn [Big-Bone] son of Nerth [Strength], Gwaeddan son of Cynfelyn Ceudawg, Pwyll Half-Man, Dwn the Unbruised Chieftain, Eiladar son of Lord Llarcan, Cynedyr the Wild son of Hettwn Silver-Brow, Sawyl High-Head, Gwalchmei son of Gwyar, Gwalhafed son of Gwyar, Gwrhyr Interpreter of Tongues—he knew every language—and Cethtrwm the Priest. Clust son of Clustfeinad [Ear son of Hearer]—even if he were buried seven fathoms in the earth, he could hear an ant fifty miles away, as it crept out of its nest in the morning. Medyr son of Methredydd [Aim son of Aimer]—from Celliwig [in Cornwall] he could hit a wren on Esgeir Oerfel in Ireland, right between the legs. Gwiawn Cat's Eye, who could cut out the corner of a gnat's eye without harming the eye itself. Ol son of Olwydd [Track son of Tracker]—seven years before he was born someone drove off his father's pigs, and when he grew to manhood he tracked the pigs and brought them home in seven herds. Bishop Bidwini, who would bless the food and drink.

The sweet gold-torqued daughters of this island. Not only Gwenhwyfar, greatest of the queens of this island, but Gwenhwy[f]ach her sister, and Rathtyen only daughter of Clememyl, Celemon daughter of Cei, and Tangwen daughter of Gweir Bird-Servant, Gwen the Swan daughter of Cynwal Hundred-Pigs, Eurneid daughter of Cludno of Eidyn, Eneuawg daughter of Bedwyr, Enrydreg daughter of Tuduathar, Gwenwledyr daughter of Gwaredur the Twisted, Erdudfyl daughter of Tryffin, Eurolfyn daughter of Gwdolwyn the Dwarf, Teleri daughter of Peul, Indeg daughter of Garwy the Tall, Morfudd daughter of Urien of Rheged, Gwenlliant the Fair—the magnanimous maiden—Creiddylad daughter of Lludd Silver-Hand—the maiden of most majesty who was in the three islands of Britain and their three adjacent islands—and for her sake Gwythyr son of Greidawl and Gwyn son of Nudd will always fight each other every first of May until the Day of Judgment. Ellylw daughter of

Neol Hang-Cock—and she lived three lives of men. Esyllt Fair-Neck and Esyllt Slender-Neck. Upon them all, Culhwch son of Cilydd charged his request.

THE SEARCH FOR OLWEN

Arthur said, "Well, chieftain, I have never heard of the girl about whom you speak nor of her parents. I will happily send out messengers to find her. From that night until the same one a year later, the messengers wandered. But at the end of a year, Arthur's servants still had found nothing. The chieftain Culhwch said, "Everyone else has gotten his request, yet I am still without mine. I will take my leave and your honor with me." Cei said, "Wait, chieftain, you blame Arthur too much. Come with us. Until you say she does not exist in this world or that we cannot get her, we will not abandon you."

Then Cei stood up. There was a strange thing about Cei: nine nights and nine days could he hold his breath under water; nine nights and nine days could he go without sleep. No doctor could heal a wound from Cei's sword. Cei couldn't be beaten. He could be as tall as the tallest tree in the forest when he wanted. There was another strange thing about him: when the rain was heaviest, a hand's breadth in front of his hand and a hand's breadth behind would be as dry as what was in his hand itself, so great was his body-heat; and when the cold was heaviest on his companions, he would be their kindling to light a fire.

Arthur called on Bedwyr, who never feared a mission on which Cei also went. Such was the case with Bedwyr that there was no one in this island as handsome as he, except for Arthur and Drych offspring of Cibddar. And this, too: even though he was one-handed, three warriors together never drew blood quicker on the field of battle than he did. There was another strange thing about him: his spear could still inflict a wound against nine parries.

Arthur called on Cyddelig the Guide. "Go for me on this mission with the chieftain." He was no worse a guide in a country he had never seen before than in his own.

He called on Gwrhyr Interpreter of Tongues: he knew all languages.

He called on Gwalchmei son of Gwyar because he never came home without accomplishing the mission he set out on. He was Arthur's nephew, son of his sister and his close kinsman.

Arthur called upon Menw son of Teirgwaedd: if they came to a heathen land, he would cast a spell on them, so that no one could see them and they could see everyone.

They traveled until they came to a great plateau and could see a stronghold, the biggest stronghold in the world. They traveled all that day. When they thought they were getting close to the stronghold, they were no nearer than before. However, as they came down to the same level as the ground on which it stood, they could see a vast flock of sheep without edge or end to it, and a shepherd tending that flock from the top of a mound with a jacket of skins on him and a shaggy mastiff by his side bigger than a horse of nine winters. That dog never lost a single lamb, much less a grown animal. No company of men could ever pass him without suffering deadly harm and hurt. Whatever dead tree or bush stood on the plain, his breath would burn it right down to the ground.

Cei said, "Gwrhyr Interpreter of Tongues, go speak with that man over yonder." "Cei, I only promised to go so far as you went yourself." "Let us go there together then." Menw son of Teirgwaedd said, "Don't worry about getting too close. I will cast a spell on the dog so that he will harm no one."

They came to the spot where the shepherd was. They said, "You're doing well." "May it never be better for you than for me." "By God, that's because you're in charge." "No harm can hurt me—except for my wife." "Whose sheep are those you tend, and who owns the stronghold?" "You are ignorant men. Everyone in the world knows that this stronghold belongs to Ysbaddaden Chief of Giants." "And you, who are you?" "I am Custennin the Dispossessed, and on account of my wife, Ysbaddaden Chief of Giants has robbed and ruined me. And you people, who are you?" "We are companions of Arthur, come here in search of Olwen." "Oh, men, God save you! Don't do that for the world. No one has ever left here alive who came on that errand."

The shepherd stood up to go. As he rose, Culhwch gave him a gold ring. He tried to put the ring on, but it wouldn't fit, so he put the ring into the finger of his glove and went home to give the glove to his wife. She took the ring from the glove. "Where did you get this ring, husband? You don't often come across a windfall." I went to the sea for some seafood. Then, I saw a body floating in at the turn of the tide. I have never seen a figure so handsome and from its finger I took this ring." "Alas, man, since beautiful things perish in the sea, show me that body." "Well, wife, you will see the man who owns that body here in a minute." "Who is he?" asked the woman. "Culhwch son of Cilydd son of Prince Celyddon and of Goleuddydd daughter of Prince Anlawdd, his mother, who has come to seek Olwen." She felt mixed feelings: she was glad that her nephew, her own sister's son, was coming to her, but she was sad because she had never seen anyone leave alive who had come on that errand.

They approached the gate of the court of Custennin the shepherd. The wife heard the sound of their coming and ran out joyfully to meet them. Cei grabbed a log from the woodpile as she approached, reaching out to hug their necks with both her hands. Cei put the log between her two arms. She hugged the log until it became a twisted withy. Cei said, "Well, woman, if you had hugged me like that, no woman would ever need to give me her love again. That's a wicked love!"

They came into the house and were tended to. After a while, when everyone was gathered together, the woman opened a chest in front of the hearth and out popped a curly-headed, golden-haired boy. Gwrhyr said, "It's a shame to hide such a fine boy. I know that he is not being punished for something he did wrong." The woman said, "He is all that is left. Ysbaddaden Chief of Giants has killed twenty-three of my sons. I have no more hope for this one than for the others." Cei said, "Let him accept my company, and we will not be killed, unless together." They ate. The woman said, "Why have you come here?" "We have come to find Olwen." "In the name of God, since no one has yet seen you from the stronghold, go back!" "God knows we will not go back until we see the girl. Will she come to a place where she can be seen?" "She comes here every Saturday to wash her hair, and in the washing bowl she leaves all her rings. Neither she nor her servant ever comes back for them." "Will she come here if sent for?" "God knows I will not condemn my own soul. I will not betray someone who trusts me. Only if you promise, on your good faith, that you will do her no harm will I send for her." "We promise it."

THE GIANT'S DAUGHTER

She was sent for. And she came wrapped in a robe of flame-red silk, a torque of red gold around the girl's neck, set with rich pearls and red gems. Her hair was blonder than the broom-flower. Her skin was whiter than the foam of the wave. Her palms and her fingers were whiter than the shoots of the marsh-trefoil springing up in the fine gravel of a welling spring. Not the eye of a young hawk, nor the eye of a full-grown falcon—no eye was brighter than hers. No breast of a white swan was whiter than her two breasts. Redder were her two cheeks than the rose. Whoever saw her would be filled with love for her. Four white trefoils sprang up wherever she walked. And for that reason she was called Olwen [White-Track].

She came into the house, and sat down next to Culhwch on the high seat. And when he saw her, he knew her. Culhwch said to her, "Oh, maiden, it is you whom I have loved. Will you come with me?" "I cannot do that: it would be considered a sin for both of us. My father has asked me to promise that I would not go without his consent, because he can only live until such time as I leave with a husband. However, I can give you a plan, if you will follow it. Go ask for me from my father, and however much he asks of you in return, promise to get it and you will get me. But if he doubts you at all, you will not get me, and you will be lucky to escape with your life." "I promise all of that and I will get it."

She went to her dwelling-chamber. They got up to follow her to the stronghold and killed the nine gatekeepers who were at the nine gates without a single one crying out and the nine mastiffs without even one squealing. And they went on ahead into the hall. They said, "Good wishes to you, Ysbaddaden Chief of Giants, from God and man." "And you, where are you going?" "We have come to ask for Olwen your daughter for Culhwch son of Cilydd." "Where are my bad and wicked servants?" he said. "Lift up the forks under my two eyelids so that I can see the looks of my son-in-law." This was done. "Come here tomorrow. I will give you my answer."

They got up to go, but Ysbaddaden Chief of Giants grabbed one of the three poisoned stone spears that were next to him and threw it at them from behind. And Bedwyr caught it and threw it back at him and struck Ysbaddaden Chief of Giants right through the kneecap. He said, "Cursed, cruel son-in-law, I will walk the worse uphill. As the gadfly bites, so stings the poisoned iron. Cursed be the smith who made it and the anvil on which it was hammered: it hurts!"

They spent the night in Custennin's house. And the next day with great style and with fine combs set in their hair they came into the hall. They said, "Ysbaddaden Chief of Giants, give us your daughter and you may keep her dowry and her marriage fee and her two maid-servants. But if you do not give her, it will be your death." "She and her four great-grandmothers and her four great-grandfathers are still alive—I am obliged to consult with them." "That's expected of you," they said. "We will go to dinner." As they got up, he took a second stone spear in his hand and threw it at them from behind. And Menw son of Teirgwaedd caught it and threw it back at him and struck him in the hollow of his chest so that it sprang out the small of his back. "Cursed, cruel son-in-law, as the big-headed leech sucks, so smarts the hard iron. Cursed be the forge in which it was heated! When I climb a hill there will be tightness in my chest and stomach cramps and pangs of nausea." They went on to their dinner.

They came the third day to the court and said, "Ysbaddaden Chief of Giants, don't shoot at us anymore. May no deadly harm or hurt or death befall you." "Where are my servants? Lift up the forks—my eyelids have drooped over my eyeballs—so that I can see the looks of my son-in-law." They got up, and as they did so, he took the third poisoned stone spear and threw it at them. And Culhwch caught it and threw it back, just where he aimed it, and struck him in the eyeball so that it came out the nape of his neck. "Cursed, cruel son-in-law, as long as I may be spared to live, so much the worse will be my eyesight. When I walk against the wind they will water; I will get headaches and dizziness at every new moon. Like the bite of a mad dog the poisoned iron has pierced me." They went to their dinner.

In the morning they came to the court. They said, "Stop shooting at us. Let no deadly harm or hurt or painful death befall you, or what will be even worse, if you ask for it. Give us your daughter!" "Where is the one who is said to seek my daughter?" "I am the one who seeks her, Culhwch son of Cilydd." "Come here where I can see you." A chair was placed under Culhwch, face to face with the giant.

Ysbaddaden Chief of Giants said, "You are the one who seeks my daughter?" "It is I who seeks her." "I want your promise, that you will do no worse by me than what is right." "You will have that." "When I have gotten what I will name to you, you shall get my daughter." "Name whatever you want."

"I shall."

The Conditions

"Do you see that great thicket over there?" "I do." "I want you to tear it up by the roots from the earth and burn it right down to the ground until there are only cinders and ashes left, which will be its fertilizer; and plow it and sow it until it is ripe that same morning by the time the dew dries so that it can be made into food and drink for your wedding guests and those of my daughter. And I want all this to be done in one day."

"It's easy to do that, though you think it will not be easy."

"Even though you get that done, there is something you will not get: a plowman to plow that land and to tend it, none other than Amaethon son of Don. He will not come with you of his own free will and you cannot force him."

"It's easy to do that, though you think it will not be easy."

"Even though you get this done, there is something you will not get: Gofannon son of Don to come to the edge of the field to set up the plow. He will not work of his own free will, except for a rightful king, and you cannot force him."

"That's easy."

"Even though you get this: the two oxen of Gwlwlydd Wineu, both yoked together to plow that rough soil over there properly. He will not give them of his own free will and you cannot force him."

"That's easy."

"Even though you get that: I want Melyn Gwanhwyn [Yellow-Spring] and Ych Brych [Speckled Ox] yoked together."

"That's easy."

"Even though you get that: two horned oxen, one of which is on the other side of Mynydd Bannawg [Horned Mountain] and the other of which is on this side, and the two of them yoked together in a single plow. Those are the ones, Nyniaw and Peibiaw, whom God turned into oxen for their sins."

"That's easy."

"Even though you get that: do you see that tilled slope over yonder?"

"I see it."

"When I met the mother of the girl for the first time, nine baskets of flax seed were sown in it; neither black nor white has yet come out of it and I still have that measure with me. I want to get the same amount into the new ground over there, so that there might be a white veil for my daughter's head at your wedding feast."

"That's easy."

"Even though you get that: honey that is nine times sweeter than the honey of the first swarm, without drones and without bees, to make bragget for the feast."

"That's easy."

"Even though you get that: the cup of Llwyr son of Llwyrion, which holds the best of drinks; there no vessel in the world which can hold that potent liquor, except that one. You will not get it of his own free will and you cannot force him."

"That's easy."

"Even though you get that: the basket of Gwyddneu Long-Shank—if the world gathered around it in three groups of nine men at a time, each person would find in it the food he wanted most. I want to eat from that basket on the night my daughter sleeps with you. He will not give it of his own free will and you cannot force him."

"That's easy."

"Even though you get that: the horn of Gwlgawd of Gododdin to pour out drink for us that night. He will not give it of his own free will and you cannot force him."

"That's easy."

"Even though you get that: the harp of Teirtu to entertain me that night. Whenever one wishes, it plays on its own; whenever one desires, it falls silent. He will not give it of his own free will and you cannot force him."

"That's easy."

"Even though you get that: I want the birds of Rhiannon for my entertainment that night, those that wake the dead and lull the living to sleep."

"That's easy."

"Even though you get that: the cauldron of Diwrnach the Irishman, the overseer of Odgar son of Aedd, King of Ireland, to cook food for your guests."

"That's easy."

"Even though you get that: I must wash my hair and shave my beard. I want to shave myself with the tusk of Ysgithrwyn [White Tusk], Chief of Boars. It won't cut for me unless it is taken from his living head."

"That's easy."

"Even though you get that: nobody in the world can take it from his head, except Odgar son of Aedd, King of Ireland."

"That's easy."

"Even though you get that: I won't trust anyone to keep that tusk, except Caw of Britain. Sixty counties of Britain are under him. He will not leave his kingdom of his own free will, nor can he be forced out."

"That's easy."

"Even though you get that: my beard must be softened for shaving. It will never straighten out, unless you get the blood of the Very Black Witch daughter of the Very White Witch from the Valley of Grief in the uplands of Hell."

"That's easy."

"Even though you get that: the blood will be of no use unless it is gotten hot. There is no vessel in the world that will retain the heat of the liquid put in it, except for the bottles of Gwyddolwn the Dwarf, which hold their heat from the time liquid is put in them in the east until it arrives in the west. He will not give them of his own free will and you cannot force him."

"That's easy."

"Even though you get that: some people will want milk; there is no way to get milk for everybody unless you get the bottles of Rhynnon Stiff-Beard. No liquid ever turns sour in them. He will not give them of his own free will to anyone nor can he be forced."

"That's easy."

"Even though you get that: there is no comb and scissors in the world that can cut my hair because of its stiffness, except for the comb and scissors that are between the two ears of the boar Twrch Trwyth son of Prince Taredd. He will not give them of his own free will, *etc.*"

"That's easy."

"Even though you get that: the boar Twrch Trwyth will not be hunted down until Drudwyn is gotten, the pup of Greid son of Eri."

"That's easy."

"Even though you get that: there is not a leash in the world that will hold him, except for the leash of Cors Hundred-Claws."

"That's easy."

"Even though you get that: there is not a collar in the world that can hold the leash, except for the collar of Canhastyr Hundred-Hands."

"That's easy."

"Even though you get that: the chain of Cilydd Hundred-Snatches to hold the collar and the leash."

"That's easy."

"Even though you get that: there is no hunter in the world who can keep up with that hound, except for Mabon son of Modron, who was taken away from his mother when only three nights old. No one knows where he is, what his condition is, or whether he is alive or dead."

"That's easy."

"Even though you get that: Gwyn Dark-Mane the horse of Gweddw, as swift as a wave, under Mabon to hunt the boar Twrch Trwyth. He will not give it of his own free will, *etc.*"

"That's easy."

"Even though you get that: Mabon will never be found—no one knows where he is—unless his kinsman Eiddoel son of Aer is found first, since he will be tireless in seeking him. He is his own cousin."

"That's easy."

"Even though you get that: Garselid the Irishman, who is the best hunter in Ireland. The boar Twrch Trwyth will never be hunted down without him."

"That's easy."

"Even though you get that: a leash from the beard of Dillus the Bearded, since there is nothing that will hold the two pups [of Rhymhi] except for that. And it can be of no use unless it is plucked from his face while he is still living, and plucked out with wooden tweezers. No one can do that to him while he is alive and it will be useless if he is dead, because the beard will be too brittle."

"That's easy."

"Even though you get that: there is no hunter in the world who can hold those two pups, except Cynedyr the Wild son of Hettwn the Leprous. He is nine times wilder than the wildest wild beast on the mountain. You will never get him and you will never get my daughter."

"That's easy."

"Even though you get that: the boar Twrch Trwyth will not be hunted down unless you get Gwyn son of Nudd in whom God has placed the spirit of the devils of Annwn to prevent the ruination of the world. He will not be spared from that task."

"That's easy."

"Even though you get that: no horse will help Gwyn hunt down the boar Twrch Trwyth, except for Du [Black] the horse of Moro Oerfeddawg."

"That's easy."

"Even though you get that: unless Gwilenhin King of France comes, the boar Twrch Trwyth will never be hunted down without him. It is not proper for him to leave his realm and he will never come here."

"That's easy."

"Even though you get that: the boar Twrch Trwyth will never be hunted down unless you get the son of Alun of Dyfed. He is a good unleasher."

"That's easy."

"Even though you get that: the boar Twrch Trwyth will never be hunted down unless you get [the hounds] Aned and Aethlem. They are as swift as a gust of wind; they were never unleashed upon any animal that they did not kill."

"That's easy."

"Even though you get that: Arthur and his hunters to hunt down the boar Twrch Trwyth. He is a powerful man and he will not come with you for this reason: I have him under my own control."

"That's easy."

"Even though you get that: the boar Twrch Trwyth can never be hunted down unless you get Bwlch and Cyfwlch and Syfwlch, sons of Cilydd Cyfwlch [Perfect Sword], grandsons of Cleddyf Difwlch [Unnotched Sword]: three bright flashes their three shields, three piercing points their three spears, three keen carvers their three swords. Glas [Grey], Glesig, Gleisad [Salmon]—their three dogs. Call [Clever], Cuall [Quick], Cafall [Steed]—their three horses. Hwyr Dydwg [Late-Bearer] and Drwg Dydwg [Bad-Bearer] and Llwyr Dydwg [Full-Bearer]—their three wives. Och [Alas] and Garym [Scream] and Diaspad [Shriek]—their three witches. Lluched and Neued and Eisywed—their three daughters. Drwg [Bad] and Gwaeth [Worse] and Gwaethaf Oll [Worst of All]—their three maidservants. The three men will blow their horns and all the others will start to shout until no one will care if the sky falls to the earth."

"That's easy."

"Even though you get that: the sword of Wrnach the Giant. He can never be killed except with that. He will give it to no one, neither for love nor payment, nor can you force him to."

"That's easy."

"Even though you get that: you must stay awake without sleeping at night in seeking those things and you will not manage to do that and you will not get my daughter."

"I will get horses to ride. And my lord and kinsman Arthur will get all of these things for me. And I will get your daughter and you will lose your life."

"Now be off! You are not responsible for my daughter's food or clothing. Find those things: when they are found, you will get my daughter."

THE SWORD OF WRNACH

They traveled that day until evening, when a stronghold of mortared stone came into view, the biggest stronghold in the world. Oh! A black man, bigger than three men of this world, was seen coming from the stronghold. They asked him: "Where do you come from, sir?" "From the stronghold that you see over there." "Whose is that stronghold?" "You are ignorant men. There is no one in the world that does not know to whom this stronghold belongs. It belongs to Wrnach the Giant." "What is the custom regarding hospitality for a stranger arriving at that stronghold?" "Ha, chieftain, God save you! No guest has ever left here alive. And no one is allowed in unless he brings a skill."

They approached the gate. Gwrhyr Interpreter of Tongues asked, "Is there a gatekeeper?" "There is. And you, may you keep your head, why do you ask?" "Open the gate." "I will not." "Why won't you open it?" "Knife has gone into meat and drink into horn and a crowd into Wrnach's hall. Except for a craftsman bringing his skill, it will not be opened." Cei said, "Gatekeeper, I have a skill." "What skill do you have?" "I am the best sword-polisher in the world." "I will go tell this to Wrnach the Giant and bring his answer to you."

The gatekeeper came inside. Wrnach the Giant asked, "Do you have news from the gate?" "I do. There is a company at the door of the gate and they wish to come inside."

"Did you ask if one of them had a skill?" "I did. And one of them said he could polish swords." "I have need of that. I have been looking for someone to polish my sword quite a while now; I have not found him. Let the man in, since he has come with a skill."

The gatekeeper came and opened the gate, and Cei entered by himself. And he greeted Wrnach the Giant. A chair was placed beneath him. Wrnach said, "Well, man, has the truth been told about you, that you can polish swords?" "I do that." The sword was brought to him. Cei put a striped whetstone under his armpit. "Which do you prefer, white-bladed or dark-bladed?" "Do to it whatever seems good to you, as if it were your own." He cleaned half of one side of the blade and handed it over to him: "Do you like that?" "I would like better than the wealth of my land that the whole thing were just the same. What a shame that a man like you has no partner." "Well, good sir, I do have a partner, though he does not practice this particular skill." "Who is he?" "Let the gatekeeper go out and I will describe him. The head of his spear leaps from its shaft and is of such force that it draws blood from the wind and then returns again to the shaft." The gate was opened and Bedwyr came inside. Cei said, "Bedwyr is quite capable, even though he does not practice this particular skill."

And there was a great argument among the men left outside after Cei and Bedwyr had gone inside. The young boy—the only son of Custennin the shepherd—entered with the other companions. He stuck close to them while they climbed three battlements as if these were no more than nothing to them until they got inside the stronghold. The companions said about the son of Custennin, "He is the best man!" From then on he was called Goreu [Best] son of Custennin. They went into the living quarters so they could kill those who lodged there without the giant's knowing. When the polishing of the sword was finished, Cei handed it over to Wrnach the Giant, as if to see whether his workmanship pleased him. The giant said, "The workmanship is good and I am pleased with it." Cei said, "Your sheath has damaged your sword. Give it to me to remove the wooden slats and let me make some new ones for it. And he took the scabbard from him with the sword in his other hand. He came to stand over the head of the giant as if to put the sword into the scabbard. He put the sword into the head of the giant instead, then swapped it off with a stroke. They pillaged the stronghold and took what they wanted of its treasures. On the same day at the end of a year they returned to the court of Arthur, bringing the sword of Wrnach the Giant.

Mabon son of Modron and the Oldest Animals

They told Arthur what they had done just as it happened to them. Arthur said, "Which of those conditions is it most important to seek next?" "It is most important," they said, "to seek Mabon son of Modron and he will not be found until Eiddoel son of Aer his cousin is found first." Arthur stood up with the warriors of the isle of Britain to seek Eiddoel and they came to Gliwi's outer battlement where Eiddoel was in prison. Gliwi himself was standing on the wall of the stronghold and said, "Arthur, why do you pester me and refuse to leave me alone on this crag? I have nothing good or pleasant in here, no wheat, no oats, nothing but you trying to do me harm." Arthur answered, "I have not come here to harm you, only to seek the prisoner who is with you." "I will give you the prisoner, though I had not intended to give him to anyone. And along with this, I will give you my help and support."

The men said to Arthur, "Lord, go home. You cannot march with your army to seek things as trivial as these." Arthur replied, "Gwrhyr Interpreter of Tongues, it is appropriate that you go on this mission. You know all languages and speak the same tongues as the birds and animals. Eiddoel, it is fitting that you go with my men to look for Mabon: he's your own cousin. Cei and Bedwyr, I have hope for the success of the mission on which both of you go. Go for me on this quest."

They journeyed until they came to the Blackbird of Cilgwri. Gwrhyr asked it, "In the name of God, do you know anything about Mabon son of Modron, who was taken when three nights old from between his mother and the wall?" The blackbird answered, "When I first came here, there was a smith's anvil, and for my part, I was a young bird. No work was done on it, except while my beak pecked on it every evening. Today there is not so much as a nut of it not worn away. God's vengeance on me if I have ever heard anything of the man about whom you ask. What is fitting, however, and a duty for me to do for the companions of Arthur, I will do. There is a race of creatures that God made before me. I will lead you there as your guide."

They went to where the Stag of Rhedynfre [Fern-Hill] lived. "Stag of Rhedynfre, we have come to you here, companions of Arthur, since we know of no animal older than you. Tell us, do you know anything about Mabon son of Modron, who was taken when three nights old from beside his mother?" The stag answered, "When I first came here, there was nothing but one tine on each side of my head and there were no woods here except for one sapling of oak, and that grew into an oak tree of a hundred branches and the tree fell after that and today there is nothing left but a red stump of it. From that time until today I have been here. I have heard nothing of the one about whom you ask. However, I will be your guide, since you are companions of Arthur, to where there is an animal whom God created before me."

They came to the place where the owl of Cwm Cawlwyd lived. "Owl of Cwm Cawlwyd, we are companions of Arthur. Do you know anything about Mabon son of Modron who was taken when three nights old from beside his mother?" "If I knew it, I would tell it. When I first came here, the big valley you see was a wooded glen and a race of men moved into it and cut it down and another forest grew up in it. And this is the third forest. And now the roots of my wings are mere stumps. From that time until today I have heard nothing of the one about whom you ask. However, I will guide the companions of Arthur until you come to where lives the oldest animal that is in this world and the most-traveled, the Eagle of Gwern Abwy."

Gwrhyr said, "Eagle of Gwern Abwy, we have come to you, companions of Arthur, to ask you whether you know anything about Mabon son of Modron who was taken when three nights old from beside his mother?" The eagle said, "I came here a long time ago, and when I first arrived, there was a stone from the top of which I used to peck at all the stars above. Now it is not a hand's breadth in height. From that time until today I have been here and I have heard nothing of the man about whom you ask—except that one time, I went looking for food as far as Lake Llyw, and when I came there I struck my claws into a salmon, thinking to get my food from it for a good while, but he pulled me down into the depths until with great difficulty I escaped him. Then I did this—I and all my kinsmen—we mobbed him and tried to destroy him, but he sent emissaries to make peace with me and he came to me to take 50 fish-spears out of his back. Unless he knows something about the man you seek, I know of no one who will. However, I will guide you to where he is."

They came to where he was. The eagle said, "Salmon of Lake Llyw, I have come to you with companions of Arthur to ask if you know anything about Mabon son of Modron, who was taken when three nights old from beside his mother?" "As much as I know, I will tell. With every incoming tide I swim upriver until I come right up to the wall of Caer Loyw [Gloucester] and I have never gotten as much harm in my life as I have gotten there. And so you may believe me, let one of you come between my two shoulders here." So Cei and Gwrhyr Interpreter of Tongues got on between the two shoulders of the salmon. And they traveled until they came to the other side of the wall from the prisoner, so that they could hear crying and moaning from inside the wall. Gwrhyr asked, "Who is crying in this house of stone?" "Oh sir, there is good reason to lament for anyone who is in here. Mabon son of Modron is here in prison and no one has been imprisoned in such a painful captivity as I, neither the captivity of Lludd Silver-Hand nor the captivity of Greid son of Eri." "Do you have hope that you may be freed with gold or silver or worldly wealth, or only by force and fighting?" "Whatever is gotten of me will be gotten by force."

They turned back from there and came to where Arthur was. They told him where Mabon son of Modron was imprisoned. Arthur called up the warriors of this island to go to Caer Loyw where Mabon was in prison. Cei and Bedwyr went on the two shoulders of the fish. While Arthur's warriors were fighting around the stronghold, Cei broke through the wall and carried out the prisoner on his back, still fighting with the men as before. Arthur came home with Mabon free.

The Two Pups of Rhymhi

Arthur asked, "Which of the conditions should we seek next?" "It is best to seek the two pups of the bitch Rhymhi." "Is it known," he said, "where she is?" "She is," said one, "in

Aber Deu Gleddyf." Arthur came to the house of Tringad in Aber Gleddyf and asked him, "Have you heard about her here? What shape is she?" "In the shape of a she-wolf," he said, "and she roams about with her two pups. She has often killed my stock and she is down in Aber Gleddyf in a cave.

This is what Arthur did, he sent his ship Prydwen by sea and others by land and hunted down the bitch and so surrounded her and her two pups. And God turned them back into the shape of dogs for Arthur. Arthur's army then departed by ones and by twos.

THE FLAX SEED

And as Gwythyr son of Greidawl was one day traveling over a mountain, he could hear wailing and bitter moaning, and it was a dreadful noise to hear. He rushed toward it and as he arrived there he drew his sword and struck a [burning] anthill to the earth and so saved them from the fire. And the ants said to him, "Take God's blessing and ours upon you and that which no man can ever move, we will come to move it for you." After that they came with the nine baskets of flax seed that Ysbaddaden Chief of Giants had required of Culhwch, in full measure, without any of it lacking, except for a single flax seed—and a lame ant brought that one in before nightfall.

THE BEARD OF DILLUS

When Cei and Bedwyr were sitting on the top of Pumlumon on Carn Gwylathyr in the strongest wind in the world, they looked all around and saw a great smoke towards the south, far from them, but not blowing at all in the wind. And then Cei said, "By the hand of my friend, look at that fire fit for a warrior." They hurried toward the smoke and drew closer, watching that place from a distance until they saw Dillus the Bearded roasting a wild boar. Yes indeed, he was the largest warrior who had ever fled from Arthur. Then Bedwyr said to Cei, "Do you recognize him?" "I do," answered Cei, "look at him, that's Dillus the Bearded. No leash in the world will hold Drudwyn the pup of Greid son of Eri except for a leash from the beard of the man you see over there. And it won't be of any use either, unless it is plucked from his face with wooden tweezers while he is still alive, since it will be brittle if he is dead." "Do we have a plan for that?" asked Bedwyr. "Let's let him eat his fill of the meat," said Cei, "and after that he will fall asleep." While he was doing that, they were making wooden tweezers. When Cei knew for sure that Dillus had fallen asleep, he dug a pit under his feet, the biggest in the world, and struck him a huge blow with immeasurable force and pushed him into the pit until they managed completely to pluck out his beard with the wooden tweezers. And after that they finished him off.

And from there the two of them went to Celliwig in Cornwall bringing the leash from the beard of Dillus the Bearded and Cei handed it over to Arthur. And then Arthur sang this verse:

> Cei made a leash
> From the beard of Dillus son of Eurei.
> If he were still alive, you'd be dead.

And because of this Cei grew angry until it was with difficulty that the warriors of this island made peace between Cei and Arthur. But even so, neither in Arthur's need nor at the slaying of his men, did Cei concern himself with his service from that moment on.

Gwythyr son of Greidawl and Gwyn son of Nudd

And then Arthur asked, "Which of the conditions is it best to seek next?" "It is best to seek Drudwyn the pup of Greid son of Eri."

Not long before that, Creiddylad daughter of Lludd Silver-Hand had run off with Gwythyr son of Greidawl. But before she slept with him, Gwyn son of Nudd came and took her away by force. Gwythyr son of Greidawl raised an army and came to fight Gwyn son of Nudd, but he was beaten by Gwyn, who captured Greid son of Eri and Glinneu son of Taran [Thunder] and Gwrgwst Half-Bare and Dyfnarth his son. And he captured Penn son of Nethawg and Nwython and Cyledyr the Wild his son. And he killed Nwython and cut out his heart and forced Cyledyr to eat his father's heart and for that reason Cyledyr went insane. Arthur heard about this and came to the North Country and called Gwyn son of Nudd to him. Arthur freed from their captivity the noblemen Gwyn held and made peace between Gwyn son of Nudd and Gwythyr son of Greidawl. This is the peace that was made: to let the girl stay at home with her father unmolested by either party and for Gwyn and Gwythyr to fight every first of May from that day forward until Judgment Day. And whoever won on Judgment Day, let him take the girl.

And after those noblemen had made peace in this manner, Arthur got Mygdwn the horse of Gweddw and the leash of Cors Hundred-Claws.

Ysgithrwyn Chief of Boars

After that Arthur went to Llydaw [Brittany] with Mabon son of Mellt [Lightning] and Gwarae Golden-Hair to seek out the two pups of Glythfyr the Breton. And after getting them Arthur went into the west of Ireland to seek out Gwrgi [Man-Dog] Seferi and Odgar son of Aedd King of Ireland who was with him. And from there Arthur went to the North Country and captured Cyledyr the Wild, and went to seek out Ysgithrwyn Chief of Boars. And Mabon son of Mellt went with the two hounds of Glythfyr the Breton in his hand and also Drudwyn the pup of Eri. And Arthur himself went on the hunt with his hound Cafall [Horse] in his hand. And Caw of Britain mounted Llamrei, Arthur's mare and brought the boar to bay. And wielding a small hand-axe, Caw of Britain charged the boar and split its head into two halves. And Caw took the tusk. It was not the dogs that Ysbaddaden had named who took the boar, but Arthur's own hound Cafall.

Menw son of Teirgwaedd

And after the slaying of Ysgithrwyn Chief of Boars, Arthur went with his men to Celliwig in Cornwall. And from there, Menw son of Teirgwaedd went to reconnoiter the treasures between the ears of the boar Twrch Trwyth, because it would be so nasty to go and fight with him, unless he actually had those treasures on him. It was true, however, that he was there. He had devastated a third part of Ireland. Menw went to find the boar and his piglets. He caught sight of them in Esgeir Oerfel in Ireland. And Menw transformed himself into the shape of a bird and landed on the top of the boar's lair and tried to snatch one of the treasures from between his ears. But for all that, he got nothing but one of his bristles. The boar started up full of anger and shook himself so that some of his venom splashed Menw. And from then on Menw was never completely well.

THE CAULDRON OF DIWRNACH

Then Arthur sent a messenger to Odgar son of Aedd King of Ireland to ask for the cauldron of Diwrnach the Irishman, his overseer. Odgar asked him to give it, but Diwrnach answered, "God knows, even if he would be better off from one look at it, he will not get it." So Arthur's messenger returned from Ireland with a "no." Arthur set off with a small force and boarded Prydwen his ship and came to Ireland and sought out the house of Diwrnach the Irishman. The army of Odgar saw their strength and after they had eaten and drunk their fill, Arthur asked for the cauldron. Diwrnach said that if he were able to give it to anyone, he would have given it at the word of Odgar King of Ireland. After his saying "no" to them, Bedwyr grabbed the cauldron and put it on the back of Hygwydd, Arthur's servant—that man was brother by the same mother of Cacamwri, another servant of Arthur; his job was always to carry Arthur's cauldron and make a fire under it. Llenlleawg the Irishman grabbed Caledfwlch and swung it in a circle and killed Diwrnach the Irishman and his whole force. The armies of Ireland came and fought with them. And when those armies had fled the field completely, Arthur and his men boarded his ship in plain view of them with the cauldron full of the treasures of Ireland. And they landed at the house of Llwydeu son of Cel Coed in Porth Cerddin in Dyfed, where there's still a pool just the same size as the cauldron.

THE HUNTING OF THE BOAR TWRCH TRWYTH

And then Arthur gathered whatever warriors there were in the three islands of Britain and their three adjacent islands, and which were in France and Brittany and Normandy and the Summer Country, and all the picked dogs and famous horses there were. And he went with all those forces to Ireland and there was great fear and trembling on account of that in Ireland. After Arthur came ashore, the saints of Ireland approached him and asked for his protection. And he gave them his protection and they laid their blessing on him. The men of Ireland came to Arthur to pay him a tribute of food. Arthur came to Esgeir Oerfel in Ireland to the place where the boar Twrch Trwyth was with his seven piglets. The dogs were let loose on him from every side. The Irishmen fought with the boar that day until evening. Nevertheless, he destroyed the fifth part of Ireland. The next day Arthur's war-band fought with the boar: except for the bad they got from him, they got nothing good. The third day Arthur himself fought with the boar, nine nights and nine days. He killed nothing but one piglet of the swine. The men asked Arthur what was the story of that pig.

He answered, "He was a King, but for his sins God turned him into a swine."

Arthur sent Gwrhyr Interpreter of Tongues to seek a word with the boar Twrch Trwyth. Gwrhyr went in the shape of a bird and landed on the top of his lair and that of his seven piglets. Gwrhyr Interpreter of Tongues asked him, "By the one who made you into this shape, if you are able to speak, I entreat you to come speak with Arthur." Grugyn Silver-Bristle replied—all his bristles were like silver wings—wherever he went in woods or field it seemed as if his bristles glistened. Grugyn gave this answer, "By the one who made us in this shape, we will not do that and we will say nothing to Arthur. God has already done plenty of bad to us by making us into this shape, without you coming to fight with us as well." "I tell you that Arthur will be forced to fight you for the comb and the razor and the scissors that are between the two ears of the boar Twrch Trwyth." Grugyn answered: "Unless you take his life, those treasures will not be gotten. Tomorrow morning we will set out from here, and let us go to Arthur's own country and do there all the harm we can!"

The pigs set out across the sea towards Wales and Arthur and his men and horses and dogs boarded Prydwen and in the twinkling of an eye they sighted them ahead. The boar Twrch Trwyth came ashore at Porth Cleis in Dyfed. Arthur arrived in Mynyw that night. In the morning their passing through was reported to Arthur and he caught up with the boar killing the cattle of Cynwas Staff-Point, after killing all the men and animals of Deu Gleddyf before Arthur arrived.

When Arthur got there, the boar Twrch Trwyth had already set off for Preselly. Arthur arrived there with the armies of the world. Arthur sent his men Ely and Trachmyr into the hunt with Drudwyn the pup of Greid son of Eri in his own hand, and Gwarthegyd son of Caw from another direction with the two dogs of Glythmyr the Breton in his hand, and Bedwyr with Arthur's dog Cafall in his hand. All the warriors ranged along the two banks of the River Nyfer. The three sons of Cleddyf Dyfwlch arrived, men who had won great fame by killing Ysgithrwyn Chief of Boars. But then the boar Twrch Trwyth left Glyn Nyfer and came to Cwm Cerwyn, and made a stand there. And then he killed four of Arthur's champions: Gwarthegyd son of Caw and Tarawg of Allt Clwyd [Rock of Clyde] and Rheiddwn son of Eli Adfer and Isgofan the Generous. And after killing these men, he made another stand against them in that place and killed Gwydre son of Arthur and Garselid the Irishman and Glew son of Yscawd and Iscawyn son of Panon. And then the boar Twrch Trwyth, too, was wounded.

The next morning at the break of day some of the men caught up with him. But then he killed Huandaw and Gogigwr and Penpingion, the three servants of Glewlwyd Great-Grip, until God knows he had no servant in the world to help him, apart from Llaesgymyn alone, a man for whom no one was better off. And after that the boar Twrch Trwyth killed lots of men of the country, including Glwyddyn the Builder, Arthur's master builder. And then Arthur caught up with him in Peluniawg, but the boar Twrch Trwyth killed Madawg son of Teithion, Gwyn son of Tringad son of Nefed, and Eiriawn Penlloran. And from there he went to Aber Tywi. And then he made a stand against them and killed Cynlas son of Cynan and Gwilenhin King of France. Then he went into Glyn Ystu, and the men and dogs lost sight of the boar.

Arthur called Gwyn son of Nudd to him and asked him if he knew anything about the boar Twrch Trwyth. He answered that he knew nothing. All the companions went to hunt the swine there, all the way to Dyffryn Llychwr. And Grugyn Silver-Bristle charged them along with Llwydawg Gofynniad and they killed the hunters until none of them were left alive except for one man. So Arthur came with his forces to where Grugyn and Llwydawg were and then set loose on them all the dogs that have been named. And at the outcry that then ensued and at the baying of the hounds, the boar Twrch Trwyth came to defend his piglets. And from the time they had all crossed the sea together from Ireland up to that very moment, he had not yet seen them. He was attacked by men and dogs. He tried to go to Mynydd Amanw when one of his piglets was killed. And then it went life for life with him, and then the pig Llawin was killed. And then another of his piglets was killed, Gwys by name. And then the boar Twrch Trwyth went into Dyffryn Amanw, and his piglets Banw and Bennwig were killed there. None of his piglets left that place with him, except for Grugyn Silver-Bristle and Llwydawg Gofynniad.

From there they went as far as Llwch Ewin where Arthur caught up with the boar Twrch

Trwyth. Then he made a stand. And then he killed Echel Great-Thigh and Garwyli offspring of Gwyddawg Gwyr and lots of other men and dogs, too. And then they went over to Llwch Tawy. And then Grugyn Silver-Bristle split off from them and Grugyn went from there on to Din Tywi. And from there he went into Ceredigiawn with [the hounds] Eli and Trachmyr after him, and a multitude following them as well. And he came to Garth Grugyn and there Grugyn Silver-Bristle was killed in their midst, but he had killed Rhuddfyw Rhys and lots of others with him. And then Llwydawg went on to Ystrad Yw and there the men of Brittany charged him and then he killed Peisawg the Tall King of Brittany and both Llygatrudd Emys and Gwrbothu, Arthur's uncles, brothers of his mother. And then the pig Llwydawg Gofynniad was killed.

The boar Twrch Trwyth then went between Tawy and Ewyas. Cornwall and Devon were called up by Arthur to muster at Aber Hafren [the mouth of the Severn River], and Arthur said to the warriors of this island, "The boar Twrch Trwyth has killed many of my men. By the courage of my men, he will not go into Cornwall while I am still alive. I will not chase him further, but will go against him myself, life for life. Do what you can." So they followed his plan to send a body of horsemen with the dogs of this island to Ewyas. And from there they doubled back to the Severn and there the surviving veteran warriors of this island surprised the boar Twrch Trwyth and drove him one way or another into the Severn. And Mabon son of Modron rode Gwyn Mygdwn the horse of Gweddw into the Severn, along with Goreu son of Custennin and Menw son of Teirgwaedd, in between Lake Lliwan and Aber Gwy [the mouth of the Wye]. And Arthur charged the boar with the champions of Britain. Osla Big-Knife attacked and Manawydan son of Llyr and Cacamwri Arthur's servant and Gwyngelli, and they closed in all around him. And first they grabbed him by his feet, and pulled him down into the Severn until it was pouring over him. Mabon spurred his horse up to the one side of the boar and snatched his razor, while from the other side Cyledyr the Wild charged on another horse right into the Severn and took his scissors. But before the comb could be taken, the boar Twrch Trwyth touched the bottom with his feet and from the moment he found purchase, neither dog nor man nor horse could keep up with him until he got away into Cornwall.

Whatever bad was gotten in trying to take the treasures he had with him, even worse was gotten in trying to save the two men from drowning. Two quernstones dragged Cacamwri back into the depths as he was being pulled out. The knife of Osla Big-Knife had fallen out of its sheath while he was running after the boar and he had lost it; and as he was being pulled out of the river, his sheath filled with water so that he was dragged back down into the depths.

Then Arthur went with his men until he caught up with the boar Twrch Trwyth in Cornwall. Whatever bad had been gotten from him before was child's play compared with what they got from him then in trying to snatch the comb. From one bad thing to the next was the getting of that comb from him. And then the boar Twrch Trwyth was chased out of Cornwall and driven right into the sea. And it has never been known where else he went and [the two hounds] Aned and Aethlem still swimming after him. And from there Arthur went to bathe himself and rest in Celliwig in Cornwall.

THE VERY BLACK WITCH

Arthur asked, "Are there any of those conditions left to get?" One of the men said, "There is, the blood of the Very Black Witch daughter of the Very White Witch from the

Valley of Grief in the uplands of Hell." Arthur set out for the North Country and came to the old crone's cave. And it was the idea of Gwyn son of Nudd and Gwythyr son of Greidawl to send Cacamwri and his brother Hygwydd in to fight with the crone. And as they came into the cave the witch attacked them and grabbed Hygwydd by the hair of his head and threw him to the floor beneath her. And Cacamwri grabbed her by the hair of her head and pulled her off Hygwydd to the floor, upon which she turned on Cacamwri and beat them both soundly and stripped off their weapons and drove them out squealing and squalling. And Arthur got angry at the sight of his two servants almost killed and started to enter the cave.

And then Gwyn and Gwythyr said to him, "It is neither pretty nor pleasant for you to be seen wrestling with a witch. Send Tall Amren and Tall Eiddil into the cave." So they went. And whatever the difficulties the first two had, it was a worse for these two, so that God knows not one of the four could have walked away from that place, if all four had not been loaded onto Llamrei, Arthur's mare. And then Arthur himself rushed the entrance to the cave and from the entrance threw his knife Carnwennan at the witch and sliced her in half so that she fell as two tubs. And Caw of Britain took the blood of the witch and kept it with him.

Conditions Met

And then Culhwch set off with Goreu son of Custennin and those who wished ill to Ysbaddaden Chief of Giants, bringing the stipulated things to his court. And Caw of Britain came to shave off his beard, skin and flesh down to the bone, and his two ears as well. And Culhwch asked, "Have you been shaved, man?" "I have," he replied. "And your daughter, is she mine now?" "She is," he said. "But don't thank me for that: thank Arthur, the man who did it for you. Of my own free will, you would never have gotten her. And it is now high time to take my life." And then Goreu son of Custennin grabbed him by the hair of his head and dragged him back behind the mound and struck off his head and stuck it on a stake on the battlement. And then they took over the stronghold and its territory.

And that night Culhwch slept with Olwen. And she was his only wife for the rest of his life. And the armies of Arthur dispersed, each man to his own country.

And that's how Culhwch won Olwen daughter of Ysbaddaden Chief of Giants.

Chrétien de Troyes. *Perceval* (The Story of the Grail)

Translated by WILLIAM W. KIBLER

Chrétien de Troyes, active in the last quarter of the twelfth century, is unquestionably one of the most original and influential writers in all of French literature. Not only did he invent the Arthurian verse romance with its chivalric quests, but he created some of its most enduring and influential characters and themes, notably the love affair between Sir Lancelot and Arthur's queen Guenevere and the legend of the Grail. Both of these themes enjoyed tremendous success in the centuries after Chrétien, in French as well as in many of the other languages of Western Europe. It is not an exaggeration to say that everything written about King Arthur, Queen Guenevere, and the Knights of the Round Table until at least the end of the sixteenth century, derives ultimately from Chrétien.

In addition to some minor works generally attributed to him, he is the author of five lengthy verse romances: *Erec and Enide*, *Cligés*, *Yvain* (The Knight with the Lion), *Lancelot* (The Knight of the Cart), and *Perceval* (The Story of the Grail). Although we don't know why, the last seventh of the *Lancelot* was completed by another poet; and the *Perceval*, which is dated to the 1180s, was left unfinished at about 9,000 lines. Its dedicatee, Phillip of Flanders, died in the Holy Land in 1191. His death, or possibly Chrétien's own, could explain its lack of closure.

The *Perceval* tells how a naïve Welsh squire rose to prominence through combat and love, then failed in his quest at the Grail castle when he didn't ask the questions he should have. Due to his failure, great misfortune spread through Arthur's lands, affecting especially those whom a good knight should protect: single maidens, widows, orphans, and the dispossessed. The mysteries of the Grail remain unexplained by Chrétien, although many later attempts—both medieval and modern—have been made to elucidate them. Selections from one of the most impressive of these, the *Perlesvaus*, appear later in this volume.

The stories of Perceval and the grail were most likely independent of one another before Chrétien combined them in memorable form. Many of the motifs he used can be found earlier in classical and Celtic literature, but Chrétien reshaped them for his own purposes, in line with his own aesthetic preferences and the tastes of his own period. His genius lay in combining the magical and fantastic elements of his sources with keenly observed contemporary mores to create an atmosphere of wonder and mystery that remains nonetheless securely anchored in a recognizable twelfth-century "present."

The Story of the Grail

He who sows little, reaps little,
but he who wishes to reap plentifully
casts his seed on ground
that will increase his fruit a hundredfold;   4

for good seed withers and dies
in worthless soil.
Chrétien sows and casts the seed
of a romance that he begins,
and sows it in such a good place
that it cannot fail to be bountiful,
since he does it for the most worthy man
in all the empire of Rome:
that is, Count Philip of Flanders,
who surpasses Alexander
whom they say was so great.
But I shall prove that the count
is much more worthy than he,
for Alexander had amassed within himself
all the vices and wickedness
of which the count is pure and free.
   The count does not listen
to wicked gossip or prideful words,
and if he hears evil spoken of another,
no matter whom, it grieves him.
The count loves true justice,
loyalty, and Holy Church,
and despises all baseness.
He is more generous than one can imagine,
for he gives without hypocrisy or deceit,
in accord with the Gospel injunction
that states: "Let not your left hand
know the good your right hand does."
But the receiver of his largesse knows,
as does God, who sees all secrets
and knows all that is hidden
deep within one's heart and soul.
   Why does the Gospel state:
"Hide your good deeds from your left hand?"
The left hand, according to tradition,
stands for vainglory,
which comes from false hypocrisy.
And what does the right hand stand for?
Charity, which does not boast of
her good deeds, but hides them
so that only He whose name
is God and Charity knows of them.
God is Charity, and he who abides
in Charity, according to Holy Writ
(St. Paul states it and I read it there),
abides in God and God in him.
Know truly therefore that the gifts
given by the good count Philip
are gifts of charity;
for he consults no one
except his noble, honest heart,
which urges him to do good.
Is he not more worthy than
Alexander, who cared not
for charity or any good deeds?
Indeed yes, have no doubt!
Therefore Chrétien's efforts will not
be in vain, since he strives and aims
by command of the count
to rhyme the best story
that's ever been told in royal court:
it is the Story of the Grail,
whose book was given him by the count.
Hear now how he acquits himself of it.
   It was in the season when trees flower,
shrubs leaf out, meadows grow green,
and birds in their own tongue
sing sweetly in the mornings,
and everything is aflame with joy,
that the son of the widow lady
of the deep Waste Forest
arose. Then effortlessly
he placed the saddle upon
his hunter and, taking
three javelins, left
his mother's manor.
He thought that he would go to see
some harrowers in his mother's service,
who were harrowing her oats
with twelve oxen and six harrows.
As soon as he entered the forest
his heart leapt within his breast
because of the fair weather
and the songs he heard
from the joyful birds:
all these things brought him pleasure.
Because of the sweet calm weather
he lifted the bridle from his hunter's head
and let it wander along
grazing through the fresh green grass.
Being a skilled thrower,
he took to casting
his javelins all around him,
sometimes behind, sometimes before,
sometimes low and sometimes high,
until he heard five armed knights
coming through the woods,
in armor from head to toe.
And the approaching knights' armor
made a great racket,
for the branches of oak and hornbeam
often slapped against the metal.
Their hauberks all clanked,

108 their lances knocked against their shields,
and the metal of hauberks and
the wood of shields resounded.
The boy heard but could not see
112 the swiftly advancing knights;
he marveled and said: "By my soul,
my lady mother spoke the truth
when she told me that devils are
116 more frightening than anything in the world.
She instructed me to make
the sign of the cross to ward them off,
but I scorn her teaching
120 and indeed I won't cross myself;
instead, I'll strike the strongest of them at once
with one of the javelins I'm carrying
so that none of the others, I believe,
124 will dare approach me."
Thus spoke the boy to himself
before he saw them.
But when he caught sight of them
128 coming out of the woods,
he saw the glittering hauberks
and the bright, shining helmets,
the lances and the shields,
132 which he had never seen before,
and he beheld the green and scarlet
glistening in the sunshine,
and the gold and blue and silver:
136 he found it most fair and noble.
Then he said: "Lord God, I give you thanks!
These are angels I see before me.
Ah! in truth I sinned grievously
140 and did a most wicked thing
in saying they were devils.
My mother did not lie to me
when she told me that angels were
144 the most beautiful creatures alive,
except God, who is the most beautiful of all.
Yet here I see God Almighty in person, I think,
for one of them, so help me God,
148 is more than ten times
more beautiful than any of the others.
And my mother herself said
that one must believe in God
152 and adore, worship, and honor Him;
so I shall adore that one there
and all the angels with him."
He flung himself to the ground at once
156 and recited the whole creed
and the prayers he knew
that his mother had taught him.
And the leader of the knights
160 saw it and said: "Stand back,
for the sight of us has made
this youth fall to the ground in fright.
If we all approach him
164 together, I think he would be
so frightened that he would die
and not be able to answer
any questions I might put to him."
168 They halted while their leader
rode swiftly toward the boy,
and greeted and reassured him,
saying: "Don't be afraid, young man!"
172 —"I'm not, by the Savior
I believe in," replied the youth.
"Are you God?"—"No, upon my word."
—"Who are you, then?"—"I am a knight."
176 —"I've never before met a knight,"
said the boy, "nor seen one,
nor ever heard tell of one;
but you are more beautiful than God!
180 Would that I were like you,
so shining and so well formed!"
Upon hearing these words, the knight
drew near him and asked:
184 "Have you seen in this clearing today
five knights and three maidens?"
But the boy had his mind made up
to inquire about other matters:
188 he reached out for the knight's lance,
took it, and asked: "Dear sir,
you who are called 'Knight,'
what is this you carry?"
192 —"Well, I can see that I've come
to the right place!" said the knight.
"I'd intended, my fair friend,
to get information from you,
196 but you're the one asking me.
I'll tell you: it's my lance."
—"Would you say you launch it
as I do my javelins?"
200 —"Not at all, young man. You're such a dolt!
One thrusts with it instead."
—"Then any one of these three
javelins you see here is better,
204 because I can kill as many

birds and beasts as I want or need,
and I can kill them from as far away
as one can shoot a crossbow."
208 —"I'm not interested in this, young man;
but answer me about the knights.
Tell me if you know where they are,
and whether you saw the maidens."
212 The boy grabbed the bottom
of his shield and spoke forthrightly:
"What's this and what's it used for?"
—"Young man, this is some trick!
216 You're leading me on to other subjects
I didn't ask or inquire about!
I intended, so help me God,
to get information from you
220 rather than have you draw it from me—
but you want me to inform you!
Yet I'll tell you, come what may,
because I've grown to like you.
224 What I'm carrying is called a shield."
—"It's called a shield?"—"Exactly," he said,
"and I should never despise it,
for it is so true to me that,
228 if anyone thrusts or shoots at me,
it stands firm against all blows:
that is the service it renders me."
At that moment, those who had lagged
232 behind came swiftly up the path
toward their lord and said
to him at once: "My lord,
what is this Welshman telling you?"
236 —"He doesn't know his manners,
so help me God," replied the lord,
"because he won't answer anything
I ask him in a straightforward way;
240 instead, he asks the name of everything
he sees, and what it is used for."
"My lord, you must be aware
that all Welshmen are by nature
244 more stupid than beasts in the field:
this one is just like a beast.
A man's a fool to tarry beside him,
unless he wants to while away
248 his time in idle chatter."
—"So help me God, I don't know,"
the knight replied. "But before I leave
I'll tell him everything he wants to know;
252 otherwise I'll never leave!"
Then he asked him anew:

"Young man, don't be upset if I insist:
tell me whether you have
256 seen or encountered the five knights,
and also the maidens."
But the boy held onto him
by the edge of his hauberk and pulled:
260 "Now tell me," he said, "dear sir,
what is this you're wearing?"
—"Young man," he replied, "don't you know?"
—"No I don't."—"It's my hauberk, young man,
264 and it is as heavy as iron—
for it is made of iron as you can see."
—"I don't know anything about that,
but it's very beautiful, so help me God.
268 What do you use it for? What good is it?"
—"Young man, that's easy to explain.
If you tried to throw a javelin
or shoot an arrow at me
272 you couldn't do me any injury."
—"Sir knight, I hope God won't let
the hinds and stags have such hauberks,
for I wouldn't be able to kill any
276 and could never hunt them again."
And the knight asked him once more:
"Young man, as God is your help,
can you give me any information
280 about the knights and maidens?"
And the boy, who lacked instruction,
said to him: "Were you born like this?"
—"No indeed, young man, it's impossible
284 for anyone to be born like this,"
—"Then who fitted you out in this fashion?"
—"Young man, I'll tell you who."
—"Then tell me."—"Most willingly.
288 It hasn't been five full days
since King Arthur knighted me
and gave me all these trappings.
But now you tell me what became of
292 the knights who passed by here
escorting the three maidens:
were they proceeding slowly, or were they in flight?"
He answered him: "My lord, look now
296 at the woods that encircle
the top of that mountain.
There lie the passes of the river Doon."
—"And what of them, good brother?"
300 —"My mother's harrowers are there,
who are sowing and plowing her lands.

And if these people passed by there,
and if they saw them, they would tell you."
304 And the knights said that they would accompany
the boy there, if he would take them
to those who were harrowing the oats.
So the young man took his hunting horse
308 and went to where the harrowers
were harrowing the plowed ground
where the oats were sown.
And when they saw their master
312 they trembled in fright.
And do you know why?
Because they saw armed knights
coming along with their master;
316 and they were well aware that if these knights
had explained to him what knighthood was,
he would want to become a knight
and his mother would go mad with grief,
320 for they had sought to keep him
from ever seeing knights
or learning of their ways.
And the boy said to the ox-drivers:
324 "Have you seen five knights
and three maidens pass this way?"
—"This very day they went
through these woods," replied the ox-drivers.
328 And the boy said to the knight
who had spoken to him at such length:
"My lord, the knights and maidens passed this way.
332 But now tell me news
of the king who makes knights,
and where he's most often found."
—"Young man," he said, "I wish to tell you
336 that the king is staying in Carlisle,
and it hasn't been
more than five days since he was there,
for I was there and saw him.
340 And if you don't find him there,
someone will surely tell you where he is;
he'll not have gone too far."
At that the knight galloped off,
344 for he was most eager
to catch up with the others.
And the boy was not slow
in returning to his manor,
348 where his mother was grieving
and sad of heart because of his delay.
She was filled with joy the moment she saw him, nor could she
352 conceal the joy she felt,
for like a deeply loving mother
she ran toward him calling out:
"Fair son! fair son!" more than a hundred times.
356 "Fair son, my heart was most
distressed because of your delay.
I've been overwhelmed with grief
and almost died of it.
360 Where have you been so long today?"
—"Where, mother? I'll tell you
honestly, with no lie,
for I've experienced great joy
364 because of something I saw.
Did you not used to tell me
that our Lord God's angels
are so very beautiful that Nature
368 never made such a beautiful creature,
nor is there anything so fair in all the world?"
—"Fair son, I say it still.
It's true and I repeat it."
372 —"Hush, mother! Have I not just seen
the most beautiful things there are
going through the Waste Forest?
They are more beautiful, I think,
376 than God or all his angels."
His mother took him in her arms
and said: "Fair son, I commend you to God,
for I am most afraid on your account:
380 you have seen, I'm sure,
the angels men complain of,
who kill whatever they come upon."
—"Not at all, mother, no, not at all!
384 They say they are called knights."
His mother fainted at this word,
when she heard him say "knight."
And after she had recovered,
388 she spoke like a woman in despair:
"Ah, woe is me, what misfortune!
Fair sweet son, I had hoped
to keep you so far from knighthood
392 that you'd never hear tell of knights
nor ever see one!
You were destined for knighthood,
fair son, had it pleased God
396 to protect your father
and others close to you.

There was no worthier knight,
no knight more feared or respected,
400 fair son, than your father
in all the Isles of the Sea.
You can well boast
that neither his lineage nor mine
404 is any disgrace to you,
for I too am from a knightly line,
one of the best in this land.
In the Isles of the Sea there was
408 no finer lineage than mine in my day;
but the best have fallen on hard times—
and it is widely known
that misfortune often comes
412 to noble men who cultivate
great honor and prowess.
Cowardice, shame, and sloth
never seem to fall on hard times;
416 it is always the good who do.
Your father, though you do not know it,
was wounded through his thighs
so that he was maimed in body.
420 The great lands and great treasures
he held as a nobleman
were all laid waste,
and he fell into great poverty.
424 After the death of Utherpendragon,
who was king and father of good King Arthur,
the nobles were wrongfully
impoverished, disinherited,
428 and cast into exile.
Their lands were laid ruin
and the poor people abused;
those who could flee, fled.
432 Your father had this manor
here in this wild forest;
he couldn't flee, but he quickly
had himself brought here in a litter,
436 for he couldn't think where else to flee.
And you, a child at the time,
had two very handsome brothers.
You were tiny, still nursing,
440 barely over two years old.
When your two brothers were grown,
on the advice and counsel of their father
they went to two royal courts
444 to receive their armor and horses.
The elder went to the king
of Escavalon and served him
until he was knighted.
448 And the other, the younger,
went to King Ban of Gomeret.

Both youths were dubbed
and knighted on the same day,
452 and on the same day set forth
to return to their home,
for they wanted to bring happiness to me
and to their father, who never saw them again,
456 for they were defeated in arms.
Both died in combat,
which has brought me great grief and sadness.
A strange thing happened to the elder:
460 the crows and rooks
pecked out both his eyes.
So the people found them both dead.
Your father died of grief for his sons,
464 and I have suffered a very bitter
life since he passed on.
You were all the consolation
that I had, and all the comfort,
468 for none of my loved ones remained.
God had left me nothing else
to bring me joy and happiness."
The boy paid scarcely any attention
472 to what his mother said to him.
"Give me something eat," he insisted.
"I don't know what you're talking about,
but I would gladly go
476 to the king who makes knights;
and I will go, no matter what."
His mother detained him as long as possible
And held him back;
480 she outfitted and dressed him
in a coarse canvas shirt
and breeches made in the style
of Wales, where breeches and hose
484 are of one piece, I believe;
and he had a cloak and hood
of buckskin fastened about him.
Thus did his mother equip him.
488 She delayed him three days, no more;
her wheedling could detain him no longer.
Then his mother felt a strange sadness;
she kissed him and hugged him tearfully,
492 saying: "Now I feel a great sadness,
fair son, as I see you about to leave.
You will go to the king's court
And will ask him to give you arms.
496 There will be no objection,

I know, and he'll give them to you.
But when you start trying out
those weapons, how will it go then?
500 Since you've never used weapons
nor seen anyone else using them,
how will you manage?
Poorly, to be sure, I fear!
504 You will lack skill in everything,
and it's not surprising, I think,
since no one can know what he hasn't learned.
But it is surprising when one doesn't learn
508 what is often seen and heard.
Fair son, I want to give you some advice
that you would do very well to heed;
and if it pleases you to remember it,
512 great profit can come to you.
Before long you'll be a knight, son,
so I believe, if it pleases God and I approve.
Should you encounter, near or far,
516 a lady in need of aid,
or a maiden in distress,
make yourself ready to aid
them, if they ask for your help,
520 for it is the most honorable thing to do.
He who fails to honor ladies
finds his own honor dead inside him.
Serve ladies and maidens
524 and you'll be honored everywhere.
And if you ask a woman for her love,
be careful not to annoy her
by doing anything to displease her.
528 He who kisses a maiden gains much;
but if she grants you a kiss,
I forbid you to go any further,
if you'll refrain for my sake.
532 But if she has a ring on her finger,
or an alms purse at her belt,
and if she gives it to you for love
or the asking, I'll not object
536 to you wearing her ring.
I give you leave to take the ring
and the alms purse.
Fair son, I have something more to tell you:
540 never keep company with anyone for very long,
whether at an inn or on the road,
without asking his name;
learn his name well,
544 for by the name one knows the man.
Fair son, speak to gentlemen,
keep company with gentlemen:
gentlemen never lead astray
548 those who keep their company.
Above all I want to beg you
to pray to our Lord
in chapel and church
552 to give you honor in this world
and grant you so to act
that you may come to a good end."
—"Mother, what is a chapel?"
556 —"A place where one worships
Him who made heaven and earth
and placed man and beast upon it."
—"And what's a church?"—"This, son:
560 a most holy and beautiful building
with relics and treasures,
where they sacrifice the body
of Jesus Christ, the Holy Prophet,
564 whom the Jews greatly defiled:
He was betrayed and wrongfully condemned,
and suffered the pains of death
for men and women alike,
568 whose souls went to hell
when they left their bodies,
and He delivered them.
He was bound to the stake,
572 beaten, and then crucified,
and wore a crown of thorns.
I urge you to go to churches
to hear Masses and Matins,
576 and to worship this Lord."
—"Then I'll gladly go
to chapels and churches
from now on," said the boy.
580 "This I pledge to you."
At that there was no further delay;
the boy took his leave and his mother wept.
His horse was already saddled.
584 The youth was outfitted in the fashion
and manner of the Welsh:
he had pulled on coarse rawhide buskins,
and as always wherever he went
588 he carried three javelins.
He intended to bring his javelins,
but his mother took two away from him
so he wouldn't appear so clearly Welsh;
592 she would happily have taken away
all three, had it been possible.

	In his right hand he carried		I'll go pray to Him, upon my word,
	a willow switch to strike his horse.		to give me something to eat this day,
596	His mother, who loved him dearly,	648	for I'll be in great need of such."
	kissed him tearfully as he left		Then he came the tent and found it open.
	and begged God to watch over him.		He saw in the middle of the tent
	"Fair son," she said, "God be with you.		a bed covered with a silken spread.
600	May He give you, wherever you go,	652	Upon the bed a young girl
	more joy than remains with me."		was sleeping all alone;
	When the boy was but		her attendants were far away:
	a stone's throw distance away,		her maidens had all gone
604	he looked back and saw that his mother	656	to gather fresh flowers
	had fallen at the head of the bridge		to scatter through the tent,
	and was lying in a faint		as was their custom.
	as if she had dropped dead.		When the youth entered the tent
608	But he whipped his hunter	660	his horse stumbled so hard
	across the crupper with his switch,		that the girl heard it,
	and the horse bore him		awakened, and was startled.
	swiftly on without stumbling		And the boy, untutored,
612	through the great dark forest:	664	said: "Maiden, I greet you
	he rode from morning		just as my mother taught me.
	until the day dimmed.		My mother instructed me
	He slept in the forest that night		to greet maidens
616	until the light of day appeared.	668	wherever I found them."
	The next morning the boy arose		The maiden trembled in fear
	to the singing of the birds, remounted,		of the boy who appeared mad to her,
	and rode on purposefully		and thought herself a perfect fool
620	until he saw a tent	672	for having let him find her alone.
	pitched in a beautiful meadow		"Young man," she said, "be on your way.
	beside the stream from a spring.		Flee, lest my lover see you."
	The tent was wondrously beautiful:		—"First I'll kiss you, by my head,"
624	one side was scarlet	676	said the boy, "whether you like it or not,
	and the other striped with golden bands;		because my mother instructed me to."
	on top was a gilded eagle.		—"I'll never kiss you, to be sure,"
	The sun struck bright		said the maiden, "not if I can help it!
628	and blazed upon the eagle,	680	Flee, lest my lover find you,
	and the whole meadow was bright		for if he finds you, you are dead!"
	from the glow of the tent.		The boy had strong arms
	All around the tent,		and embraced her clumsily
632	which was the most beautiful in the world,	684	because he knew no other way:
	there were bowers, arbors, and shelters		he stretched her out beneath himself,
	built in the manner of the Welsh.		but she resisted mightily
	The boy went toward the tent		and squirmed away as best she could.
636	and exclaimed before he reached it:	688	But her resistance was in vain,
	"My God, here I behold your house!		for the boy kissed her repeatedly—
	I would do wrong		twenty times as the story says—
	were I not to go to worship you.		whether she liked it or not,
640	My mother spoke the truth	692	until he saw on her finger a ring
	when she said to me that a church		set with a shining emerald.
	is the most beautiful thing there is,		"My mother also told me," he added,
	and told me never to pass		"to take the ring from your finger,
644	a church without going to worship	696	but not to do anything more to you.
	the Creator in whom I believe.		Now give me the ring; I want it!"

—"I swear you'll never get my ring,"
said the maiden, "you can be sure,
700 unless you tear it from finger."
The boy grabbed her by the wrist,
forcibly straightened out her finger,
removed the ring from it,
704 and put it on his own finger,
saying: "Maiden, I wish you well.
I'll go now quite contented,
for your kiss is much better
708 than that of any chambermaid
in all my mother's household,
because your breath is sweet."
   She wept and said: "Young man,
712 don't carry away my ring,
for I'll be ill treated if you do,
and you'll lose your life,
sooner or later, I promise you."
716 The boy did not take to heart
anything he heard her say,
and since he had not eaten
he was absolutely dying of hunger.
720 He found a little keg full of wine
and a silver goblet beside it,
and saw a new white towel
on a bundle of rushes;
724 he lifted it and found underneath
three freshly made venison meat pies.
This food was most appealing,
given the hunger that tormented him.
728 He broke open one of the meat pies
and consumed it avidly;
into the silver goblet he poured
wine, which was pleasing to the taste,
732 and drank it down in lusty gulps,
saying: "Maiden, I can't finish
these meat pies by myself today.
Come eat some, they're very good.
736 Each of us will have his own,
and there'll be a whole one left."
But she wept constantly,
no matter how he begged and called
  her,
740 and she answered not a word.
He ate as much as he wished
and drank until he'd had enough.
He promptly took his leave,
744 covered the remnants with the towel,
and commended to God the maiden
who was not pleased to hear his words:
"God save you, fair friend!" he said.
748 "For God's sake, don't be upset
if I carry away your ring,
because before I die
I'll make it up to you.
752 I'm going now with your leave."
But she wept and said she would never
commend him to God,
because she would suffer more shame
756 and grief because of him
than any wretched woman had ever
  endured,
and she would never accept any help or
  aid
from him as long he lived;
760 he should understand that he'd betrayed
  her.
So she stayed behind, weeping.
It was not long before
her lover returned from the woods.
764 He saw the tracks of the boy
who had gone his way, and was upset;
he found his sweetheart weeping,
and said: "My lady, I believe
768 by these signs I see
that a knight was here."
—"No knight, my lord, I swear to you,
but a Welsh boy,
772 uncouth, base, and naïve,
who drank as much of your wine
as he pleased and ate
some of your three meat pies."
776 —"And is that why you're crying, my
  pretty?
I wouldn't have cared if he'd
eaten and drunk everything."
—"There's more, my lord," she said.
780 "It has to do with my ring:
he's taken it and carried it off.
I'd rather be dead
than have him take it like that.'
784 Then her companion was distressed
and tormented in his heart.
"Upon my oath," he said, "this was an
  outrage!
But since he's taken it, let him have it.
788 But I believe he did more:
if there is more, don't hide it."
—"My lord," she said, "he kissed me."
—"Kissed you?"—"Yes, I assure you,
792 but it was against my will."
—"No, you liked it and were pleased by
  it!
You never tried to stop him!"
said the man, tormented by jealousy.
796 "Do you think I don't know you?

Indeed, I know you only too well!
I'm not so blind or squint-eyed
that I can't see your falseness.
800 You've set off on a wicked path
and have started up a painful road,
for your horse will never again
eat oats nor be cared for
804 until I am avenged.
And should it throw a shoe,
it'll not be reshod;
if it dies, you'll follow me on foot.
808 You'll not change
the clothes you're wearing,
but will follow me naked and on foot
until I've cut off his head—
812 Nothing less will satisfy me."
Then he sat down and ate.
 The boy rode along until he saw
a charcoal-burner approaching,
816 driving an ass before him.
"Peasant," he said, "driving that ass
before you, tell me
the shortest way to Carlisle.
820 They say that King Arthur,
whom I want to see, makes knights."
—"Young man," he answered, "in this direction
lies a castle built above the sea.
824 If you go to this castle, my good friend,
you'll find King Arthur
both sad and happy there."
—"Now I want you to tell me
828 what makes the king both sad and happy."
—"I'll tell you at once," he replied.
"King Arthur and all his army
have fought against King Ryon.
832 The King of the Isles was defeated,
and that is why King Arthur is happy;
but he is sad because his comrades
have returned to their own castles
836 where it is more pleasant to live,
and he doesn't know how they're faring:
this is the reason for the king's sadness."
The boy did not give a penny
840 for the charcoal-burner's information,
except that he did ride off along the road
that had been indicated to him,
until he saw a castle above the sea,
844 strong and fair and well-fortified.
From the gate he saw
an armed knight emerge, bearing
in his hand a golden cup.

848 He was holding his lance, his bridle,
and his shield in his left hand,
and the golden cup in his right;
and his armor, all of which was scarlet,
852 became him perfectly.
The boy saw the beautiful armor,
which was fresh and newly made.
It was pleasing to him and he said:
 "Upon my word,
856 I'll ask the king to give me this armor.
I'll be pleased if he gives it to me,
and damned if I'll ask for any other!"
Then he hurried toward the castle,
860 for he was eager to reach the court,
and soon passed near the knight.
The knight detained him
a moment and inquired:
864 "Tell me, young man, where are you going?"
—"I want to go to court," he replied,
"to ask the king for your armor."
—"Young man," he said, "that's a fine idea!
868 Go swiftly, then, and return as fast,
and say this to that wicked king:
if he doesn't want to pay me homage
for his land, he must give it to me
872 or send a champion to defend it
against me, for I say that it is mine.
And so that he'll believe your words,
remind him that I snatched
876 this cup I am carrying from him
just now, with his wine still in it."
He should have found another to do his mission,
for the young man had not heard a word he said.
880 He did not slow down until he reached court,
where the king and his knights
were seated at table.
The main hall was at ground level,
884 and the boy entered on horseback
into the long, wide hall,
which was paved in marble.
King Arthur was seated
888 dejectedly at the head of a table;
and all the knights were eating
and talking among themselves,
except for Arthur, who was disheartened and silent.
892 The boy came forward
but did not know whom to greet,

	since he did not recognize the king,
	until Yonet, who was holding
896	a knife in his hand, came trowards him.
	"Squire," said the boy, "you coming there
	with the knife in your hand,
	show me which of these men is the king."
900	Yonet, who was very courteous,
	replied: "Friend, there he is."
	The boy went to him at once
	and greeted him in his manner.
904	The king was downcast and answered not a word,
	so the boy spoke to him again.
	The king remained downcast and silent.
	"Upon my word," the boy then said,
908	"this king never made a knight!
	How could he make knights
	if you can't get a word out of him?"
	Immediately the boy made ready to depart;
912	he turned his hunter's head,
	but, like the untutored fellow he was,
	he brought his horse so close to the king
	—I tell no lie—that he knocked
916	the king's cap of fine cloth
	from his head onto the table.
	The king turned his still lowered head
	in the young man's direction,
920	abandoned his serious thoughts,
	and said: "Fair brother, welcome.
	I beg you not to take it ill
	that I failed to answer your greeting.
924	My anger prevented a reply,
	for the greatest enemy I have,
	who hates and distresses me most,
	has just laid claim to my land
928	and is so impertinent as to state
	that he'll have it, whether I like it or not.
	He's called the Red Knight
	from forest of Quinqueroy.
932	And the queen had come here
	to sit in my presence,
	to see and to comfort
	these wounded knights.
936	The knight would never
	have angered me by words alone,
	but he snatched away my cup
	and raised it so insolently
940	that he spilled all the wine in it
	right on the queen.
	After this dreadful deed
	the queen returned
944	to her chambers, where she is
	morified with anger and grief.
	So help me God, I don't think
	she'll come out alive."
948	The boy did not give a fig
	for anything the king told him,
	nor did his grief or the shame done
	the queen make any impression on him.
952	"Make me a knight, sir king," he said,
	for I wish to be on my way."
	The eyes of the rustic youth
	were bright and laughing in his head.
956	None who saw him thought him wise,
	but all who observed him
	considered him handsome and noble.
	"Friend," said the king, "dismount
960	and give your hunter to this
	squire, who'll watch over it
	and do whatever you ask.
	I swear to God that all will be done
964	in accord with my honor and your profit."
	And the youth replied:
	"The knights I met in the clearing
	never dismounted,
968	yet you want me to dismount!
	By my head, I'll not dismount,
	so get on with it and I'll be on my way."
	—"Ah!" said the king. "Good dear friend,
972	I'll gladly do it
	to your profit and my honor."
	—"By the faith I owe the Creator,"
	said the boy, "good sir king,
976	I'll never be a knight
	if I'm not a Red Knight.
	Grant me the armor of the knight
	I met outside your gate,
980	the one who carried off your golden cup."
	The seneschal, who had been wounded,
	was angered by what he heard
	and said: "Right you are, friend!
984	Go and snatch his armor from him
	right now, for it belongs to you.
	You were no fool
	to come here and ask for it!"
988	—"Kay," said the king, "for the love of God,
	you are too eager to speak ill,
	and it doesn't matter to whom!
	This is a wicked vice in a gentleman.

992	Though the boy is naïve, still he may be of very noble line; and if his folly comes from poor teaching, because he had a low-bred master,
996	he can still prove brave and wise. It is a wicked thing to mock another and to promise without giving. A gentleman should never undertake
1000	to promise anything to another that he cannot or will not grant him, for he might then earn the enmity of this person who would otherwise have been his friend,
1004	but who, once the promise has been given, expects it to be kept. So by this you can understand that it is better to refuse a man something
1008	than to give him false hope, for to tell the truth he who makes promises he doesn't honor mocks and deceives himself,
1012	because it turns his friend's heart from him." Thus spoke the king to Kay. As the boy turned to leave, he saw a maiden,
1016	fair and noble, whom he greeted. She returned his greeting with a laugh, and as she laughed she said to him: "Young man, if you live long enough,
1020	I think and believe in my heart that in this whole world there will never be, nor will anyone ever acknowledge, a better knight than yourself.
1024	This I think and feel and believe." The maiden had not laughed in six full years or more, yet she said this so loudly
1028	that all heard her. And Kay, greatly upset by her words, leapt up and struck her so forcefully with his palm on her tender cheek
1032	that he knocked her to the ground. After slapping the maiden, he turned and saw a court jester standing beside a fireplace;
1036	he kicked him into the roaring fire

	because he was furiously angry at having heard the jester often say: "This maiden will not laugh
1040	until she has seen the man who will become the supreme lord among all knights." The jester cried out and the maiden wept,
1044	but the boy tarried no longer; without a word to anyone he set off after the Red Knight. Yonet, who was well acquainted
1048	with all the best roads and who often carried news to court, hurried alone and unaccompanied through an orchard beside the hall
1052	and out a postern gate until he came straightway to the path where the Red Knight was awaiting knightly adventure.
1056	The boy swiftly approached to claim his armor; and the knight as he waited had put down the golden cup
1060	on a block of dark stone. When the boy had come near enough to be heard, he shouted: "Take off
1064	your armor! King Arthur commands you not to wear it any more!" And the Red Knight asked him: "Boy, does anyone dare come forth
1068	to uphold the king's cause? If anyone does, don't hide it from me." —"What the devil is this? Sir knight, are you mocking me
1072	by not removing my armor? Take it off at once, I order you!" —"Boy," he replied, "I'm asking you if anyone is coming on the king's behalf
1076	to do combat against me." —"Sir knight, remove this armor at once, or I'll take it off you myself, for I'll not let you keep it any longer.
1080	Be certain that I'll attack you if you make me say it again." Then the Red Knight grew furious. He raised his lance with both hands
1084	and struck the boy such a mighty blow across the shoulders with the shaft of his lance that it drove him down

1088 over the neck of his horse;
the boy became irate
when he felt himself injured
by the blow he'd taken.
1092 With his best aim he let fly
his javelin at the knight's eye:
before he could react, the javelin pierced
the knight through his eye and brain,
1096 and came out the back of his neck
amid a gush of blood and brains.
The Red Knight's heart failed in agony,
and he fell forward full-length upon the ground.
1100 The boy dismounted,
placed the knight's lance to one side
and lifted his shield from off his shoulders,
but he could not manage
1104 to remove his helmet from his head
because he did not know how to grasp it.
He also wanted to ungird
his sword, but he did not know how
1108 and could not pull it from its scabbard,
so he gripped the scabbard and pulled and tugged.
Yonet began to laugh
when he saw the boy struggling like this.
1112 "What's going on, friend?" he asked.
"What are you doing?"—"I don't know.
I thought your king
had given me these arms,
1116 but I think I'll have to carve up
this dead knight into little morsels
before getting any of his armor,
because it adheres so tightly
1120 to the corpse that inside and outside
are as one, it seems to me,
so tightly do they cling together."
—"Now don't you worry about a thing,"
1124 said Yonet, "for I'll separate it
easily, if you wish me to."
—"Then do it quickly," said the boy,
"and give it to me without delay."
1128 Yonet undressed the knight at once
right down to his big toe,
leaving neither hauberk nor hose of mail,
nor helmet on his head, nor other armor.
1132 But the boy did not want to take off
his own clothing and refused,
in spite of all Yonet's pleadings,
to don a very comfortable tunic
1136 of padded silken material
that the knight, when he was alive,
had worn beneath his hauberk;
nor could Yonet persuade him to remove
1140 the rawhide buskins from his feet.
He just said: "What the devil! Are you mocking me?
Do you think I'll change
the good clothes just made for me
1144 by my mother for this knight's clothing?
Do you want me to trade
my thick canvas shirt
for this thin chemise?
1148 My jacket, which keeps out the water,
for this one that wouldn't stop a drop?
May the man be hanged
who'd ever exchange
1152 his good clothing for someone else's bad!"
It is a difficult task to teach a fool.
In spite of every urging,
he did not want to take anything except the armor.
1156 Yonet laced up his mail leggings for him
and strapped on the spurs
over his rawhide buskins;
then he put the hauberk on him,
1160 of which there was no finer,
and placed the helmet,
which fit him perfectly, over the coif,
and showed him how to gird on
1164 the sword so that it swung loosely.
Then he placed the boy's foot in the stirrup
and had him mount the knight's charger:
he had never before seen a stirrup
1168 and knew nothing about spurs,
having used only switches or whips.
Yonet brought the shield
and lance and gave them to him.
1172 Before Yonet left, the boy
said: "Friend, take
my hunter away with you,
for he's a fine horse and I give him to you
1176 because I don't need him any longer;
and take the king his cup
and greet him for me;
and tell the maiden
1180 whom Kay struck on the jaw
that if I can, before I die

I hope to cook her such a dish
That she'll consider herself well avenged."
1184 Yonet replied that he would return
the king's cup and deliver
the young man's message faithfully.
Then they parted and went their own
ways.
1188 By the main door Yonet entered the hall
where the barons were assembled;
he returned the cup to the king,
saying: "Sire, cheer up,
1192 for your knight who was here
sends back your cup to you."
—"What knight are you talking about?"
asked the king, who was still filled
1196 with anger.—"In the name of God, sire,"
said Yonet, "I'm talking about the boy
who left here a short while ago."
—"Are you talking about that Welsh boy
1200 who asked me for the red-tinted
armor of the knight who caused me
the greatest shame he possibly could?"
inquired the king.
1204 —"Sire, truly I am talking about him."
—"And how did he get my cup?
Did the Red Knight like or respect him
so much that he freely gave it to him?"
1208 —"No, the boy made him pay dearly
for it by killing him."
—"How did this come about, fair
friend?"
—"I don't know, my lord, except that I
saw
1212 the Red Knight strike him
with his lance and injure him gravely,
and then I saw the boy strike him
with a javelin through the eye-slit
1216 so that blood and brains
spilled out from beneath his helmet
and he lay stretched out dead on the
ground."
Then the king addressed the seneschal:
1220 "Ha! Kay, what harm you've caused me
this day!
By your venomous tongue,
which has spoken many an idle word,
you've driven from me a knight
1224 who today has done me a great service."
—"My lord," said Yonet to the king,
"by my head, he sends word by me
to the queen's handmaiden,
1228 whom Kay struck in anger
and out of hatred and jealousy of himself,
that he will avenge her if he lives
long enough and has the opportunity to
do so."
1232 The jester, sitting beside the fire,
heard these words, jumped to his feet,
and came merrily before the king,
leaping and dancing for joy,
1236 and saying: "Sir king, so help me God,
the time of your adventures is nearing.
You will often witness
cruel and harsh ones,
1240 and I swear to you
that Kay can rest assured
that he will regret his feet and hands
and his wicked, foolish tongue,
1244 because before forty days have passed
the young knight will have avenged
the kick Kay gave me,
and the blow he struck the maiden
1248 will be dearly paid for
and properly avenged,
for he'll break his right arm
between the shoulder and elbow—
1252 he'll carry it in a sling from his neck
for half a year, and well deserved!
He can no more escape this than death."
These words so enraged
1256 Kay that he nearly died
of wrath and, in his anger,
he could scarcely keep from killing
the jester in front of the whole court.
1260 But because it would displease the king
he refrained from attacking him.
And the king said: "Ah, Kay!
How angry you've made me this day!
1264 Had someone instructed the boy
and taught him enough of weaponry
that he could use his shield
and lance a little, no doubt
1268 he would have made a fine knight.
But he doesn't know a thing
about weapons or anything else,
and couldn't even draw
1272 his sword if he needed to.
Now he's sitting armed upon his steed
and will encounter some blackguard
who won't hesitate to injure him
1276 in order to win his horse;
he'll be dead or crippled before long!
Because he's so simple-minded and
uncouth
he doesn't know how to defend himself,
1280 And his enemy will easily defeat him."

So the king lamented, mourned,
and felt sorry for the young man,
but he could gain nothing by it,
1284   and so fell silent.
    Meanwhile the boy rode on
without delay through the forest
until upon the flatlands
1288   he came to a river that was
wider than a crossbow's shot,
for all the waters had drained into it
and flowed now through its bed.
1292   He crossed a meadow
toward the raging waters,
but he did not set foot in them,
for he saw that they were dark and deep
1296   and swifter than the Loire.
He rode along the riverbank
across from a high rock cliff,
and opposite him the water
1300   lapped against the foot of the rock.
Upon the rocks, on a slope
that dropped down to the water,
was built a fine and mighty castle.
1304   Where the river became a bay,
the boy turned to his left
and saw the castle towers appear,
which to him seemed to be born
1308   and spring forth from the castle walls.
Rising in the middle of the castle
was a high and mighty tower;
there where the waters of the bay
1312   fought with the tide,
the footings of a mighty barbican
were washed by the sea.
At the four corners of the walls,
1316   built of solid square-cut stones,
were four low turrets
which were strong and fair.
The castle was very well situated
1320   and quite comfortable within.
Before the round entrance tower
stood a bridge over the water
made of stone, sand, and lime.
1324   The bridge was strong and high
with battlements all around.
In the middle of the bridge was a tower,
and on the near end a drawbridge,
1328   built and ordained
for its rightful purpose:
a bridge by day and a gate by night.
The boy rode towards the bridge.
1332   A gentleman robed in ermine
was strolling on the bridge,
awaiting the approaching boy.
The gentleman was holding
1336   a short staff in his hand
to appear more distinguished,
and was followed by two
squires without cloaks.
1340   As he approached, the boy remembered well
what his mother had taught him,
for he greeted him and said:
"Sir, my mother taught me this."
1344   —"God bless you, dear brother,"
said the gentleman, who saw by his speech
that he was a naïve simpleton.
He added: "Dear brother, where are you from?"
1348   —"Where? From King Arthur's court."
—"What did you do there?"—"The king,
may God bless him, made me a knight."
—"A knight? So help me God,
1352   I never thought he'd be doing that
in the present circumstances;
I thought the king would be concerned with
other things than making knights.
1356   Now tell me, my good young man,
who gave you this armor?"
—"The king gave it to me."
—"Gave it? How?" And he told him
1360   just as you have heard in the tale.
If anyone were to tell it again
it would be boring and wearisome,
for no story improves by repetition.
1364   Then the gentleman asked him
how skilled he was with his horse.
"I can make it run up hills and down,
just as I could run
1368   my hunter, when I had it,
that I took from my mother's house."
—"Now tell me, fair friend,
what you know how to do with your armor."
1372   —"I know how to put it on and off
just as the squire armed me,
after he'd stripped the armor
from the man I'd killed.
1376   It's so light on my body
that it doesn't hurt me at all."
—"By God, I'm proud of this,"
said the gentleman, "and pleased to hear it.

1380	Now don't be offended if I ask what duty brought you this way." —"Sir, my mother taught me to go up to gentlemen,
1384	to take advice from them, and to believe what they tell me, for profit comes to those who believe them." The gentleman replied: "Fair brother,
1388	blessed be your mother, for she raised you well. But do you want to say something else?" —"Yes."—"And what?"—"This and no more:
1392	that you give me lodging this day." —"Most willingly," said the gentleman, "if you'll grant me a boon that will bring you great profit, as you'll see."
1396	—"And what is that?" he asked.—"That you believe your mother's advice and mine." —"In faith," he said, "I grant it." —"Then dismount." And he dismounted.
1400	One of the two squires who had come there took his horse and the other removed his armor, leaving him in the coarse robe,
1404	the buskins, and the roughly sewn and ill-fitting buckskin cloak that his mother had given him. Then the gentleman had himself fitted
1408	with the sharp steel spurs the young man had been wearing, mounted the boy's horse, hung the shield by its strap
1412	from his own neck, took the lance, and said: "Friend, learn now about weapons and take heed how you should hold the lance
1416	and spur your horse and rein him in." Then he unfurled the pennon and showed and taught him how he should grip his shield.
1420	He let it hang a little forward so that it rested on the horse's neck, put the lance in its support, then spurred the horse, which was worth a hundred marks of silver,
1424	for none ran more swiftly or willingly or with greater might. The gentleman was very experienced with shield, horse, and lance,
1428	for he had practiced with them since boyhood; everything the gentleman did pleased and delighted the young man. When he had gone through
1432	all his maneuvers before the boy, who had observed them all very carefully, he returned to the youth with lance raised and asked:
1436	"Friend, could you handle the lance and shield like that, and spur and guide your horse?" And he replied at once
1440	that he would not care to live another day, nor possess lands or riches, until he could do as well. "What one doesn't know can be learned,
1444	if one is willing to pay attention and work," said the gentleman. "My dear friend, every profession requires effort, devotion and practice:
1448	with these three one can learn everything. And since you've never used weapons nor seen anyone else use them, there's no shame or blame
1452	if you don't know how to use them." Then the gentleman had him mount and the young man began to bear the lance and shield as properly
1456	as if he had always frequented the tournaments and wars and had wandered through every land seeking battle and adventure,
1460	for it came naturally to him; and since Nature was his teacher and his heart was set upon it, nothing could be difficult
1464	for which Nature and his heart strove. With the help of these two he did so well that the gentleman was delighted and thought to himself
1468	that had this young man worked with arms all his life he would truly have been a master. When the boy had done his round,
1472	he rode back before the gentleman with lance raised

just as he had seen him do,
and spoke: "Sir, did I do well?
1476 Do you think that I can learn
if I'm willing to take the pain?
My eyes have never beheld anything
I've yearned for so much.
1480 I truly want to know
as much as you do about knighthood."
—"Friend, if your heart is in it,"
said the gentleman, "you'll learn much
1484 and never experience any difficulty."
Three times the gentleman mounted the horse,
three times he demonstrated the weapons
until he had shown him all he knew
1488 and all there was to show,
and three times he had the young man mount.
The last time he said to him:
"Friend, if you were to meet
1492 a knight, what would you do
if he struck you?"—"I'd strike him back."
—"And if your lance splintered?"
—"If that happened I'd have no choice
1496 but to rush at him with my fists."
—"Friend, that's not what you should do."
—"Then what should I do?"—"Pursue him with your sword and fence with him."
1500 Then the gentleman thrust his lance upright into the ground before him,
for he was very eager
to teach him more about weapons
1504 so he'd be able to defend himself well
with the sword if he were challenged,
and attack with it when need arose.
Then he grasped the sword in his hand:
1508 "Friend," he said, "this is the way
you'll defend yourself if someone assails you."
—"So help me God," the boy replied,
"no one knows more about this than I do,
1512 because I often practiced hitting
pads and shields at my mother's house
until I was weary from it."
—"Then let's return now to my lodgings,"
1516 said the gentleman, "for there's nothing more to do;

and tonight you'll have proper lodgings,
whether anyone objects or not."
Then they went on side by side,
1520 and the boy said to his host:
"Sir, my mother taught me
never to go with any man
or keep his company for long
1524 without asking his name.
So if her advice was proper,
I want to know your name."
—"My dear friend," said the gentleman,
1528 "I'm called Gornemant of Gohort."
They continued on towards his lodgings,
walking hand in hand.
A squire came unsummoned
1532 to the bottom of the staircase
carrying a short mantle.
He hurried to dress the boy in it
so that after the heat of exercise
1536 he would not catch a harmful cold.
The gentleman had large and splendid
lodgings and handsome servants.
The meal was nobly and well
1540 prepared and splendidly laid out.
The knights first washed,
then sat down to eat;
and the gentleman had the youth
1544 sit beside him and made him eat
from the same bowl as himself.
I'll say no more about how many
courses they had or what they were,
1548 only that they had plenty to eat and drink.
I'll say no more about the meal.
After they had risen from table,
the gentleman, who was most courteous,
1552 begged the boy seated beside him
to stay for a month. Indeed,
if he wished, he would gladly
detain him a full year,
1556 and would teach him in the meanwhile
such things, if he were pleased to learn them,
as he should know in time of need.
And the boy responded afterwards:
1560 "My lord, I don't know if I'm close
to the manor where my mother lives,
but I pray God to guide me there
so that I might behold her again,
1564 for I saw her fall in a faint
at the head of the bridge before the gate,

and I don't know whether she's alive or dead.
I'm well aware she fainted
1568 in grief at my departure,
and for this reason
until I know how she is
I cannot tarry for long,
1572 so I must be off tomorrow at dawn."
The gentleman saw there was no point
insisting and kept his silence.
Without further words they retired to rest,
1576 because the beds were already prepared.
The gentleman arose early
and came to the boy's bed,
where he found him still lying.
1580 He had a shift and linen underclothing
brought there for the boy,
and red-dyed hose
and a cloak of violet silk
1584 which had been woven in India.
He had them brought to him
to wear, and said:
"Friend, you shall wear this clothing
1588 you see here, if you want my guidance."
And the boy replied: "Dear sir,
surely you don't mean that!
Aren't the clothes my mother made me
1592 better than any of these?
Yet you want me to wear these!"
—"Young man," said the gentleman,
"by my head, yours are worse!
1596 You assured me, dear friend,
when I brought you here,
that you would heed my every command."—"And so I shall,"
1600 said the boy. "I'll never oppose
you in anything at all."
He hesitated no more in putting on the new clothing,
and left aside those his mother had made him.
1604 The gentleman leaned over
and attached the boy's right spur
(custom once dictated that
he who made another a knight
1608 should attach his spur).
There were many other squires
present, and everyone who could
came to give him a hand with his armor.
1612 And the gentleman took the sword,
girded it on him and kissed him,
saying that with the sword
he had given him the highest order
1616 that God had set forth and ordained,
that is, the order of knighthood,
which must be maintained without villainy.
And he added: "Young man, remember
1620 that if you are ever compelled
to do combat with any knight,
there is one thing I want to beg you:
if you get the upper hand
1624 and he can no longer defend himself
or hold out against you,
you must grant him mercy
rather than killing him outright.
1628 And be careful not to be
too talkative or prone to gossip.
Anyone who is too talkative
soon discovers he's said something
1632 that brings him reproach;
the wise man states and declares:
'He who talks too much commits a sin.'
Therefore, dear brother, I forbid you
1636 to talk too much. And I beseech you,
if you find a maiden or woman—
be she damsel or lady—
who is disconsolate in any way,
1640 you would do right to console her
if you know how to console her
and are able to do so.
And do not scorn
1644 another thing I would teach you,
for it must not be scorned:
go gladly to church
and pray to Him who made all things
1648 to have mercy on your soul
and to keep you a true Christian
in this earthly life."
And the youth said to the gentleman:
1652 "May you be blessed, dear sir,
by all the popes of Rome,
for I heard my mother say the same thing."
—"Dear brother, you must never again say,"
1656 continued the gentleman, "that your mother
taught or instructed you.
I don't blame you one bit
for having said it up till now,
1660 but henceforth, begging your pardon,
I urge you to correct yourself,

	for if you say that any more		
	people will take you for a fool.		
1664	Therefore I urge you to refrain from saying that."		
	—"Then what shall I say, dear sir?"		
	—"You can say that the vavasor		
	who attached your spur		
1668	taught and instructed you."		
	And the boy promised		
	that he would never again		
	as long as he lived speak		
1672	a word of any master but him,		
	for he thought that that was good advice.		
	The gentleman then blessed the young man,		
	raising his hand high above him		
1676	and saying: "Dear sir, God save you!		
	Be off, and may God guide your steps,		
	since it does not please you to delay."		
	The new knight left		
1680	his host and was very impatient		
	to reach his mother		
	and find her alive and well.		
	He set off into the deep forests,		
1684	where he was more at home		
	than on the open fields,		
	and rode until he saw		
	a strong and mighty castle.		
1688	Outside its walls there was nothing		
	but the sea, a river, and wasteland.		
	He hastened toward the castle		
	until he came before its gate;		
1692	but he had to cross such a fragile		
	bridge before passing to the gate		
	that he thought it would barely hold him.		
	The knight stepped onto the bridge		
1696	and crossed it without incurring		
	any injury, harm, or shame.		
	He reached the gate		
	but found it locked;		
1700	he did not knock softly		
	or whisper, but beat upon it		
	so hard that immediately		
	a thin and pale maiden		
1704	came to the windows of the main hall		
	and said: "Who is calling there?"		
	The new knight looked up at		
	the girl and said: "Fair friend,		
1708	I am a knight who begs you		
	to let me enter		
	and give me lodging for the night."		
	—"Sir," she replied, "you shall have it,		
1712	but you'll not be pleased.		

Nonetheless, we'll prepare you
the best lodgings we can."
Then the maiden withdrew
1716 and the new knight waiting at the gate
was afraid they were keeping him too long,
so he began to shout once more.
Immediately four men-at-arms came
1720 bearing large battle-axes on their shoulders,
and each had girded on his sword.
They unbolted the gate
and said: "My lord, enter."
1724 Had the men-at-arms been in good health
they would have been handsome indeed,
but they were so weakened by
famine and sleepless nights
1728 that they were wondrously changed.
And just as he found the land wasted
and impoverished outside the walls,
he found things no better within,
1732 for everywhere he went
he saw the streets laid waste
and the houses in ruins,
for there was no man or woman to be seen.
1736 There were two churches in the town,
which had both been abbeys:
one for distraught nuns,
the other for impoverished monks.
1740 He did not find the churches
well decorated or in good repair;
rather, their walls were cracked
and broken, their steeples were in ruins,
1744 and their doors were open
by night as by day.
No mill was grinding or oven baking
anywhere within the castle walls,
1748 and there were no bread or cakes,
nor anything at all one could sell
to earn a penny.
Thus he found the town desolate,
1752 without bread or pastry,
without wine, cider, or beer.
The four men-at-arms led him
to a slate-roofed hall, where they
1756 helped him dismount and remove his armor.
Immediately a squire descended
the steps from the great hall,
carrying a gray mantle;
1760 he placed it over the knight's shoulders

while another squire led his horse
to a stable where there was scarcely
any grain, straw, or hay,
1764 for there were no provisions in the castle.
The others had him pass
before them up the stairway
leading to the magnificent great hall.
1768 Two gentlemen and a maiden
came forward to greet him.
The two men's hair was graying
but not yet altogether white;
1772 they would have been vigorous
and at the peak of their strength
had it not been for their cares and hardships.
And the maiden was more charming,
1776 more splendid, more graceful
than sparrowhawk or parrot:
her cloak and tunic were
of rich black silk flecked with gold,
1780 and the edgings of ermine
showed no signs of wear.
The collar of her cloak
was trimmed with black and gray sable,
1784 which was of perfect length and cut.
And if ever before I have described
the beauty God formed
in a woman's face or body,
1788 I would like to try another description
that would never vary from the truth:
her hair flowed free
and was so lustrous and blond
1792 that anyone who saw it
might mistake it, if that were possible,
for strands of purest gold.
Her forehead was white, high, and as smooth
1796 as if it had been moulded by hand,
or as if it had been carved
from stone, ivory, or wood.
Her eyes, under dark eyebrows
1800 and set wide apart, were
laughing and bright, shining and narrow.
Her nose was straight and long,
and the rosiness of the cheeks
1804 on her white face was more pleasing
than crimson on silver.
God made her an unsurpassed marvel
to dazzle men's hearts and minds;
1808 never since has He made
her equal, nor ever before.

When the new knight saw her,
he greeted her and she, and the two knights
1812 with her, returned his greetings.
The damsel took him
courteously by the hand
and said: "Dear sir, your lodgings
1816 tonight certainly won't be suited
to a gentleman.
If I were to tell you
all of our sad condition,
1820 it is possible you'd think
that I did it from discourtesy
to induce you to leave.
But if it pleases you, come with me
1824 and accept the lodgings such as they are,
and may God grant you better tomorrow."
So she led him by the hand
into a private room,
1828 which was long and wide and beautiful.
They sat down together
on an embroidered coverlet of samite
that was spread across a bed.
1832 Four knights, then five and six,
came into the room, sat down
all in a group, and said nothing.
They looked at the knight who sat
1836 beside their lady without saying a word;
he refrained from speaking
because he recalled the lesson
the gentleman had given him.
1840 Meanwhile the six knights
whispered at length among themselves.
"Heavens," they all said, "I wonder
if this knight is mute.
1844 It would be a real pity,
for a more handsome knight was never born:
how good he looks beside my lady,
and she, too, at his side.
1848 If they were not both silent,
he is so handsome and she so beautiful
that no knight or lady
was ever more suited for the other.
1852 It appears that the two of them
were destined by God for one another,
since He's brought them here together."
Everyone in the room there
1856 was conversing in this manner,
and the damsel kept waiting
for him to speak of anything at all,
until she clearly saw and understood

1860	that he would not speak a word to her
	unless she addressed him first.
	So she said most courteously:
	"Sir, where did you come from today?"
1864	—"My lady," he replied, "I spent last night
	in a gentleman's castle,
	where I had fine and noble lodgings:
	he has five strong and excellent towers,
1868	one large and four small.
	I cannot describe it all in detail,
	nor do I know the name of the castle,
	but I do know for a fact that the gentleman
1872	is called Gornemant of Gohort."
	—"Ah! dear friend," said the maiden,
	"your words are welcome
	and courteously spoken.
1876	May the Lord God reward you
	for calling him a gentleman.
	You never spoke a truer word,
	for he *is* a gentleman, by St. Richier,
1880	this I can assure you;
	and know that I am his niece,
	though I've not seen him for a long while.
	And indeed, since you left
1884	your home you've not met
	a finer gentleman, of this I'm sure.
	He welcomed you happily
	and joyfully, as only a noble
1888	and courteous gentleman can, who is
	powerful, rich, and well-to-do.
	But here there are no more than five crumbs,
	which another uncle, who's a prior—
1892	a very holy and religious man—
	sent me to eat this night,
	and a little cask full of brandy.
	There's no other food herein,
1896	except a roebuck that one of my servants
	killed this morning with an arrow."
	Then she ordered the tables
	to be set, and they were,
1900	and everyone sat down to supper.
	Supper there did not last long,
	but it was consumed with hearty appetites.
	After eating they went their separate ways.
1904	Those who had kept watch the night before
	remained within to sleep,
	while those who were to keep watch
	over the castle that night went to their posts—
1908	fifty men-at-arms and knights
	kept watch that night.
	The others made every effort
	to make their guest feel comfortable:
1912	the man in charge of his bed
	brought him white sheets,
	a costly coverlet, and a pillow for his head.
	That night the knight
1916	had all the comfort and delight
	one could hope for in a bed,
	except the pleasure
	of a maiden's company, if he pleased,
1920	or a lady's, had it been permitted.
	But he knew nothing of these pleasures
	and never thought of them at all,
	so he promptly fell asleep,
1924	having not a care in the world.
	But his hostess had no rest
	within the closed space of her chamber.
	While he slept peacefully, she worried,
1928	for she could offer no defense
	against an imminent attack.
	She tossed and turned constantly,
	upset and distressed.
1932	Finally she put on a short robe
	of red silk over her chemise
	and bravely and courageously
	started on her mission,
1936	which was not an idle one,
	for she was determined to go
	to her guest and tell him
	a part of her troubles.
1940	She arose from her bed
	and left her chamber
	so frightened that all her limbs
	were trembling and her body was bathed in sweat.
1944	Weeping she left her room
	and came, still weeping and sighing,
	to the bed where the knight was asleep.
	She knelt down and leaned over him,
1948	weeping now so copiously
	that her tears dampened his whole face;
	she did not dare do anything more.
	She wept so much that he awakened,
1952	astounded and amazed
	at finding his face all damp,
	and beheld her kneeling
	beside his bed, embracing

1956	him tightly around the neck;
	and he was courteous enough
	to take her in his arms
	at once and draw her to him.
1960	He said to her: "My beauty, what's the matter?
	What has brought you here?"
	—"Ah, gentle knight, have pity on me!
	In the name of God and His Son,
1964	I beg you not to despise me
	for having come here,
	or for being nearly naked.
	I meant no folly,
1968	no wickedness or evil,
	for there is nothing living in this world
	so sorrowful or distraught
	that I am not more sorrowful still.
1972	Nothing I have is pleasing to me,
	for I am constantly plagued by troubles.
	I am so miserable
	that I'll not live to see another night
1976	beyond this one tonight,
	nor another day beyond tomorrow;
	I'll kill myself instead.
	Of three hundred knights and ten
1980	who garrisoned this castle
	there are but fifty left,
	for Anguingueron,
	a most evil knight and
1984	seneschal of Clamadeu of the Isles,
	has led away, killed,
	and imprisoned forty-eight of them.
	I'm as upset about those
1988	in prison as those he killed,
	for I know they'll die there,
	since they can never escape.
	So many noble men have died for my sake
1992	that it's right that I should suffer too.
	Anguingueron has laid siege
	to this castle for an entire winter
	and summer without departing,
1996	and every day his army grows,
	while ours is diminished
	and our supplies depleted,
	until there's not enough left here
2000	to feed a bee.
	We are now in such a state
	that tomorrow, without God's help,
	this castle, which can no longer be defended,
2004	will be surrendered to him
	and me with it, as his prisoner.

	But truly, before he takes me alive,
	I'll kill myself; then he'll have me dead
2008	and I'll not care if he carries me off.
	Clamadeu, who hopes to have me,
	will not possess my body
	till it's devoid of life and soul,
2012	for I keep in one of my jewelry boxes
	a knife of flawless steel
	that I intend to plunge into my body.
	That is all I had to tell you;
2016	now I'll go back
	and let you rest."
	The new knight will soon be able
	to win glory if he has the courage:
2020	she had come to shed tears over his face
	for no other reason,
	in spite of what she pretended,
	than to inspire in him
2024	the desire to undertake
	the battle, if he dared,
	to defend her and her lands.
	And he said to her: "Dear friend,
2028	cheer up this night:
	take comfort, weep no more,
	draw close to me here
	and wipe the tears from your eyes.
2032	Tomorrow God will grant you a better day,
	if He pleases, than you've predicted.
	Lie down in this bed beside me,
	it's wide enough for both of us;
2036	you won't leave me again today."
	She said: "If it pleases you,
	I'll stay." And he kissed her
	and held her tightly in his arms.
2040	He placed her gently and comfortably
	beneath the coverlet,
	and she let him kiss her,
	and I do not believe it displeased her.
2044	Thus they lay side by side
	with lips touching all night long,
	until morning came and day dawned.
	He brought her so much comfort
	that night
2048	that they slept with lips touching
	and arm in arm until day broke.
	At dawn the maiden
	returned to her own chamber.
2052	Without servant or chambermaid
	she dressed and prepared herself,
	awakening no one.
	Those who had kept watch at night

2056 came and woke up the others
and roused them from their beds
as soon they saw the light of day.
They all arose without delay.
2060 The maiden returned
at once to her knight
and addressed him courteously:
"Sir, may God give you a good day today!
2064 I truly believe that you'll
not stay a long while here.
There can be no question of your staying;
and I'll not take it ill if you go,
2068 for it would not be gracious of me
to be upset by your departure,
for we have brought you no comfort
and shown you no honor here.
2072 And I pray God that He prepare
you better lodgings,
with more bread, wine, salt,
and other good things than there are here."
2076 And he said: "My beauty, I'll not
look for any other lodging today.
First, if I can, I'll bring peace
throughout your lands.
2080 If I discover your enemy outside,
it will distress me if he remains there longer
to torment you in any way.
But if I defeat and kill him,
2084 in recompense I ask
that you give me your love;
I'll accept no other payment."
The maiden replied coyly:
2088 "Sir, you've just requested
a pitiful thing of little value.
But if it were denied you,
you'd think me proud,
2092 so therefore I don't wish to refuse you.
And yet don't say
that you'd go forth
to die for me on condition that
2096 I become your sweetheart,
as that would be most unfortunate;
you are not strong or old
enough, I assure you,
2100 to hold your own
in skirmish or battle
against a knight so strong and tall
and so hardened by combat
2104 as the one awaiting you out there."
—"This very day you'll see if that is so," he said,
"for I'll go forth to fight with him.
No words of yours can stop me."
2108 She pretended by her words to discourage him,
though in fact she wished him to fight;
but it often happens
that one hides one's true desires
2112 when one finds someone
keen to enact them,
in order to increase his desire to do so.
Thus she behaved cleverly,
2116 by discouraging him from doing
what she had planted in his heart to do.
The new knight called for
his arms, which were brought to him.
2120 The gate was opened before him
and he was armed and mounted
upon a horse that had been
made ready for him in the square.
2124 Everyone who was present
showed signs of grief and said:
"My lord, may God be with you
on this day and punish
2128 Anguingueron the seneschal,
who has laid waste to this whole land."
Men and women alike wept.
They accompanied him to the gate,
2132 and as they saw him leave the castle
they said as with a single voice:
"Dear sir, may the one true Cross
on which God let His own Son suffer
2136 protect you today from death,
difficulty, or capture,
and bring you back safely
to where you will find comfort,
2140 happiness, and pleasure."
Thus they all prayed for him.
The besieging host saw him approaching
and pointed him out to Anguingueron,
2144 who was sitting before his tent,
firm in the belief that the castle
would be surrendered to him before nightfall,
or that someone would come forth
2148 to engage him in single combat.
He had already laced on his mail leggings,
and his men were in high spirits,
believing they had already conquered
2152 the castle and all its lands.
As soon as Anguingueron saw the knight,

	he had himself armed at once	2204	But then he remembered
	and rode toward him swiftly		the gentleman who had taught him
2156	on his large and powerful horse,		never to kill a knight
	saying: "Young man, who sends you here?		knowingly once he'd defeated
	Tell me what you are up to.	2208	and gotten the best of him.
	Have you come to make peace or fight?"		Anguingueron repeated: "My dear friend,
2160	—"And you, what are you doing in this land?"		don't be so haughty
	he demanded. "You tell me first:		as to refuse me mercy.
	why have you killed the knights	2212	I assure you and concede
	and laid waste the whole countryside?"		that you've got the better of me
2164	Then Anguingueron replied		and are an excellent knight,
	in a proud and haughty tone:		but not so good that a man
	"I demand that the castle be opened	2216	who hadn't seen us fight it out,
	to me today and the keep surrendered,		but who knew the two of us,
2168	for it has been denied me too long.		would ever believe that you alone
	And my lord shall have the maiden!"		could have slain me in single combat.
	—"Cursed be these words," said the youth,	2220	But if I bear witness
	"and the man who spoke them!		that you defeated me in arms
2172	Instead, you'll have to abandon		before all my men outside my own tent,
	every claim you've made against it,"		my word will be believed
	—"By Saint Peter," said Anguingueron,	2224	and your fame will be acknowledged
	"you're plying me with lies!		greater ever than any knight's.
2176	It's often the innocent one		And if you have a lord
	who has to pay the penalty."		who has rendered you some service
	The youth was growing angry;	2228	you have not yet repaid,
	he fixed his lance in its support		send me to him and I'll go
2180	and the two charged one another		on your behalf to tell him
	as fast as their steeds could carry them.		how you've defeated me in arms,
	With all the power of their anger	2232	and I'll yield myself prisoner to him
	and all the strength of their arms		to do with as he pleases."
2184	they split their lances in two		—"Cursed be anyone who asks for more!
	and showered splinters all around.		And do you know where you'll go?
	Anguingueron alone fell,	2236	To this castle, and you'll say
	wounded through his shield,		to the beauty who is my love
2188	with his arm and side		that never again as long as you live
	in terrible pain.		will you bring her harm,
	And the youth, not knowing how	2240	and you'll deliver yourself
	to continue on horseback, dismounted.		wholly and completely to her mercy."
2192	When his feet touched ground		Anguingueron replied: "Kill me then,
	he drew his sword and laid on again.		for she would have me killed,
	I cannot describe to you in every detail	2244	since she wants nothing so much
	what happened to each knight,		as my death and downfall,
2196	nor all their blows one by one,		for I helped kill her father
	but the battle lasted a long while		and have made her even angrier
	and the blows were powerful	2248	by killing or capturing
	until at last Anguingueron fell.		all her knights this past year.
2200	The young knight pursued him fiercely		He who sends me to her
	until he begged for mercy,		damns me to a cruel punishment;
	and the youth said there could be	2252	he couldn't imagine a worse fate for me!
	no question of mercy.		But if you have any other friend,
			or other sweetheart, who doesn't
			desire to do me ill, then send me there,

2256	for this lady would not fail
	to take my life if she got hold of me."
	So then he told him he should go
	to a gentleman's castle,
2260	and gave him the man's name.
	In all the world there was no mason
	who could have described more accurately
	the castle than he described it to him:
2264	he praised the river and bridge
	and the corner towers and keep
	and the strong walls surrounding it
	so accurately that Anguingueron realized
2268	that he wished to send him a prisoner
	to the place where he was hated most.
	"Dear sir," he said, "I'll be no safer
	there where you're sending me now.
2272	So help me God, you are intent on
	sending me to a wicked end by enemy hands,
	for I killed one of his brothers
	in this same war.
2276	Kill me yourself, good noble friend,
	rather than make me go to him.
	It will be my death if you drive me there."
	The young knight said: "Then you'll go
2280	to be imprisoned at King Arthur's court,
	and you'll greet the king for me
	and tell him on my behalf
	to have someone show you the maiden
2284	whom the seneschal Kay struck
	because she favored me with her laughter.
	You'll surrender yourself to her
	and tell her at once, if you please,
2288	that I pray God not to let me die
	before I am able to avenge her."
	Anguingueron replied that he would be pleased
	to render him this service.
2292	Then the victorious knight
	headed back toward the castle;
	the vanquished knight set off for prison,
	after having his standard lowered
2296	and lifting the siege
	so that not a man remained before the town.
	People poured forth from the castle
	to welcome back the young knight,
2300	but they were very disappointed
	that he had not taken the head
	of the knight he'd defeated
	and brought it to them.
2304	In high spirits they helped him dismount
	and disarmed him by a horse block,
	saying: "My lord, since you didn't bring Anguingueron back alive,
2308	why didn't you cut off his head?"
	And he replied: "My lords, in faith
	that would not have been wise, I believe:
	because he had killed your relatives
2312	I wouldn't have been able to stand warrant
	that you wouldn't kill him in spite of me.
	Once I had gotten the better of him,
	it wouldn't have been right for me
2316	not to show him mercy.
	Do you know how I showed him mercy?
	If he keeps his oath to me, he'll go
	as a prisoner to King Arthur."
2320	Just then the damsel approached,
	full of joy at the sight of him,
	and took him to her chamber
	to rest and take his ease.
2324	And she did not refuse him
	her kisses and embraces;
	in lieu of food and drink
	they sported, kissed, caressed,
2328	and spoke together pleasantly.
	Meanwhile Clamadeu was foolishly thinking
	as he neared the castle that he would win it
	without any opposition,
2332	when he met along the road
	a grief-stricken squire
	who told him the news
	of his seneschal Anguingueron.
2336	"In the name of God, sir, it goes very badly,"
	said the squire, who was so distraught
	he was pulling out his hair with both fists.
	Clamadeu asked: "What's the matter?"
2340	And the squire responded: "Upon my word,
	your seneschal has been defeated
	in single combat and has gone off
	to become a prisoner at King Arthur's court."

| 2344 | —"Who did this, squire, tell me?
How could this happen?
Where did the knight come from
Who could defeat such a valiant
| 2348 | and noble man in single combat?"
He answered: "Good my lord,
I don't know who the knight was,
but I do know that I saw him
| 2352 | sally forth from Biaurepaire
dressed in red armor."
—"So what do you advise me to do now?"
asked Clamadeu, nearly beside himself with rage.
| 2356 | "What, sir? Go back,
for if you continue onwards
I don't think it would do you good."
On hearing these words, an elderly
| 2360 | somewhat grizzled knight, who had been
Clamadeu's mentor, came forward and said:
"Young man, your words are ill chosen.
He should follow wiser
| 2364 | and better advice than yours.
He'd be a fool to believe you;
I advise him to press onwards."
Then he added: "My lord, do you
| 2368 | want to know how you can have
both knight and castle?
I'll tell you exactly what to do,
and it will be very simple:
| 2372 | within the walls of Biaurepaire
there is neither food nor drink,
and the knights are weak;
but we are strong and healthy
| 2376 | and suffer neither hunger nor thirst
and can withstand a mighty battle
if those within dared
sally forth to meet us.
| 2380 | We'll send twenty knights
prepared to joust before the gate.
The knight who is enjoying
his sweet friend Blancheflor's company
| 2384 | will want to prove himself
against greater odds than he should
and will be captured or killed,
because the enfeebled knights
| 2388 | will provide him little aid.
The twenty will do nothing
but divert them
until we can surprise them
| 2392 | by attacking up this valley
and circling their flank."

—"Upon my word," said Clamadeu,
"I fully approve this plan of yours.
| 2396 | We have here a select company:
four hundred fully armed knights
and a thousand well-equipped foot soldiers;
it will be like capturing a troop of dead men."
| 2400 | Clamadeu sent twenty knights
before the castle gate
with pennons and banners
of every shape and form
| 2404 | unfurled to the wind.
When the castle's defenders saw them,
they opened the gates wide
at the youth's request,
| 2408 | and before them all he rode forth
to do battle with the knights.
With boldness, strength, and courage
he attacked the whole troop of them.
| 2412 | Those he struck did not find
him to be an apprentice at arms.
That day his lance's tip
was felt in many a bowel.
| 2416 | One he pierced in the chest, another in the breast,
one had his arm broken, another his shoulder blade;
this one he killed, that one he struck down,
this one he unhorsed, that one he captured.
| 2420 | The prisoners and horses he gave
to those of his companions who needed them.
Then they saw Clamadeu's main force
advancing up the valley—
| 2424 | four hundred fully armed knights
to support the thousand foot soldiers,
who occupied a large portion
of the battlefield near the open gate.
| 2428 | The attackers beheld the great slaughter
of their men by the young knight
and charged straight for the gate
in confusion and disarray;
| 2432 | the defenders held their position
fast up before their gate
and opposed them bravely.
But they were weak and few in number,
| 2436 | while the attacking army
grew in strength as the last columns arrived,

until finally the defenders could hold no
   longer
and had to retreat inside their castle.
2440 From above the gate archers fired
on the swarming mass of men,
which was struggling furiously
to gain entrance to the castle,
2444 until at last a troop of them
managed to force its way in.
But the defenders dropped the
   portcullis
as they passed below,
2448 and it crushed and killed
all those whom it struck in its descent;
Clamadeu had never seen anything
that brought him so much grief,
2452 for the portcullis had killed many
of his men; and he, locked without,
was now powerless to move,
for a hastily conceived assault
2456 would have been wasted effort.
And his mentor, who counseled him,
said: "My lord, it is no surprise
when misfortune strikes a noble man:
2460 good and evil fortune are distributed
according to the will of God.
You've lost, that's all there is to it,
but there's no saint without his feast
   day.
2464 The storm has tested you,
your troops are reduced
and the defenders have won,
but rest assured that they'll lose yet.
2468 You may pluck out both my eyes
if they hold out for two days more.
The keep and castle will be yours,
and they'll all beg for your mercy.
2472 If you can remain here
just for today and tomorrow,
the castle will be in your hands;
even the maiden who has refused you
2476 for so long will beg you
in God's name to deign to have her."
Then those who had brought tents
and pavilions had them pitched,
2480 and the others camped out
and made whatever arrangements they
   could.
Those within the castle
disarmed the knights they had captured.
2484 They did not lock up their prisoners in
   irons
or in dungeons, but only had them swear
on their word as knights
not to attempt to escape
2488 nor ever seek to do them harm.
So this was how they settled matters.
   That very day a ship,
heavily laden with wheat and filled
2492 with other provisions had been driven
across the waters by a powerful storm;
it was God's will that it come
whole and undamaged to the foot of the
   castle.
2496 When they saw it, those within the
   walls
sent down to inquire of the sailors
who they were and what they had come
   to seek.
The envoys from the castle
2500 went down at once to the ship
and asked the sailors who they were,
where they had come from, and where
   they were going.
And they replied: "We are merchants
2504 carrying provisions to sell.
We have plenty of bread, wine,
salt pork, cattle and pigs
for slaughter, if you need any."
2508 The townspeople exclaimed: "Blessed
be God who gave the wind its power
to bring you sailing in our direction,
and may you be most welcome!
2512 Haul forth, for we'll buy everything
at whatever price you set;
come quickly to receive your payment,
for you'll be hard put
2516 to receive and count
the bars of gold and silver
that we'll give you for the wheat;
and for the wine and meat
2520 you'll have a cartful of precious metal
and more, if need be."
Both the buyers and the sellers
did good business on that day.
2524 They saw to the unloading of the ship
and had all the provisions carried up
for the relief of the castle.
   When the inhabitants of the castle
   saw
2528 them arriving with the provisions
you can well believe they were
   overjoyed,
and as quickly as they possibly could
they had a meal prepared.
2532 Clamadeu could now dally

as long as he wanted outside their walls,
for those within had cattle and pigs
and salt bacon aplenty,
2536 and wheat enough to last till the harvest.
The cooks were not idle;
the boys lit the fires
in the kitchens to cook the food.
2540 Now the young knight could tarry
beside his sweetheart at his ease.
She embraced him and he kissed her,
and each brought joy to the other.
2544 The great hall was no longer silent,
but filled with noise and laughter:
everyone was cheered up
by the long-awaited meal,
2548 and the cooks worked until
all those famished people
were able to sit down and eat.
After eating they all arose.
2552 But Clamadeu and his men
were dismayed, for they had heard
of the good fortune of those in the castle,
and many said that they should
2556 depart since there was no longer
any way to starve out the castle
and their siege was pointless.
But Clamadeu, livid with rage,
2560 without consulting anyone
sent a messenger to the castle
to inform the Red Knight
that until noon tomorrow
2564 he could find him alone on the plain
readied for single combat, if he dared.
When the maiden heard this challenge
delivered to her lover,
2568 she was saddened and distressed;
and when the knight sent back word
that since Clamadeu had requested
the battle, he would have it no matter what,
2572 the maiden's sorrow was
aggravated and increased;
but I do not believe he would desist
for any sorrow she might feel.
2576 Everyone in the castle begged him
not to do battle with Clamadeu,
whom no knight had ever before
defeated in single combat.
2580 "My lords, you'll do well
to hold your peace," said the youth,
"for nothing in this world
nor any man's pleas will stop me."

2584 Thus he cut short the discussion,
for they dared oppose him no longer;
they went instead to bed and rested
until the sun rose the next morning.
2588 Yet they were all filled with sadness,
unable as they were to find words
to change their young lord's mind.
All night long his sweetheart
2592 begged him not to go
do battle, but to stay in peace,
for Clamadeu and his men
were no longer any threat to them.
2596 But all her pleadings were in vain,
and that is a strange thing,
for there was much sweetness
in her blandishments,
2600 since with every word she kissed him
so sweetly and softly
that she slipped the key
of love into the lock of his heart.
2604 Yet she was totally incapable
of persuading him
not to enjoin battle;
instead, he called for his arms.
2608 The squire to whom he had entrusted them
brought them as quickly as he could.
As they armed him,
men and women alike were filled with grief;
2612 he commended them all
to the King of Kings,
then mounted the Norwegian steed
that had been brought forward for him.
2616 He did not remain long among them,
but set forth at once
and left them to their grief.
When Clamadeu saw him coming,
2620 about to do battle against him,
he was so filled with foolish presumption
that he assumed he would knock him
from his saddle in an instant.
2624 The heath was fair and level
and there were but the two of them,
for Clamadeu had dismissed
and sent away all his people.
2628 Each combatant had fixed his lance
in the support before his saddle-bow,
and they charged one another
without challenge or warning.
2632 Each knight had a sharp ashen lance,

strong and yet easy to handle,
and their horses charged full speed.
The two knights were powerful
2636 and harbored a mortal hatred for one another:
when they struck, their shield-boards cracked, their lances splintered,
and they drove each other to the ground;
2640 but both leapt quickly to their feet,
hurried again to the attack,
and fought for a long while
on equal terms with their swords.
2644 I could tell you all about it
if I set myself to do so,
but I do not want to waste my efforts,
since one word is as good as twenty.
2648 In the end Clamadeu was compelled
in spite of himself to beg for mercy
and to grant the youth everything he asked,
just as his seneschal had done;
2652 but nothing could compel him
to accept imprisonment in Biaurepaire
any more than had his seneschal,
nor would he go to the gentleman's
2656 magnificently situated castle
for all the riches of Rome.
But he was quite ready to swear
to constitute himself a prisoner
2660 of King Arthur and to carry
to the maiden whom Kay had insolently struck
the young knight's message:
that he intended to avenge her,
2664 no matter whom it might displease,
if God granted him the strength to do so.
Afterwards he had Clamadeu swear
that before dawn the next day
2668 all those whom he had imprisoned
in his dungeons would be set free;
that so long as he lived,
if any army lay siege to Biaurepaire,
2672 he would come to its relief, if he could;
and that the damsel would never again
be troubled by him or by his men.
Thus defeated, Clamadeu returned
2676 to his own land; and when he arrived there
he ordered that all the prisoners
be released to return
unimpeded to their lands.

2680 No sooner had he given the order
than it was carried out:
the prisoners came forth at once
and left that land
2684 with all their belongings,
for nothing was held back.
Clamadeu set off alone
in another direction.
2688 In those days it was the custom—
as we find it written in the annals—
that a knight had to render himself
prisoner with all his equipment
2692 just as he left the combat
where he had been defeated,
without removing
or putting on anything.
2696 Clamadeu in just this way
set off after Anguingueron,
who was headed for Disnadaron,
where King Arthur was to hold court.
2700 Back in the castle of Biaurepaire
there was great rejoicing
upon the return of those
who had spent years in cruel confinement.
2704 The great hall and the knights' quarters
were frenzied with excitement;
the bells of all the chapels
and churches pealed joyfully,
2708 and every monk and nun
gave prayerful thanks to God.
Men and women danced rounds
through every street and square.
2712 Throughout the whole town people rejoiced
that they were no longer under siege or attack.
Meanwhile Anguingueron pursued
his route, followed by Clamadeu,
2716 who slept in the same lodgings as his seneschal
exactly three nights later.
He was able to follow his tracks
all the way to Disnadaron in Wales,
2720 where King Arthur was holding
high court in his halls.
They saw Clamadeu approaching,
still in his battle armor as custom required,
2724 and he was recognized by Anguingueron,
who had already recounted and delivered

his message upon his arrival
at court the other night,
2728 and who was being retained there
for the kings's household and council.
He saw his lord covered with
red blood, yet recognized him
2732 and shouted out at once:
"My lords, my lords, behold this wonder!
Believe me when I tell you that the knight
with the red armor has sent
2736 this knight you see before you.
He's defeated him, I'm certain of this,
because I see him covered in blood.
I can see the blood from here
2740 and I recognize the knight, too,
for he is my lord and I, his man.
He is called Clamadeu of the Isles
and I thought him to be
2744 a knight without peer
in all the empire of Rome.
Yet many a good man has his misfortunes."
So spoke Anguingueron
2748 as Clamadeu was approaching,
and the two ran to greet one another
and met in the center of the courtyard.
It was at Pentecost,
2752 and the queen was seated
beside King Arthur at the head of the dais.
There were counts and dukes and kings,
and many queens and countesses;
2756 and it was the moment
after all the Masses had been celebrated
and the ladies and knights had returned from church.
Kay strode to the center of the hall
2760 without his mantle, holding
in his right hand a staff;
he had a cap of fine cloth
over his blond hair,
2764 which had been plaited into a braid—
there was no more handsome knight in the world,
but his beauty and prowess
were spoiled by his evil tongue.
2768 His cloak was of a colorful
and expensive silken material;
he wore an embroidered belt
whose buckle and links were
2772 all of gold—I recall it well,
for the story bears witness to it.
Everyone stepped aside
as he strode through the hall;
2776 they all feared his evil words
and malicious tongue and made way for him:
a man is a fool not to fear
public slander,
2780 whether it is spoken in jest or earnest.
Everyone within the hall was so afraid of
Kay's malicious words
that no one spoke to him.
2784 While they all watched, he strode
right up to where the king was seated
and said: "My lord, if you please,
it is now time for you to eat."
2788 —"Kay," said the king, "leave me be,
for I swear by the eyes in my head
that I'll not partake of food on such a great feast,
whether I am holding high court or not,
2792 until some worthy news comes my way."
While they were conversing in this fashion,
Clamadeu entered the hall
to deliver himself to imprisonment,
2796 armed still as custom required,
and said: "May God protect and bless
the best king living,
the noblest and worthiest,
2800 as everyone who has heard tell
of his many good works
constantly bears witness!
Now attend to me, fair sir,
2804 for I must deliver my message:
though it is painful to acknowledge,
I admit that I have been sent here
by a knight who defeated me.
2808 I have no choice but to surrender
myself prisoner to you on his behalf.
And if anyone were to ask me
if I know his name,
2812 I would answer no;
but I can tell you
that his armor is red
and he says you gave it to him."
2816 —"Friend, so help you God,"
replied the king, "tell me truly
whether he is in good shape,
happy, healthy, and well."
2820 —"Yes, you may be certain of that,
my good lord," said Clamadeu,

"for he's the best knight
I've ever met.
2824 He told me to speak
to the maiden who laughed for him,
and who was insulted
grievously by Kay's slap;
2828 and he said he would avenge her
if God grants him the strength."
When the jester heard these words,
he leapt for joy and shouted:
2832 "My lord king, so help me God,
the slap will soon be avenged,
and don't think it far-fetched
when I say there's no way
2836 Kay won't have his arm broken
and his collar-bone dislocated."
Kay, upon hearing these words,
thought them utter foolishness,
2840 and you can be sure it was not cowardice
that prevented his challenging the jester,
but respect for the king's honor.
The king shook his head
2844 and said: "Ah! Kay, I'm very distressed
that he's not here with me!
It's your evil tongue that drove him
away, and I grieve for it."
2848 With these words Girflet arose
by order of the king,
along with my lord Yvain, who brings honor
to all who accompany him,
2852 and the king told them
to escort the knight and bring him
into the chambers where the queen's
damsels were making merry,
2856 and Clamadeu bowed low before Arthur.
Those whom the king had commanded
brought him into the chambers
and pointed out the damsel to him,
2860 and he told her the message
just as she wished to hear it,
for she was still suffering
from the slap upon her cheek.
2864 She had recovered fully
from the pain of the slap,
but she had not overcome
or forgotten the insult,
2868 for only a coward overlooks
the shame or insults done him:
pain passes and shame endures
in a sturdy upright person,
2872 but cools and dies in a coward.

After Clamadeu had delivered his message,
the king attached him for life
to his court and household.
2876 Meanwhile, the youth who had fought
Clamadeu for the lands and the maiden—
his beautiful love Blancheflor—
was taking his ease and delight beside her.
2880 Both she and the land
could have been his had he wished
and had his thoughts not been elsewhere,
but he was intent on other things:
2884 he remembered his mother
whom he had seen fall in a faint,
and he wanted to go to see her
more than anything else.
2888 But he dared not take leave of his lady,
for she refused and denied him
and commanded all her people
to beg him to stay.
2892 But all their pleadings were in vain,
except that he did promise them
that if he found his mother alive
he would bring her back with him,
2896 and from that day on he would rule
the land—of this they could be sure.
And if she were dead, he would likewise return.
And so he set off on his way
2900 and promised to return,
leaving his noble sweetheart
very sorrowful and distressed,
and all the others with her.
2904 As he left the town
there was such a procession with him
that it seemed like Ascension Day
or like a Sunday,
2908 for all the monks came along,
attired in silken copes,
and all the nuns in their veils;
everyone was saying to him:
2912 "My lord, since you brought us
out of exile and returned us to our homes,
it is no wonder that we grieve
when you wish to leave us so soon:
2916 our sadness should be overwhelming,
and indeed it could not be greater."

And he said to them: "You must
not weep any longer.
2920 I shall return, with God's help,
so there is no point in weeping.
Don't you think it is proper
for me to go to see my mother,
2924 who was living all alone in a wood
called the Waste Forest?
I shall come back, whether she wishes it
or not: nothing will prevent my return.
2928 If she's alive, I'll make her
a veiled nun in your church;
and if she's dead, you shall sing
a Mass each year for her soul,
2932 so that God might place it with the faithful
in the bosom of holy Abraham.
Reverend monks and you, dear ladies,
have no cause for grief,
2936 for I'll offer generous gifts for the repose
of her soul, if God brings me back."
With that the monks and nuns
and all the others returned to the city,
2940 and he rode on, lance at the ready,
as fully armed as the day he came.
He continued along his way all day
without meeting a living soul,
2944 neither man nor woman,
who could show him the way.
And he prayed unceasingly
to Almighty God, the heavenly Father,
2948 to let him find his mother
alive and healthy,
if it were His will.
And this prayer lasted
2952 until he reached a river
carving its way down a hillside.
He looked at the deep and rushing waters
and dared not attempt to cross.
2956 He said: "Ah! Almighty God,
if I could cross this river
I feel sure I'd find
my mother if she's still alive."
2960 So he rode along the bank
until he neared a large boulder
sitting in the water
and blocking his path.
2964 Then he caught sight of a boat
drifting down-river
with two men in it.
He stopped and waited,
2968 thinking they would eventually
come as far as where he was.
But the two of them stopped
in midstream and stayed perfectly still,
2972 for they had anchored fast.
The man in front was fishing
with a line, baiting his hook
with a little fish,
2976 somewhat larger than a minnow.
The knight, not knowing what to do
or how to cross,
greeted them and inquired:
2980 "Tell me, my lords, is there
a ford or bridge across this river?"
And the one who was fishing replied:
"Not at all, brother, upon my word;
2984 nor is there a boat, I assure you,
larger than the one we're in,
and it wouldn't hold five men.
For twenty leagues upstream or down,
2988 there's no way to get a horse across,
for there's no ferry, bridge, or ford."
—"Then tell me, in God's name,
where I can find lodging."
2992 And he replied: "You'll need
that and more, I believe.
I'll give you lodging tonight.
Go up through that cleft
2996 cut into the rock,
and when you reach the top
you'll see in a valley before you
a house where I live,
3000 near the river and woods."
The young knight climbed
until he reached the top of the hill;
and when he was at the summit
3004 he looked all around him
and saw only sky and earth,
and said: "What have I come for?
Deceit and trickery!
3008 May God bring shame today
on him who sent me here.
He sent me on a wild goose chase
when he told me I'd see
3012 a house when I came up here!
Fisherman, you did me great dishonor
when you told me this,
if you said it out of malice."
3016 But just then he caught sight of
the top of a tower in a valley below him.
From there to Beirut you could not find
a finer or better situated one.

3020	It was square in construction, of dark stone,
	with two turrets flanking it.
	The hall was in front of the keep,
	and galleries in front of the hall.
3024	The youth headed down in that direction,
	exclaiming that the man who had sent
	him there had guided him well.
	So he praised the fisherman
3028	and no longer called him deceitful,
	disloyal, or lying,
	now that he had found lodgings.
	He rode toward the gate,
3032	before which he found
	a lowered drawbridge.
	He crossed over the bridge
	and four squires hastened towards him:
3036	two of them helped him remove his armor,
	the third took charge of his horse
	and gave it hay and oats,
	while the fourth robed him
3040	in a fresh new mantle of scarlet.
	Then they led him toward the galleries
	which, I assure you, were more splendid
	than any that could be sought
3044	or seen from there to Limoges.
	The youth waited in the galleries
	until the lord of the castle sent
	two squires there to summon him,
3048	and he accompanied them
	into the great hall, which was square in shape,
	as long it was wide.
	In the middle of the hall he saw
3052	a handsome nobleman with graying hair
	seated upon a bed.
	His head was covered
	by a cap of sable, black as mulberry,
3056	with a purple peak,
	and his robe was of the same material.
	He was leaning on his elbow
	before a very large fire
3060	of dry logs, flaming bright
	between four columns.
	Four hundred men could
	easily sit around that fire,
3064	and each would have a comfortable spot.
	A tall, thick, and broad
	brass chimney was supported
	on those strong columns.
3068	The two squires who were escorting his guest
	came before their lord,
	flanking him on either side.
	When the lord saw him approaching
3072	he greeted him at once,
	and said: "Friend, don't be offended
	if I don't rise to welcome you,
	for it is not easy for me to do so."
3076	—"In God's name, sir," he replied,
	"say no more, I am not at all offended,
	as God gives me health and happiness."
	To do his guest honor, the gentleman
3080	rose as much as he was able,
	and said: "Friend, come over here
	and don't be frightened of me;
	sit down confidently
3084	at my side, for so I command you."
	The youth sat down beside him
	and the nobleman continued: "Friend,
	where did you come from today?"
3088	—"Sir," he said, "this morning I left
	Biaurepaire, so it is called."
	—"So help me God," said the nobleman,
	"you've ridden a great distance today,
3092	You must have set off this morning
	before the watchman sounded the dawn."
	—"No," said the youth, "I assure you
	that the hour of prime had already been sounded."
3096	As they were conversing in this way,
	a squire entered by the door.
	He was carrying a sword
	hanging by straps from his neck;
3100	he handed it to the noble lord,
	who unsheathed it halfway
	and saw clearly where it had been made,
	for it was engraved upon the blade;
3104	he also saw that it was made
	of such good steel
	that it could not be broken
	except in a single perilous circumstance
3108	known only to him
	who had forged and tempered it.
	The squire who had brought it
	said: "My lord, the blond maiden,
3112	your beautiful niece,
	sent you this gift;
	you've never beheld a finer sword,
	in its length and weight, than this one here.
3116	You may bestow it upon whomever you choose,

but my lady would be most pleased
if it were given to someone
who would use it well,
3120 for the man who forged it
made only three, and he will die
before being able to make
another sword after this one."
3124 Immediately the lord invested the stranger
among them with the sword
by placing over his shoulders its straps,
a great treasure in themselves.
3128 The sword's pommel was of gold,
the best from Arabia or Greece;
its scabbard was of Venetian goldsmith's art.
In all its splendor
3132 the lord gave it to him
and said: "Dear brother, this sword
was ordained and destined for you,
and I am eager for you to have it.
3136 Put it on now and draw it."
He thanked him
and strapped it on loosely,
then drew it shining from its scabbard;
3140 after he had held it a moment
he replaced it in its scabbard.
I assure you it was magnificent
by his side and better in his grip,
3144 and it was clear that in time of need
he would wield it bravely.
Behind him he saw squires
standing about the blazing fire:
3148 he caught sight of the one in charge
of his armor and handed him
the sword to keep.
Then he sat down again beside the lord,
3152 who paid him every honor.
Within that hall the light
from the burning candles was as bright
as one could find in any castle.
3156 As they were speaking of one thing and another,
a squire came forth from a chamber
gripping a white lance
by the middle of its shaft;
3160 he passed between the fire
and those seated upon the bed,
and everyone in the hall saw
the white lance with its white point,
3164 from whose tip there issued
a drop a blood,
and this red drop flowed
down to the squire's hand.
3168 The youth who had come there that night
observed this marvel,
but refrained from asking
how it came about,
3172 for he recalled the admonishment given
by the gentleman who had knighted him,
who taught and instructed him
not to talk too much;
3176 he was afraid that if he asked
they would consider him uncouth,
and so he did not ask.
Then two other squires entered
3180 holding in their hands candelabra
of pure gold, crafted with enamel inlays.
The young men carrying the candelabra
were extremely handsome.
3184 In each of the candelabra
were at least ten candles burning.
A maiden accompanying
the two young men was carrying
3188 a grail in her two hands;
she was beautiful, noble, and richly attired.
After she had entered the hall
carrying the grail,
3192 the room was so brightly illuminated
that the candles lost
their brilliance like stars
when the sun rises, or the moon.
3196 After her came another maiden,
carrying a silver carving platter.
The grail, which preceded,
Was of fine pure gold;
3200 set in the grail were
precious stones of every kind,
the best and costliest
to be found in earth or sea:
3204 the grail's stones were finer
than any others in the world, beyond a doubt.
The grail passed by like the lance;
they passed before the bed
3208 and into another chamber.
The young knight watched them pass by
but did not dare ask
who was served from the grail,
3212 for in his heart he always kept
the wise gentleman's advice.
Yet I fear that this may cause him harm,
for I have heard it said

3216	that at times it is just as wrong
	to keep too silent as to talk too much.
	Whether for good or for ill
	he did not ask or inquire anything of them.
3220	The lord of the castle ordered his squire
	to bring water and prepare the tablecloths.
	Those whose duty it was
	did these things as they were accustomed.
3224	The lord and his young guest washed
	their hands in warm water,
	and two squires carried in
	a broad ivory table:
3228	as the story relates,
	it was all of a single piece.
	They held it a moment
	before their lord and the youth,
3232	until two other squires came
	bearing two trestles.
	The wood of the supports
	had two excellent qualities:
3236	the trestles would last forever
	since they were of ebony,
	a wood no one need fear
	would ever rot or burn,
3240	for ebony would do neither.
	The table was placed upon these
	supports, with the tablecloth over it.
	What could I say about the cloth?
3244	No pope, cardinal, or papal legate
	ever ate off one so white.
	The first course was a haunch
	of venison cooked in its fat with hot pepper.
3248	Claret and dry wines were not lacking,
	easy to sip from golden goblets.
	Before them a squire carved
	the haunch of peppered venison
3252	which he had brought within his reach
	upon the silver carving platter,
	and he set the pieces before them
	on whole loaves of flat bread.
3256	Meanwhile the grail
	passed again before them,
	and again the youth did not ask
	who was served from the grail.
3260	He held back because the nobleman
	had so gently warned him
	not to talk too much, and he
	bore this warning constantly to heart.
3264	But he kept more silent than he should have,
	because with each course that was served
	he saw the grail pass by
	before him completely uncovered.
3268	But he did not learn who was served from it,
	though he wanted to know,
	and said to himself that he would be sure
	to ask one of the court squires
3272	before he left there,
	but he would wait until morning
	while he was taking leave of the lord
	and all the rest of his household.
3276	So the question was put off,
	and he set his mind to drinking and eating.
	The wine and food were delicious
	and agreeable, and were served
3280	at table in generous portions.
	The meal was fine and good:
	the nobleman was served that evening
	with food fit for a king,
3284	count or emperor,
	and the young knight with him.
	After the meal the two
	stayed a long while in conversation.
3288	As squires were preparing the beds,
	baskets of all the finest fruits
	were served them:
	dates, figs and nutmeg,
3292	cloves and pomegranates,
	and electuaries for dessert,
	with Alexandrian gingerbread,
	pliris and arcoticum
3296	resontif and stomaticum.
	Afterwards they had a variety of drinks:
	sweet wine without honey or pepper,
	good mulberry wine, and clear syrup.
3300	The youth was in wonder at all this,
	for he had never experienced anything like it;
	and the nobleman said to him: "Friend, now it is time for bed.
3304	Don't be offended if I leave you
	to go into my own chambers to sleep;
	and whenever you are ready
	you may lie down out here.
3308	I have no strength in my body
	and will have to be carried."
	Four strong and nimble servants
	promptly came forth from a chamber,
3312	seized by its four corners the coverlet

that was spread over the bed
on which the nobleman was lying,
and carried it to where they were ordered.
3316 Other squires remained with
the youth to serve him,
and saw to his every need.
When he requested, they removed
3320 his shoes and clothing and bedded
him down in fine white linen sheets.
And he slept until morning,
when dawn had broken
3324 and the household was awake.
But he saw no one there
when he looked around,
and so he had to arise alone,
3328 although it bothered him to do so.
Since he saw he had no choice,
he arose, for there was nothing else to do,
and pulled on his shoes without help;
3332 then he went to don his armor,
which he found at the head of the dais,
where it had been left for him.
After having armed himself fully,
3336 he went toward the doors of chambers
he had seen open the night before;
but his steps were wasted,
for he found them tightly closed.
3340 He shouted and knocked for a long while:
no one opened or gave a word in answer.
After having shouted a good deal,
he tried the door to the great hall:
3344 finding it open,
he went down the steps,
where he discovered his horse saddled
and saw his lance and shield
3348 leaning against the wall.
He mounted and rode all about,
but he found none of the servants
and saw no squire or serving boy.
3352 So he went straight to the gate,
where he found the drawbridge lowered;
it had been left like that
so that nothing might prevent him
3356 from crossing over it unimpeded
whenever he came there.
When he found the bridge lowered,
he thought perhaps the squires
3360 had gone into the forest
to check the traps and snares.

He made up his mind
to set off at once after them
3364 to see whether any of them would explain
to him why the lance bled
(if it were possible for him to know),
and tell him where the grail was carried.
3368 Then he rode off through the gate,
but before he had crossed the bridge
he felt it drawing up under
the hooves of his horse;
3372 but the horse made a great leap,
and if he had not done so
both horse and rider
would have come to grief.
3376 The youth turned around
to see what had happened
and saw that the drawbridge had been raised;
he shouted out, but no one answered.
3380 "Say there," he said, "whoever raised
the bridge, speak to me!
Where are you that I can't see you?
Come forward where I can see you
3384 and ask you about something
I want to know."
But he wasted his time shouting like this,
for no one would reply.
3388 Then he headed for the forest
and found a path on which
he discovered fresh hoofprints
of horses recently passed by.
3392 "This makes me think," he said to himself,
"that those I'm seeking passed this way."
He rode swiftly through the forest
following the tracks as far as they went,
3396 until he saw by chance
a maiden beneath an oak tree
crying, weeping, and lamenting
like a woman in distress:
3400 "Wretched me!" she exclaimed,
"I was born in an evil hour!
Cursed be the hour I was begotten
and the day I was born,
3404 for I've never before been made
so miserable by anything!
So help me God, I shouldn't have
to hold my dead lover in my arms;
3408 it would have been far better
if he were alive and I were dead!

Why did Death, which tortures me,
take his soul instead of mine?
3412 When I behold the one I most love
lying dead, then what is life to me?
With him dead, indeed I have
no interest in my life or body.
3416 So come, Death, and take my soul,
and let it be a servant and companion
to his, if he'll deign to accept it."
    Her grief was caused
3420 by a knight she held in her arms,
whose head had been cut off.
The youth, after catching sight of her,
rode right up to where she sat.
3424 As he came before her he greeted her
and she, with head still lowered and
    without
ceasing her lament, returned his
    salutation.
And the youth asked her:
3428 "My lady, who has slain
this knight lying in your lap?"
—"Dear sir," said the maiden,
"a knight killed him just this morning.
3432 But your appearing here
is truly surprising:
as God is my witness, they say
that one could ride
3436 for twenty-five leagues in the
    direction
from which you're coming
without finding a good,
honest, and proper lodging place,
3440 yet your horse's belly
is so full and his coat so shining,
that he couldn't appear more satisfied
or his coat smoother
3444 had he been washed and combed
and given a bed of hay and oats.
And it appears to me
that you yourself have had
3448 a comfortable and restful night."
—"Upon my word," he said, "I was
as comfortable as I could possibly be,
and if it shows, it's only right,
3452 for if you were to shout out
loudly from here where we are,
it could be clearly heard
there where I slept last night.
3456 You must not know this country well
or have traveled through it all,
for without a doubt I had
the best lodgings I've ever enjoyed."

3460 —"Ah, my lord! Did you sleep then
in the castle of the noble Fisher King?"
—"Maiden, by our Lord and Savior,
I don't know if he is a fisherman or a
    king,
3464 but he is most noble and courteous.
I can tell you no more,
except that late last night I came upon
two men sitting in a boat
3468 rowing slowly along.
One of the men was rowing
while the other was fishing with a hook,
and this latter showed me the way to his
    house
3472 last night and gave me lodging."
And the maiden said: "Dear sir,
I can assure you that he is a king,
but he was wounded and maimed
3476 in the course of a battle
so that he can no longer manage alone,
for he was struck by a javelin
through both thighs,
3480 and is still in so much pain
that he cannot ride a horse.
Whenever he wants to relax
or to go out to enjoy himself
3484 he has himself put in a boat
and goes fishing with a hook:
this is why he's called the Fisher King.
And he relaxes in this way
3488 because he cannot tolerate the pain
of any other diversion:
he cannot hunt for game or fish,
but he has his hunters,
3492 his archers, and his gamesmen
who hunt his forests for him.
That is why he likes to stay
in this hidden retreat,
3496 for there's no retreat in the world
more suited to his needs,
and he has had a mansion built
that is worthy of a noble king."
3500 —"My lady," he said, "upon my word,
what you say is true,
for I was in awe last night
as soon as I was brought before him.
3504 I kept a little distance from him,
and he told me to be seated
beside him and not to consider
him too proud for not rising
3508 to greet me, since he didn't have
the means or strength.
And I went to sit beside him."

3512	—"Indeed he did you great honor to have you sit beside him. And as you were sitting beside him, tell me whether you saw
3516	the lance with the tip that bleeds, though it has neither blood nor veins." "Yes, upon my word, I did see it!" —"And did you ask why
3520	it bled?"—"I never spoke a word." —"So help me God, let me tell you then that you have done ill. And did you see the grail?"
3524	—"Quite clearly."—"Who carried it?" —"A maiden."—"Where did she come from?" —"From a chamber."—"And where did she go?"
3528	—"She entered another chamber." —"Did anyone precede the grail?" —"Yes."—"Who?"—"Only two squires." And what were they holding in their hands?"
3532	—"Candelabra full of candles." "And who came after the grail?" "Another maiden."—"What was she holding?"
3536	—"A small silver carving platter." —"Did you ask the people where they were going in this manner?" —"No question came from my mouth."
3540	—"So help me God, now it's even worse! What is your name, friend?" And the youth, who did not know his name, guessed and said he was called
3544	Perceval the Welshman. Though he didn't know if that were true or not, he spoke the truth without knowing it. And when the damsel heard him,
3548	she stood up before him and said as in anger: "Your name is changed, fair friend!" —"To what?"—"To Perceval the wretched!
3552	Ah, unlucky Perceval, how unfortunate you were when you failed to ask all this, because you would have brought great succor
3556	to the good king who is maimed: he would have totally regained use of his limbs and ruled his lands, and much good would have come of it! But understand this now: much suffering
3560	will come to you and others. And understand this too: it befell you because you sinned against your mother, who died of grief on your account.
3564	I know you better than you do me, because you do not know who I am. I was raised with you for many years in your mother's house;
3568	I am your first cousin and you are mine. I am pained as much because of your misfortune
3572	in failing to have asked what is done with the grail and where it's carried, as I am for your mother's death or the death of this knight,
3576	whom I loved and held dear because he called me his dearest friend and loved me like a good and faithful knight."
3580	—"Ah, cousin," said Perceval, "if what you tell me is true, tell me how you know it." —"I know it," said the damsel,
3584	"as truly as one who saw her buried in the ground." —"May God in His goodness have mercy on her soul!" said Perceval.
3588	"You've brought me terrible news. And since she's buried in the ground, what reason have I to continue on, for I had set off only
3592	because I wished to see her again? I must change my course, and if you wish to come with me, I'd be truly pleased,
3596	for I assure you that this dead knight will no longer bring you aid. The dead to the dead, the living to the living.
	Let us go on, you and I, together. It seems foolish to me for you to watch alone over a corpse;
3600	let us pursue his killer, and I say and swear to you that either he will force me to surrender or I him, if I manage to overtake him."
3604	And the maiden, who could not hold back

the grief she felt in her heart,
said to him: "Dear friend, I can't possibly
go off in your company
3608 or leave my knight
until I have buried him.
If you'll heed my suggestion,
follow that cobbled road over there,
3612 for that is the path taken
by the wicked and boastful knight
who killed my sweet love.
But so help me God, I haven't
3616 told you this because I want
you to go after him,
though I do wish him grief
as much as if it were me he'd killed.
3620 But where did you get that sword
hanging at your left side,
which has never spilled a drop of blood
or been drawn in time of need?
3624 I know well where it was made
and the name of him who forged it.
Be careful, don't trust it,
since it will surely fail you
3628 when you enter the fray
and shatter to pieces."
—"Fair cousin, one of my host's
nieces sent it to him last evening,
3632 and he gave it to me.
I consider it a fine gift,
but if what you've told me is true,
you've given me cause to worry.
3636 Tell me now, if you know:
if it were broken
could it ever be repaired?"
—"Yes, but it would be difficult.
3640 If you knew the way
to the lake beyond Cotouatre,
there you could have it reforged,
retempered, and repaired.
3644 If by chance you go there,
go only to Trabuchet's shop;
he's the smith who made it,
and if he cannot repair it,
3648 it will never be repaired
by any man alive.
Be careful that no one else touches it,
for they could never restore it properly."
3652 —"Indeed, if it were to break,"
said Perceval, "I would regret it dearly."
Then he left and she remained,
for she did not wish to leave the knight
3656 whose death had brought such sorrow
to her heart.

Perceval followed the tracks
he found along the trail
until he overtook a lean and weary
palfrey
3660 shuffling along ahead of him.
The palfrey was so thin and wretched
that Perceval thought
it had fallen into evil hands.
3664 It seemed to be
as overworked and ill-fed
as a horse that's hired out,
which is overtaxed by day
3668 and poorly cared for at night.
Just so did the palfrey appear.
It was so thin that it trembled
as if suffering from glanders;
3672 its mane had all fallen out
and its ears drooped down.
Soon it would only be good as food
for the hounds and mastiffs,
3676 since there was nothing but hide
hanging over its bones.
The lady's saddle on its back
and the bridle on its head
3680 were in the same sorry state.
And riding on it was the most
wretched girl you'd ever seen.
Yet she'd have been fair and noble enough
3684 had she had better fortune,
but she was in such a bad state
that there was not a palm's breadth
of good material in the dress she wore,
3688 and her breasts hung out
through the tears.
The dress was held together here and
   there
with knots and crude stitches,
3692 and her skin looked lacerated as though
it had been torn by lancets,
and it was pocked and burned
by heat and wind and frost.
3696 Her hair was loose and she wore
no hood, so that her face showed,
with many an ugly trace
left by tears rolling
3700 ceaselessly down her cheeks;
they flowed across her breasts
and out over her dress
down to her knees.
3704 Anyone in such affliction
might well have a very heavy heart.
As soon as Perceval saw her
he rode swiftly in her direction,

3708	and she gathered her dress around to cover her flesh. But holes appeared everywhere, for as soon as she covered one up	3760	I sweat with anguish whenever anyone stops or looks at me." —"In truth," said Perceval,
3712	a hundred others opened. Perceval rode up to her in her pale and miserable state, and as he neared	3764	"I was unaware of having wronged you. I assure you I didn't come here to cause you shame or injury, but because my path led in this direction;
3716	he heard her woefully lament her troubles and affliction: "My God, may it not please You to let me live long in this state!	3768	and since I've seen you so miserable, poor, and naked, my heart will not be happy again until I learn the truth:
3720	I've been miserable for so long, I've suffered so many woes, and I've not deserved it! My God, since you know	3772	what adventure has reduced you to this sad and painful state." —"Ah, sir," she said, "have pity! Say no more, just fly from here and leave me in peace!
3724	that I've not deserved any of this, may it please You to send me someone to lift me from this misery, or deliver me Yourself from him	3776	Sin has made you tarry here, but it would be best for you to hurry on!" —"I'd like to know," he replied, "what fear or threat would make
3728	who makes me live in such disgrace. In him I find no mercy, yet I cannot escape him alive and he refuses to kill me.	3780	me flee when no one is pursuing me." —"Sir," she said, "don't be offended, but flee while you still have the chance, before the Haughty Knight of the Heath,
3732	I don't understand why he desires my company in this state, unless he just enjoys my disgrace and misfortune.	3784	who seeks nothing but combat and battle, should catch us here together, for if he found you with me
3736	Even if he had absolute proof that I deserved this misery, still he should have pity on me now that I've suffered so long—	3788	he'd surely kill you on the spot. He becomes so angry when anyone stops me that if he gets back in time he beheads all those
3740	if I were at all pleasing to him. But surely I don't please him when he forces me to follow after him in such misery and shows no concern."	3792	who speak to me (he killed a knight only a short while ago), but first he tells each one why he holds me in such disgrace
3744	Then Perceval, who had overtaken her, said: "Fair one, may God protect you!" When the damsel heard him, she lowered her head and said softly:	3796	and put me in such misery." Even as they were speaking the Haughty Knight came out of the woods charging like a thunderbolt
3748	"Sir, for your words of greeting may your heart have whatever it deserves, though I have no right to say so." And Perceval, blushing	3800	across the sands and dust, shouting: "You will pay for lingering with this girl! Rest assured that your end has come
3752	with shame, replied: "Fair friend, what do you mean? I'm absolutely certain that I never saw you before	3804	for having detained and delayed her a single step. But I won't kill you before I've told you what shame
3756	or did you any harm." —"You have," she said, "and I am so miserable and full of woe that no one should greet me.		

3808	and evil deed she did to cause me
	to make her live in such disgrace.
	Listen now and you'll hear the tale.
	"Recently I went off into the woods
3812	leaving this damsel—
	the only one I ever loved—
	alone in one of my tents;
	then by chance along came
3816	a young Welshman.
	I don't know where he was headed,
	but he managed to force her
	to kiss him, so she told me.
3820	If she lied to me, what harm is there in it?
	But even if he kissed her against her will,
	didn't he take advantage of her afterwards?
	Indeed yes, and no one will ever believe
3824	he kissed her without doing more,
	for one thing leads to another:
	if a man kisses a woman and nothing more,
	when they are all alone together,
3828	I think there's something wrong with him.
	A woman who lets herself be kissed
	easily gives the rest
	if someone insists upon it;
3832	and even if she resists,
	it's a well-known fact
	that a woman wants to win
	every battle but this one:
3836	though she grabs a man by the throat,
	and scratches and bites him till he's nearly dead,
	still she wants to be conquered.
	She puts up a fight, but is eager for it;
3840	she is so afraid to give in
	she wants to be taken by force,
	but then never shows her gratitude.
	Therefore I believe this Welshman lay with her.
3844	And he took from her a ring of mine
	that she wore upon her finger;
	and carried it off, which makes me angry!
	But before that he drank and ate his fill
3848	of a hearty wine and three meat pies
	I had put aside for myself.
	But now my love has a splendid reward, as you can see.
3852	One who makes a mistake must pay for it,
	so it won't happen again.
	You can imagine my anger
	when I returned and learned what had happened.
3856	And I swore, and rightly so,
	that her palfrey would have
	no oats and would not be
	reshod or groomed,
3860	and that she would have no other
	tunic or mantle than what she was wearing then,
	until I had defeated,
	killed and decapitated
3864	the one who'd raped her."
	When Perceval had heard him out,
	he answered point for point:
	"Friend, rest assured
3868	that she has done her penance,
	for I am he who kissed her
	against her will, and she was upset by it.
	And I am he who took the ring from her finger,
3872	but I did no more than that;
	and I swear to you that I ate
	one and a half of the three meat pies,
	and drank as much wine as I pleased:
3876	in this I did nothing foolish.'
	—"By my head," said the Haughty Knight,
	"now I am astounded at you
	for admitting to these things!
3880	You are deserving of death
	since you've truly confessed."
	—"My death is not so near
	as you think," answered Perceval.
3884	Then without another word
	they charged at one another
	and struck with such fury
	that both lances shattered
3888	and the two knights were knocked
	from their saddles to the ground.
	But they leapt immediately to their feet
	drew their shining blades,
3892	and struck mighty blows.
	The battle was long and hard,
	but it seems to me a waste of effort
	to give more details of it,
3896	except to say that they fought
	until the Haughty Knight of the Heath
	admitted defeat and asked for mercy.
	Then Perceval, ever mindful
3900	of the words of the gentleman
	who urged him never to kill

a knight who had begged for mercy,
said: "Knight, upon my word,
3904 I'll never show mercy for you
until you show it for your sweetheart,
for she never deserved
the punishment you inflicted
3908 upon her, this I swear to you."
　　He who loved her more than his own eye
said: "Good sir, I wish to make it
up to her according to your counsel:
3912 whatever you command of me
I'm ready to do.
My heart is sad and darkened
for the suffering I made her bear."
3916 —"Go quickly now," he said,
"to your nearest manor house
and have her bathed leisurely
until she's healed and healthy.
3920 Then make ready and escort her,
dressed in her finest attire,
to King Arthur's court; greet him in my name
and cast yourself upon his mercy,
3924 equipped in your armor just as you are here.
If he asks who sent you,
tell him you were sent by
the one he made a Red Knight
3928 on the advice and counsel
of my lord Kay the seneschal.
And you must acknowledge to the court
the sufferings and hardships
3932 you forced the damsel to endure;
announce it to all present
so that everyone will hear,
even the queen and her maidens—
3936 and there are many beautiful ones with her.
But I prize one above all others, who,
because she favored me with her laughter,
was given such a slap by Kay
3940 that she was quite stunned.
I command you to seek her out
and tell her on my behalf
that I'll never under any circumstances
3944 attend any court held by King Arthur
until I have avenged the insult
in a way to make her joyful and happy."
The Haughty Knight said he would go there
3948 willingly and tell her

everything Perceval had enjoined him,
delaying only long enough
to let his sweetheart recover
3952 and then be clothed
in an appropriate fashion.
Then he kindly offered to take
Perceval himself somewhere to recover,
3956 in order to heal and dress
his injuries and wounds.
"Go now, and may good fortune be with you,"
said Perceval. "Watch over her well,
3960 for I'll seek shelter elsewhere."
　　No further words were spoken;
both Perceval and the Haughty Knight
set off without further ado.
3964 That evening the knight had his lady
bathed and richly attired,
and he gave her such tender care
that her beauty was soon restored.
3968 Afterwards they rode together
straight to Caerleon
where King Arthur was holding court:
it was a small gathering,
3972 for there were only
three thousand worthy knights in attendance.
Before them all the Haughty Knight,
who was escorting his damsel,
3976 came forward to surrender himself
to King Arthur, and said when he stood
before him: "Sire, I am your prisoner
to do with as you please,
3980 and this is very right and proper,
for so I was commanded
by the youth who requested
the red armor from you, and received it."
3984 As soon as the king heard this,
he knew precisely what he meant:
"Remove your armor, good sir," he said.
"May he who offered you as a gift to me
3988 have joy and good fortune,
and may you feel welcome.
For his sake you will be held dear
and honored in my dwelling."
3992 —"Sire, I have something else to say
before I remove my armor.
I would like to request
that the queen and her maidens
3996 come forward to hear this news
I have brought you,

for I'll not give my message
until she who was struck
4000 upon the cheek for having
laughed a single time comes forward—
she did no more wrong than this."
Then he spoke no more,
4004 and the king understood that he must
summon the queen into his presence.
He sent for her and she came,
along with all her maidens,
4008 hand in hand and two by two.
 When the queen was seated
beside her lord King Arthur,
the Haughty Knight of the Heath
4012 addressed her: "My lady, a knight
who defeated me in single combat
and whom I highly esteem sends you
    greetings.
I don't know what more to tell about
    him,
4016 except that he sends you my sweetheart,
this maiden here beside me."
 —"Friend, I am most grateful to him,"
said the queen. And he related to her
4020 all the wickedness and shame
he had made his lady endure for so long,
and the sufferings she had undergone,
and why he had done this to her:
4024 he told her everything, hiding nothing.
Afterwards they pointed out to him
the maiden the seneschal Kay had struck,
and he said to her: "He who sent me here
4028 commanded me, fair maiden,
to greet you in his name
and not to move one foot
until I've told you
4032 that he swears in the name of God
never on any occasion to come
to a court held by King Arthur
until he has avenged you
4036 for the slap and insult
you suffered on his account."
 As soon as the jester heard this,
he leapt to his feet and exclaimed:
4040 "Kay, may God bless me!
You'll really pay for it now, Kay,
and the time is fast approaching!"
 After the jester, the king spoke to
    Kay:
4044 "Ah, sir Kay! How courteous you were
in mocking the young knight!
Your mockery has driven him away
and I never expect to see him again."

4048 Then the king had his knight prisoner
sit down before him;
he freed him from his sentence
and then had him disarm.
4052 My lord Gawain, who was seated
at the king's right hand, asked:
"In God's name, sire, who can it be
who defeated such a great knight
4056 as this in single combat?
In all the Isles of the Sea
I've never seen or known
or heard tell of any knight
4060 who could rival this knight here
in chivalry and feats of arms."
 —"Dear nephew," said the king,
"I don't know him, though I've seen
    him before.
4064 When I saw him, I thought so little of
    him
that I didn't even inquire who he was.
And he told me
to make him a knight immediately.
4068 I saw that he was handsome and
    agreeable,
so I said: 'Gladly, brother.
But dismount for a while
until someone can bring you
4072 a suit of golden armor.'
But he said he wouldn't accept it
and would never dismount
until he had red armor.
4076 And he said another amazing thing:
that he didn't want any armor
except that worn by the knight
who had carried off my golden goblet.
4080 And Kay, who was surly then
and still is and always will be,
and who never has anything pleasant to
    say,
said to him: 'Brother, the king
4084 makes you a gift of that armor,
so you should go claim it at once!'
Not understanding the sarcasm,
the young knight took it in earnest
4088 and pursued and killed the knight
with a javelin he threw at him.
I don't know how the mêlée
and combat started,
4092 except that the Red Knight
from the forest of Quinquercy
struck the youth, I don't know why,
with his lance in a contemptuous
    manner,

4096	and the youth struck him
	right through the eye with his javelin
	and killed him and took his armor.
	Since that day he has served me so well
4100	that I swear by St David,
	whom they worship and pray to in Wales,
	that I'll not sleep two consecutive nights
	in the same hall or chamber
4104	until I see him,
	if he's alive on land or sea.
	I'll set off at once in search of him."
	Once the king had made this oath,
4108	they were all persuaded
	there was nothing to do but go.
	You should have seen all the bed clothes,
	coverlets, and pillows being packed,
4112	trunks filled, packhorses loaded,
	the many carts and wagons piled high,
	for they did not skimp on the number of
	tents, pavilions, and shelters:
4116	a wise and learned clerk
	could not write down in a day
	all the equipment and provisions
	that were readied instantly.
4120	The king set forth from Caerleon
	as if he were going off to war,
	followed by all his barons;
	and the queen, in equal pomp
4124	and dignity, brought all her maidens,
	leaving not one behind.
	That evening they pitched camp
	in a meadow beside a forest.
4128	Before morning it snowed heavily,
	for it was very cold in the land.
	Perceval arose at dawn
	as was his custom
4132	to go off in search
	of chivalric adventures,
	and he came straight into
	the frozen, snow-covered meadow
4136	where the king's retinue was camped.
	But before he reached the tents,
	a flock of geese that had been
	blinded by the snow flew over.
4140	He heard and caught sight of them,
	for they had been scared up
	by a falcon that had swooped down upon them at full speed,
4144	until it found one that had become

	separated from the flock;
	it attacked and struck her so hard
	that she fell to the earth;
4148	but since it was very early, the falcon flew off
	without seizing his prey.
	Perceval began to spur his steed
	to where he had observed the attack:
4152	the goose had been wounded in the neck
	and bled three drops of blood,
	which spread upon the white snow
	with a natural color.
4156	The goose was not hurt badly enough
	to remain lying on the ground
	until Perceval reached there,
	and it had flown away before he came.
4160	When Perceval saw the snow disturbed
	where the goose had lain,
	and the blood still visible,
	he rested upon his lance
4164	to behold this sight,
	for the blood mingled with the snow
	resembled the rosy blush
	of his lady's cheeks.
4168	He became lost in contemplation:
	the red tone of his lady's cheeks
	in her white face were like
	the three drops of blood
4172	against the whiteness of the snow.
	As he gazed upon this sight,
	it pleased him so that he felt as if
	he were beholding the fresh color
4176	of his fair lady's face.
	Perceval mused upon the drops
	throughout the dawn hours and spent
	so much time that when the squires
4180	came out of their tents and saw him there,
	they thought he was sleeping.
	While King Arthur was still
	lying asleep in his tent,
4184	the squires encountered
	before the king's pavilion Sagremor,
	who, because of his hot temper,
	was called Sagremor the Unruly.
4188	"Say there," he said, "don't hide it from me:
	why have you come here in such a hurry?"
	—"Sir," they replied, outside this camp
	we came upon a knight
4192	sleeping upon his warhorse."

—"Is he armed?"—"In faith, yes."
—"I'll go speak to him," he said,
"and bring him to court."

4196 Sagremor ran immediately
to the king's tent and awakened him.
"My lord," he said, "there on the heath
is a knight asleep on his horse."

4200 The king ordered him to be off,
and urged and commanded him
to bring back the knight without fail."
    Sagremor immediately ordered

4204 that his horse be brought forth,
and called for his armor.
All was done as soon as he commanded,
and he had himself well armed at once.

4208 In full armor he left camp
and rode until he came to the knight.
"Sir," said, "you must come
to court." But Perceval did not move

4212 and acted as if he had not heard him.
Sagremor spoke again, but still
there was no reply; so he became angry
and said: "By the Apostle Peter,

4216 you'll come now whether you like it or not!
I'm sorry I asked you
politely, for I can tell
that I wasted my words."

4220 Then he unfurled the pennon
that was rolled around his lance;
his horse started beneath him
and took its position to one side;

4224 and Sagremor told the knight to stand ready,
for he would strike him if he failed
to defend himself. Perceval looked up
and saw him charging full speed;

4228 he ceased his musings
and spurred against him.
When the two met,
Sagremor's lance shattered

4232 while Perceval's stayed straight and whole,
striking him with such might
that he was brought down in the middle of the field.
His horse promptly fled

4236 towards the tents with its head in the air.
Those who were now stirring
within the tents saw the horse,
and many among them were distressed;

4240 and Kay, who could never
refrain from speaking ill,
said sardonically to the king: "Fair sir,
see how Sagremor's returning!

4244 He's got the knight by the bridle
and is bringing him back against his will!"
—"Kay," said the king, "it's not good
for you to mock gentlemen in this manner.

4248 Go yourself, so we can see
how you'd do better than he."
—"My lord," said Kay, "I'm very happy
that you are pleased for me to go,

4252 since I'll certainly force him
to return with me, whether he likes it or not,
and I'll make him tell us his name."
    Then he had himself carefully armed.

4256 When he was armed, he mounted and rode
towards the knight, who was so intent
upon the three drops he was contemplating
that he was heedless of anything else.

4260 And he shouted to him from far off,
"Vassal, vassal, come to the king!
You'll come, upon my word,
or you'll pay for it dearly!"

4264 When Perceval heard this threat,
he turned his horse's head
and urged it to a full gallop
with his steel spurs.

4268 Each was eager for the victory,
so they met with unrestrained force.
Kay struck him, putting
all his strength behind the blow,

4272 and his lance split like bark.
Perceval did not flinch,
but struck upon the boss of Kay's shield;
he threw him down hard upon a rock,

4276 dislocating his collar-bone
and breaking the bone of his right arm
between the shoulder-blade and elbow
as if it had been a dry twig—

4280 just as the jester
had often foretold would happen:
the jester's prophecy was perfectly true.
Kay fainted from the pain

4284 and his fleeing horse trotted
straight for the tents.
The Britons saw the horse
returning without the seneschal;

4288 squires rushed to their horses,

and knights and ladies began to stir:
when they found the seneschal in a faint
they all thought he was dead.
4292 Then all the lords and ladies began
to mourn for him most deeply.
Perceval was once again resting on his lance
and contemplating the three drops.
4296 But the king was very upset
by the wounds his seneschal had received:
he was sad and angry,
until they told him not to worry
4300 because Kay would recover fully
if they found him a healer
who knew how to relocate his collar-bone
and set a broken arm.
4304 The king, who had a tender feeling
for Kay and cherished him in his heart,
sent him a most learnèd healer
and three maidens trained by him,
4308 who set his collar-bone
and bound his arm
so the broken bones would knit together.
Then they carried him to the king's tent
4312 and consoled the sovereign,
assuring him that Kay would fully recover
and that he need not worry about a thing.
My lord Gawain said to Arthur:
4316 "Sire, as God is my witness,
you are well aware
and have always said
that it is not right
4320 for a knight to interrupt another's thoughts, whatever they might be,
as these two knights have done.
And whether they were wrong in this,
4324 I don't know, but it is certain
that they have come to grief.
The knight was contemplating
some loss he had suffered,
4328 or perhaps his lady has been carried off
and he is sad and dispirited.
But if it is your pleasure,
I'll go to watch how he behaves,
4332 and if I find at some point
that he's abandoned his reverie,
I'll bid and urge him
to come to you here."

4336 On hearing these words Kay grew angry
and said: "Ha! my lord Gawain,
so you'll lead the knight here by the reins,
whether he likes it or not!
4340 It's all fine and good if he'll let you,
and you can get away without a fight.
You've captured many a knight in just this way!
When the knight's worn out
4344 and has had enough of fighting,
that's when the brave fighter
asks permission to go after him!
Gawain, a hundred curses upon my neck
4348 if you're not so crazy
that one can learn a lot from you!
You know all kinds of
flattering and polished words to use;
4352 you'll trick the king with
deceitful and arrogant talk:
a curse upon anyone who'd believe you,
for you don't fool me!
4356 You could win this fight
in a silken tunic:
you won't even have to draw
your sword or break a lance.
4360 You're so conceited
that if your tongue is able
to say 'Sire, may God bless you
and give you good health and long life,'
4364 he'll do whatever you want.
I'm not telling you anything you don't know,
for you can mollify him
just like stroking a cat,
4368 and everyone will say: 'See how bravely
my lord Gawain is fighting!' "
—"Ah, sir Kay," Gawain replied,
"you might have spoken more kindly.
4372 Are you trying to take out
your wrath and anger on me?
Upon my word, my good friend,
I will bring him back if I can,
4376 and I won't have my arm broken
and my collar-bone dislocated,
for I don't care for such wages."
—"Go now, nephew," said the king,
4380 "for you've spoken most courteously.
Bring him back if you can,
but wear all your armor,
for you mustn't go forth unarmed."
4384 Sir Gawain, who was renowned
and esteemed for all his virtues,

	had himself armed at once, mounted	4436	and let me tell you that it was he
	upon a strong and experienced horse,		who just jousted with you,
4388	and came directly to the knight		and though you are unaware of it,
	who was resting upon his lance:		the joust cost him
	he was still not weary	4440	a broken right arm
	of his pleasing reverie,		and a dislocated collar-bone."
4392	even though the sun had		—"Then," said Perceval, "I've honored
	melted away two of the drops of blood		the maiden whom Kay slapped."
	that had lain upon the snow,	4444	When my lord Gawain heard this
	and was even then melting away the third.		he was startled and surprised,
4396	Because of this the knight		and said: "Sir, so help me God,
	was not so lost in contemplation as before.		it is you the king has come to find!
	My lord Gawain approached him	4448	What is your name, my lord?"
	at a gentle amble and said		—"Perceval, my lord; and what is yours?"
4400	in an unthreatening tone,		—"Sir, know truly that
	"My lord, I would have		I was named Gawain at my baptism."
	greeted you if I had known	4452	—"Gawain?"—"Indeed yes, good sir."
	your heart as well as I do mine,		Perceval was overjoyed
4404	but at least I can tell you		and said: "My lord, I have heard
	that I am a messenger of the king,		good things told of you in many places
	who summons you and requests through me	4456	and I have been very eager
	that you come to speak with him."		for the two of us to become acquainted,
4408	—"There have already been two,"		if this is pleasing to you."
	said Perceval, "who tried to take		—"Indeed," replied my lord Gawain,
	my life and lead me away	4460	"I'm sure that this is no less pleasing
	as if I were their prisoner.		to me than to you, but more so."
4412	I was so lost in contemplation		And Perceval answered: "Upon my word,
	of a most pleasing thought		then I'll gladly go with you where
	that anyone who tried to stop me	4464	you wish, for that is right,
	was not looking to his own good,		and I am most honored
4416	for before me in this place		now to be your friend."
	were three drops of fresh blood		Then they went to embrace one another.
	that made the white snow sparkle.	4468	They began to unlace
	Looking at them, I thought		their helmets, coifs and ventails
4420	I could see the fresh color		and to pull off their chain mail.
	of my sweet love's face,		Then they headed for camp rejoicing;
	and I never wanted to stop."	4472	squires who had been posted
	—"Indeed," said my lord Gawain,		on a hill as lookouts observed
4424	"this was no vulgar thought,		their mutual delight
	but a most sweet and courtly one,		and came running to the king.
	and whoever disturbed your heart	4476	"My lord, my lord," they said,
	was an arrogant fool.		"in faith, my lord Gawain
4428	But now I am most eager		is bringing the knight here,
	to learn what you wish to do:		and they are delighted to be together."
	if it is not displeasing to you,	4480	All who heard the news
	I would gladly take you to the king."		came forth from their tents
4432	—"Now tell me first,		and went out to greet them;
	fair dear friend," said Perceval,		and Kay said to the king, his lord:
	"if the seneschal Kay is there."	4484	"Your nephew, my lord Gawain,
	—"Upon my word, he is indeed,		has won the honors of the battle.

The fight was tough
and frightfully dangerous, and I'm not
 lying,
4488 for he's returning just as
bold and hardy as when he left,
since he didn't strike a single blow
or feel a blow from anyone.
4492 He won't say a word to deny it.
How right for him to have the honors,
and for everyone to say he did
what neither of us was able
4496 to accomplish, even though
we gave our best efforts!"
So Kay spoke his mind, just as
he always did, whether right or wrong.
4500 My lord Gawain did not wish
to bring his companion fully armed
to court, but disarmed:
he had him disarmed in his own tent,
4504 and one of his chamberlains
brought Perceval a robe from his trunk
which he presented him to wear.
When he had donned
4508 the cloak and mantle,
which suited him perfectly,
the two of them came hand in hand
to the king, who was seated before his
 tent.
4512 "Sire," said my lord Gawain
to the king, "I bring you,
I believe, the knight you've
been eager to see
4516 these past two weeks.
He's the one you spoke so much about
and the one you came to find.
Here he is, I present him to you."
4520 —"Dear nephew, my thanks to you,"
said the king, so pleased to see Perceval
that he leapt to his feet to greet him,
saying: "Dear sir, be most welcome!
4524 I beg you to inform me
by what name I should address you."
—"Upon my word, I'll not hide it from
 you,
good sir king," said Perceval.
4528 "I am called Perceval the Welshman."
—"Ah, Perceval, my dear friend,
now that you've come to my court,
I don't want you ever to leave.
4532 Since the first time I saw you
I have been very upset on your account
because I didn't know the success
that God had destined for you.

4536 Yet the maiden and the jester
whom the seneschal Kay struck
had predicted it accurately,
so that all the court knew of it.
4540 You have perfectly fulfilled
their prophecies in every respect,
let there be no doubt of this,
for I have heard true reports
4544 of your deeds of chivalry."
    As he was speaking the queen
entered, having heard news of
the knight who'd come.
4548 As soon as Perceval saw her
and was told that it was she,
and saw she was followed by the maiden
who had laughed when she beheld him,
4552 he went up to them at once
and said: "May God give joy and honor
to the most beautiful and best
of all the ladies in the world,
4556 as all who see her or who
have ever seen her bear witness."
And the queen responded:
"And we are glad to have found you,
4560 a knight whose noble prowess
and good deeds are well attested!"
Then Perceval greeted the
damsel, the one who had laughed,
4564 and said as he embraced her:
"My beauty, if ever you're in need,
I shall be the knight
who will never fail to come your aid."
4568 And the maiden thanked him.
    Great was the joy that the king,
the queen, and all the barons
made over Perceval the Welshman
4572 as they returned with him
that night to Caerleon.
And all night they revelled,
and all the next day,
4576 until on the third day they saw
a damsel approaching
on a tawny mule, holding
a whip in her right hand.
4580 The damsel had her hair twisted
into two tight black braids
and, if the words are true
as they are given in the book,
4584 there was never a creature so ugly
even in the bowels of Hell.
You've never seen iron
as black as her neck and hands,
4588 and this was nothing

compared to the rest of her ugliness.
Her eyes were two holes,
as tiny as a rat's eyes;
4592 she had a nose like a monkey's or a cat's,
and the lips of an ass or ox.
Her teeth were the color
4596 of egg yolk, flecked with red,
and she had the beard of a goat.
She had a hump in the middle of her chest,
her backbone was twisted,
and her hips and shoulders
4600 were well made for dancing;
she was humpbacked and had legs
twisted like two willow wands:
just perfect for leading the dance!
4604 The damsel drove her mule
straight up before the king:
such an ugly damsel had never before
been seen at the court of any king.
4608 She greeted the king
and all the assembled barons
except Perceval alone,
to whom she spoke from her tawny mule:
4612 "Ah, Perceval! Fortune is bald
behind and hairy in front.
Cursed be anyone who'd greet you
or who'd wish you well,
4616 for you didn't catch hold of Fortune
when you met her!
You entered the castle of the Fisher King
and saw the bleeding lance,
4620 but it was so much effort for you
to open your mouth and speak
that you couldn't ask
why that drop of blood
4624 flowed from its white iron point!
And you didn't ask or inquire
what rich man was served
from the grail you saw.
4628 Wretched is the man who sees
that the propitious hour has come
but waits for a still better one.
And you are that wretched man,
4632 for you saw that it was the time and place
to speak, yet held your silence!
You had plenty of time to ask!
Cursed be the hour you kept silent,
4636 because if you had asked,
the rich king who suffers so
would already be healed of his wound
and would be ruling in peace
4640 over the land he'll never again rule.
And do you know what will happen
since the king will not rule
and won't be healed of his wounds?
4644 Ladies will lose their husbands,
lands will be laid waste
and maidens will remain
helpless orphans;
4648 many a knight will die.
All these troubles will come because of you."
Then the damsel addressed the king:
"King, do not be offended if I leave,
4652 for tonight I must find
lodgings far from here.
I don't know whether you've heard
tell of the Proud Castle,
4656 but that's where I must go tonight.
In that castle there are
five hundred and sixty-six worthy knights,
and I assure you that not one
4660 lacks the company of his sweetheart,
a fair and courtly noble lady.
I tell you all this
because no one who goes there
4664 will fail to find a joust or battle:
anyone wishing to perform deeds of chivalry
will find them there for the asking.
And if anyone should wish to be esteemed
4668 the best knight in all the world, I believe I know
the spot, the very piece of earth,
where he could best win that honor,
if he were bold enough to attempt it.
4672 There is a damsel besieged
on the peak below Montesclere.
Whoever can lift the siege
and free the maiden
4676 will win great glory:
if God grants him good fortune,
he will garner all the praise
and be able to gird on without fear
4680 the Sword with the Strange Straps."
Then the damsel ceased speaking,
having said all she was pleased to say,
and left without another word.
4684 My lord Gawain leapt up
and said that he would go

and do all in his power to free the maiden.
And Guiflet, the son of Doon, said
4688 that if God would grant him aid
he would go to the Proud Castle.
"And I'll not stop,"
said Kahedin, "until I've reached
4692 the top of Mount Perilous."
But Perceval swore a different oath,
saying that he would not spend two nights
in the same lodgings as long he lived,
4696 nor hear word of any dangerous passage
that he would go to cross,
nor learn of a knight reputed better
than any other, or even two,
4700 that he would test himself against him,
until he had learned who was served
from the grail and had found
the bleeding lance
4704 and been told the true reason
why it bled; for no hardship
would he abandon his quest.
Thus as many as fifty knights
4708 stood up and swore
and affirmed before one another
that they would undertake whatever
battle or adventure they learned about,
4712 no matter how dangerous the land it was in.
And as they were making ready
and arming themselves throughout the hall,
Guinganbresil strode through the entryway
4716 to the great hall, carrying
a shield with an azure bend
upon a field of gold.
The bend covered precisely
4720 a third of the shield.
Guinganbresil recognized the king
and greeted him as was proper,
but instead of greeting Gawain
4724 he charged him with felony,
saying: "Gawain, you killed
my lord, and you struck him
without issuing a challenge.
4728 For this you are disgraced and shamed,
and I accuse you of treason.
May all the barons acknowledge
that I've spoken nothing but the truth."
4732 On hearing these words, my lord Gawain,

covered with shame, leapt to his feet,
but his brother, Agravain the Haughty,
sprang forth and restrained him:
4736 "For the love of God, dear sir," he said,
"do not disgrace your lineage.
I swear to defend you myself
against the shame and outrage
4740 of which this knight accuses you."
Gawain replied: "Brother, no man
but myself must come to my defense:
I alone must defend myself,
4744 since he accuses only me.
And if I had known of any wrong
I had committed against this knight,
I would gladly have sued for peace
4748 and offered such amends
as all his friends and mine
would have acknowledged satisfactory.
But since he has uttered this outrage,
4752 I accept his challenge and will defend myself
here or there, anywhere he pleases."
Guinganbresil said he would prove
the foul and wicked treason
4756 at the end of forty days
before the King of Escavalon,
who in his thoughts and opinion
was more handsome than Absalom.
4760 "And I swear to you," said Gawain,
"that I'll follow after you at once
and there we shall see who's right."
Guinganbresil set off immediately
4764 and my lord Gawain made ready
to follow him without delay.
Anyone who had a good shield and good lance,
a good helmet and good sword,
4768 offered them to him, but he refused
to have anything that wasn't his own.
With him he took seven squires,
seven warhorses, and two shields.
4772 Before he left the court,
there was much grieving for him—
many a breast was beaten, many a hair torn out,
and many a face scratched;
4776 even the most level-headed of the ladies
showed their sorrow for him.
Many men and women wept for him,
but my lord Gawain set off.
4780 You will hear me tell at length
of the adventures with which he met.

First of all he saw
a troop of knights cross
4784 a clearing, and he asked
a squire who had
a shield hanging at his neck
and who was coming along alone after them
4788 leading a Spanish warhorse:
"Squire, tell me, who are these knights passing here?" And he replied:
"Sir, it is Meliant de Liz,
4792 a bold and hardy knight."
—"Are you his squire?"—"No, sir, I'm not.
My lord is called Traet d'Anez,
and he's every bit as worthy."
4796 —"Upon my word," said my lord Gawain
"I know Traet d'Anez well.
Where is he going? Hide nothing from me."
—"Sir, he is going to a tournament
4800 in which Meliant de Liz
has challenged Tiebaut of Tintagel,
and I suggest that you join with
Tiebaut against his adversaries."
4804 —"Heavens," said my lord Gawain then,
"wasn't Meliant de Liz raised
in Tiebaut's manor?"
—"Yes, sir, so help me God.
4808 His father dearly loved Tiebaut
as his liegeman and trusted him so much
that as he lay upon his deathbed
he commended his young son to him.
4812 And Tiebaut raised and watched over him as dearly as he could,
until he began to seek the love
of one of his daughters;
4816 and she said she would never grant him her love
until he had become a knight.
And so with high hopes
4820 he had himself knighted
and returned to renew his suit.
'By my faith,' said the maiden,
'you cannot have my love
4824 until you've jousted and performed enough feats of arms in my presence
to earn my love,
for things that are had for nothing
4828 are not nearly so sweet and delightful as those paid dearly for.

Challenge my father to a tourney
if you care to win my love,
4832 for I want to know without a doubt
that my love would be well placed
if it were placed in you.'
"So he has undertaken the tournament
4836 just as she proposed,
because love has such mastery
over those in its service
that they would never dare refuse
4840 anything it might command of them.
You'd be making a great mistake
not to side with those in the castle,
for they'll have real need of your support
4844 if you're willing to help them."
Gawain said: "Friend, be on your way,
you'd do well to follow your lord
and stop saying these things."
4848 The squire set off at once,
and my lord Gawain rode on:
he headed directly for Tintagel,
as there was no other route.
4852 Tiebaut had assembled
all his family and his cousins,
and had summoned all his neighbors,
and they had all come,
4856 high and low, young and old.
But Tiebaut had found no one
among his privy council
who favored war against his lord,
4860 for they were all very afraid
that Meliant was out to destroy them completely.
So Tiebaut had had all the entries
to the castle filled and walled up;
4864 the gates were solidly blocked
with heavy rocks and mortar,
and there was no entrance
except a small postern gate
4868 whose door was so impregnable
that it had not been walled shut.
The door, built to last forever,
was of copper and locked by a bar:
4872 there was enough iron in that door
to load down a heavy cart.
My lord Gawain, preceded by all
his equipage, came to this door,
4876 for he had to pass through the castle
or turn back, since
there was no other path or road
for seven long leagues around.

4880	When he saw the postern closed, he rode out onto a clearing below the keep, which was enclosed by a palisade, and dismounted beneath an oak tree		my lord Gawain's equipage, and they thought at first
4884	from which he hung his shields. Those in the castle saw this, and many there were saddened that the tournament had been delayed.	4928	that there were two knights, because they saw the two shields hanging from the oak tree. And when they had taken their places,
4888	But in the castle there was an old vavasor—very wise and respected, powerful because of his lands and lineage— and whatever advice he gave,	4932	the ladies said they were fortunate because they could watch these two knights arming before them. Thus they talked among themselves,
4892	no matter how it worked out in the end, was always followed by those in the castle. He had seen Gawain and his men approaching, for they had been pointed out to him at a distance,	4936	and there were several who said: "Dear God, this knight has so much equipment and so many horses that there's more than enough for two,
4896	before they had entered the fenced clearing. He went to speak with Tiebaut and said: "Sir, so help me God, I believe I've seen	4940	yet there's no other knight with him. What will he do with two shields? No knight's ever been seen to carry two shields at the same time,
4900	two knights coming this way, who are companions to King Arthur. Two brave knights are valuable to us, for either one of them could win a tourney.	4944	so it would be a great surprise if this one knight were to carry both these shields." While the ladies were conversing
4904	For my part I advise you to enter confidently into this tournament, for you have good knights,	4948	the knights rode forth, and Tiebaut's elder daughter, who was the occasion for the tournament, climbed to the top of the tower.
4908	good men at arms, and good archers who'll kill their horses, and I am certain that they'll come to do battle before this gate.	4952	With her was her younger sister, who dressed herself in such elegant sleeves that she was called The Maiden with the Small Sleeves,
4912	If their pride leads them here, the victory will be ours and theirs the loss and suffering." Upon the advice of his aged counselor	4956	and this name was embroidered along her sleeves. With Tiebaut's two daughters all the ladies and maidens had climbed to the top of the towers,
4916	Tiebaut gave leave to all to arm themselves and sally forth if they so desired. The knights were heartened by this;	4960	and the tournament was just now assembling in front of the castle. But there was no knight as handsome as Meliant de Liz,
4920	squires ran to fetch armor and to saddle and lead out the horses. The ladies and maidens went to sit in the highest places	4964	according to his sweetheart's words to the ladies all around her: "My ladies, truly no knight I've ever seen has pleased me more
4924	to observe the tournament, and below them in the plain they saw	4968	than Meliant de Liz— why should I lie to you about this? Is it not a comfort and delight to behold such a splendid knight?
		4972	A knight so handsome cannot help but sit well in his saddle and wield his lance and shield with the best."

But her sister, who was seated beside her,
4976 said that there was a more handsome knight.
Her elder sister became angry
and rose to strike her;
but the ladies pulled her away
4980 and restrained and stopped her
from hitting her sister,
which made her most upset.
Then the tournament began,
4984 where many a lance was broken,
many a sword blow landed,
and many a knight struck down.
You can be sure that those who jousted
4988 with Meliant de Liz paid dearly,
for every knight who faced his lance
was thrown to the hard earth;
and if his lance shattered,
4992 he paid out heavily with his sword,
and he did better
than any knight on either side.
And his sweetheart was so delighted
4996 that she could not refrain from saying:
"My ladies, his deeds are wondrous to behold!
You've never seen or heard tell
of any to equal them!
5000 Behold the best young knight
you've ever laid eyes upon,
for he is more handsome and a better fighter
than anyone else at the tournament."
5004 Her little sister countered: "I see
a more handsome and better knight, I think."
Her sister, enflamed with ire,
rushed upon her and said hotly:
5008 "You brat! How could you
be so impertinent
as to dare criticize
anyone whom I had praised?
5012 Let this blow teach you
to keep silent in the future!"
Then she slapped her so hard
that her fingers left their stamp upon her face,
5016 but the ladies who were there
rebuked her strongly and pulled her away.
Afterwards they too spoke of
my lord Gawain among themselves.
5020 "Heavens," said one of the damsels,

"what's keeping that knight under
the hornbeam from putting on his armor?"
Another, more rash, answered:
5024 "He's sworn not to participate."
And a third added afterwards:
"He's a merchant, don't say any more
about his participating in the tournament:
5028 he's brought all those horses to sell."
—"No, he's a money-changer," said the fourth.
"He doesn't have any intention of sharing
these goods he's brought with him
5032 among the poor knights here today.
Don't think I'm lying to you:
it's money and dishes
he's got in those chests and trunks."
5036 —"To be sure, you've got wicked tongues,"
said the younger sister, "and you're all wrong.
Do you think a merchant would carry
as stout a lance as he has?
5040 Indeed you make me die with shame
by saying such evil things.
By the faith I owe the Holy Spirit,
he seems more like a champion
5044 than a merchant or money-changer:
he's a knight, and looks the part!"
And all the ladies replied as one:
"Fair friend, though he may seem
5048 to be a knight, he isn't,
and he only pretends to be
so he can avoid
taxes and customs duties.
5052 He's a fool, though he thinks himself so clever,
because he'll be caught for this
like a thief and convicted
of base and stupid larceny.
5056 He'll soon have a rope around his neck!"
My lord Gawain clearly
heard their mockery and understood
what the ladies were saying about him;
5060 he was very upset and ashamed.
But he recalled, and rightly so,
that he had been accused of treason
and must go to defend his honor,
5064 for if he failed to join battle
as he had sworn to do,

he would shame himself first of all,
and his family even more so.
5068 So since he was afraid
of being injured or captured,
he hesitated to enter the fray,
though he was very eager to do so,
5072 because with each passing minute he saw
the tournament getting bigger and more
  prestigious.
And Meliant de Liz was asking for
stouter lances to joust better.
5076 All day long until evening
the tournament continued before the
  gate:
whoever won carried off his winnings
to where he thought them to be safest.
5080 The ladies caught sight of
a tall, bald squire who was holding
a broken lance shaft and approaching
with a bridle over his shoulders.
5084 One of the ladies called him a simpleton
and shouted to him:
"Sir squire, so help me God,
you must be a crazy fool
5088 to enter this fray to steal
lance heads and bridles
and those shafts and cruppers.
And you suppose you're a good squire!
5092 You can't think much of yourself
to risk your life like that, when I see
right below us in this meadow goods
that are unprotected and unguarded.
5096 A man's a fool not to look to his own
  gain
whenever he has a chance to do so.
Here's the most easy-going
knight who was ever born,
5100 for even if you plucked out all
his whiskers, he wouldn't move!
So don't settle for petty profits:
you'd do better to take
5104 all those horses and that equipment,
for he won't do a thing to stop you!"
So he went straight into the meadow
and struck one of the horses
5108 with his broken lance and said: "Vassal,
aren't you hale and hardy?
Why do you watch all day
without doing anything, not even
5112 breaking a lance or splitting a shield?"
—"So what is it to you?
Perhaps you'll yet learn
why I've stood aside,

5116 but by my head it won't be now,
for I wouldn't deign to tell you.
So go from here, be on your way
and see to your own affairs!"
5120 Then the squire left him at once,
and there was no one after him who
  dared
say anything that might offend Gawain.
The tournament ceased for the day;
5124 but many a knight had been captured
and many a horse killed;
the attackers had fought the more
  bravely,
but the defenders had won more booty,
5128 and as they separated both sides swore
to meet again on the morrow
in the field and continue the
  tournament.
   And so they separated at night
5132 and all those who had emerged
from the castle returned there.
My lord Gawain went there too
and entered the castle after the others;
5136 before the gate he met
the gentleman vavasor
who had advised his lord
to commence the tournament,
5140 who courteously and politely
invited Gawain to take lodgings there,
saying: "Sir, your lodgings
are all prepared in this castle.
5144 If you please, stay with us today,
for if you continued further
you'd not find good lodgings this night.
Therefore I urge you to stay."
5148 —"I'll stay, good sir,
by your leave," said my lord Gawain,
"for I've heard many worse offers."
The vavasor took him
5152 to his own house and asked him about
  one thing
and another, and what was meant
by his not bearing arms with them
all that day in the tournament.
5156 And he told him everything:
that he had been accused of treason
and must keep from being captured,
injured, or wounded
5160 until he could free himself
from the disgrace that had been cast
  upon him.
And he would dishonor himself
and all his friends by his delay,

5164	if he were unable to come in time
	to the battle to which he'd been challenged.
	The vavasor esteemed him more highly
	and said he was grateful to him:
5168	if this was his reason for avoiding
	the tournament, he had done right.
	So the vavasor led him to
	his manor and they dismounted.
5172	Meanwhile the people of the court
	continued to heap blame upon Gawain
	and spoke of how
	their lord was going to capture him;
5176	and his elder daughter
	did all she could to malign him,
	out of hatred for her sister:
	"Father," she said, "I am well aware
5180	that you lost nothing today;
	on the contrary, I believe you've won
	rather more than you realize,
	and I'll tell you how:
5184	you'd be a fool not to have
	your men go seize him.
	The man who brought him into the city
	won't dare try to defend him,
5188	for he's a most evil trickster:
	he's had shields and lances brought in
	and horses led in by their reins,
	thus by-passing the customs duties
5192	because he looks like a knight:
	this is how he travels freely
	as he goes about his business.
	But give him what he deserves!
5196	He has taken lodgings
	with Garin, son of Bertha.
	He passed by here not long ago
	and I saw him leading him off."
5200	And so she did her best
	to cause shame to my lord Gawain.
	Her father mounted his horse at once,
	for he wanted to go himself.
5204	He headed straight to the manor
	where my lord Gawain was staying.
	When his younger daughter
	saw him set off in this fashion,
5208	she stole away through a back door,
	not wishing to be seen,
	and went straight and quickly
	to my lord Gawain's lodgings
5212	at the manor of Garin, son of Bertha,
	who had two very beautiful daughters.
	When the maidens saw
	their young mistress coming,
5216	it was their duty to welcome her joyfully,
	which they did in all sincerity:
	each took her by a hand
	and led her in gaily,
5220	kissing her eyes and lips.
	Meanwhile Sir Garin, who was neither poor
	nor impoverished, had remounted
	and set off for the court
5224	with his son Bertran,
	as was their custom,
	for they wished to speak with their lord.
	But they met him along the way,
5228	and Sir Garin greeted the vavasor
	and asked him where he was going,
	to which the lord replied that he wished
	to enjoy the festivities at his manor.
5232	"Indeed, this is no displeasure
	or pain to me," said Sir Garin,
	"and while you're there you can see
	the most handsome knight in the world."
5236	—"By my faith, I'm not going there for that,"
	said the lord. "Instead, I'll have him seized:
	he's a merchant and wants to sell
	horses, yet he pretends he's a knight."
5240	—"What! this is a most wicked accusation
	I hear you making!" said Sir Garin.
	"I am your liegeman and you're my lord,
	but I now renounce my homage
5244	and that of all my lineage.
	I defy you here and now
	rather than suffer this indignity
	to occur in my manor."
5248	—"I have no such intention,"
	said the lord, "so help me God.
	Your guest and your house
	will have only honor from me;
5252	but not, I swear to you,
	because I've been advised or counseled
	to do such a thing."
	—"I thank you sincerely," said the vavasor,
5256	"and it will be a great honor for me
	to have you come to see my guest."
	And so they joined company
	and they rode along together
5260	until they came to the manor
	where my lord Gawain was staying.

When my lord Gawain saw them,
like the proper knight he was
5264 he rose and said, "Welcome!"
They both returned his greeting
and then sat down beside him.
Then the gentleman who was
5268 lord of that land asked him
why he had stood aside all day
after coming to the tournament,
and had not entered the fray.
5272 My lord Gawain did not deny
that it might be considered wrong and shameful,
but then he explained at once
that a knight had accused him
5276 of treason, and that he was going
to defend his honor at a royal court.
"You have an honorable excuse, sir,
without any doubt," said the lord.
5280 "Where will this combat be held?"
—"My lord," he said, "I must go
before the king of Escavalon,
and I trust I'm headed straight in that direction."
5284 —"I'll give you an escort
who'll take you there," said the lord.
"And since you must cross
through very barren land,
5288 I'll give you provisions to take
and horses to carry them."
My lord Gawain replied
that he had no need of this gift,
5292 for if he could find any for sale,
he had money enough for food
and good lodgings wherever he went,
and whatever else he might need.
5296 Therefore he sought nothing from him.
At this the lord turned to leave,
but as he was leaving he saw his younger
daughter coming the other way,
5300 and she immediately clasped
my lord Gawain's leg
and said: "Dear sir, listen to me!
I have come before you to lay claim
5304 against my sister for having hit me:
uphold my rights, if you please."
My lord Gawain, who did not understand
what this was about, remained silent;
5308 but he placed his hand upon her head
and the girl grasped it
and said: "I tell you, dear sir,

that I lay claim before you against my sister,
5312 for whom I bear no love or affection,
because today she's caused me great
shame on your account."
—"And what is this to me, my pretty?
What rights can I uphold for you?"
5316 The lord, who had taken his leave,
heard what his daughter requested
and said: "Daughter, who told you
to come make your claim before knights?"
5320 And Gawain said: "My good sir,
is she your daughter then?"
—"Yes, but don't pay any attention
to what she says," answered the lord.
5324 "She's a child—a silly, foolish thing."
—"Indeed," said my lord Gawain,
"then I'd be very ill-mannered
not to do what she wants.
5328 Tell me at once,
my sweet and noble child,
what rights I can secure for you
against your sister, and how."
5332 —"Sir, just for tomorrow,
if you please, you could bear arms
in the tourney for love of me."
—"Tell me then, dear friend,
5336 if ever you've requested
anything of a knight before?"
—"No, my lord."—"Don't pay any attention
to what she says," said her father.
5340 "Don't listen to her foolishness."
But my lord Gawain replied:
"Sir, as God is my helper,
she has spoken well
5344 for such a little girl,
and I'll not refuse her request.
Rather, since it pleases her,
I'll be her knight for a while tomorrow."
5348 —"I thank you, fair dear sir!"
said she who was so happy
she bowed down at his feet.
Then they parted without saying more.
5352 The lord carried his daughter
before him on his palfrey's neck
and asked her what had been
the cause of this quarrel;
5356 she told him the truth
from beginning to end
and said: "Sir, I was very upset
because my sister claimed

5360 that Meliant de Liz was
the best and most handsome of all,
yet I had seen this knight
in the meadow below,
5364 and I couldn't keep myself
from replying to her and saying
that I had seen one more handsome
than Meliant.
And because of that my sister called me
5368 a silly brat and pulled my hair—
a curse upon anyone who enjoyed that!
I'd let both my tresses be cut off
at the back of my neck,
5372 though it would destroy my beauty,
if only I could be sure that
tomorrow morning in the combat
my knight would defeat Meliant de Liz:
5376 that would put an end to his praises,
which the lady my sister keeps singing!
She never stopped talking about him
today,
which upset all the ladies—
5380 but from a great gale falls little rain!"
—"Sweet daughter," said the gentleman,
"I order and permit you
to send him out of courtesy
5384 some sign of your affection,
either your sleeve or wimple."
And she modestly replied:
"Most willingly, since you say so.
5388 But my sleeves are so little
I wouldn't dare send them to him;
I'm afraid that if I sent him one
he wouldn't think much of it."
5392 —"My daughter, I'll see to this,"
said her father. "Now don't fret,
for I'm glad to do it."
As they talked he carried her along
5396 in his arms, happy to be
holding and hugging her,
until at last they came to his palace.
And when the elder daughter saw him
5400 coming with her sister in his arms,
her heart was filled with anger
and she said: "Sir, where has my sister
been,
the Maiden with the Small Sleeves?
5404 She knows lots of tricks and ruses,
for she's practiced them a long while.
Where did you bring her from just
now?"
—"And what do you wish to make of
it?" he asked.

5408 "You'd do well to keep quiet.
She's worth more than you.
By hitting her and pulling her hair
you've made me angry.
5412 You haven't behaved properly at all!"
The elder sister was crushed
because her father had
reprimanded and scolded her so.
5416 Meanwhile, he had a piece of red
samite
taken from one of his coffers
and had a long, wide sleeve
made from it at once;
5420 then he called his daughter
and said: "My daughter, get up early
tomorrow and go
to the knight before he stirs.
5424 Give him this new sleeve as a token
of love, and he'll wear it
when he goes to the tournament."
And she answered her father
5428 that as soon as she saw the dawn break
she intended to be awake,
dressed, and ready to go.
Her father left on hearing this
5432 and she, filled with happiness,
begged all her ladies-in-waiting
not to allow her to sleep
late in the morning,
5436 but to awaken her promptly
when they saw the dawn,
if they wished to retain her favor.
And they did exactly as she asked,
5440 for as soon as they saw
dawn break in the early morning
they awoke and dressed her.
The maiden arose early
5444 and went all alone
to where my lord Gawain was staying.
But she was not there so early
that they'd not already arisen
5448 and gone to church
to hear Mass sung for them.
The damsel awaited them
at the vavasor's manor
5452 until they'd said all their prayers
and fulfilled their spiritual obligations.
After they returned from church
the maiden rushed to my lord Gawain
5456 and said: "May God protect you
and give you honor on this day!
Please wear this sleeve I give you
as a token of my love."

5460	—"Gladly, my friend, and I thank you for it," said my lord Gawain. After this the knights did not tarry in donning their armor.
5464	They gathered in their armor outside town, and the damsels and all the ladies of the castle climbed once more to the top of the walls
5468	to watch the groups of brave and hardy knights assemble. Ahead of them all, Meliant de Liz charged hotly toward the opposing camp,
5472	having left his companions some hundred and fifty meters behind. The elder sister caught sight of her lover and could not restrain
5476	her tongue: "My ladies, look at that knight, who's the lord and flower of chivalry!" Then my lord Gawain charged
5480	as fast as his horse could carry him directly at Meliant, who showed no fear, but shattered his lance to pieces. And my lord Gawain's blow,
5484	which knocked him sharply to the ground, caused him great injury. Then Gawain reached for Meliant's horse, took it by the bridle, and gave it
5488	to a squire, telling him to go to the one in whose honor he was fighting and tell her that he sent her the first prize he had won that day,
5492	for he wanted her to have it. The squire led the horse with its saddle to the maiden, who had clearly seen, from where she was
5496	at a window in the keep, Sir Meliant de Liz fall. She said: "Sister, now you can see Sir Meliant de Liz, whom you've bragged on
5500	so much, lying on the ground! Everyone will have to admit that what I said yesterday was right! So help me God, now we can see
5504	that there's one who's better than he!" She went on deliberately provoking her sister in this fashion until she lost her head
5508	and said: "Shut up, you brat! If I hear you say another word today I'll hit you so hard your feet won't hold you up!"
5512	—"Goodness, sister! Remember God," replied the younger sister. "Since I've spoken the truth, you've no cause at all to hit me!
5516	Upon my oath, I clearly saw him defeated, just as you did yourself, and I think he still doesn't have the strength to get back up.
5520	And even if you die of shame, I still say there's not a lady here who can't see him lying there on his back with his legs in the air."
5524	Her sister would have slapped her had she not been restrained; but the ladies around her would not let her strike her.
5528	Just then they saw the squire coming, leading the horse with his right hand. He found the maiden seated at a window and presented her the horse.
5532	The maiden thanked him more than sixty times and had the horse led off, while the squire returned to convey her gratitude
5536	to his lord, who appeared to be the lord and master of the tournament, for there was no knight so skillful who, if he matched lances against him, was not thrown from his stirrups.
5540	Never before had Gawain been so intent upon winning horses. He presented four that day, which he won with his own hands:
5544	he sent the first to the younger sister; another to the vavasor's wife, whom he pleased immensely;
5548	one of the vavasor's two daughters received the third, the other the fourth. After the tournament the knights reentered town by the main gate;
5552	my lord Gawain had carried off the honors on both sides, though it was not yet midday when he left the combat.

5556	On his return my lord Gawain was accompanied by so many knights that the whole street was filled, and everyone who followed him		took him by the foot, kissed it, and commended him to God.
5560	wanted to ask and inquire who he was and where he came from. He met the younger maiden just before the door of her manor;	5608	And my lord Gawain asked her what she meant by this, and she replied that she had kissed
5564	her only reaction was to help steady his stirrup while she greeted him, saying: "Five hundred thanks, dear sir."	5612	his foot because she wanted him to remember her wherever he might go. And he said to her: "Have no fear,
5568	He knew exactly what she meant and replied to her nobly: "I'll be white-haired and gray, my dear, before I fail in	5616	fair friend, for so help me God, I'll never forget you after I've left here." He departed as soon as he'd taken leave
5572	your service, wherever I may be. And no matter how far I may be from you, if ever I learn you need my help, nothing at all could prevent	5620	of his host and the others, who all commended him to God. That night my lord Gawain lay in a small monastery,
5576	my coming at the first summons." —"I thank you sincerely," said the damsel. While they were conversing, her father came into the square	5624	where he had all that he needed; and very early the next day he was riding along his way when he saw as he passed
5580	and did everything in his power to persuade my lord Gawain to stay the night and take lodgings with him, but first he begged and requested him	5628	some wild beasts grazing at the edge of a forest. He ordered his squire, who was leading one of his horses—the best he had—
5584	to tell him his name, if he would. My lord Gawain refused to stay, but told him: "Sir, I am called Gawain;	5632	and carrying a strong and stiff lance, to stop; then he told him to bring the lance and to harness up the charger
5588	I've never refused to reveal my name anywhere it was asked, but I've never given it unless I was first asked for it."	5636	he was leading with his right hand, and to take and lead his palfrey instead. His squire did not hesitate, but immediately handed over to him
5592	When the lord heard that it was my lord Gawain, his heart was filled with joy and he said to him: "My lord, please stay	5640	his horse and lance. Gawain set off after the hinds, hunting them with such skill and cunning that he overtook a white one
5596	and accept my service tonight. Until now I've not served you in any way, but I can swear to you I've never in my life seen	5644	beside a thorn bush and laid his lance across its neck. The hind leapt like a stag and fled; Gawain followed
5600	a knight I'd rather honor." He begged him repeatedly to stay, but my lord Gawain refused his every prayer.	5648	and pursued her and was about to catch her fast and stop her when his horse threw a shoe completely off a front hoof.
5604	And the younger sister, who was neither discourteous nor foolish,	5652	My lord Gawain rode on to overtake his supply horses, but it upset him to feel his horse stumbling under him;
		5656	he did not know what made it lame,

unless perhaps a stick had struck its
    foot.
He called his squire Yvonet at once
and ordered him to dismount
5660 and care for his horse,
for it was limping badly.
Yvonet did as he was ordered:
he lifted its foot high
5664 and discovered it was missing a shoe,
and said: "Sir, it needs to be reshod.
There's nothing to do but walk it
gently until we are able to find
5668 a smith who can reshoe it."
Then they rode along until they saw
people pouring out from a castle
and coming along the road.
5672 In front were people in short robes,
boys on foot leading hounds,
and afterwards came huntsmen
carrying sharp pikes;
5676 then there were archers and foot
    soldiers,
carrying bows and arrows;
and after them came the knights.
Following all the other knights
5680 were two mounted on chargers,
one of whom was just a youth
and the most handsome of all.
This one alone greeted my lord Gawain,
5684 taking him by the hand
and saying: "Sir, stay with me.
Go on in the direction from which I've
    come
and take lodgings at my manor.
5688 It is already high time
to seek shelter, if you don't mind.
I have a most courteous sister
who will be happy to welcome you,
5692 and this lord you see beside me
will take you there." He turned then
to his friend: "Go along, my dear
    companion,
for I'm sending you with this lord,
5696 to take him to my sister.
Greet her first,
then tell her that I order her
by the love and great fidelity
5700 that should exist between herself and
    me,
that if ever she loved a knight,
she should love and cherish this one
and do as much for him
5704 as she would for me, her brother:

she should offer him
entertainment and good company
until we have returned.
5708 Once she has suitably
taken charge of him,
come swiftly to fetch us,
for I wish to return
5712 to keep him company
as soon as I possibly can,"
    The knight set off at once,
taking my lord Gawain there
5716 where everyone bore him a mortal
    hatred;
but he was not recognized
because they had never before seen him,
so he did not know the danger he faced.
5720 He observed the site of the castle,
which overlooked an arm of the sea,
and saw that its walls and keep
were so strong it feared no assault.
5724 He looked over all the town,
peopled with excellent citizens,
and the booths of the money-changers
covered with gold and silver coins,
5728 and saw the squares and the streets
all filled with fine workers
engaged in as many diverse jobs
as there are different occupations:
5732 one made helmets, another hauberks,
one made saddles, another shields,
one made reins, another spurs,
and yet another furbished swords.
5736 Some fulled cloth, while others wove
and combed and clipped it;
yet others melted down gold and silver
for beautiful and costly metalwork;
5740 cups, goblets, and bowls,
and jewelry inlaid with enamel,
rings, belts, and clasps.
It was easy to believe that every day
5744 was the day of the fair in town,
filled to overflowing with so much
    wealth:
with wax, pepper and grains,
and gray and variegated pelts,
5748 and every sort of merchandise.
    They stopped from time to time
and looked at all these things,
but finally they reached the keep
5752 and squires came forth to take
all their harnass and equipment.
The knight entered the keep
alone with my lord Gawain

	and led him by the hand		carressed, hugged, and kissed
5756	to the maiden's chamber,		by the man whom you should
	where he said to her: "Fair friend,		most hate in all the world!
	your brother sends you greetings	5812	Foolish, unfortunate woman,
5760	and commands you to honor		you are behaving in accord with your nature!
	and serve this knight.		You should be pulling out his heart
	Don't do it grudgingly,		with your hands rather than your lips!
	but just as whole-heartedly	5816	If your kisses have touched his heart,
5764	as if you were his sister		you've lifted his heart from his breast,
	and he your brother.		but you'd have done much better
	Be careful not to skimp		to have ripped it out with your hands:
	in fulfilling all his desires,	5820	that's what you should have done,
5768	but be generous, noble, and good.		if a woman could do anything right!
	See to him now, for I must follow		A woman's not a woman
	my lord into the woods."		if she hates evil and loves the good;
	And she, who was delighted, said:	5824	they're wrong to call her a woman,
5772	"A blessing upon him who sends me		for she's unworthy of the name woman
	such excellent company as this!		if she loves only the good.
	He surely loves me dearly		But I can see you're a true woman,
	to lend me a companion such as he.	5828	because this man seated beside you
5776	Dear sir," continued the maiden,		killed your father, yet you're kissing him!
	"please take a seat here beside me.		As long as a woman can have her pleasure,
	Since you appear fair and noble		she doesn't care about anything else."
	and since my brother wishes me to,	5832	With these words he rushed away
5780	I'll offer you good companionship."		before my lord Gawain
	The knight turned at once to go		could say anything to him.
	and stayed with them no more.		And the maiden fell to the stone floor
	My lord Gawain remained behind,	5836	and lay a long while in a faint;
5784	having no objection at all		my lord Gawain gathered her in his arms
	to being left alone with the maiden,		and raised her up, pale and discolored
	who was most courteous and attractive.		by the shock she had had.
	She was so well raised that she was sure	5840	When she had recovered
5788	no one would keep an eye on her		she said: "Ah! we are both dead!
	even though she was alone with him.		I shall die unfairly today because of you,
	The two of them spoke of love,		and you, I fear, because of me.
	for had they talked of other things	5844	I feel sure the common folk
5792	it would have been a great waste.		of this town will come here shortly;
	My lord Gawain sought her love		soon there will be more than ten thousand of them
	and implored her, saying he would be		gathered in front of this tower.
	her knight for all his life;	5848	But there are arms enough within
5796	and she did not refuse him,		with which I'll equip you at once.
	but gladly granted him her love.		One nobleman can easily defend
	Meanwhile a vavasor had entered,		this keep against an entire army."
	who was to bring them sorrow:	5852	She hurried to fetch his armor,
5800	he recognized my lord Gawain,		for she was not feeling at all secure.
	and found them kissing one another		When she had armed him fully,
	and bringing each other much pleasure.		both she and my lord Gawain
	The moment he saw this happiness,	5856	were less afraid,
5804	he could not restrain his tongue,		
	but shouted out for all to hear:		
	"Woman, shame on you!		
	May God destroy and damn you,		
5808	for you are letting yourself be		

160   PART II: ARTHURIAN ROMANCE

```
        except that as luck would have it
        there was no shield to be found;
        so my lord Gawain made a shield from
5860    a chessboard and said: "Friend,
        I don't want you to look for any other
           shield for me."
        Then he overturned the chessboard,
        which had ivory pieces, ten times
           heavier
5864    than other pieces and of the hardest
           bone.
        Henceforth, whatever might happen,
        he felt he could hold
        the door and entry to the keep,
5868    for he had belted on Excalibur,
        the best sword ever made,
        which cut iron as if it were wood.
        Meanwhile his accuser had left
5872    and had found, seated side by side,
        an assembly of his neighbors,
        the mayor and councilmen,
        and many other town dwellers,
5876    who all seemed in fine fettle,
        for they were hardy and well-fed.
        He came running toward them
        shouting: "Take up arms, my lords,
5880    and let's go capture the traitor
        Gawain, who killed my lord!"
        —"Where is he? Where is he?" they all
           shouted.
        —"Upon my word," he said,
5884    "I've found Gawain, that proven traitor,
        in this tower taking his pleasure,
        kissing and hugging our lady,
        and she offers no resistance at all,
5888    but puts up with him and enjoys it.
        So come along and we'll capture him:
        if we can deliver him to my lord
        we will have served him well.
5892    The traitor well deserves
        to die shamefully,
        but capture him alive, nonetheless,
        for my lord would rather have him alive
5896    than dead, and that's not wrong,
        for a dead man has nothing to fear.
        So rouse the whole town
        and do what you must!"
5900    The mayor stood up at once,
        and all the councilmen after him.
        There you could see angry peasants
        taking up hatchets and pikes:
5904    one took a shield without arm-straps,
        another a door, another a basket.
```

```
        The town crier sounded the alarm
        and everyone gathered together.
5908    The church bells rang through the town
        so that no one would miss the call;
        even the poorest among them grabbed
        pitchfork, scythe, pickaxe, or club.
5912    Even on a snail hunt in Lombardy
        they don't make that much racket!
        The lowliest peasant came
        carrying some sort of weapon.
5916    My lord Gawain is a dead man
        if Almighty God does not help him!
        The damsel bravely
        readied herself to aid him
5920    and shouted to the mob:
        "Be off with you!" she said, "rabble,
        mad dogs, filthy wretches!
        What devils called you together?
5924    What do you want? What are you after?
        May God never bring you joy!
        So help me God, you'll never take
        the knight who's here with me—
5928    I don't know how many of you will be
        injured or killed instead, if God be with
           us.
        He didn't coming flying in here
        or enter by some secret passage:
5932    my brother sent him as a guest
        to me, and heartily implored me
        to treat him as I would treat
        my brother himself.
5936    And do you consider me wicked
        if at his request I keep him
        company, and bring him joy and solace?
        Listen to me if you will:
5940    I welcomed him with joy for no other
           reason,
        and I never committed any folly.
        So I am all the more angry at you
        for having so greatly dishonored me
5944    by drawing your swords
        against me at my chamber door,
        and you can't even say why!
        And if you can give a reason,
5948    you haven't told me yet,
        which is a greater insult still!"
        While she was speaking her mind,
        they splintered the door
5952    by hammering it with axes
        and finally split it in two.
        But Sir Gawain the doorkeeper
        held out strongly from within:
5956    with sword in hand he made
```

the first to enter pay so dearly
that the others were terrified
and none dared advance.
5960 Each one looked out for himself,
because each feared for his own head.
No one was bold enough to approch,
for they were all afraid of the doorkeeper;
5964 no one dared lift a hand against him
or take a single step forward.
The damsel took the chessmen
that were lying on the stone floor
5968 and flung them furiously at the mob.
She tore at her hair and flailed about
and swore in her wrath
that she would see them all destroyed,
5972 if she could, before she died.
But the townspeople withdrew,
promising to bring the tower down
upon them if they did not surrender.
5976 And they defended themselves better and better
by hurling the huge chessmen down upon them.
Most turned tail and ran,
for they could not withstand their assault.
5980 Since they did not dare attack or fight
at the door, which was too well defended,
they began to dig under the keep
with steel picks to bring it down.
5984 If you please, take my word that the door
was so narrow and low
that two men couldn't pass through it together without great difficulty;
5988 thus, a single good man
could easily hold and defend it:
there was no need to call for
a better doorkeeper
5992 to slaughter unarmed peasants
and split their skulls to the teeth.
   The lord who had offered lodgings to Gawain
knew nothing of any of this,
5996 but was returning as rapidly as he could
from the woods where he'd been hunting.
The mob was still trying to undermine
the keep with steel pickaxes.
6000 Suddenly Guinganbresil appeared,
I do not know by what chance,
riding swiftly into the castle,
and was completely dumbfounded
6004 at the noise and hammering
he heard being made by the peasants.
He had no idea
that my lord Gawain was in the tower,
6008 but as soon as he learned it
he ordered that no one
dare be so bold—
if he valued his life—
6012 as to dislodge a single stone.
But they said they would not stop
on his account, and would bury him,
too, under the ruins that day
6016 if he were in there with Gawain.
And when he saw that his order
would be ignored, he determined
to seek out the king
6020 and bring him to see
this havoc created by the townspeople.
The king was just returning from the woods,
and when he met him Guinganbresil said:
6024 "My lord, you have been greatly disgraced
by your mayor and councilmen,
for they've been attacking your keep
since this morning and are pulling it down.
6028 If they don't make amends and pay for it,
I'll never respect you again.
I had charged Gawain
with treason, as you well recall,
6032 and it is he whom
you are lodging in your house;
yet it is right and proper,
since you have made him your guest,
6036 that he not be shamed or dishonored."
And the king answered Guinganbresil:
"Trusted advisor, he won't be
as soon as we get there.
6040 What has happened to him
has made me very upset and angry.
If my people bear him a mortal hatred
it is no surprise to me;
6044 but for honor's sake I'll keep him
from being injured or captured,
since I've offered him lodging."
So they approached the tower
6048 which they found surrounded by a mob
raising a great din.

The king ordered the mayor to leave
and take all the people with him:
6052 they all left, and not a one remained,
since it was the mayor's wish.
In the square there was a vavasor,
a native of the town,
6056 who gave counsel throughout the land
because he was a man of very great wisdom.
"My lord," he said, "at this moment
you need loyal and good advice.
6060 You should not be surprised
that they have laid siege here
to the man who treasonously
killed your father, for,
6064 as you know, the people
rightly bear him a mortal hatred.
But because you've offered him lodgings
he must be protected and safeguarded
6068 from capture and death.
And the truth of the matter is
that Guinganbresil himself, here present,
who accused him of high treason
6072 at the king's court, is the one
who must protect and safeguard him.
This much is clear:
Gawain has come to defend himself
6076 at your court; but I suggest
that this battle be postponed for a year
and that my lord Gawain go
in search of the lance whose point
6080 bleeds constantly, from which
the last drop can never be wiped clean.
Either he brings you this lance
or he must surrender himself
6084 your prisoner here, as he is now.
Then you'd have a better reason
to keep him your prisoner
than you would have at present;
6088 yet I don't believe you could
find any task difficult enough
that he could not manage to do it.
A man should impose the harshest conditions
6092 he can imagine on his enemy:
I cannot suggest a better way
for you to belabor your enemy."
The king accepted this advice.
6096 He came to his sister in the tower
and found her full of anger.

His sister rose to meet him,
together with my lord Gawain,
6100 who did not flush or tremble
or show any signs of fear.
Guinganbresil stepped forward
and greeted the maiden,
6104 who had grown pale;
then he spoke these proud words:
"Sir Gawain, Sir Gawain,
I had offered you safe conduct,
6108 but I never told you
to be so bold
as to enter any castle
or town belonging to my lord,
6112 but to avoid it, if you please.
So you cannot complain
of what has happened to you here."
And the wise vavasor said:
6116 "Sir, so help me God,
all of this can be made good.
Who's to be blamed
if the townspeople assaulted him?
6120 We'd be trying to decide this
until the great Judgment Day.
So let it be settled
as my lord king here present wishes:
6124 he has commanded me to speak,
and I propose that you both
postpone this battle for one year,
if neither of you objects,
6128 and that my lord Gawain go forth
after having sworn an oath
to my lord that he will deliver to him
within one year and no more
6132 the lance whose point weeps
with the clear blood it sheds.
And it is written that in time it will
come to pass that all the kingdom of Logres,
6136 which was once the land of ogres,
will be destroyed by this lance.
My lord the king wishes
to have this oath and promise."
6140 —"Indeed," said my lord Gawain,
"I'd rather let myself languish
seven years in prison, or even die,
than swear this oath to you
6144 or give you my word upon it.
I'm not so afraid of death
that I'd not prefer to suffer
and die an honorable death
6148 than live in shame, having broken my word."

—"Good sir," said the vavasor,
"it will not bring you shame,
and your honor will not suffer
6152 if you express your oath as I propose:
you will swear to do all
in your power to seek the lance;
if you do not find the lance,
6156 you'll return to this tower
and be absolved of your oath."
—" I am prepared to take the oath," said he,
"exactly as you have stated it."
6160 A very precious reliquary
was brought out to him at once,
and he swore an oath
to do everything in his power
6164 to seek the bleeding lance.
Thus the battle was
postponed for one year
between Guinganbresil and himself:
6168 he escaped a great peril
when he avoided this one.
Before he left the tower keep
he took leave of the maiden
6172 and told all his squires
to return to his land
with all of his horses
except Gringalet.
6176 Weeping, the squires left
their lord and rode off.
I do not care to speak further
of them or of their grief.
6180 At this point the tale ceases
to tell of my lord Gawain
and begins to speak of Perceval.
Perceval, the story relates,
6184 had lost his memory so totally
that he no longer remembered God.
Five times April and May passed—
that was five full years—
6188 without his having entered a church
or adored God or His Cross.
Five years he remained in this way,
yet for all this he never ceased
6192 pursuing deeds of chivalry;
he sought out the most difficult,
treacherous and unusual adventures,
and found enough
6196 to test his valor;
he never undertook any venture
that he was unable to accomplish.
He sent sixty worthy knights
6200 as prisoners to King Arthur's court

in the course of the five years.
So he passed the five years
without ever thinking of God.
6204 At the end of the five years
it happened that he was riding
through a deserted region,
armed as usual in full armor;
6208 he met three knights
and, with them, as many as ten ladies,
their heads covered by hoods;
they were all walking barefoot
6212 and wearing hairshirts.
The ladies were quite surprised
to find him fully armed
and bearing his shield and lance,
6216 since to secure the salvation of their souls
they were doing penance on foot
for the sins they had committed.
One of the three knights
6220 stopped him and said: "My good sir,
do you not believe in Jesus Christ,
who set forth the New Law
and gave it to Christians?
6224 Indeed, it is not proper or good,
but very wrong, to bear arms
on the day when Jesus died."
And Perceval, who was so troubled
6228 in his heart that he had no idea
of the day or hour or time,
said: "What day is it today, then?"
—"What day, sir? You don't know!
6232 It is Good Friday,
when one should worship
the Cross and weep for one's sins,
for today the Man was hung upon the Cross
6236 who was sold for thirty pieces of silver.
He who was guiltless of any sin
beheld the sins that ensnared
and stained all mankind,
6240 and became man for our sins.
It is true that He was God and man,
that the Virgin gave birth to a Son
conceived by the Holy Spirit,
6244 in whom God assumed flesh and blood,
and His divinity was concealed
under flesh of man. All this is certain.
And whoever does not believe this
6248 will never see Him face to face:
He was born of the Virgin lady
and took the soul and body of man
in addition to His Holy Divinity;

6252	and on a day like today, in truth, He was nailed upon the Cross and delivered all His friends from Hell. This was truly a holy death,	6300	sighing deep within his heart because he felt he had sinned against God and was very sorry for it. Weeping, he went toward the thicket,
6256	which saved the living and brought the dead back to life. The wicked Jews, whom we should kill like dogs, hurt themselves	6304	and when he came to the hermitage he dismounted and removed his armor. He tied his horse to a hornbeam and entered the hermit's cell.
6260	in their malice and did us great good when they raised Him on the Cross: they damned themselves and saved us. All those who believe in Him	6308	In a small chapel he found the hermit with a priest and a young cleric—this is the truth— who were just beginning the service,
6264	should be doing penance on this day: No man who believes in God should bear arms today in field or path." —"And where are you coming from dressed like this?"	6312	the highest that can be said in Holy Church, and the sweetest. Perceval knelt down as soon as he entered the chapel,
6268	asked Perceval.—"Sir, from close by here, from a good man, a holy hermit who lives in this forest, and who is such a holy man	6316	and the good hermit called him to him, for he saw he was humble and penitent, and saw the tears flowing from his eyes right down to his chin.
6272	that he lives solely by the glory of God." —"In God's name, my lords, what were you doing there?" What did you request? What were you seeking?"	6320	And Perceval, who was very much afraid that he had sinned against Almighty God, took the hermit by the foot, bowed before him, and with hands clasped
	—"What, sir?" said one of the ladies.	6324	begged him to give him absolution, for he was in great need. And the good hermit told him to make his confession,
6276	"We asked forgiveness for our sins, and we confessed them to him. We fulfilled the most important duty that any Christian can do	6328	for he would never be forgiven if he did not first confess and repent. "Sir," said Perceval, "It has been over five years
6280	who truly wishes to please God." What Perceval had heard made him weep, and he wanted to go speak with the holy man.	6332	since I have known where I was going, and I have not loved God or believed in Him, and all I have done has been evil."
6284	"I would like to go there," he said, "to the hermit, if I could know the path and way." —"My lord, if you wish to go there,		—"Ah, dear friend," said the worthy man, "tell me why you acted in this manner,
6288	keep right to this path before you, over which we came through this thick and deep forest, and take careful note of the branches	6336	and pray God to have mercy upon the soul of His sinner," —"Sir, I was once at the manor of the Fisher King, and I saw the lance
6292	we wove together with our hands as we came through the woods: we made these signs so that no one would lose his way	6340	whose point bleeds beyond a doubt, and I never asked about this drop of blood I saw suspended from the white iron tip.
6296	while going to see this holy man." Then they commended one another to God and asked no more questions. Perceval set out upon the path,	6344	I've done nothing since then to make amends. I never learned who was served from the grail I saw;

| | since that day I've suffered such affliction
6348 that I would rather have died;
| I forgot Almighty God
| and never implored Him for mercy,
| and I've not consciously done anything
6352 to merit His forgiveness."
| "Ah, fair friend," said the good man,
| "now tell me your name."
| And he answered, "Perceval, sir."
6356 At this word the hermit sighed,
| for he recognized his name,
| and said: "Brother, a sin of which
| you are unaware has caused you much hardship:
6360 it is the sorrow your mother felt
| when you departed from her,
| for she fell in a faint on the ground
| at the head of the bridge before the gate,
6364 and she died from this sorrow.
| Because of this sin of yours
| it came about that you did not ask
| about the lance or the grail,
6368 and much hardship has resulted for you.
| And understand that you
| would not have lasted until now
| had she not commended you to God;
6372 but her prayer was so powerful
| that God watched over you for her sake
| and kept you from death and imprisonment.
| Sin stopped your tongue
6376 when you saw the lance
| that bleeds unceasingly pass before you
| and failed to ask its purpose;
| when you did not inquire who is served
6380 from the grail, you committed folly.
| He who is served from it is my brother.
| Your mother was his sister and mine,
| and the rich Fisher King, I believe,
6384 is the son of the king
| who is served from the grail.
| And do not think he is served
| pike or lamprey or salmon.
6388 A single Host that is brought
| to him in that grail sustains
| and brings comfort to that holy man—
| such is the holiness of the grail!
6392 And he is so holy
| that nothing more sustains his life
| than the Host that comes in the grail.
| Twelve years he has lived like this,
6396 without ever leaving the room

into which you saw the grail enter.
Now I wish to impose
your penance for this sin."
6400 —"Dear uncle, this is what I desire,"
said Perceval with all his heart.
"Since my mother was your sister,
you should call me nephew
6404 and I call you uncle, and love you the more."
—"That is true, dear nephew, but listen now:
if pity has gripped your soul
you must feel penitent within
6408 and go each day to do penance
in church before going anywhere else,
and that will bring you blessings.
Let nothing deter you from this duty:
6412 if you are anywhere near
a church, chapel, or altar,
go there as soon as the bells ring,
or earlier if you are awake.
6416 This will never hurt you;
rather, it will improve your soul.
And if Mass has begun
your visit will be even better.
6420 Stay there until the priest
has said and sung it all.
If you do this with a true heart,
you will yet improve yourself
6424 and win honor and salvation.
Believe in God, love God, worship God;
honor gentlemen and noble ladies;
rise in the presence of the priest—
6428 it is an easy thing to do
and God truly loves it,
because it is a sign of humility.
If a maiden seeks your aid,
6432 or a widow or orphan,
help her, and you will profit.
This is the full penance
that I want you to do for your sins
6436 if you wish to regain the graces
you used to enjoy.
Tell me now if you are willing."
—"Yes," he said, "most willing."
6440 —"Now I enjoin you to remain
here with me two full days,
and in penitence to take
only such nourishment as I do."
6444 Perceval agreed to this
and the hermit whispered
a prayer into his ear,
repeating it until he knew it well.

6448	And in this prayer were		to seek his glory and honor,
	many of the names for Our Lord,		had climbed this hillock.
	all the best and holiest,	6500	Then he looked beneath the oak
	which man's mouth should never utter		and saw a damsel sitting,
6452	except in peril of death.		who would have seemed very beautiful to him
	After he had taught him the prayer,		
	he forbade him ever to say it		had she been happy and joyful,
	except in the gravest of perils.	6504	but she had dug her fingers
6456	"Nor shall I, sir," said Perceval.		into her tresses to pull out her hair
	So he remained and heard		and was showing every sign of grief.
	the service, and his heart filled with joy;		She was lamenting for a knight
	after the service he worshiped	6508	whose eyes, forehead, and lips
6460	the Cross and wept for his sins.		she was kissing repeatedly.
	And that night for supper		When my lord Gawain approached her
	he had what the hermit liked,		he saw the knight was wounded:
	but there were only herbs	6512	his face was cut up
6464	chervil, lettuce, and watercress—		and he had a very grievous
	and barley and oat bread,		sword gash in the middle of his head;
	and clear spring water;		blood was flowing freely
	and his horse had straw	6516	down both his sides.
6468	and a full bucket of barley.		The knight had fainted repeatedly
	Thus Perceval acknowledged		from the pain he suffered,
	that God was crucified		until finally he lost consciousness.
	and died on Good Friday.	6520	When my lord Gawain came there,
6472	On Easter Sunday Perceval		he could not tell whether he was dead or alive,
	very worthily received communion.		
	The tale no longer speaks		so he said: "My beauty, do you think
	of Perceval at this point;		this knight you're holding will survive?"
6476	you will have heard a great deal	6524	—"Sir," she replied, "you can see
	about my lord Gawain		that his wounds are so serious
	before I speak of Perceval again.		that he could die from the least of them."
	After escaping from the tower		And Gawain said to her: "My sweet friend,
6480	where he had been attacked by the mob,		
	my lord Gawain rode until he came,	6528	awaken him, if you don't mind,
	between nine in the morning and noon,		for I wish to ask him news
	to the foot of a hillock		of the affairs of this land."
6484	upon which he saw a tall and mighty oak,		—"Sir, I won't awaken him,"
	thick with leaves that cast a deep shadow.	6532	said the maiden. "I'd let myself
			be ripped to pieces first,
	He saw a shield hanging from the oak		for I've never loved a man so dearly
	with a straight lance beside it.		and never will again as long as I live.
6488	He hurried toward the oak	6536	Since I see him sleeping peacefully
	until he saw beside it		I'd be a wretch and fool
	a small Norwegian palfrey;		if I did anything
	and he was quite surprised,		that might cause him to complain of me."
6492	for it was most unusual,		
	it seemed to him, to find a palfrey	6540	—"Upon my word, then I'll awaken him,"
	together with a shield and arms.		
	Had the palfrey been a charger,		said my lord Gawain.
6496	he might have presumed that some squire,		Then with the butt
			of his lance he touched
	who had gone off through the countryside	6544	the knight's spur; the knight was not upset

at being awakened in this fashion,
because Gawain had nudged his spur
so very gently that he did not hurt him;
6548 instead the knight thanked him and said:
"My lord, I thank you five hundred times
for having nudged and awakened
me in such a courteous manner
6552 that I've felt no pain at all.
But for your own safety I urge you
not to proceed beyond this spot,
for that would be a great folly.
6556 Take my advice and stay here."
—"Stay here, my lord? Why should I?"
—"I'll tell you, upon my faith,
since you wish to hear it.
6560 No knight who crossed these fields
or took these paths has ever returned,
for this is the frontier of Galloway:
no knight can ever cross it
6564 and return with his life;
and no knight has ever returned
except me, but I'm so grievously
wounded that I don't think
6568 I'll live to see the evening.
I encountered a knight who was
bold and brave and strong and proud:
I'd never before encountered such a bold one
6572 or tested myself against one so strong.
Therefore I advise you to turn back
rather than descend this hillock."
—"Upon my word," said my lord Gawain,
6576 "it would be a base choice to turn around:
I didn't come here to turn back.
It would be imputed as
the worst sort of cowardice
6580 if I were to turn back
after having chosen this road:
I'll go forward until I discover
why no one can return."
6584 —"I clearly see you are determined to go,"
said the injured knight,
"and you will go, since it is your desire
to increase and enhance your honor.
6588 But if it would not displease you,
if God should grant you the honor
to return this way—
which no knight at any time
6592 has ever had, nor do I believe
that anyone ever will,
in any event, either you or any other—
I would like to beseech you
6596 to ascertain, if you please,
whether I am dead or alive,
or if I'm better off or worse.
If I am dead, in charity
6600 and in the name of the Holy Trinity
I beseech you to take care
of this maiden and to see
that she is not disgraced or abused.
6604 And may it please you to do so,
for God never made or conceived of
a more noble, better bred,
more courteous, or more gracious damsel.
6608 I believe she is very sad now
on my account, and rightly so,
for she sees me near to death."
My lord Gawain assured him
6612 that if imprisonment or other
unforeseen misfortune did not detain him,
he would return there to him
and give the maiden
6616 the best counsel he could.
And so he left them and rode on
across plains and through forests
until he saw a mighty castle,
6620 to one side of which was a port
filled with many ships.
The castle, which was splendid indeed,
was worth scarcely less than Pavia.
6624 Beyond it were the vineyards,
and a mighty river flowed
around all the walls
down to the sea:
6628 thus the castle and town
were entirely enclosed by it.
My lord Gawain entered
the castle by crossing a bridge,
6632 and when he had ridden up
to the strongest place in all the castle,
in a garden beneath an elm
he found a maiden all alone
6636 gazing in a mirror at her face
and neck, which were whiter than snow.
Her head was encircled by a narrow band
embroidered with golden threads.
6640 My lord Gawain spurred his horse
to a canter towards the maiden,

and she shouted to him: "Slow down!
slow down, sir! Take it easy,
6644 you're riding like a fool!
You shouldn't hurry so
and quicken your horse's pace:
only a fool rushes up for no reason."
6648 —"Maiden," said my lord Gawain,
"may you be blessed by God!
Tell me now, dear friend,
what you were thinking
6652 when you cautioned me
to slow down, and for no reason?"
—"I do have one, I swear, sir knight,
for I know just what you are thinking."
6656 —"What then?" he asked.—"You want
to grab me and carry me down this hill
across your horse's neck."
—"That's right, damsel."
6660 —"I knew it well," said she.
"Cursed be you for thinking that!
Be careful never to try
to put me on your horse!
6664 I'm not one of those silly girls
that knights sport with
and carry away on their horses
when they go out seeking adventure.
6668 You'll never carry me on your horse!
Nonetheless, if you dared,
you could take me off with you.
If you are willing to take the trouble
6672 to go fetch me my palfrey
from this garden plot,
I'll go along with you until
you encounter in my company
6676 misfortune and grief
and trials and shame and woe."
—"And is anything more than courage needed
for these trials, fair friend?" he asked.
6680 —"I don't believe so,
vassal," answered the damsel.
—"Ah, damsel, where can I leave
my horse if I cross to the garden,
6684 for he could never
pass over that plank I see."
—"It's true he couldn't, sir, so give
him to me and cross on foot.
6688 I'll care for your horse
as long as I'm able to restrain him.
But hurry back,
because I couldn't do much
6692 if he became restive

or were taken from me by force
before your return."
—"What you say is true," he replied.
6696 "If he's taken from you or escapes
I'll not hold you responsible,
and you'll never hear me say otherwise."
So he entrusted his horse to her
6700 and departed, but he decided
to carry all his arms with him,
for if he were to find anyone in the orchard
who wished to deny or keep him
6704 from fetching the palfrey,
there would be a fight or battle
before he returned without it.
Then he crossed over the plank
6708 and found a gathering of many people,
who were looking at him in amazement
and saying: "May a hundred devils burn you,
maiden, for such an evil deed!
6712 May you go to perdition,
for you've never loved a noble man!
You've caused many a one to lose
his head, and it's a very great pity.
6716 Sir knight, you intend to lead away
the palfrey, but you don't yet realize
the troubles that await you
if you lay a hand upon it!
6720 Ah, sir knight, why do you keep coming closer?
Truly you would never come near it
if you realized the great shame,
the great trials and sufferings
6724 that will befall you if you lead it away."
The men and women said this
because they all wanted to warn
my lord Gawain not to go to the palfrey,
6728 but to turn back instead.
Though he heard and understood them well,
he would not abandon his quest on this account.
He pressed forward and greeted the crowd
6732 and they all, men and women alike, returned
his salutation, though it seemed
that all of them were
in great anguish and distress.
6736 My lord Gawain advanced
to the palfrey, held out his hand,

	and tried to take it by the bridle,
	for it was saddled and bridled.
6740	But there was a huge knight seated
	beneath a leafy olive tree
	who said: "Knight, you've wasted
	your efforts coming for the palfrey.
6744	Only false pride could make you
	reach out your hand for it now;
	nonetheless I don't wish
	to forbid or oppose you
6748	if you really want to take it.
	But I advise you to leave,
	for if you take it you'll encounter
	strong opposition elsewhere."
6752	—"I'll not stop for this reason,
	dear sir," said my lord Gawain,
	"because the lady admiring herself in a mirror
	beneath that elm tree sent me,
6756	and if I don't take it back to her now,
	then what did I come to seek?
	I would be disgraced throughout the land
	as a coward and failure."
6760	—"Then you will suffer for it,
	good brother," said the huge knight,
	"because by God the Almighty Father
	to whom I commend my soul,
6764	no knight ever dared take it—
	as you intend to take it—
	who did not suffer for it
	by having his head chopped off.
6768	This I fear will happen to you.
	And if I forbade you to take it
	I meant no harm by it,
	for you can lead it away, if you wish:
6772	don't stop on my account,
	or because of anyone you see here.
	But you will suffer evil consequences
	if you dare take it out of here.
6776	I don't advise you to do so,
	for you would lose your head."
	My lord Gawain did not delay
	even a single instant after these words.
6780	He drove the palfrey, whose head
	was half black and half white,
	in front of him across the plank;
	it had no difficulties crossing,
6784	for it was well trained and schooled
	and had done it many times.
	My lord Gawain took it
	by its rein, which was silk,
6788	and came straight to the tree

	where the damsel was gazing in her mirror.
	She had let her mantle
	and wimple fall to the ground
6792	so that one could better admire
	her face and body.
	My lord Gawain turned over
	the saddled palfrey to her,
6796	saying: "Come along now, maiden,
	and I'll help you mount."
	—"May God never let you claim,
	no matter where you go," said the maiden,
6800	"that you took me in your arms!
	If you ever held any part
	of me with your bare hand,
	or touched me or fondled me,
6804	I would think myself shamed.
	It would bring me much dishonor
	if it were ever said or known
	that you touched my bare flesh.
6808	I dare say I'd rather have
	the flesh and skin sliced
	right to the bone at that spot!
	Leave me the palfrey at once.
6812	I can easily get on by myself,
	for I've no need of your help.
	And may God permit me to see
	what I want to happen to you this day;
6816	before nightfall I'll have cause to rejoice!
	Go wherever you wish,
	for you'll not get any closer than you are
	to my person or my clothing,
6820	and I'll follow faithfully
	until you are overwhelmed
	by some great shame or misfortune
	on my account,
6824	for I am absolutely sure
	that I'll cause you to come to grief:
	it is as unavoidable as death."
	My lord Gawain listened
6828	to everything the haughty damsel
	told him without replying a word;
	he just gave her her palfrey
	and she let him have his horse.
6832	My lord Gawain leaned over,
	intending to pick up
	her mantle and help her put it on,
	but the damsel glared at him,
6836	unafraid as she was
	and quick to insult a knight:
	"Vassal," said she, "what business do you have
	with my mantle or wimple?

6840	By God, I'm not half
	as naïve as you think I am!
	I have absolutely no desire
	for you to undertake to serve me,
6844	for your hands are not clean enough
	to hold anything I'd wear
	or put around my head.
	Would you dare touch anything
6848	destined for my eyes or mouth,
	or for my forehead or face?
	May God never honor me again
	if I ever exhibit even the least
6852	desire to accept your service."
	So the maiden mounted,
	after lacing on her clothing herself,
	and said: "Now, knight, go
6856	wherever you wish
	and I'll follow along closely
	until I see you shamed on my account;
	and that will be today, if God pleases."
6860	My lord Gawain kept his peace
	and did not reply a single word.
	Shamefaced he mounted, and off they set;
	he turned back, with head hung low,
6864	towards the oak tree where he had left
	the maiden and the knight,
	who was in great need of a doctor
	to heal his wounds.
6868	And my lord Gawain knew
	more about healing wounds than anyone.
	In a hedgerow he saw an herb
	that was excellent for relieving pain
6872	from wounds, and he went to pick it.
	After picking the herb, he rode on
	until he again found
	the maiden weeping beneath the oak tree;
6876	and she told him as soon as
	she saw him: "My noble sir,
	I fear that this knight is dead,
	for he can no longer hear anything."
6880	My lord Gawain dismounted
	and found that his pulse was
	steady and that his mouth
	and cheeks were still warm.
6884	"Fair maiden," he said, "this knight
	is alive, you can be certain of it,
	for he has a steady pulse and is breathing well.
	And if his wounds are not fatal,
6888	I've brought him an herb
	which, I believe, will be of much help to him,
	and which will relieve some
	of the pain from his injuries
6892	as soon as it touches him;
	one cannot place a better herb
	upon a wound, for according to
	the book, its strength is such
6896	that if it is placed on the bark
	of a tree that's been injured,
	as long as it isn't completely withered,
	the roots will grow again
6900	and the tree will once more be able
	to leaf out and flower.
	My lady, your friend
	will be in no danger of dying
6904	once this herb is placed upon
	his wounds and bound tightly.
	But I'll need a clean wimple
	to make a bandage."
6908	—"I'll give you one immediately,"
	said she who was heartened by his words,
	"this very one I'm wearing on my head,
	for I've brought no other with me here."
6912	She removed the clean,
	white wimple from her head,
	and my lord Gawain cut it into strips,
	which was the proper procedure,
6916	and used it to bind the herb
	he had gathered over all his wounds;
	and the maiden helped him
	as best she was able and knew how.
6920	My lord Gawain did not move
	until the knight sighed
	and spoke these words: "May God watch over
	the one who restored my speech,
6924	for I was in great fear
	of dying without confession.
	The devils had come in procession
	to seek my soul.
6928	Before my body is buried
	I dearly wish to confess my sins.
	If I had a mount to ride,
	I know a nearby chaplain
6932	to whom I'd go and tell
	all my sins in confession
	and take communion;
	I would no longer fear death
6936	once I had made my confession
	and received communion.
	But please do me a favor now,
	if it is not too much trouble:

6940	give me the nag that squire is on,	6992	that I struck you, as God is my witness—
	who's trotting along in this direction."		but you did speak rudely!"
	When my lord Gawain heard this,		—"Now I won't stop until I tell you
	he turned and saw		how I intend to repay you;
6944	a hideous squire approaching.	6996	you'll lose the hand and arm
	What was he like? I'll tell you:		with which you gave me that blow,
	his hair was tangled and red,		for it will never be forgiven!"
	bristly and sticking straight up		In the meantime the wounded knight,
6948	like the spines of an enraged boar;		
	his eyebrows were the same,	7000	whose heart had been greatly weakened,
	and they covered his nose		regained his power of speech
	and all his face down to his moustache,		and said to my lord Gawain:
6952	which was twisted and long.		"Let this squire be, dear sir,
	He had a harelip and broad beard,	7004	for you'll never hear him say
	forked and then curled,		a word to your honor.
	a short neck and high chest.		Leave him, it's for the best,
6956	My lord Gawain was eager		but first bring me his nag;
	to go to him to find out	7008	then take this maiden
	whether he could have his nag,		you see here beside me,
	but first he said to the knight:		steady her palfrey
6960	"My lord, so help me God,		and help her mount,
	I don't know who the squire is.	7012	for I no longer wish to remain here.
	I'd rather give you seven chargers,		If I can, I'll mount this nag
	if I had them here with me,		and then look for someone
6964	than his poor horse, such as it is."		to whom I can confess my sins,
	—"My lord," he replied, "rest assured	7016	for I don't intend to stop
	that he is seeking nothing so much		until I receive the last rites,
	as to harm you, if he can."		confess my sins, and take communion."
6968	And my lord Gawain moved		My lord Gawain seized the nag
	toward the approaching squire	7020	at once and handed its reins
	and asked him where he was going.		to the knight, who had
	The uncouth squire said		regained his sight;
6972	to him: "Vassal, what's it to you		he looked at my lord Gawain
	where I'm going or where I'm coming from?	7024	and recognized him for the first time.
			My lord Gawain took
	Whatever road I'm taking,		the damsel and placed her
	a curse upon you!"		courteously and graciously
6976	My lord Gawain immediately	7028	upon the Norwegian palfrey.
	gave him his just deserts:		While he was helping her into the saddle,
	he struck him with open palm,		
	and since he was wearing gauntlets		the knight took my lord Gawain's horse
6980	and struck him purposefully,		and mounted, then began
	he toppled him from his saddle.	7032	to make it prance all around.
	And when he tried to stand back up,		My lord Gawain looked up
	he stumbled and fell down again,		and saw him galloping across the hillside;
6984	and fainted seven or more times		
	in less space—and this is the truth—		he was astounded and began to laugh,
	than the length of a pinewood lance.	7036	and with good humor said to him:
	When he finally regained his feet,		"Sir knight, upon my word,
6988	he said: "Vassal, you struck me!"		it's very foolish of you
	—"Indeed I did," replied my lord Gawain,		to make my horse leap about like that.
	"but I didn't hurt you very much;	7040	Dismount and give it to me,
	yet I'm sorry nonetheless		

for you could easily hurt yourself
and cause your wounds to reopen."
And he answered: "Hold your tongue, Gawain!
7044 You'd be smart to take the nag,
for you've lost your charger.
I made him prance to test him out,
and now I'll take him as my own."
7048 —"Hey! I came here to help you,
and you would harm me in return!?
Don't take my horse,
for that would be treachery!"
7052 —"Gawain, whatever might happen to me,
I don't regret this act;
I'd like to rip your heart
from your belly with my two hands."
7056 —"This reminds me of a proverb,"
said my lord Gawain, "which states:
'Stick out your neck for someone and
he'll break it.'
But I really want to know
7060 why you'd like to rip out
my heart and why you've taken my horse,
for I never sought to do you harm,
nor ever did in all my life.
7064 I don't believe I've done
anything to deserve this;
I don't think I've ever seen you before."
—"You have, Gawain; you saw me
7068 when you brought me great dishonor.
Don't you recall the knight
you tormented so
and forced against his will
7072 to eat for a month with the hounds,
his hands tied behind his back?
Know that you acted foolishly,
for now it will bring you disgrace."
7076 —"Are you then Greoreas,
who took the damsel by force
and did with her what you would?
Yet you knew perfectly well
7080 that maidens are protected
in King Arthur's land.
The king has given them safe conduct,
and watches over and protects them.
7084 No, I don't think, and I refuse to believe,
that this is why you hate me
and seek to do me ill,
for I acted in accord with the law
7088 that is established and set
throughout the kingdom."

—"Gawain, you punished me
on that occasion, I remember it well;
7092 so now you must
suffer what I choose to do:
I'll ride off on Gringalet,
it's the best vengeance I can have now.
7096 You'll have to trade him for the nag
of the squire you struck down,
for you'll get nothing else in exchange."
At that Greoreas left him
7100 and set off after his sweetheart,
who was riding away rapidly,
and he followed her at full speed.
Then the malevolent maiden laughed
7104 and said to my lord Gawain:
"Vassal, vassal, what will you do?
After what's happened one can truly say
that a few fools flourish still!
7108 I'm perfectly aware that it's wrong of me
to follow you, so help me God,
but wherever you turn
I'll gladly follow.
7112 I just wish that nag you took
from the squire were a mare!
You know why I wish that?
Because it would be even more
disgraceful."
7116 Immediately my lord Gawain mounted
the ridiculous trotting nag,
for he had no better option.
The nag was an extremely ugly beast:
7120 it had a thin neck, an outsized head
with long floppy ears,
and it was so long in the tooth
that they kept one lip from closing to
7124 within two fingers' breadth of the other.
Its eyes were weak and poor,
its feet eaten away, and its thin flanks
were all cut up by spurs.
7128 The nag was scrawny and long,
with a thin crupper and distended spine.
The reins and headstall
of its bridle were of frayed rope;
7132 the saddle had no blanket pad
and was far from new; the stirrups
were so short and so weak
that Gawain did not dare use them.
7136 "Ha! Things are going well indeed!"
said the spiteful maiden.
"Now I'll be delighted and happy
to go wherever you wish,
7140 because it is quite right and proper now

that I follow after you
for a week or two,
or three weeks or a month!
7144 Now that you're so well equipped
and seated on such a fine horse
you really look like a knight
who should be escorting a maiden!
7148 So the first thing I want is to amuse myself
by observing your misfortunes:
try spurring your nag a bit
to see how it goes!
7152 But don't be frightened,
he's awfully swift and spirited!
I'll follow you, for it is sworn
that I'll never quit you
7156 until you are truly disgraced,
and there's no way to avoid it."
And he replied: "Fair friend,
you may say what you please,
7160 but it isn't proper for a girl
to be so evil-tongued
beyond the age of ten;
instead she should be polite,
7164 courteous, and well-mannered."
—"Unfortunate knight,
I have no interest in lessons from you;
ride on and hold your tongue,
7168 for now you're exactly the way
I wanted to see you."
So they rode on until evening,
and neither of them said anything more.
7172 Gawain rode on, with the maiden after,
and no matter how hard he tried
he could not discover how to get
his nag to run or gallop.
7176 Like it or not, it just walked along,
for if he touched it with his spurs
it gave him a dreadful ride,
jostling his insides so much
7180 that in the end he could not bear
for it to go faster than a walk.
So he rode upon the nag
through lonely and uninhabited forests
7184 until he came to a flat plain
crossed by a deep river,
which was so wide that no stone
could be shot across the river
7188 by mangonel or catapult,
nor bolt by any crossbow.
On the other side of the water sat
a very well designed, very strong,
7192 and very splendid castle.

There is no reason for me to lie about it:
the castle sat upon a cliff
and was so well fortified
7196 that no finer fortress was ever beheld
by eye of mortal man;
and upon a bare rock
was set a great hall
7200 all of dark-colored marble.
There were a good five hundred open windows
in the great hall, and a hundred of them
were filled with ladies and damsels
7204 gazing out into the meadows
and flowering orchards in front of them.
Most of the damsels
were wearing clothes of samite,
7208 and most had donned
tunics of many hues
and silken robes with golden threads.
The maidens were standing
7212 before the windows,
and those outside could see them
from the waist up
with their lustrous hair and noble bodies.
7216 And the evilest creature in the world,
who was directing my lord Gawain,
came straight to the riverbank,
then stopped and dismounted
7220 from her little dappled palfrey;
on the shore she found a boat
chained to a stone mooring
and locked with a key.
7224 In the boat was an oar,
and upon the mooring
was the key that locked the boat.
The damsel, who had an evil heart
7228 within her breast, entered the boat,
followed by her palfrey,
which had done this many times before.
"Vassal," said she, "dismount
7232 and come aboard after me
with your nag
that's thinner than a chick;
then pull up the ship's anchor,
7236 for you'll soon be in a real fix
if you don't cross over this water at once,
or can't get away quickly."
—"Tell me, damsel, why is that?"
7240 —"Don't you see what I see,
sir knight? If you saw it,
you'd flee at once."
My lord Gawain immediately

7244	turned his head, saw
	a knight coming across the clearing
	in full armor, and asked
	the maiden: "Now if you don't mind,
7248	tell me who that is seated
	upon my own horse that was stolen from me
	by the traitor whose wounds
	I healed this morning."
7252	—"By St. Martin, I'll tell you,"
	said the maiden gaily,
	"but you can be sure
	that nothing would make me tell you
7256	if I saw it could help you at all.
	But since I am sure
	he comes to do you ill,
	I'll not hide his identity from you:
7260	he is the nephew of Greoreas,
	sent here by him to follow you;
	and I'll tell you why,
	since you've asked me:
7264	his uncle has ordered him
	to pursue you until he's killed you
	and brought your head back to him.
	This is why I urge you to dismount
7268	unless you want to wait and be killed.
	Climb aboard and escape."
	—"I'll certainly never flee because of him, damsel.
	No, I'll wait for him here."
7272	—"I'll not try to stop you,"
	said the damsel. "I'll hold my peace,
	because you'll put on a fine show
7276	before all those comely
	and attractive maidens
	leaning out those windows.
	Your presence makes the game more exciting,
	and they've come here on your account.
7280	You can imagine how happy they'll be
	when they see you stumble!
	You look just like a gallant knight
	ready to joust with another."
7284	—"Whatever it might cost me,
	maiden, I'll never flinch,
	but will go straight to meet him,
	because I'd be very happy
7288	if I could recover my horse."
	Then he headed for the clearing
	and turned his nag's head
	toward the knight who was
7292	spurring across the sands.
	As my lord Gawain awaited him,
	he thrust his feet so forcefully
	into the stirrups that he broke
7296	the left one clean off;
	so he abandoned the right one
	and awaited the knight just so,
	for the nag refused to budge;
7300	no matter how hard he spurred,
	he could not get it to move.
	"Alas!" he said. "A nag
	is a poor mount for a knight
7304	when he wants to joust!"
	Meanwhile the other knight
	charged directly toward him
	on his sure-footed steed and struck him
7308	such a blow with his lance
	that it bent, then shattered to pieces,
	leaving the point in Gawain's shield.
	And my lord Gawain struck
7312	the upper edge of the knight's shield,
	hitting it so hard that his lance
	passed through the shield and hauberk,
	upending him on the fine sand;
7316	then my lord Gawain reached out, took hold
	of his horse, and leapt into the saddle.
	This good fortune delighted him:
	his heart was so filled with joy
7320	that never in his life had he
	been so encouraged by one such success.
	He returned to the maiden
	who had gotten into the boat,
7324	but he did not find
	either her or the boat;
	he was most displeased
	to have lost track of her,
7328	for he didn't know what had become of her.
	While Gawain was thinking about the maiden,
	he saw a punt heading towards him
	from the direction of the castle,
7332	piloted by a boatman;
	and when he reached shore,
	the boatman said: "Sir, I bring you
	greetings from those damsels,
7336	and they also urge you
	not to keep what belongs to me;
	return it to me, if you please."
	Gawain answered: "May God bless
7340	the whole company of damsels
	and yourself as well.

I will never be the cause of your losing
    anything
to which you have a rightful claim:
7344 I have no desire to wrong you.
But what property are you requesting of
    me?"
—"Sir, I have seen you
defeat a knight
7348 whose charger I am entitled to have.
If you don't wish to wrong me,
you must return the horse to me."
Gawain replied: "Friend, I'd be
    reluctant
7352 to turn over this property to you,
for then I'd have to proceed on foot."
—"What, sir knight! Then
these damsels that you see
7356 will find you very disloyal
and consider it most wicked of you
not to return to me my property;
it has never happened, and no one has
    ever said,
7360 that a knight has been defeated
at this port without my having
his horse, if I knew of his defeat.
Or, if I didn't have the horse,
7364 I never failed to get the defeated
    knight."
My lord Gawain said to him:
"Friend, you are free to take
the knight and have him for yourself."
7368 —"Upon my word," said the boatman,
"he's not that badly injured.
I think even you
would have a hard time capturing him
7372 if he decided to resist you.
But anyway, if you're man enough,
go capture him and bring him to me
and your debt to me will be paid."
7376 —"Friend, if I dismount,
can I trust you
to keep my horse faithfully for me?"
—"Yes, certainly," he replied.
7380 "I'll keep it in trust
and willingly return it to you,
for I'll never wrong you
in anything as long as I live—
7384 this I pledge and swear to you."
—"And I," said Gawain, "believe you
on your pledge and oath."
Immediately he climbed down from his
    horse
7388 and gave it to the boatman, who took it

and said he would watch it faithfully.
My lord Gawain set off
with sword drawn toward his enemy,
7392 who was at the end of his strength,
for he had been deeply wounded in his
    side
and had lost a lot of blood.
My lord Gawain advanced towards him.
7396 "Sir, there's no need to hide it from
    you,"
said the grievously injured man.
"I'm so badly wounded
that I cannot bear any more.
7400 I've lost a large amount of blood
and surrender to your mercy."
—"Now get up from there," said
    Gawain.
With great difficulty he stood up,
7404 and my lord Gawain took him
to the boatman, who thanked him.
And my lord Gawain begged him,
if he had any news of the maiden
7408 whom he had been escorting there,
to tell him which direction
she had taken. He said:
"Sir, don't concern yourself
7412 with the maiden or where she went,
because she's not a maiden:
she's worse than Satan,
for she has had many a knight's head
7416 chopped off at this port.
But if you'll heed my advice,
you'll come to my house this day
and accept such lodgings as I can
    provide.
7420 It would not be to your advantage
to linger upon this shore,
for this is a wild land
full of great wonders."
7424 —"Friend, since you so advise me,
I wish to heed your counsel,
whatever it might bring."
He followed the boatman's advice and,
7428 leading his horse after him,
he boarded the punt and they set off
and reached the other shore.
The boatman's house was near
7432 the water, and was so good
and comfortable that a count
would be well received there.
The boatman escorted his guest
7436 and his prisoner and was
as happy as he could possibly be

My lord Gawain was served
with everything befitting a gentleman:
7440 he had plover and pheasant
and partridge and venison for supper;
and the wines were strong and clear,
both white and red, young and vintage.
7444 The boatman was very happy
with both his prisoner and his guest.
After they had eaten, the table was removed
and they washed their hands again.
7448 That night my lord Gawain had
host and lodgings to his liking,
for he was very pleased and delighted
with the boatman's hospitality.
7452 In the morning, as soon as
he could see the day breaking,
my lord Gawain arose as he should
and as was his custom.
7456 The boatman too, for the sake
of friendship, also arose,
and the two of them were soon
leaning out the windows of a turret.
7460 My lord Gawain gazed at the countryside,
which was most beautiful:
he beheld the forests and the plains
and the castle on the cliff.
7464 "My dear host," he said, "if you don't object,
I'd like to ask and inquire of you
who is lord of this land
and of that castle up there?"
7468 And his host replied without delay:
"Sir, I don't know."—"You don't know?
That's a surprise, because you told me
you are in the service of the castle
7472 and are well paid for it,
yet you don't know who's lord of it!"
—"I can truthfully tell you," he said,
that I don't know now and never have."
7476 —"Good host, then tell me now
who defends and guards the castle."
—"Sir, it is well guarded
by five hundred longbows and crossbows,
7480 which are always drawn and ready.
They are so ingeniously set up
that if anyone were to attack
they'd keep shooting indefinitely
7484 and never be exhausted.
I'll tell you this much about the situation:
there is a queen, a very noble,
rich, and wise lady,
7488 who's of the highest lineage.
The queen, with all
her great treasures of gold and silver,
came to dwell in this land,
7492 and she had this strong manor
you see before you built.
And she brought with her
a lady she loves so much
7496 that she calls her queen and daughter;
and this second lady also has a daughter,
who is in no way a shame
or disgrace to her lineage,
7500 and I don't think there's a more beautiful
or gifted princess under heaven.
The hall is very well protected
by magic and enchantment,
as you'll soon learn
if it pleases you to be told.
A learned astronomer,
whom the queen brought with her,
7508 created such a great marvel
in that palace on the hill,
that you've not heard the equal of it:
no knight can enter there,
7512 or stop for any time at all,
or stay alive within it
if he is filled with covetousness
or has within him any stain
7516 of pride or avarice.
Cowards and traitors cannot endure,
nor can perjurers or recreants:
these all perish so quickly
7520 that they cannot live there even a moment.
Yet there are many squires within,
who have come from many lands
to serve here and win their arms;
7524 there are easily as many as five hundred,
some with beards, others not:
a hundred without beard or moustache,
another hundred with growing beards,
7528 and a hundred who shave and trim
their beards every week.
There are a hundred with hair whiter
than lamb's wool,
and a hundred who are turning gray;
7532 and there are elderly ladies
without husbands or lords,
who have very wrongly been disinherited
from lands and possessions

7536 after the deaths of their husbands;
and there are orphaned damsels
abiding with the two queens,
who treat them with very great respect.
7540 Such are the people who frequent the castle,
and all are waiting for
an absurd, impossible event:
they are awaiting a knight
7544 who'll come there to protect them,
to restore their inheritances to the ladies,
to give husbands to the maidens,
and to make the squires knights.
7548 But the sea will turn to ice
before they find a knight
who can stay within the great hall,
for he would have to be perfectly
7552 wise and generous, lacking all covetousness,
fair and noble, bold and loyal,
with no trace of wickedness or evil.
If such a knight were to come there,
7556 he could rule in the hall
and return their lands to the ladies
and bring many wars to their ends.
He could marry off the maidens,
7560 confer knighthood on the squires,
and in no time rid the hall
of its magic spells."
This news pleased and delighted
7564 my lord Gawain immensely.
"My dear host," he said, "let's ride down there.
Have my horse and arms
brought to me at once,
7568 for I don't want to tarry here any longer.
I'm eager to be off."—"Sir, which way?
As God is your protection, stay with me today,
tomorrow, and a few days more."
7572 —"Dear host, I cannot stay at this time,
but may your house be blessed!
I'll go instead, with God's aid,
to see the ladies up there
7576 and behold the marvels of the hall."
—"Silence, my lord! Please God,
you mustn't do anything so rash!
Take my advice and stay here."
7580 —"Enough, dear host. You must think
I am weak and cowardly!
May God forsake my soul
if I accept such advice!"

7584 —"Upon my word, sir, I'll say no more,
for it would be wasted effort.
Since you're so intent upon going,
you'll go, though it upsets me;
7588 and it is I who must escort you,
for I assure you that no other escort
would be of any avail to you.
But I wish to ask a boon of you."
7592 —"What boon, good host? I'd like to know."
—"First you must grant it."
—"Good host, I'll do your will
as long as it doesn't bring me dishonor."
7596 Then he ordered them to bring him
his horse from the stable,
all saddled and ready to ride,
and he called for his arms,
7600 which were brought to him.
He armed, mounted, and set off,
and the boatman in turn
mounted upon his palfrey,
7604 for he intended to give him a loyal escort
to where he himself was loath to go.
They rode to the foot of the stairs
in front of the great hall,
7608 where they found a peg-legged man
sitting alone upon a pile of freshly cut grass;
his artificial leg was of silver,
finely inlaid with gold
7612 and striped with alternating bands
of gold and precious stones.
The hands of the peg-legged man
were not idle, for he was holding
7616 a knife with which he was busily
whittling a piece of ash.
The man did not address
those who passed before him,
7620 nor did they say a word to him.
The boatman drew my lord Gawain
to him and asked: "Sir,
what do you make of this peg-legged man?"
7624 —"His artificial leg is not aspen wood,
I'd swear," said my lord Gawain,
"for what I see is quite beautiful."
—"In the name of God," said the boatman,
7628 "the peg-legged man is wealthy,
with large and handsome properties!
You would already have heard some news
that would have been most distressing

7632	were I not accompanying you
	and serving as your escort."
	So the two of them passed by him
	and came to the great hall,
7636	with its very high entry-way.
	Its gate was splendid and beautiful,
	for the hinges and catches were
	of pure gold, so the source tells.
7640	One of the doors was ivory,
	with beautifully carved panels;
	the other door was ebony,
	likewise with carved panels;
7644	and each was highlighted
	by gold leaf and magical gems.
	The stone floor of the great hall was
	green and red, dark blue and black,
7648	of many diverse colors,
	all carefully worked and polished.
	In the middle of the hall was a bed,
	in which there was not a speck of wood,
7652	for everything was gold
	except for the cords alone,
	which were all of silver.
	I am not lying about the bed,
7656	for at each point where the cords crossed
	there hung a little bell;
	over the bed was spread
	a large samite embroidery.
7660	To each of the bedposts
	was affixed a carbuncle,
	which cast as much light
	as four brightly burning candles.
7664	The bed's legs were carved figures
	of little dogs with grimacing jowls,
	and the dogs were set on four wheels
	that rolled so smoothly
7668	that you could push the bed
	with one finger and roll it
	all the way across the room.
	To tell the truth, the bed was so unusual
7672	that none like it had ever been made
	for count or king, nor ever would be.
	The hall was all hung with silk,
	and I want you to believe me
7676	when I say the walls were not
	of soft plaster but marble,
	with glass windows above
	so clear that if you were attentive
7680	you could see through the glass
	everyone passing through the door
	and entering the hall.
	The glass was stained
7684	with the most costly and finest colors
	one could conceive of or create.
	But I do not wish to describe
	or tell about everything.
7688	The hall had some four hundred
	closed windows, and a hundred open.
	My lord Gawain carefully
	inspected the hall
7692	from top to bottom and to every side.
	When he had seen it all,
	he called to the boatman
	and said: "Good host, I don't see
7696	anything here that would
	make one fear
	to enter this hall.
	Now tell me what you meant
7700	when you warned me so insistently
	not to come and see it.
	I wish to sit and rest
	a little upon this bed,
7704	for I've never seen such a splendid one."
	—"Ah, dear sir! May God keep you
	from going near that place!
	If you do approach it,
7708	you'll die the most horrible death
	ever any knight experienced."
	—"Good host, then what should I do?"
	—"What, sir? I'll tell you,
7712	since I see you're eager
	to stay alive.
	When you decided to come to this place,
	I asked you for a boon before we left
7716	my house, but you didn't know what it was.
	Now I wish to collect the boon:
	you are to return to your land
	and tell your friends
7720	and the people of your country
	that you've seen a hall
	more splendid than any you know,
	more splendid than anyone knows!"
7724	—"Though you seem to be suggesting this
	for my benefit, good host, it would be
	like admitting I'd lost God's favor
	and been disgraced as well.
7728	No, nothing will prevent me
	from sitting upon the bed
	and beholding the maidens
	I saw last evening leaning
7732	out over those window ledges."
	Like a man pulling back to deliver a harder blow,

	the boatman replied: "You'll not see a one
	of those maidens you've mentioned!
7736	Go back out now
	just as you came in,
	for it is no good at all
	for you to see them;
7740	yet, so help me God,
	the damsels, queens, and ladies
	who are in those rooms
	can see you even now
7744	through these glass windows."
	—"Upon my word," said my lord Gawain,
	"even if I cannot see the maidens
	at least I'll sit upon the bed,
7748	because I do not think or believe
	that such a bed was made
	except for a worthy man
	or noble lady to rest upon;
7752	so by my soul I'll sit upon it,
	whatever may be the outcome!"
	When the boatman saw he was unable
	to stop him, he said no more;
7756	but he could not bear to remain in the hall
	long enough to watch him
	sit upon the bed, so he went his way
	saying: "My lord, I'm very upset
7760	and saddened you must die,
	for no knight has ever sat
	upon this bed who didn't die,
	because it is the Bed of Marvels,
7764	whereon no one sleeps or dozes
	or rests or sits
	and then arises alive and well:
	it is a great pity
7768	that you will offer your life in pledge
	without hope of ransom or recovery.
	Since neither affection nor argument
	can persuade you to leave this place,
7772	may God have mercy on your soul,
	for my heart could never bear it
	were I to see you die."
	With that he left the great hall.
7776	And my lord Gawain sat
	upon the bed in his full armor,
	with his shield strapped over his shoulders.
	As he sat down
7780	the cords screeched
	and all the bells rang,
	filling the whole hall with noise.
	All the windows flew open,
7784	and the wonders were revealed
	and the enchantments appeared,
	for bolts and arrows
	flew in through the windows,
7788	and more than five hundred
	struck my lord Gawain's shield.
	He did not know who'd attacked him,
	for the enchantment was such
7792	that no one could see
	from which direction the arrows came,
	nor the archers who shot them.
	And you can well imagine
7796	the great racket made by the stretching
	of so many crossbows and longbows.
	At this moment my lord Gawain would have given
	a thousand marks not to have been there.
7800	But in short order the windows
	reclosed without anyone touching them,
	and my lord Gawain pulled out
	the bolts that were stuck
7804	in his shield, several of which
	had wounded his body
	and caused the blood to gush forth.
	Before he had pulled them all out,
7808	he was subjected to another trial:
	a peasant struck a door
	with a club, and the door opened
	and a very ravenous,
7812	strong, fierce, and wondrous lion
	leapt from a room through the door
	and attacked my lord Gawain
	with great viciousness and savagery;
7816	it dug its claws full length
	into my lord Gawain's shield
	as if it were wax,
	and drove him to his knees.
7820	But he jumped up at once and drew
	his good sword from its scabbard
	and struck such a blow that he
	cut off its head and both forepaws.
7824	My lord Gawain was delighted
	to see both its paws hanging
	on his shield by the claws—
	he could see the paws on one side
7828	and the claws sticking through on the other.
	After killing the lion,
	he sat back down upon the bed,
	and his host returned
7832	to the hall with a beaming face,
	found him sitting on the bed,

	and said: "Sir, I assure you		to consider you their rightful lord
	you have nothing more to fear.		and to come serve you one and all.
7836	Remove all your armor,		I offer you my service
	because the marvels of the great hall	7888	before all others without deceit,
	have been forever stilled		and these maidens coming here
	by your coming here.		all consider you their lord,
7840	You'll be served and honored		for they have long hoped for your coming.
	by young and old	7892	Now they are happy when they behold
	herein, may God be praised!"		the best of all gentlemen.
	At that floods of squires came up,		Sir, there is nothing more to say, for we are
7844	all very handsomely clad in tunics;		all prepared to serve you."
	they all fell to their knees,	7896	With these words they all knelt
	saying: "Dear good kind sir,		down and bowed to him,
	we offer you our services;		for they had all sworn themselves
7848	you are the one we have		to his service and glory.
	long been awaiting and hoping for,	7900	He had them arise
	though it seems that you have been		at once and be seated,
	a very long time coming to us."		for they were very delightful to behold,
7852	Immediately one of them came forward		not only because they were beautiful
	and began to remove his armor,	7904	but more especially because they had made
	and others went to stable		him their prince and their lord.
	his horse, which was still outside.		He was happy, and had never been happier,
7856	And as he was being disarmed,		for the honor God had bestowed upon him.
	a very beautiful and attractive	7908	Then the maiden came forward
	maiden, who had a golden band		and said: "My lady sends you
	upon her head, and whose hair		this robe to put on before she
7860	was as blond as gold,		sees you, because she believes,
	or more so, entered the room.	7912	being filled as she is
	Her face was white, and Nature		with courtesy and wisdom,
	had highlighted it		that you have undergone
7864	with a pure and rosy tint.		great sufferings and tribulations.
	The maiden was very graceful,	7916	So put it on, and see
	beautiful and elegant, tall and erect;		if it is a good size for you,
	and she was followed by other		because it is prudent to dress warmly
7868	very noble and beautiful maidens.		against the cold after the heat of exercise,
	And there came a single young squire,	7920	lest you become numb and chilled.
	who had a robe over his shoulders,		That is why my lady the queen
	a cloak, mantle, and surcoat.		sends you an ermine robe:
7872	The mantle was lined in ermine		so that the cold won't harm you,
	and sable black as mulberries,	7924	for blood congeals in the veins
	and the outside		when a man shivers after the heat of exercise,
	was of a splendid red material.		just as water turns to ice."
7876	My lord Gawain marvelled		And my lord Gawain replied,
	at the maidens he saw approaching	7928	like the most courteous man in the world:
	and he could not stop himself		"May the all-perfect Lord
	from leaping to his feet to greet them,		
7880	saying: "Welcome, fair maidens!"		
	And the one who came first bowed to him		
	and said: "Good dear sir,		
	my lady the queen sends you greetings		
7884	and has ordered all her people		

save my lady the queen,
and you, too, for your kind words,
7932 your courtesy, and your charm.
I believe the lady who has
such a courteous messenger must be wise indeed;
she is well aware of what a knight
7936 needs and requires
when she—and I thank her for it—
sends me a robe to wear.
Please thank her sincerely for me."
7940 —"I assure you I shall gladly
do so," said the maiden.
"And while you are waiting, you may
dress and gaze out over
7944 the countryside through these windows;
or, if you like, you can climb
up into this tower to see
the forests, plains, and rivers
7948 until I have returned."
With that the maiden departed.
My lord Gawain dressed himself
in the very costly robe
7952 and fastened the neck with a clasp
that was hanging at the collar.
Then he wished to go see the view
from the tower.
7956 Accompanied by the boatman,
he climbed a spiral staircase
along the wall of the vaulted hall
until they reached the top of the tower
7960 and could see the surrounding countryside,
more beautiful than words can describe.
My lord Gawain gazed at all
the rivers and flatlands,
7964 and the forests full of wild game;
then he looked at the boatman
and said: "Good host, so help me God,
I'd love to stay here
7968 to go hunting and shooting
in these nearby forests."
—"My lord, you'd do well to speak
no more of this," said the boatman,
7972 for I've often heard it told
that it was vowed and determined
that whoever God would love so dearly
that the people of this castle would proclaim him
7976 their master and lord and protector,

would never again, whether rightly or wrongly,
be able to leave this manor.
Therefore you must not speak
7980 of hunting or shooting;
here is where you'll stay:
you'll never leave this castle again."
—"Good host," he said, "speak no more of this!
7984 You'll drive me out of my mind
if I hear you say that again!
So help me God, I couldn't live here
for as many as seven days,
7988 any more than for seven score years,
if I didn't have the possibility
of leaving whenever I wanted,"
At that he came down
7992 and went back into the great hall
very angry and upset;
he sat back down upon the bed
with a sorrowful and downcast face,
7996 until the maiden returned
who had been there before.
When my lord Gawain saw her,
he stood up to meet her
8000 and greeted her at once,
though he was still ill-tempered.
She noticed that his words
and countenance were much altered,
8004 and it certainly appeared from his face
that something had vexed him;
but she did not dare let on she knew,
and said: "Sir, whenever you please
8008 my lady will come to see you.
The dinner is prepared
and you can eat, if you wish,
either down here or up there."
8012 My lord Gawain replied:
"My pretty, I don't wish to eat.
May I be cursed
if I eat or have any pleasure
8016 before I've heard other news
which I really need to hear
to cheer me up."
Much abashed, the maiden
8020 returned at once to the queen,
who motioned to her
and asked: "What news,
sweet granddaughter?" said the queen.
8024 "In what state, in what mood
did you find the good lord
whom God has given us?"
—"Ah, my lady, honored queen,

8028 my heart is mortally wounded
because the only words one can elicit
from the noble and highborn knight
are words of wrath and anger.
8032 Nor can I tell you the reason why,
for he didn't tell me and I don't know
and I didn't dare ask him.
But I can well assure you
8036 that the first time I saw him
today I found him so polite,
so talkative, so happy,
that I couldn't hear enough
8040 of his words or see enough
of his handsome face.
But all of a sudden he is so changed
that I think he'd rather be dead,
8044 for everything he hears annoys him."
—"Don't worry, grand-daughter,
for he'll calm down completely
as soon as he sees me:
8048 no matter how great the anger in his heart,
I'll swiftly banish it
and put great joy in its place."
Then the queen stirred
8052 and came into the great hall,
along with the other queen
who was delighted to accompany her,
and after them trailed
8056 a good hundred and fifty damsels
and at least as many squires.
As soon as my lord Gawain
saw the queen coming
8060 hand in hand with the other queen,
his heart guessed and told him
that this was the queen
about whom he had heard tell.
8064 This was easy to divine
on seeing the white tresses
that hung down over her hips;
she was clad in a white silk gown
8068 with golden flowers, delicately woven.
As soon as my lord Gawain saw her
he was not slow to approach her;
he greeted her and she him,
8072 saying: "Sir, after you
I am lady of this palace.
I yield you its lordship,
for you have well deserved it.
8076 But are you from the household
of King Arthur?"—"My lady, I am indeed."

—"And are you, I'd like to know,
one of the knights of the king's watch,
8080 who have done so many deeds of prowess?"
—"I am not, my lady."—"As you say.
Then tell me, are you
a Knight of the Round Table,
8084 one of the most worthy in the world?"
—"My lady," he answered, "I wouldn't dare
say that I'm one of the most worthy.
I don't count myself among the best,
8088 nor do I think I'm one of the worst."
And she replied: "Noble sir,
these are most courteous words I hear,
when you don't accord yourself the praise
8092 due the best, nor the blame due the worst.
But tell me now about King Lot:
how many sons did he have by his wife?"
—"Four, my lady."—"Tell me their names."
8096 —"My lady, Gawain is the eldest;
the second is Agravain,
the Proud Knight with strong hands;
Gaheris and Gareth
8100 are the names of the last two."
And again the queen spoke:
"Sir, as God is my support,
it seems to me those are their names.
8104 Would to God they were all
here with us now!
Tell me now, do you know
King Urien?"—"Yes, my lady."
8108 —"Does he have a son at court?"
—"Yes, my lady, two very renowned sons.
One is called my lord Yvain,
the courteous and well-mannered:
8112 I find him so wise and courteous
that it makes me happier all day long
when I can see him in the morning.
And the other is also called Yvain,
8116 but he's not his full brother,
so they call him the Bastard,
and he defeats all knights
who oppose him in battle.
8120 At court they are both
very noble, very wise, and very courteous."
—"Dear sir," said she, "and how
goes it with King Arthur now?"

8124 —"Better than he ever was before:
he's healthier, happier, and stronger."
—"Upon my word," she said, "that's not surprising,
for he's still a child, King Arthur.
8128 If he's a hundred, he's no more;
he couldn't be a day over that.
But there is still more I'd like to learn
from you: please tell me
8132 about the bearing and comportment
of the queen, if it's not too much trouble."
—"Indeed, my lady, she is so courteous
and so beautiful and so full of wisdom
8136 that God has not created a land or region
where one could find a wiser lady.
No lady has been so esteemed
since God formed the first
8140 woman from Adam's rib;
and she is very rightly so acclaimed.
Just as the wise master
instructs the little children,
8144 so my lady the queen
teaches and instructs everyone,
for every good thing has
its source and origin in her.
8148 It is impossible for anyone
to depart unhappy from my lady,
for she knows each person's worth exactly,
and what must be done
8152 in order for her to please him;
no man behaves well or honorably
without having learned it from my lady,
and no man, however miserable,
8156 leaves my lady's presence sad."
—"Nor will you leave my presence sad, sir."
—"My lady," he said, "I can well believe you,
because before I saw you
8160 I didn't care what I did,
I was so sad and downcast.
But now I am as happy and joyful
as I could possibly be."
8164 —"Sir, by the God who gave me life,"
said the queen with the white tresses,
"your happiness will double
and your joy constantly increase,
8168 and never again will they desert you.
And now that you are cheered up,
dinner has been prepared;
you may eat whenever you are ready

8172 and wherever you please:
you may eat up here if you wish,
or, if you prefer, you may come
down to eat in the chambers below."
8176 —"My lady, I would not like
to trade this hall for any chambers,
for I have been told that
no knight ever sat or ate here."
8180 —"No, my lord, none ever
emerged alive or stayed alive
for even the shortest while."
—"My lady, then I shall eat here
8184 if you give me your permission."
—"Sir, I give it gladly,
and you will be the first
knight ever to eat here."
8188 At that the queen departed,
leaving a good hundred and fifty
of her most beautiful maidens with him.
They dined beside him in the great hall,
8192 serving him and providing him
with whatever he desired.
More than a hundred squires served
at dinner, some of whom were
8196 all white-headed, others were
greying, and others not;
still others had neither beard
nor moustache, and two of these
8200 latter knelt together before him,
one carving his meat for him
and the other pouring his wine.
My lord Gawain had the boatman
8204 sit beside him to eat;
and the dinner was not short:
it lasted longer than one of
the days around Christmas,
8208 for dark night had fallen
and many large torches were lit
before the meal was finished.
During dinner there was much
8212 conversation, and afterwards,
before going to bed, many rounds were danced;
they all wearied themselves making merry
over their dearly beloved lord.
8216 And when he was ready for bed,
he lay down upon the Bed of Marvels.
A damsel placed
a pillow under his head
8220 which helped him sleep comfortably.
The next day when he awoke
they readied for him
a robe of ermine and samite.

8224	The boatman came to his bedside
	in the morning and had him arise,
	dress, and wash his hands.
	Clarissant, the worthy, the beautiful,
8228	the comely, the wise, the eloquent,
	was also present at his rising.
	Then she went to the chamber
	of her grandmother the queen,
8232	who hugged her and asked:
	"Granddaughter, by the faith you owe me,
	has your lord arisen yet?"
	—"Yes, my lady, long ago."
8236	—"Where is he, my beautiful granddaughter?"
	—"My lady, he went up into the turret
	and I don't know whether he's come back down."
	—"Granddaughter, I wish to go to him,
8240	and, if it pleases God, today he will experience
	only joy, happiness, and pleasure."
	The queen stood up immediately,
	eager as she was to go to him.
8244	She found him high up
	gazing from the windows of a turret
	and watching a maiden
	and a fully armed knight
8248	who were making their way across a meadow.
	As he was watching them,
	the two queens came up
	side by side behind him;
8252	they found my lord Gawain
	and the boatman each at a window.
	—"Good morning to you, sir,"
	said both of the queens.
8256	"May the Glorious Father who made
	His daughter His mother
	bring you a happy and joyful day."
	—"My lady, may He who sent
8260	His Son to earth to save mankind
	accord you great happiness.
	But if you will,
	come here to this window
8264	and tell me who can be
	that maiden coming this way,
	accompanied by a knight
	with a quartered shield?"
8268	—"I'll gladly tell you,"
	said the queen as she looked.
	"May Hell fires burn her:
	it's the one who came here last evening with you.
8272	But don't pay any heed to her,
	for she's too proud and wicked.
	And I pray you not to pay heed either
	to the knight she's brought with her,
8276	for without a doubt he is
	the boldest knight of all:
	when he fights it is not for sport,
	because I've seen him defeat and kill
8280	many a knight at this port."
	—"My lady," he said, "with your permission, I'd like to go
	speak with the maiden."
8284	—"Sir, may it not please God for me
	to permit you to harm yourself.
	Let the malevolent maiden
	go about her own business.
8288	So help me God, you'll not leave
	your hall on such a foolish mission.
	And you must never again leave here
	unless you wish to do us wrong."
8292	"Heavens, noble queen!
	Now you've upset me greatly.
	I shall never be happy in this hall
	if I cannot leave it when I will.
8296	May it not please God for me
	to remain a prisoner here too long!"
	—"Ah, my lady," said the boatman,
	"let him do whatever he wants.
8300	Don't keep him against his will,
	for he might die of grief."
	—"Then I will let him leave,"
	said the queen, "provided he swears that,
8304	if God protects him from death,
	he will return here this very night."
	—"My lady," said Gawain, "do not worry,
	for I'll return if I am able.
8308	But I ask and request a boon of you,
	if you are willing to grant it:
	that you not ask my name
	for seven days, if you don't mind.
8312	—"Since that is your pleasure, my lord,"
	replied the queen, "I'll refrain from asking,
	for I do not wish to incur your hatred.
	Yet had you not forbidden me to,
8316	the first thing I would have requested
	would have been for you
	to tell me your name."
	So they climbed down from the turret,

8320	and squires ran up bringing his armor to arm him. His horse was led forth; fully armed he mounted it		My lord Gawain accepted his oath of surrender and turned him over to the awaiting boatman.
8324	and rode to the port accompanied by the boatman, and together they entered a boat and crossed so swiftly	8372	Meanwhile the malevolent maiden had gotten off her palfrey. Gawain came up to her and greeted her, saying: "Mount up, fair friend,
8328	that soon they reached the other shore, where my lord Gawain disembarked. And the other knight addressed the merciless maiden:	8376	I'm not going to leave you here; no, I'm taking you back with me over this river I must cross." —"Ah, knight!" she said,
8332	"Tell me, my friend, do you know this knight who's coming toward us fully armed?" And the maiden said: "Not at all,	8380	"look at how happy and proud you are! But you'd have had more than you could handle if my friend had not been
8336	but I do know that he's the one who escorted me to this place yesterday." And he responded: "So help me God, he's the one I was looking for!	8384	weakened by old wounds: your proud words would have been silenced, your babbling tongue hushed, and you'd have been checkmated into silence. Now tell me the truth:
8340	I was very much afraid he had escaped me, for no knight born of woman has ever crossed the frontier of Galloway	8388	do you think you're more worthy than he because you've defeated him? It often happens, as you well know, that the weak overcome the strong.
8344	and lived to boast anywhere that he's come back, if I have seen him and found him in front of me.	8392	But if you were to leave this port and come with me to that tree and undertake a task that my friend,
8348	This knight too will be captured and held prisoner, since God has let me see him." The knight immediately grasped his shield, spurred his horse,	8396	whom you've taken prisoner in the boat, did for me whenever I wanted, then I would truly acknowledge
8352	and charged without a word of warning. And my lord Gawain headed toward him and struck a blow that gravely wounded him in the arm and side;	8400	that you were more worthy than he, and would no longer bear you ill will." —"If I have to go no farther than that tree, maiden," he replied, "nothing will prevent my doing your will."
8356	but he was not fatally injured, for his hauberk held so well that the iron could barely penetrate it, though a finger's length	8404	And she said: "May it please God that I never see you return alive!" At that they set off on the way, she in front and he behind,
8360	at the very tip did enter his body and knocked him to the ground. He got up, alarmed to see his blood gushing from his arm and side	8408	while the maidens and ladies in the palace tore their hair and ripped and scratched themselves, saying: "Ah, wretched women,
8364	over his white hauberk. He rushed at Gawain with his sword, but became fatigued so quickly that he could not continue	8412	why are we still alive when we watch the knight who was to have been our lord going to his death and disgrace?
8368	and had to beg for mercy.		

8416	The malevolent maiden, that vile creature,
	is leading and escorting him
	to the place whence no knight returns!
	Alas! How soon we are wretched again
8420	after just finding happiness,
	for God had sent us
	a knight of unsurpassed goodness,
	lacking in no virtues,
8424	whether courage or anything else."
	In this manner the ladies
	lamented for their lord, whom they saw
	following after the evil damsel.
8428	She and my lord Gawain came
	beneath the tree, and when they were there
	my lord Gawain called to her:
	"Maiden," he said, "tell me now
8432	whether I've fulfilled my obligation:
	if you want me to do more,
	I'll do so if I'm able,
	rather than lose your good graces."
8436	Then the maiden said to him:
	"Do you see that deep ford
	with the very high banks?
	My friend used to cross there."
8440	—"I don't know where the ford is:
	the water's too deep, I'm afraid,
	and the bank is too high all around
	for one to go down it."
8444	—"I knew you wouldn't dare
	enter the ford," said the maiden.
	"I certainly never supposed
	that you'd be brave enough
8448	to dare to cross it,
	for this is the Perilous Ford
	that only the bravest of the brave
	dares cross."
8452	Immediately my lord Gawain
	led his horse to the edge
	and looked at the deep water below
	and the sheer vertical banks.
8456	But the river was narrow,
	so when my lord Gawain saw it
	he said to himself that his horse
	had leapt over many a wider chasm,
8460	and he recalled having heard
	it said in many places
	that the knight who could cross over
	the deep waters of the Perilous Ford
8464	would be accounted the best in the world.
	So he drew back from the river,
	then came springing forward full speed to jump over; but he failed,
8468	for he had not made a good jump
	and fell right into the middle of the ford.
	But his horse swam until it felt
	solid footing for all four hooves;
8472	it gathered itself for a jump,
	sprang, and leapt
	to the top of the steep bank.
	When it had reached the bank
8476	it was so tired
	that it could not stir at all;
	my lord Gawain was obliged
	to dismount, and he found
8480	his horse to be totally exhausted.
	As soon as he had dismounted
	he decided to remove
	the saddle, which he turned
8484	on its side to dry.
	After the blanket had been removed,
	he wiped the water from his horse's
	back, sides and legs.
8488	Then he resaddled his steed, remounted,
	and rode along at a walking pace
	until he saw a lone knight
	hunting with a sparrow-hawk.
8492	Preceding the knight through the meadow
	were three small bird dogs.
	The knight was more handsome
	than can be described in words.
8496	As he approached him, my lord Gawain
	greeted him and said:
	"Dear sir, may the God who made you
	more handsome than any other creature
8500	grant you joy and good fortune."
	And he was swift to reply:
	"You are handsome and good yourself!
	But tell me, if you don't mind,
8504	how you managed to leave
	that malevolent maiden alone over there.
	Where did her companions go?"
	—"Sir," said Gawain, "a knight
8508	with a quartered shield was
	escorting her when I met her."
	—"What did you do to him?"—"I defeated him in arms."
	—"And what became of the knight then?"
8512	—"The boatman led him away,

for he told me he was to have him."
—"Indeed, good sir, he told you the truth.
The maiden was my sweetheart,
8516 but she wasn't such as would
ever deign to love me
or to call me her lover,
nor did she ever favor me in anything,
8520 for I loved her against her will
after having taken her from a lover
she took everywhere with her:
I killed him and brought her with me
8524 and strove to serve her.
But my services were to no avail,
for as soon as she was able
she found the occasion to leave me
8528 and made that knight from whom
you've just taken her her friend.
He is not a knight to be scorned,
so help me God: he is very bold,
8532 yet he never was one
who dared to come anywhere
he thought he might encounter me.
Today you have done something
8536 no knight ever before ventured;
and since you dared do it,
your great prowess has won you
praise as the best knight in the world.
8540 It took tremendous courage
to leap into the Perilous Ford,
and you can be sure
that no knight had ever come out of it before."
8544 —"Sir," he said, "then the damsel lied to me when she said,
and had me believe as true,
that her friend crossed it once
8548 a day for love of her."
—"Did the liar say that?
Ha! she should be drowned herself,
for she is possessed of the devil
8552 to tell you such a monstrous lie!
She hates you, I can't deny it,
and that devil—may God damn her!—
wanted to have you drowned
8556 in the deep and treacherous waters.
Now give me your oath here
and I will give you mine:
if you wish to ask anything of me
8560 I'll never hide from you
the truth, if I know it,
whether it be to my joy or sadness;
and you will likewise swear

8564 that you will never lie to me
about anything I wish to ask of you,
if you know the truth to tell me."
Both swore this oath,
8568 and my lord Gawain began
by asking the first question:
"Sir," said he, "I wish to ask you
about a citadel I see over there:
8572 to whom does it belong and what is it called?"
—"Friend," he said, "I'll tell you
the truth about that citadel:
it is so completely mine
8576 that I owe nothing to anyone else
and give homage for it to God alone.
It is called Orqueneles."
—"And what is your name?"—
"Guiromelant."
8580 —"Sir, I've heard it said
that you are brave and worthy,
and lord over a vast land.
And what is the name of the maiden
8584 about whom no good is spoken,
either near or far,
as you yourself bear witness?"
—"I can truly attest," he replied,
8588 "that it's best to stay far from her,
for she's very wicked and full of scorn;
that is why she is called the Haughty Maid
of Logres, where she was born,
8592 and from whence she was brought as a child."
—"And what is the name of her friend
who went, whether he wished to or not,
as a prisoner of the boatman?"
8596 —"Friend, I assure you
that he is a fabulous knight
who is called the Haughty Knight
of the Stone at the Narrow Way
8600 and he defends the passes into Galloway."
—"And what is the name
of that strong and fine castle
from which I sallied forth today,
8604 and where I ate and drank last evening?"
At this question Guiromelant
turned away in sadness
and began to ride off.
8608 Gawain called him back:
"Sir, sir, speak to me!
Remember your oath."
Guiromelant stopped,

8612	turned his head towards him, and said: "May the hour I saw you and swore my oath to you be shamed and accursed!		because, thank God, I cut off its head and both feet.
8616	Be gone, I absolve you of your oath and ask you to absolve me of mine, because I had thought to ask you for news about that castle,	8664	What do you think of this proof?" At these words Guiromelant dismounted as swiftly as he could, knelt before Sir Gawain with hands clasped,
8620	but it seems to me you know as much about the moon as you do about it." —"Sir," replied Gawain, "I slept there last night in the Bed of Marvels,	8668	and begged him to pardon the foolish things he had said. "I forgive you completely," said Gawain. "Mount up again." Guiromelant remounted,
8624	which is unlike any other bed, and whose equal has never been seen." —"Upon my word," he said, "I am amazed by what you tell me!	8672	still ashamed of his ill-considered words, and said: "Sir, so help me God, I did not believe that there was any knight,
8628	What a pleasure and delight to hear your fabrications, for you're as much fun to listen to as any teller of tales:	8676	near or far, who could win the honor that has come to you! Tell me now if you saw the white-haired queen,
8632	you're a storyteller, I see it all now! Yet at first I thought you were a knight and that you'd done some feats of valor there.	8680	and whether you asked her who she is and where she's from." —"I never thought to ask," he said, "but I did see her and speak to her."
8636	But go ahead and tell me anyway of any bold deeds you did there, and what you saw there." And my lord Gawain told him:	8684	—"I shall tell you who she is," he said. "She's the mother of King Arthur." —"By the faith I owe God and His might,
8640	"Sir, when I sat upon the bed there was a great tumult in the hall, and don't think I'm lying to you, for the bed cords screeched	8688	if I remember right, King Arthur hasn't had a mother for a long while— not for a good sixty years or more, I believe."
8644	and bells, which were hanging from them, rang. Then the windows, which had been closed, all opened by themselves;	8692	—"Yet it is true, sir, that she's his mother. When Utherpendragon, his father, was laid to rest, it happened that Queen Igerne came into this land, bringing
8648	and sharp bolts and polished arrows struck my shield, and the claws of a huge, ferocious, and crested lion, which had long been	8696	all her wealth, and upon this rock she had the castle built and the splendid and beautiful hall I've heard you describe.
8652	kept chained in another chamber, remained caught in it. The lion was released and set upon me by a peasant;	8700	And I know that you saw the other queen, the grand and beautiful lady who was wife to King Lot and mother
8656	it sprang towards me and struck my shield with such force that it became stuck to it by its claws and couldn't withdraw them.	8704	of the knight I'd like to see damned— mother of Gawain!"—"Of Gawain, dear sir? I know him well, and I dare say that this Gawain has not had a mother
8660	If you don't believe my story, just look here at the claws	8708	for at least these past twenty years."

—"Yet it is she, sir, have no doubt.
She followed her mother here
and was heavy with child,
8712 bearing the very beautiful and noble
damsel who is my sweetheart
and the sister—I'll not hide it from
 you—
of him whom I'd like God to shame,
8716 for truly he'd no longer have
his head if I had him
within my grasp as you are now;
I would defeat him
8720 I'd cut it off at once,
and even his sister couldn't stop me
from ripping out his heart
with my bare hands, I hate him so!"
8724 —"You don't love in the same manner
I do, by my soul," said my lord Gawain.
"If I loved a maiden or lady,
for love of her I would love
8728 and serve all her family."
—"You're right, I admit it.
But when I think of Gawain
and of how his father killed mine,
8732 I cannot wish him well at all.
And Gawain himself killed
with his own hands a valiant and brave
knight who was my first cousin:
8736 I've never had the opportunity
to avenge him in any way.
Please do me a service:
go back to that castle
8740 and take this ring for me
to my sweetheart and give it to her.
I want you to go on my behalf
and tell her that I so trust
8744 and believe in her love for me,
that I know she'd prefer that her brother
Gawain die a bitter death
than that I should injure
8748 even my smallest toe.
Please greet my sweetheart for me
and give her this ring
from me, her lover."
8752 Then my lord Gawain put
the ring on his smallest finger
and said: "Sir, upon my word,
you have a wise and courteous
 sweetheart,
8756 a gentle woman of high lineage,
beautiful, noble, and high born,
if she behaves in just
the way you've said."

8760 The knight replied: "Sir, you will be
 doing me
a great service, I assure you,
if you take my ring as a gift
to my darling sweetheart,
8764 for I love her very deeply.
I will reward you for it
by telling you the name
of this castle, as you've asked:
8768 the castle, if you don't know,
is called the Rock of Champguin.
There many a fine cloth and bolt
of scarlet is dyed green or red,
8772 and much material is bought and sold.
 "Now I've told you what you wished
without word of falsehood,
and your questions have been good
 ones.
8776 Will you ask me anything more?"
—"Nothing, my lord, except for your
 leave."
And he answered: "Sir, if it's not
too much trouble, tell me
8780 your name before I grant you leave."
And my lord Gawain said to him:
"Sir, so help me God,
my name will never be hidden from you.
8784 I am the one you hate so much,
I am Gawain."—"You are Gawain?"
—"Indeed, the nephew of King Arthur."
—"In faith, then, you are very bold,
8788 or very foolhardy, to tell me your name,
knowing that I bear you a mortal hatred.
Now I'm quite troubled and annoyed
that I don't have my helmet laced on
8792 and my shield slung from my shoulder,
for if I were armed
as you are, you could be sure
I'd cut off your head instantly,
8796 and nothing could persuade me to spare
 you.
But if you dare to wait for me,
I'll go collect my arms
and return to fight against you,
8800 and I'll bring three or four men
to witness our battle.
Or, if you prefer, we can
put off our combat for a week,
8804 and on the seventh day return
fully armed to this spot,
and you should summon the king,
the queen, and all their people,

8808	and I'll summon all my people
	from throughout the land;
	thus our battle won't be fought
	in secret, but will be observed
8812	by everyone who'd wish to see it,
	because a battle between two worthy men,
	which they all say we both are,
	should not be fought secretly,
8816	but is best witnessed
	by many knights and ladies.
	And when one of us wearies
	everyone will know,
8820	so the victor will have
	a thousand times more glory
	than he would if he alone knew of it."
	—"Sir," said my lord Gawain,
8824	"I'd gladly settle for less
	if it were possible and you'd agree
	that there be no battle.
	And if I've wronged you in any way,
8828	I'll very gladly make amends
	before your friends and mine
	so that all will be made right and good."
	And he said: "I can't understand
8832	how anything could be right
	if you don't dare fight me.
	I've offered you two alternatives,
	choose whichever you prefer:
8836	if you dare, wait here
	and I'll go fetch my arms,
	or else send for all your supporters
	to be ready in seven days,
8840	for I've heard it said
	that at Pentecost King Arthur
	will hold his court at Orkney,
	which is but two days travel from here.
8844	Your messenger can find
	the king and all his people assembled there;
	you'd do well to send there,
	for a day's respite is worth a hundred sous."
8848	Gawain replied: "So help me God,
	the court will surely be there;
	you are well informed.
	And I swear by my hand
8852	that I'll send word to him tomorrow,
	or before I close my eyes to sleep."
	—"Gawain," said he, "I'd like
	to guide you to the best bridge in the world.
8856	The waters here are so swift and deep

	that no one alive can ford them
	or leap across to the other shore."
	And my lord Gawain replied:
8860	"No matter what might happen,
	I won't look for a ford or bridge.
	I'll go directly back
	to the wicked damsel
8864	as I have promised her,
	rather than incur her wrath."
	Then he spurred his horse and it leapt
	completely across the water
8868	without incident.
	When the maiden who had
	slandered him so with her unkind words
	saw him returning towards her,
8872	she tied her horse
	to the tree and came towards him on foot;
	her heart and feelings had changed,
	for she greeted him at once
8876	and said she had come
	to beg forgiveness for her wickedness,
	since he had endured so much for her sake.
	"Dear sir," she said, "listen now:
8880	I'd like to tell you, if you don't mind,
	why I've been so haughty
	toward all the knights of this earth
	who've tried to escort me.
8884	That knight—may God destroy him!—
	who spoke to you on the other shore
	wasted his love upon me.
	He loved me, but I hated him,
8888	because he caused me great pain
	by killing—I'll not hide it from you—
	the knight whose sweetheart I was.
	Then he thought he could honor me
8892	by persuading me to love him,
	but this was to no avail,
	for as soon as I was able
	I escaped from him
8896	and attached myself to the knight
	whom you stole away from me today,
	though I never cared a whit for him.
	But ever since death separated me
8900	from my first love,
	I've been behaving foolishly,
	and have been so rude of tongue
	and so wicked and foolish,
8904	that I never paid any heed
	to whom I was insulting,
	but did it deliberately,
	because I hoped to find

8908	someone so rash that I could make him angry and irate enough to slash me all to pieces, for I've long wished to be dead.	8956	where they all sat down. And my lord Gawain took his sister, seated her beside himself on the Bed of Marvels,
8912	Dear sir, punish me now so severely that no maiden who hears news of my punishment will ever again dare insult a knight."	8960	and said to her in a whisper: "Damsel, I bring you a ring from across this river, with a sparkling green emerald.
8916	—"Fair one," he said, "what is it to me to punish you? May it never please the Son of God Almighty for me to cause you pain.	8964	A knight sends it to you as a token of his love, and he greets you and says you are his sweetheart." —"Sir," said she, "I believe it well.
8920	Mount up now and don't delay: let us be off to this fortress. There's the boatman at the port waiting to take us across."	8968	But if I love him at all I'm his sweetheart from afar, for he's never seen me nor I him except across these waters.
8924	—"My lord, I will do your bidding from beginning to end," said the maiden. Then she climbed up onto the little long-maned palfrey's saddle,	8972	Though he gave me his love long ago, and I thank him for it, he's never crossed this river; but his messengers have implored me
8928	and they rode to the boatman, who ferried them across the water without any trouble or difficulty. And the ladies and maidens,	8976	so ardently that I've granted him my love, I'll not deny it. But I'm no more his sweetheart than that." —"Ah, pretty one! He's just now boasted
8932	who been lamenting my lord Gawain most bitterly, saw him approaching, and on his account all the squires in the palace had been mad with grief;	8980	that you would much rather see dead my lord Gawain, who is your own blood brother, than for him to injure his toe."
8936	but now they showed more joy than anyone had ever known before. The queen was seated in front of the great hall in expectation of his arrival;	8984	—"Heavens, sir! I'm astonished he could say such a foolish thing! By God, I never thought he was so ill-mannered!
8940	she had had all her maidens join hands together to dance and begin the merry-making. In his honor they began	8988	It was very impertinent of him to send me such a message. Alas, my brother doesn't even know I was born, and has never seen me.
8944	to sing, dance, and do rounds; and he came and dismounted in their midst. The ladies and the damsels and the two queens embraced him	8992	Guiromelant has lied!" While the two of them were speaking thus and the ladies observed their demeanor, the elderly queen sat down
8948	and spoke joyfully with him; amid great festivity they removed the armor from his legs, arms, feet, and head. Next they extended a joyful welcome	8996	beside her daughter and said to her: "Fair daughter, what do you think of this lord who is sitting beside your daughter, my granddaughter?
8952	to the maiden he had brought with him; they all served her for Gawain's sake, but not at all on her own account. They entered gaily into the great hall	9000	He's been whispering to her for a long time, about I don't know what, but I like it and it wouldn't be right for you to object, for it's a sign of his great nobility

9004 that he is attracted to the most beautiful
  and wisest woman
 in this hall, as is only right.
 May it please God that he marry her
9008 and that she please him as much
 as Lavinia did Aeneas."
 —"Ah, my lady," said the other queen,
 "may God grant him to love her
9012 as a brother loves his sister,
 and may he so love her and she him
 that the two become as one flesh."
 By her prayer the lady intended
9016 for him to love her and take her as his
  wife:
 she did not recognize her own son.
 Yet they will be like brother and sister,
 sharing no other kind of love.
9020 Once they have both learned
 that she is his sister and he her brother,
 their mother will experience a great
  happiness
 different to what she anticipated.
9024 After my lord Gawain had spoken
 for a while with his beautiful sister,
 he stood up and summoned
 a squire he saw to his right,
9028 the one who seemed the most
 eager and worthy and helpful,
 the wisest and most clever
 of all the squires in the hall.
9032 Gawain went into a private chamber,
 followed only by the squire.
 When they were both inside,
 Gawain addressed him: "Young man, I
  think
9036 you are a worthy, wise, and clever
  squire.
 I'm going to tell you a secret,
 and I warn you that it will be
 to your advantage to keep it well.
9040 I intend to send you to a place
 where you'll be happily welcomed."
 —"Sir, I'd rather have
 my tongue ripped from my throat
9044 than for a single word
 to escape my mouth
 that you would prefer be kept hidden."
 —"Brother," said Gawain, "then you
  shall go
9048 to my lord King Arthur,
 for I am called Gawain, his nephew.
 The way is neither long nor difficult,
 because the king is holding
9052 his Pentecost court
 in the city of Orkney.
 If the journey there costs
 you anything, I'll reimburse you.
9056 When you come before the king
 you'll find him very upset,
 but when you greet him
 in my name, he'll be filled with joy.
9060 Everyone who hears the news
 will be happy.
 You will say to the king that, by the faith
 he owes me as a lord to his vassal,
9064 nothing must prevent
 my finding him, on the fifth day
 of this feast, camped
 in the meadow below this tower;
9068 and he must come with as many people,
 both high-born and commoners,
 as are in attendance at his court,
 for I've engaged to do battle
9072 against a knight who has no trace of
  respect
 either for myself or for King Arthur:
 this knight is Guiromelant,
 who hates me with a mortal hatred.
9076 Likewise you will say to the queen
 that she must come by the great faith
 we bear one another,
 for she is my lady and my friend.
9080 She will not fail to come
 as soon as she receives the news;
 and tell her that for love of me
 she must bring with her all the ladies
9084 and maidens who are at court that day.
 Only one thing worries me:
 you might not have a good hunting
  horse
 to take you swiftly there."
9088 The squire replied that he had access to
 a large, swift, strong, and good horse
 that he could take as if it were his own.
 "I'm glad to hear that," said Gawain.
9092 Then the squire led Gawain
 straight to the stables
 and brought forth several
 strong and rested hunters,
9096 one of which was equipped
 to ride and travel,
 for he had just had it reshod
 and it lacked neither saddle nor bridle.
9100 "Upon my word, squire," said my lord
  Gawain,
 "you have everything you need.

Go now, and may the King of Kings
watch over your going and your coming
9104 and keep you on the right path."
So he sent off the squire
and accompanied him as far as the river,
where he ordered the boatman
9108 to ferry him across.
The boatman took him across
without any effort on his part,
for he had plenty of oarsmen.
9112 After crossing the river
the squire found the right path
that led to Orkney,
for anyone who knows how to ask directions
9116 can travel anywhere in the world.
My lord Gawain returned
to his palace, where he sojourned
amidst much joy and revelry,
9120 for everyone there loved him.
The queen had hot baths
prepared in five hundred tubs,
and had all the squires get in them
9124 to bathe themselves and soak.
Robes had been sewn for them,
which were brought forth to them
when they stepped from the baths:
9128 the cloth was woven with golden threads
and the linings were ermine.
The squires stood vigil all night long
in the church until after matins,
9132 without ever kneeling down.
In the morning my lord Gawain
with his own hands placed the right spur
on each of them, belted on their swords,
9136 and dubbed each squire a knight.
Afterwards he had a company
of five hundred new knights.
Meanwhile the squire rode
9140 until he came to the city
of Orkney, where the king was
holding a court as befitted the day.
The crippled and mangy beggars
9144 who saw him approaching

said: "This squire has an urgent mission:
I think he's coming from far away
with wondrous news for the court.
9148 Whatever he may say, he'll find
the king deaf and dumb,
for he's quite upset and sad.
And who will be there
9152 to offer counsel after he's heard
what the messenger has to say?'
—"Go on," they said. "What business is it
of ours to talk of advising the king?
9156 You ought to be worried,
dismayed, and saddened
at having lost the knight
who presented us all with clothing in God's name,
9160 and from whom we received everything
in charity and alms."
Thus throughout the city
the poor people lamented the loss
9164 of my lord Gawain, whom they all loved dearly.
The squire passed through the crowds
and rode on until he found
the king seated in his palace,
9168 with a hundred counts, a hundred dukes,
and a hundred kings seated around him.
Arthur was sad and downcast
to see all his many barons
9172 and no sign of his nephew;
he fainted in his great distress.
The first to reach the king
was certainly not slow,
9176 since they all rushed to help.
My lady Lore, who was seated
on a balcony, heard
the lamentations throughout the hall.
9180 She came down from the balcony,
overcome with emotion,
and went straight to the queen.
When the queen saw her
9184 she asked her what was the matter....

Perlesvaus (Le Haut Livre du Graal): Selections

Translated by WILLIAM W. KIBLER

When Chrétien de Troyes, probably around 1180, composed his *Conte du Graal (Story of the Grail)* its hero, Perceval the Welshman, was a naïve youth who set off on a seemingly impossible search: for a grail. It was not yet The Grail, much less The Holy Grail. It was only a simple serving platter on which were some strange foodstuffs. But it was accompanied by a mysterious procession involving maidens, candelabra, a bleeding lance, and bright light. Struck speechless by the sight, Perceval failed to ask the purpose of the grail, which only much later he learned was to provide sustenance to a maimed king, Perceval's own grandfather. Chrétien never completed his romance, so we will never truly know what it all means—if, indeed, even he did. But almost immediately afterwards other writers, enamored no doubt of this inchoate tale, began to compose sequels and conclusions, interpreting its strange events in their own fashion and to their own purposes. One of the most significant of these was Robert de Boron who, about a decade after Chrétien, transformed the grail into The Holy Grail, making explicit what was at most only suggested in Chrétien's tale. For him, the Grail was the cup of the Last Supper, used also to collect Christ's blood as he hung on the Cross. It was Robert, too, who explained how the Grail came to be in Britain, brought there by Bron, the Rich Fisher as well as the brother-in-law of Joseph of Arimathea. Continuing the process of Christianization, the anonymous poets of the *First* and *Second Continuations* of the *Conte du Graal*, writing in the last decade of the twelfth century, identified the bleeding lance with the lance used by Longinus to pierce Christ's side.

Early in the thirteenth century, an anonymous author composed a radically new prose version of the Perceval legend and Grail quest. It is centered on three traditional Arthurian heroes, Gawain, Lancelot, and Perceval (now renamed Perlesvaus) and takes up the story roughly at the point Chrétien left off. It is unapologetically Christian in its inspiration, full of allegory, and militant in its desire to see the New Law (Christianity) replace the Old (Judaism). Usually called simply *Perlesvaus*, it is perhaps better entitled *Le Haut Livre du Graal*. There exist today two complete manuscripts (Oxford, Bodleian Library, Hatton 82 and Brussels, Bibl. roy. 11145) as well as several fragments, the most important of which (Paris, Bibl. Nat. fr. 1428) serves as the basis of the present translation. It is divided into eleven Branches (or chapters) and runs to over 400 printed pages in each of the modern editions.[1] For this volume, we have chosen to reproduce the entire first Branch, as well as significant portions of Gawain's, Lancelot's, and Perlesvaus's visits to the Grail Castle. The intervening and subsequent narrative will be briefly filled in by summaries (in brackets). Page references in parentheses are to the Strubel edition.

[Branch I.² The story begins after Perceval's fatal first visit to the Grail Castle, as recounted by Chrétien. Arthur's realm is now in disarray, because the king himself no longer practices the regal virtues of honor and largess. Arthur determines to make amends. At a chapel in the forest he witnesses the mystery of transubstantiation, where he gains strength to defeat the devil incarnate. Typical of the *Perlesvaus* are the strange and bloody dream of Cahus, the vision of the transubstantiation, the barbarous allegorical battle against the Black Knight, and the evocation of Perlesvaus's past.]

* * *

Here begins the story of the most holy vessel called the Grail, which received the precious blood of the Savior on the day He was crucified to save mankind from Hell: Josephus composed it for posterity at the summoning of an angel's voice so that the truth might be known, through his writings and testimony, about the knights and worthy men who suffered grief and pain in bearing witness to the religion of Jesus Christ, which He established through his own crucifixion and death.

The High Book of the Grail begins in the name of the Father, the Son, and the Holy Spirit. These three persons are one being, and this being is very God, and from God comes the High Story of the Grail; and all those who hear it should pay heed and put aside all the wickedness they have in their hearts, for it will be most profitable to all those who hear it with their hearts. Josephus tells us this holy tale in order to recall the deeds of the worthy men and good knights, and for the lineage of a Good Knight who lived after the crucifixion of Our Lord. He was a good knight without fault, for he was chaste and virginal of body, bold and mighty of heart, endowed only with good qualities. He kept his own counsel and, to look at him, you would not have thought him so brave. Because of a very few words he hesitated to speak, so many misfortunes befell Great Britain that all the islands and all the land fell into great sadness; but later he restored them to joy through his chivalrous deeds. He was a good knight by right, for he was of the lineage of Joseph of Arimathea. This Joseph was the uncle of his mother and had been seven years in the service of Pontius Pilate; the only reward he asked for his service was to remove the body of Christ from the Cross. When this request was granted, it seemed very great to Joseph, but small indeed to Pilate, for Joseph had served him very well and, if he had asked for gold or land or riches, Pilate would gladly have given these to him. He granted him the gift of the Savior's body because he thought Joseph would drag it vilely through the city of Jerusalem after he had lowered it from the Cross, and then leave the body in some filthy place outside the city. But such was not the good knight's intention; instead, he honored the body as much as he could and placed it in the Holy Sepulcher, keeping the holy lance that had wounded him in the side, and the most holy vessel, in which those who believed in him and feared him gathered the blood that flowed from the wounds He received on the Cross (128).

The Good Knight for whom this high story is related was of this lineage. His mother's name was Iglai; his uncles were the Fisher King, the King of the Lowly People, called Pelles, and the King of Deadly Castle; this latter was as evil as the other two were good, and he was extremely evil; these three were his uncles on his mother Iglai's side, who was a loyal and good woman; the Good Knight had a sister named Dandrane. On his father's side, the lineage began with Nicodemus. Gay the Fat of the Hermits' Cross was the father of Julain the Fat of the Vales of Camelot. This Julain had eleven brothers, all good knights as was he; and all were knights for only twelve years, and all died in arms through their valor in their desire to promote the religion that had been newly established. There were twelve brothers: Julain the Fat was the eldest, Gosgallians came next, Brun Brandalis was third, Bertolai the Bald was fourth, Brandalus of Wales was fifth, Elinant of Escavalon was sixth, Calobritius the seventh, Meralis of the Palace Meadow was eighth, Fortunat of the Red Heath was ninth, Melairman of Albany the tenth, Galerian of the White Tower was eleventh, Aliban of the Desolate City was twelfth. All these brothers died in arms in the service of the Holy Prophet who established Holy Faith by his death, and they subjugated his enemies by their power. Josephus the good scribe tells us that this Good Knight, whose name and nature you will hear, was descended from these two lineages, whose names and account you have heard.

The authority of texts tells us that after Our Lord's crucifixion no earthly king did more to advance the cause of faith in Jesus Christ than did King Arthur of Britain, alone and with the good knights who lived at his court. Good King Arthur, after the crucifixion of Our Lord, was as I shall tell you: he was a powerful king who believed in God, and many fine adventures happened at his court; and he had the Round Table, which was favored with the best knights in the world. After the death of his father, King Arthur reigned more mightily and splendidly than ever any king had done, such that all the princes and all the barons imitated him for his goodness. King Arthur ruled ten years in the manner I have told you and no earthly king was as praised as he, until a weakening impulse overcame him and he began to lose interest in the largess he had formerly shown. He no longer wished to hold open court at Christmas, nor at Easter, nor at Pentecost. The knights of the Round Table, when they saw his favors growing less, began to leave and abandon his court. From three hundred seventy knights he once had in his household, no more than twenty-five remained. Adventures no longer happened at his court. All the other princes withheld their own largess, because they saw the king so lax. Queen Guinevere was so grief-stricken she did not know what to do with herself (132).

King Arthur was at Carduel one Ascension Day. He arose from table and paced the hall from one end to the other; looking up, he saw the queen seated at a window. The king sat down beside her, looked her in the face, and saw that tears were streaming from her eyes. "My lady," said the king, "what's the matter? Why are you crying?"—"Sire," said she, "it is right that I weep. Nor should you be joyful."—"My lady, indeed I am not."—"Sire," said she, "you are right. On a day like today I've seen so many knights at your court that they could scarcely be counted. Now there are so few every day that it brings me great shame, and no adventures happen any more. I am very fearful that God has forgotten you."—"Indeed, my lady," said the king, "I no longer have any desire to bestow largess or do anything that brings honor; rather, my desire has become weakness of heart, and I know that this causes me to lose my knights and the love of my friends."—"Sire," said the queen, "if you go to the chapel of St. Augustine, which is in the White Forest and can only be found through adventure, I believe that upon your return you will have renewed desire to do good, for if anyone prays to God with a sincere heart, no matter how disconsolate, God will listen and help."—"My lady," replied the king, "I'll go there most willingly. I have heard others speak of it just as you've described, and for three days now I've wanted to go there."—"The place is very dangerous, my lord," said she, "and the chapel full of adventures, but the worthiest hermit in all of Wales has his cell beside the chapel, where he lives only through the glory of God."—"My lady," said the king, "I must go there fully armed and without a knight for company."—"Surely you could take a squire with you," said the queen.—"My lady," replied the king, "I dare not, for the place is dangerous, and the more people you bring, the more cruel the adventures."—"Sire," said she, "you will take a squire because I wish you to do so and, if it please God, this will bring you only good."—"Be it as you wish, my lady," said the king, "but I fear that this will bring me ill."—"May God forbid that it do so, my lord!"

The king rose from the window seat, and then the queen. The king looked up and saw before him a tall, strong, and handsome young squire. His name was Cahus, and he was the son of Yvain the Bastard. "My lady," the king said to the queen, "I'll take this youth with me, if you agree."—"I do agree," said Guinevere, "because I've heard good things said of him." The king summoned the youth, who came and knelt before him. The king had him rise and said: "Cahus, you will sleep this night in this hall, and you will see that my horse is saddled at dawn and my armor ready, for I wish to set off at that very hour. You will come with me, alone."—"Sire," replied the squire, "it will be as you wish."

It was nearing vespers; the king and queen retired to bed. After dinner was finished in the hall, the knights returned to their lodgings. The squire remained in the hall; he chose not to remove his clothing or shoes, for the night seemed short and he wanted to be ready in the morning at the king's command.

The squire lay down as I've told you and in his first sleep he dreamt that the king had left without him. Very frightened, the squire ran to his horse, put on its saddle and reins, laced on his spurs, and girded his sword; it seemed to him in his dream that he rushed forth from the castle full speed after King Arthur. After having ridden a long way, he entered a vast forest and thought he saw in the path before him the tracks of the king's horse. He followed the trail a great distance until he came to a clearing in the forest, where he thought the king must have dismounted, or about there, because the trail had disappeared. On the right he saw a chapel in the clearing, and around it he saw a large cemetery with many sarcophagi, or so it seemed to him. In his dream he decided to go toward the chapel because he thought the king had entered there to pray. He rode that way and dismounted. Once dismounted, he tied up his horse and entered the chapel. He saw no one anywhere in the chapel except a single knight who was lying on a litter; he was covered with a fine silk cloth and there were four wax candles burning around him, set in four golden candelabra. The youth was very astonished to find this body left there all alone, for it was attended only by holy statues. And he was even more astonished not to find the king, for he did not know which way to look for him. He unfixed one of the candles, took the candelabrum and put it between his britches and his thigh, left the chapel, and remounted his horse. He rode past the cemetery, left the clearing, entered the forest, and decided that he would ride until he found the king (138).

As he was setting off, there appeared before him a man who was dark and ugly, even taller on foot than the squire was on horseback; he held a large, sharp, double-bladed knife in his hand, so it seemed. The youth spurred up to him and asked: "You, coming there—have you met King Arthur in this forest?"—"No," said he, "but I have met you, and I'm quite happy about it, since you left the chapel like a thief and traitor; you have stolen the golden candelabrum, which honored the knight who is lying dead in the chapel. I want you to give it back to me, so I can return it; otherwise, I challenge you."—"I swear to you," said the squire, "that I'll never return it, but will take it to give as a gift to King Arthur."—"And I swear," said the other, "that you'll pay very dearly for it if you don't return it to me at once." Then the youth spurred his horse, intending to ride on, but the other attacked him, striking his right side with his sword and driving it in up to the handle. The squire, who had dreamt all this while sleeping in the great hall at Carduel, awoke and shouted: "Holy Mary! Help me! Help me, for I am slain!"

The king, the queen, and the chamberlain heard the shout. The latter arose with a start and said to the king: "Sire, you can set off now, it's day." The king had his clothing and boots put on, while the squire shouted as loudly as he could: "Bring me a priest, I'm dying!" The king hurried to him, and the queen and the chamberlain brought many bright torches. The king asked him what was the matter, and the youth told him just what he had dreamt. "Ah," said the king, "is this a dream?"—"Yes, my lord," he said, "and it has proven to be dreadfully true." He raised his left arm. "Look here, sire: you can see the knife that is plunged into me up to its handle." Then he placed his hand on his britches where the golden candelabrum was hidden; he pulled it out and showed it to the king. "My lord," he said, "I have been slain because of this candelabrum, which I offer to you as a gift." The king took the candelabrum and admired it greatly, for never had he seen such a splendid one. The king showed it to the queen. "My lord," said the youth, "do not pull the sword from my side until I have made my confession." The king called his chaplain and had him hear his confession and give him the last rites. The king himself pulled out the sword and the youth's soul left him as he did so. The king arranged for the funeral service and had him placed in a splendid casket and buried. The youth's father, Yvain the Bastard, was deeply grieved at his son's death. At the father's bidding, King Arthur had the golden candelabrum given to St. Paul's in London, which had been recently founded, because the king wished that this wondrous adventure be widely known and that there be prayers in the church for the soul of the squire who was killed on account of the candelabrum (140).

The king put on his armor in the morning, as I had started to tell you, to set off for the chapel of St. Augustine. The queen asked him: "My lord, who will go with you?"—"My lady," he replied, "I will have no companion but God. You can know by this adventure which has just happened, that God does not wish to have anyone go with me."—"Sire," said she, "may God watch over you and bring you safely back; may He give you the will to do good, through which your honor, which is greatly diminished, might be restored."—"My lady," he answered, "may God hear you!" His warhorse was brought to him and he mounted, fully armed, at the mounting block. My lord Yvain the Bastard gave him his shield and sword. When the king was fully appareled he seemed, by the looks of him, a bold and mighty knight. As he rose powerfully in his stirrups, the saddle-horn tensed and the horse—though strong and swift—strained under him; he jabbed with his spurs and the horse gave a mighty leap beneath him. The queen was at the windows of the great hall and as many as twenty-five knights had come to the mounting block. As the king was leaving, the queen asked: "My lords, what do you think of the king? Does he not seem worthy?"—"Indeed, my lady, he does. It is a great sadness for the world that he no longer shows his early promise, for there is no king or prince so steeped in courtesy and every largess as he, if only he behaved now as once he did." The knights grew silent then and the king rode rapidly on into the forest of wonders.

He rode all day long until, at dusk, he came into the thick of the forest where he saw a little house beside a chapel, which he thought to be a hermit's cell. The king rode in that direction and dismounted before the little house; he went in, leading his horse, which could barely fit through the door. He laid his lance upon the ground, rested his shield against the wall, unbuckled his sword and unlaced his ventail. Before him he saw some barley and grain, to which he led his horse. He then took off its harness and closed the door to the little house. It seemed to him that he heard a commotion in the chapel. Some voices were like angels, while others sounded like devils. The king wondered what this could be. He found a side door in the little house that opened onto a small cloister that led to the chapel. The king went into the tiny church and looked all about; he saw only the statues and the crucifix and did not believe the commotion came from them. The noise ceased as soon as he entered. He was amazed that the chapel was empty and wondered what had become of the hermit who resided there. The king approached the chapel altar and saw before it an open sarcophagus with the hermit, fully dressed, inside. He had a beard down to his waist and his hands were crossed over his breast; upon him lay a crucifix whose Christ figure was touched to his lips; the hermit still had life within him, though he was very near to death. The king stood a long while before the sarcophagus, gazing with pleasure at the hermit who clearly had led a saintly life. Night had fully fallen, yet the chapel was as bright as if twenty candles were burning there. The king wished to remain there until this holy man had passed. He was about to sit down before the sarcophagus when a frightening voice shouted for him to leave, for they wanted to hold a trial there and would not until he had left. Though he would have preferred to stay, the king left and returned to the little house, where he sat down on a bench the hermit used to sit upon. Then he heard the commotion start up again in the chapel, with some speaking loudly and others in whispers, and he clearly recognized that the ones were angels and the others devils. He heard the devils claiming possession of the hermit's soul, and since the decision was near they were overjoyed. The king was greatly saddened in his heart, for he heard that the angel voices were silenced. He was so depressed that he had no desire to eat or drink. While he was in this greatly depressed state, he heard the voice of a lady in the chapel, who spoke so sweetly and so forcefully that even the saddest man on hearing her would be gladdened. She said to the devils: "Get out of here! You have no right to this good man's soul, no matter what he might have done in the past. He was devoted to the service of my son and me and was doing penance in this hermitage for his past sins."—"That is true, my lady," said the devils, "but he had served us longer than you or your son, for he had spent sixty-two years and more as a highwayman and murderer in this forest. He'd only spent five years in this hermitage, yet you want to take him away from us!"—"No, I don't want to take him away from you at all, for if he had been as devoted to serving you as he was to serving us, I would have given him straight to you." The devils left, all crestfallen and sad, while the sweet Mother of God took the hermit's soul, which had left his body, and gave it to the angels to offer as a gift to her dear son in Paradise. And the angels took it and began to sing with joy. Josephus noted down this story and tells us that this good man was named Calixtus (146).

King Arthur was in the little house and heard the voices of the angels and the sweet Mother of God. He was overjoyed by it, and was most happy that the soul of the good man was carried into Paradise. The king, still fully armed, slept very little that night. He saw the bright light of dawn and went into the chapel to pray to God, thinking he would find the sarcophagus open there with the hermit's body inside. But it was not there; instead, he found it covered by the most splendid tomb anyone had ever seen, over which was an entirely red cross, and it seemed that the chapel was full of incense.

After the king had said his prayer, he returned and harnessed and saddled his horse; he mounted, took his shield and lance, rode away from the little house, and returned to the forest. He rode rapidly until about the hour of terce, when he came to one of the loveliest glades ever seen, at whose entry was a swinging gate. Before entering he looked and saw off to the right a maiden seated beneath a tree, and she was holding her mule's reins in her hand. The maiden was exceptionally beautiful. The king headed in her direction. "Fair maiden," he said, "may God grant you joy and good fortune."—"Sire," she replied, "and also to you every day."—"Fair maiden," he asked, "is there no shelter in this forest?"—"My lord, only a holy chapel and a hermitage beside the chapel of St. Augustine."—"Is it indeed the chapel of St. Augustine?"—"Yes, my lord, I am telling you the truth. But the glade and the forest around it are so perilous that any knight who goes in returns dead or maimed. Yet the place where the chapel sits is so holy that anyone who goes there downcast returns uplifted, provided he come back alive. May God watch over you, for I've not seen in a great while anyone who seemed a finer knight; it would be a great pity if you were not. Nor will I leave here until I know your fate."—"Fair maiden, if it please God, you'll see me return."—"It would make me very happy," she said. "Then would I ask news at leisure about the one I am seeking" (150).

The king rode towards the gate through which one entered the glade, passed through it, and looked to the right toward a break in the forest, where he saw the chapel and hermitage of St. Augustine. He came there and dismounted, and it appeared that the hermit was dressed to celebrate Mass. The king hitched his horse to a nearby tree and attempted to enter the chapel. Though the door was open and no one was defending it, and no one was there to stop him, still he could not enter. The king was overcome with shame. He saw a statue of Our Lord and bowed before it; he looked toward the altar and saw the holy hermit saying his Confiteor; to the right of the hermit he beheld the most beautiful child anyone had ever seen; he was wearing an alb and had on his head a golden crown studded with precious stones that gave off a bright light. To the left was a lady so beautiful that all the beautiful ladies in the world could not equal her. When the holy hermit had said his Confiteor, he went to the altar and the lady took her son and went to sit on the right side of the altar upon a splendid throne; she placed her son upon her knees and began to kiss him tenderly. "Sire," she said, "you are my father, my son, and my lord, and guardian over me and everyone." King Arthur heard these words, beheld the beauty of the lady and the child, and was astonished that she called him both her father and her son. He looked at a stained glass window near the altar and saw a burning ray of light coming through it, as soon as the Mass had begun, brighter than any sun's ray, and it came down upon the altar. The king saw it and was amazed, but he was troubled that he could not enter the chapel; but he heard, there where the holy man sang Mass, the response of the angels. When the holy Gospel had been read, the king looked toward the altar and saw that the lady took her son and placed him in the hands of the holy hermit. But the king was particularly amazed that the holy hermit did not wash his hands before receiving her offering. But there was no reason for him to be amazed, had he known the situation, for such a high offering would not have been accorded him had he not had hands and body clean of all vices. When the child was offered to him, he placed it upon the altar. Then began the Consecration of the Mass. The king knelt outside the chapel and began to pray to God and ask amends. After the Preface he looked toward the altar and it seemed to him that the priest held in his hands a man who bled from his side and from his palms and his feet, and who was crowned with thorns; he saw him as a truly human figure. After he had gazed at it a long while, a strange feeling overcame him. The king felt pity in his heart for what he had seen, and tears came to his eyes. He looked toward the altar and thought that the human figure had changed again into the child he had seen before. After the Mass was celebrated, the voice of an angel said: "Ite, missa est." The son took his mother by the hand and they vanished out of the chapel accompanied by the largest and most splendid company anyone had ever seen. The burning ray that had come through the glass window disappeared with this company.

After the holy hermit had finished the office and was disrobed, he came to the king, who was still outside the chapel. "Sire," he said to the king, "now you may enter; yet your heart could have been even more joyful had you the merit by which you could have entered at the beginning of the Mass." The king entered the chapel unchallenged. "My lord," the hermit said to him, "I know you well, as I did your father King Uther. Because of your sin you could not enter this chapel today while Mass was being celebrated. Nor will you be able to tomorrow, unless you have first made amends for your sin before God and the saint who is worshiped here. You are the richest and strongest and bravest king in the world, and you should set the example for everyone in doing good through largess and honor; yet you are instead the exemplar of wickedness for all the noble men of our day. And you will suffer greatly unless you put your life in order, as it was when you first began to reign, for your court was the most splendid of all courts, and the most open to adventures; now it has become the worst. He who slides from honor into shame is rightly downcast, whereas he who rises from shame to honor can suffer no hurtful reproach, for the honor in which he is found always saves him. But blame cannot rescue a man if he has abandoned honor for shame, for the shame and wickedness in which he finds himself prove him evil."—"I have come here to make amends," replied the king, "and to be better advised than in the past. I see clearly that this place is hallowed ground, and I ask you to pray to God to counsel me, and I will make every effort to amend my life."—"May God let you turn your life to the good," said the holy hermit, "so that you may uphold and strengthen the religion that was founded by the death of the Holy Prophet. But a great sadness has recently been brought about by a knight who was given shelter in the home of the mighty Fisher King: the Holy Grail and the Lance whose iron tip bleeds appeared to him and he did not ask what they served nor who was served by them. Since he did not ask, all lands are wracked by war and no knight encounters another in the forest without attacking him and killing him if he can; you yourself will understand this clearly before you leave this place."—"Good hermit," said the king, "may God spare me a wicked and painful death, for I came here intent upon amending my life, and I shall do so if God just permits me to return safely."—"I tell you in truth, sire," replied the hermit, "that he who has been wicked three years in forty has not been wholly good all forty years."—"Good hermit, you speak the truth," said the king. The hermit commended him to God and departed (156).

The king rushed to his horse, mounted, attached his shield over his shoulder, clasped his lance with his fist, and headed rapidly back. He had not ridden the distance of a bowshot when he saw a knight bearing wildly down upon him. The knight was seated on a large black horse and was a holding a shield and lance; the lance was thick at the end near the point, and a fierce and hideous flame was burning from the point down to the knight's fist. He lowered his lance to strike the king, but the king dodged and the knight charged by. The king then asked, "Sir knight, why do you hate me?"—"I should not love you," replied the knight.—"And why not?" said the king.—"Because," replied the knight, "you had my brother's golden candelabrum, which was wickedly stolen from him."—"Do you know, then, who I am?" asked the king.—"Yes," replied the knight, "you are King Arthur who once was good but now is evil; I challenge you as my mortal enemy." He pulled back in order to charge more swiftly, and the king saw that he would not be able to leave without a fight. He lowered his own lance when he saw the knight charging with his flaming lance. The king spurred his horse as strongly as he could and the two men charged one another with their lances lowered. They struck together so mightily that their lances bowed but did not shatter, and both men were knocked from the saddle and lost their stirrups. With fire in their eyes, they slammed their bodies and horses together; blood began to pour from the king's mouth and nose. Both pulled back and gathered their breath. The king looked at the Black Knight's flaming lance, astonished that it had not shattered when it gave him such a blow, and thought he must be a devil. The Black Knight had no intention of letting the king go yet, so he charged rapidly toward him. Seeing him approach, the king took cover behind his shield for fear of the flame and met the Black Knight with the iron tip of his lance, which struck him such a blow to the chest that he was laid flat upon his horse's crupper. Summoning all his strength, the Black Knight regained his saddle and struck such a blow to the boss of the king's shield that it pierced the wood and the sleeve of his chain mail and penetrated his arm. The king felt the wound and the burning and was filled with anger; the knight pulled out his lance, happy in his heart to learn that the king was wounded. As for the king, he was not at all happy, and he was surprised now to see that the flame had gone out. "Sire," said the Black Knight, "I ask your pardon. My lance would never have stopped burning if it hadn't been bathed in your blood."—"May God never have mercy upon me," replied the king, "if I pardon you, as long as I have strength to act." He spurred rapidly toward the Black Knight and struck him a blow with his lance that went two feet through his chest, driving both him and his horse to the ground. The king pulled out his lance and stared at the knight lying there dead upon the ground. He left him in the middle of the glade and headed for the gate (160).

As the king was departing, there was a loud din of many knights coming through the forest; it seemed that there were twenty or more. From the forest he saw them enter the clearing, armed and well mounted; they approached the knight lying dead in the glade. The king was about to go out when the girl he had left beneath the tree came toward him and said, "Ah, sire, go back and bring me the head of the knight who lies dead there." The king looked back, perceived the great danger from the many fully armed knights, and said, "Ah, maiden, do you want to kill me?"—"Certainly not, my lord, but I very much need to have his head. No knight has ever refused any boon I've asked of him, so may God grant that you not be the most wicked."—"Alas, fair maiden," replied the king, "I am sorely wounded through my shield arm."—"My lord, I am well aware of that," she answered, "but you cannot be healed if you don't bring me the knight's head."—"Then I shall make the effort, no matter what it might cost me."

The king looked across the clearing and saw that those who had come had cut the dead knight into pieces and that each of them was carrying off a foot, an arm, a hand, as they scattered through the forest. He saw that the last knight had the head impaled on the iron tip of his lance; the king rushed after him, shouting: "Sir knight, stop! Speak to me!"—"What do you want, fair sir?" said the knight.—"I ask you, by the love you bear me, to give me the head you have impaled on the tip of your lance."—"On one condition," replied the knight.— "And what is that?" inquired the king.—"That you tell me who killed the knight whose head you want."—"Is there no other way to have it?" asked the king.—"None."—"Then I'll tell you: in truth, it was King Arthur who killed him."—"Then where is he?" asked the knight.— "Look for him until you find him," said the king. "I've told you the truth; give me the head."— "Gladly," said the knight. He lowered his lance and the king took the head. The knight had a horn over his shoulder, which he put to his lips and blew. The knights who had scattered through the forest rushed back as the king left the clearing and found the maiden waiting for him. Meanwhile, the knights who had rushed back to their comrade, who had given away the head, all asked him why he had blown the horn. "Because that knight riding off there told me that King Arthur killed the Black Knight. I want you to know that," he added, "and I want us to follow him."—"We won't follow him," said the knights, "for it is King Arthur himself who is carrying off the head, and we have no power to harm him or anyone else once he has passed the gate. But you will pay for letting him escape when you had him in your grasp." They rushed upon him, killed him, sliced him into pieces, and carried off each one a piece, as they had done with the Black Knight (164).

The king passed the gate, came to the maiden who was waiting for him, and presented her the head. "Sire," she said, "many thanks."—"It was my pleasure," answered the king.— "You can dismount now," said the maiden, "you have nothing to fear outside the gate." So the king dismounted. "You can remove your chain mail without fear," she added, "and I will bind the wound in your arm, for I am the only one who can heal you." The king removed his armor. The maiden soaked a bandage with the blood that was still dripping from the Black Knight's head, bound the king's wound with it, and had him put back on his chain mail, saying: "My lord, only the blood of this knight could heal you. That is why they were taking his head and body away in pieces: they were well aware that you were wounded. And the head will be of great use to me, too, because by it I'll get back a castle that was stolen from me by treachery, unless I can find the knight I am seeking, who also is to return it to me."—"Fair maiden, who is this knight?" asked the king.—"Sire, he is the son of Julain the Fat of the Valley of Camelot, and his name is Perlesvaus."—"Why is he called Perlesvaus?" asked the king, and she answered: "My lord, when he was born they asked his father what name should be given him at baptism, and he said that he wanted him to be called Perlesvaus, because the Lord of Tides had stolen the greater part of the Valley of Camelot from him, and he wanted his son to remember this by his name, if God let him grow to become a knight. The youth was very handsome and noble, and he grew and began to frequent the forest and throw his javelins at bucks and does in the Welsh manner. His father and his mother loved him dearly. One day they all came out of their manor, which was near the forest, to relax; between the manor and the forest was a small chapel set on four marble columns; it was constructed of wood and inside was a small altar, before which was a beautiful tomb with the carving of a man upon it. My lord," continued the maiden, "the youth asked his father what man lay in this tomb, and the father replied, 'Indeed, fair son, I can't tell you, because the tomb has been here since before my father's father was born, and I've never heard of anyone who knew who was buried here, except that the writing on the tomb says that when the best knight in the world comes here the tomb will open and we will see what is inside.'"—"Fair maiden," asked King Arthur, "have many knights passed through here since the tomb was built?"—"Yes indeed, my lord, more than I could ever count, but the tomb has never stirred. When the youth heard his father's answer, he asked what a knight was. 'Fair son,' said his mother, 'you should know because of your lineage.' She told her son that he had eleven uncles on his father's side who had all been slain in combat, and each was a knight for only twelve years. My lord," the maiden told the king, "the youth replied that that wasn't his question, but rather how a knight was made. His father answered that they were the noblest men in the world, and then added: 'Fair son, they wear chain mail to protect their bodies, and helmets laced to their heads, and they carry shields and lances, and swords in scabbards to defend themselves'" (168).

"After the father had spoken these words to his son," the maiden continued, "they returned to their castle. The young man arose early the next morning; he heard birds singing and thought that he would go hunting in the forest since it was such a beautiful day. Carrying his javelins like a Welshman, he got on one of his father's hunting steeds and rode into the forest. He started a stag and pursued it some four Welsh leagues to a meadow, where he found two armed knights fighting. One had a red shield and the other a white one. He abandoned his stag hunt to observe the combat, and he saw that the Red Knight defeated the White Knight. He threw one of his javelins so hard at the Red Knight that it pierced his chain mail and passed through his body; the Red Knight fell dead. The Knight with the White Shield was overjoyed and asked the youth if this was how easily he killed knights. 'I thought,' the boy answered, 'that no one could penetrate or damage a knight's armor, or else I wouldn't have aimed my javelin at him.'" The maiden continued: "He led the knight's horse to his parents' castle. They were deeply saddened to learn of the knight he had killed, and this was right, because great sorrow came to them later as a consequence. Sire, the youth left his father's and his mother's manor and came to King Arthur's court, where the king was prompt to knight him once he knew his wishes. Afterwards he left the court and set off on adventure through every land. Now he is the best knight in the world, and I am seeking him. I would be overjoyed if I could find him. My lord, if by chance you should come across him in one of these forests—he is carrying a red shield with a white stag—tell him his father is dead and his mother will lose all her lands if he [MS BN fr. 1428 begins here] doesn't come to help her, because the brother of the Knight with the Red Shield, whom he killed in the forest with his javelin, is making war against her with the help of the Lord of the Fens."—"Fair maiden," said the king, "I would be very happy were God to let me encounter him, and I would gladly give him your message."—"My lord, I've now told you what I am seeking, so tell me your name."—"Gladly, fair maiden," said the king: "those who know me call me Arthur."—"Arthur! Is that your name?"—"Yes, fair maiden."—"So help me God, then I hate you more than before," said the maiden, "because you have the same name as the worst king in the world, and I wish he were here now, as you are. But he would never leave Carduel alone, even if he could, because he is watching to see that no one makes off with the queen, so I've been told, though I've never seen either of them. I once set off for King Arthur's court, but en route I met some twenty knights, one after the other, who all told me that his court was the most wicked in the world and that all the knights of the Round Table had fled because of its wickedness."—"Fair maiden," said the king, "that should make him very sad. I've heard that in the beginning he did much good."—"Who cares about his good beginning, when his end is so wicked? And I'm very sorry that such a handsome knight as yourself has the same name as such a wicked king."—"Fair maiden," answered the king, "one is not good because of a name, but because of one's heart."—"What you say is true," she conceded. "But still your name displeases me because it is the same as the king's. Where are you headed?"—"I shall go to Carduel, where I'll find King Arthur when I arrive."—"Splendid," she said, "like to like. Since you are headed there, you must be wicked too."—"Say what you wish, fair maiden. May God be with you."—"May God never be with you," she replied, "if you are headed to King Arthur's court" (174).

The king then remounted and set off, leaving the maiden beneath the tree. He entered the vast forest and rode as swiftly as he could toward Carduel. He had ridden some ten Welsh leagues when he heard a voice from deep in the forest, which began to shout: "Arthur, king of Great Britain, you can be very happy in your heart that God has sent me to you. He orders that you hold court as soon as you can, because the world, which has grown worse because of you and your lack of good deeds, will become better by it." The voice then grew silent, but the king was very happy in his heart by what he had heard.

The story does not speak here of any further adventure that befell the king as he returned. No, he just rode until he reached Carduel, where the queen and the knights rejoiced to see him. The king dismounted at the stone block and strode up to the great hall and had his armor removed. He showed the queen the wound to his arm, which had been deep and painful, but which was now healing nicely. The queen followed the king into their chamber, where he was dressed in a robe of silken material, a coat, a vest, and a mantle lined with ermine. "My lord," said the queen, "you have suffered much."—"My lady, worthy men must suffer so in order to have honor, for it is scarcely possible to win honor without pain." He told the queen all the adventures he had had since he left, how he had been wounded in his arm, and about the maiden who had vilified him because of his name.

"My lord," said the queen, "now you can understand that a noble, rich and powerful man should feel shame when he becomes wicked."—"My lady, the maiden certainly gave me to understand this. But I was greatly comforted by a voice I heard in the forest, which told me that God has ordered me to hold court soon, and I shall witness the finest adventure I have ever seen."—"My lord, you should rejoice that the Savior remembers you. Now do as He commands."—"Truly I shall, my lady, for never have I had a greater desire to do good, act honorably, and give generously."—"May God be praised, sire!" (176).

[Branches II-V. These branches are devoted to the chivalric adventures of Sir Gawain as he seeks the castle of the Fisher King. In Branch III he comes to Camaalot, the castle of Perlesvaus's mother, for whom he arranges a one-year truce with the evil Lord of the Fens, who is seeking to destroy her lands. Other adventures are summarized and interpreted allegorically at the Castle of Inquiry in the following selection. Typical is the adventure of the Bald Maiden, who leaves a shield and hunting dog in Arthur's castle. She explains:] "Lord Arthur, the shield ... belonged to Joseph, the good soldier who lowered God from the Cross; I offer it to you on the following conditions: that you keep the shield for a knight who will come for it, that you suspend it from this column in the middle of your great hall, and that you keep it for him. He alone can remove it and hang it from his neck, and with this shield he will win the Grail, after leaving another shield— red with a white stag—in its place. And the little dog will stay here... and will greet no one until the knight comes" (182).

[Branch VI. To prove himself worthy to enter the Grail Castle, Gawain must retrieve from the pagan king Gurguran the sword with which John the Baptist was beheaded. As the condition for winning the sword, Gawain is sent to rescue Gurguran's son from an evil giant. En route he undergoes adventures at a fountain and back at Gurguran's castle that are allegorized broadly as the sacrifice of the Eucharist. At the beginning of the following passage, Sir Gawain arrives at the Castle of Inquiry, where the adventures of the previous Branches are allegorized for him.]

That night Sir Gawain slept in the castle and the next day he left and rode many days until he came to the castle at the border of the lands of the Fisher King. He saw that the copper peasant no longer worked and that the lion was not in the doorway, and he saw that the priests and inhabitants of the castle were all processing in his direction. He dismounted. A squire was ready to take charge of his arms and horse, and he showed the sword to those approaching him. It was noon. He drew the sword and they saw that it was all bloody; they bowed down before it and chanted *Te Deum laudamus*. My lord Gawain was welcomed into the castle amid much joy. He put the sword back into its sheath and kept it close to him; he did not tell of its powers in all the places he was given lodging. The priests and the knights were delighted to see him and urged him, if God ever led him to the castle of the Fisher King and the Grail appeared before him, not to be as forgetful as the other knight; and he replied that he would do as God showed him (322).

"My lord," said the chief priest, who was very old and wizened, "you seem to me to be worn out and in great need of rest."—"I have seen many things, sir, that have astonished me and whose meaning I don't understand."—"My lord," said the priest, "this castle is called the Castle of Inquiry; you can ask the meaning of anything at all, and you will be informed, by the witness of the good scholar and hermit Josephus, who told us; and he knows it from the angel and the Holy Spirit."—"In faith," replied Sir Gawain, "I am very confused by three maidens who came to King Arthur's court carrying two heads, one of a king and one of a queen; and they brought along in a cart one hundred fifty heads of knights, some sealed in gold, others in silver, and a third of them in lead."—"That is true," said the priest, "but the maiden said that the king and the hundred and fifty knights whose heads were in the cart were betrayed by the queen, which led to their deaths. And she spoke the truth, as Josephus bears witness, for he told us in order that we not forget how Adam was betrayed by Eve along with all the people of his day, and the world to come would rue that day for evermore. Because Adam was the first man, he is called king, for he was our earthly father, and his wife was queen. The heads of knights sealed in gold represent the New Testament; the heads in silver, the Old Testament; and the heads in lead, the false religion of the Saracens. The world is made up of these three sorts of people."—"Sir, I also wonder about the castle of the Black Hermit, where they stole all the heads, and the maiden told me that the Good Knight would rescue them all when he came, though there are other people there who rue his presence."— "You are well aware," said the priest, "that both the good and the evil were sent to Hell because of the apple Eve had Adam eat. In order to release his people from Hell, God became Man and released his friends from Hell because of his goodness and power. And therefore Josephus bears witness that the castle of the Black Hermit represents Hell, and the Good Knight will rescue those within; and he witnesses that the Black Hermit is Lucifer, who is lord of Hell since he wished to be lord of Paradise. Sir, the good hermit uses this to bear witness to the New Testament, of which many men are ignorant, and he wants to use such stories to call it to mind."—"By God," continued Sir Gawain, "I am very amazed by the bald maiden who said that she would not grow her hair back until the Good Knight will have won the Grail."— "It is right that she be bald. Her baldness began at the moment the good king fell into languor because of the knight to whom he gave lodging, who did not ask the question. Baldness represents Fortune, says Josephus, which was bald before the Crucifixion of Our Lord and didn't recover her hair until the hour He redeemed his people by his suffering and death. The cart she brought after her represents her wheel, for just as the cart rolls on wheels, so Fortune pushes along the world. You can understand this clearly through the maidens who followed the cart, for the most beautiful was hurrying along on foot, the second was on a poor nag, and they were both poorly dressed, while the third had finer clothes. The shield with the red cross, which she left at King Arthur's court, represents the most holy shield of the Cross, which only God has dared to carry." My lord Gawain heard these explications, which pleased him greatly, and he thought about the shield that was hanging in King Arthur's hall and that no one dared touch or carry, as it had been told him in many places, because they were awaiting the Good Knight who was to come any day now to seek the shield (330).

"Many thanks for explaining these perplexing matters to me," said Sir Gawain to the priest. "But I was grief-stricken because of a lady who was killed by her husband on my account, though both she and I were innocent."—"My lord," said the priest, "the meaning of her death is a joyful one, for Josephus witnesses to us that the Old Law was brought down with no hope of recovery by a sword blow, and in order to bring down the Old Law God permitted himself to be wounded in the side by the sword; this blow and his crucifixion brought down the Old Law. The lady represents the Old Law. Do you wish to ask me anything else?"—"Sir," said my lord Gawain, "I met a knight in the forest who was riding backwards and who wore his armor upside-down. He said he was called The Cowardly Knight and wore his hauberk over his shoulders; but as soon as he saw me, he put his armor on correctly and rode like any other knight."—"Religion was backwards before Our Lord's crucifixion," said the priest, "but was made right as soon as He was crucified."—"There was yet another very unusual thing," continued my lord Gawain. "A knight dressed half in white and half in black came forward to joust with me, blaming me for the death of the woman slain by her husband. He added that if I defeated him, he and his men would submit to me. I conquered him and he did homage to me."—"Rightly so," explained the priest, "because the Old Law was defeated, all those who belonged to it were subjected, and will be forever more. Do you have more to ask me?"

"I am very perplexed," said Sir Gawain, "about a child who was riding a lion in a hermit's hut, and no one except the child dared approach the lion. The child was no more than seven, and the lion was very ferocious; the child was the son of the woman who was killed on my account."—"You have done well to remind me of this," said the priest. "The child represents the Savior of the world who was born into the Old Law and was circumcised, who was humble before all mankind. The lion represents the world and the people in it, as well as the beasts and the birds which only He can rule and control."

"Oh God!" exclaimed Sir Gawain, "how joyful I am in my heart for what you've told me! Sir, in the forest I found the most beautiful fountain anyone has ever seen, in which was a statue that disappeared when it saw me. A priest came forward bearing a gold vessel, which he filled with the contents of another gold vessel that was hanging from a column. Afterwards three maidens came and filled the vessel with what they were bearing; then it seemed to me that there was only one."—"My lord," said the priest, "I shall not tell you more than you have already heard. And you must consider yourself well paid: one must not reveal the mysteries of the Savior, but rather those to whom they have been given must guard them secret."

"My lord," said Sir Gawain, "I wish to ask about a king: when I brought him his dead son, he had him boiled and cooked and afterwards given as food to everyone in his land."—"He had already offered his heart to the Savior," said the priest, "and he wanted to make a sacrifice of his flesh and blood to Our Lord. For this reason he had him served to everyone in his land and wanted their thoughts to be the same as his own. In this way he uprooted all evil beliefs from his land, and none remains."—"Blessed be the hour I entered here!" exclaimed Sir Gawain.—"Amen," added the priest (334).

My lord Gawain slept in the castle that night and was well lodged. In the morning after hearing Mass, he took leave and set forth from the castle. He came one day to the most beautiful land in the world, with the most beautiful prairies and rivers that anyone had ever seen, full of wild beasts and hermit's huts. He rode until near dusk when he came to a hermit's place. The hut was so low that his horse could not enter, and the chapel was no bigger; the hermit had not come outside in some sixty years. The hermit looked out his window and said, when he saw Sir Gawain, "Welcome, my lord."—"May God bless you. Will you grant me lodging?" asked Sir Gawain.—"My lord, no one but God resides in there. No mortal man has come in with me in sixty years. But look, there before you is the castle where good knights are given lodging." — "Whose castle is it?" — "The good Fisher King's," replied the hermit, "and it is surrounded by wide moats and fully stocked, if only the lord were happy; but only good knights can lodge there." — "May God grant that I become one," said my lord Gawain. When he realized that he was near the castle, he dismounted and confessed all his sins to the hermit and truly repented. "My lord," said the hermit, "if God deigns to grant it to you, don't forget to ask the question that the other knight forgot to ask; don't be frightened by what you see at the entry to the castle, but ride boldly and worship the holy chapel that will appear to you in the castle, where the flame of the Holy Spirit descends daily for the most holy Grail and for the lance whose tip bleeds, which is adored there." — "May God give me grace to do His will!"

Sir Gawain took leave and rode until he saw the valley full of all good things, in which sat the castle where he saw the most holy chapel appear. He dismounted, knelt, bowed low and worshiped prayerfully. Then he remounted and rode until he came to a splendid tomb, covered with a fine stone slab; it was close to the castle and had the appearance of a small cemetery, for it was enclosed on all sides and there were no other tombs. As he passed by the cemetery, a voice cried out: "Don't approach the tomb, for you are not the knight who will reveal to us who lies within!" Sir Gawain rode by after hearing the voice; he neared the entrance to the castle and saw that there were three huge and horrible bridges to cross. Beneath them flowed three swift and wide currents, and it seemed to him that the first bridge was a bowshot long and not even a foot wide. The bridge seemed narrow and the water swift, wide, and deep; he did not know what he could do, for it did not seem to him that anyone could cross, whether on foot or horseback (338).

Just then an aged knight rode out of the castle and came to the head of the bridge, which was called The Needle Bridge, and shouted loudly: "Sir knight, cross over at once, for it's almost night and the people in the castle are waiting for you!" — "Ah, fair sir," said Sir Gawain, "teach me how to cross over." — "Indeed, my lord, I don't know any other way over than this bridge, at this entry, so if you want to come into the castle, then cross it without fear." My lord Gawain was ashamed that he had delayed so long and recalled what the hermit had told him, not to dread anything at the castle entrance; beyond that, he had confessed and was truly sorry for his sins, so he should be less afraid of death. Like a man thinking he is about to die, Sir Gawain blessed and crossed himself and commended his soul to God; then he spurred his horse and as soon as he started across he discovered the bridge to be large and wide, for this passage was used to test many of the knights who wished to enter the castle. He was astonished to discover that the bridge he had thought to be so narrow was in fact so wide, and after he had crossed, because it was a drawbridge it lifted magically behind him, so no one else could enter, for the water beneath was too swift. The knight withdrew beyond the second bridge and Sir Gawain rode up to cross. This one seemed as long to him as the first, with water below that was no less deep and swift. The bridge appeared to him to be made of thin, fragile, delicate ice spanning high above the water. He marveled at what he saw but was not afraid of this passage because of what he had learned at the first bridge. He rode up, commended himself to God, and when he had reached the middle saw that this bridge was the strongest and finest he had ever seen, and that its entryways were decorated with statues. After he had crossed, this bridge lifted up like the first. He looked ahead but did not see the aged knight. He reached the third bridge, which was as magnificent as the others: it had columns of marble all around with capitals on each that seemed to be of gold. Then he looked above the entryway and saw a mosaic of Our Lord upon the Cross, with his mother to one side and St. John to the other, and the images were all of gold with precious stones that sparkled like flames. And to the right he saw a most beautiful angel pointing with its finger to the chapel of the Holy Grail; in the middle of its breast was a precious stone and above its head was an inscription that said that the lord of the castle was as chaste and cleansed of all impurities as this stone. Afterwards he saw a huge, ferocious lion standing at the entryway, but as soon as it saw Sir Gawain it lay down. He passed on without incident, came into the castle, and dismounted. He rested his lance and shield against the wall of the room, climbed the marble steps, and came into a very beautiful and opulent hall, decorated all around with gilded statues. In the middle of the hall was a very high and opulent couch, at the foot of which was a very beautiful and costly chessboard, with a gilded border inset with precious stones. The squares were alternating gold and azure, and the chess pieces were not on the board. As Sir Gawain was admiring the richness and beauty of the hall, two knights came out of a room and approached him, saying, "Welcome, my lord!"—"May God grant you happiness and good fortune," replied Sir Gawain. They had him sit down upon the couch. Two squires helped him remove his armor, and then they brought him water in two golden basins to wash his face and hands. Next came two maidens who brought him an expensive robe of gold cloth and dressed him in it, saying: "My lord, look with favor on what is done for you here, because it is the lodging of good and loyal knights."—"And so I do, fair maidens," replied Sir Gawain, "and I thank you very much." Though it was dark night without and there were no candles burning, there was such brightness in the hall that it seemed lit by the sun; Sir Gawain wondered where this great light came from.

When Sir Gawain was dressed in the expensive robe, he was handsome to look at and seemed very worthy. "My lord, would it please you to come see the lord of this castle?" asked the knights. "I would be pleased to see him, my lords, and I have a most holy sword to present to him." They led him into the room where the Fisher King lay, which was all strewn with herbs and flowers and seemed very fragrant. The Fisher King was lying in a webbed bed with ivory ends; he was lying on a mattress of brocaded silk covered in expensive sable; on his head was a sable cap covered with red silk, with a gold cross. Beneath his head was a fragrant pillow, at whose corners were four luminous jewels. In the room was a copper pillar topped by an angel holding a gold cross in which was a piece of the true Cross—as long as the gold cross was tall—on which Christ was placed. The good man adored this cross. And in four golden candelabras there were four large wax candles that burned at all hours (344).

My lord Gawain approached the Fisher King and greeted him, and the king was happy to see him and made him welcome. "My lord," said Sir Gawain, "I present you the sword with which St. John was beheaded."—"Thank you, sir," replied the king. "I was well aware that you were carrying it: neither you nor anyone else could enter here without the sword, and you would not have won it if you were not most worthy." He took the sword and touched it to his mouth and face, kissing it fervently and rejoicing over it; then a beautiful maiden came to sit by his head, and he gave it to her to watch over. Two other maidens sat at his feet, gazing sweetly at him. "What is your name?" asked the king.—"My lord, I am called Gawain."—"Ah! my lord Gawain. This brightness in here now comes to us from God, for love of you. Each time a knight comes to lodge in this castle it appears like this. I would make you even more welcome than I have, if I could. But I have fallen into languor since the knight of whom you've heard lodged here. This languor overtook me because he hesitated to speak a single word. So I beg you, in God's name, to remember this, for you would rejoice greatly if you were to restore my health. This is my sister's disinherited daughter, whose lands have been taken from her, and only her brother whom she is seeking can restore them. We have been told that he is the best knight in the world, but we can find no reliable information about him."—"Sire," said the maiden to the king, "thank my lord Gawain for the honor he did my lady mother: while he was staying in her house, he restored peace to our lands and won the guardianship of our castle for a year; he placed my lady mother's five knights there to guard it with us. But now the year is just over and a dreadful war will begin anew if God doesn't protect us and I don't find my brother."—"My lady, I helped you as best I could and will help you again, if I am able to do so," said Sir Gawain, "and I would rather find your brother than all the knights in the world. But I can get no reliable information, except that I was at the cell of a hermit king and I was told not to make any noise because the best knight in the world was languishing within. The hermit told me he was called Par Lui Fais. I saw a squire groom his horse in front of the chapel and place his weapons and shield in the sunlight."—"My lord," said the maiden, "my brother is not named Par Lui Fais, but rather was baptized Perlesvaus, and those who've seen him say they've never known a more beautiful knight."—"Indeed," added the Fisher King, "I've never seen a more handsome knight than the one who stayed here, nor one who seemed better; and I know he is good, for otherwise he would not have been able to enter here. But I've been ill rewarded for lodging him, because I can no longer help myself or others. Sir Gawain, for God's sake please remember me tonight, for I have great confidence in your valor!"—"Indeed, sire, if it pleases God, I'll not do anything here for which I'd be blamed" (346).

Thereupon my lord Gawain was led into the hall where he found twelve old and hoary knights, but they did not look as old as they were, for each of them was a hundred or more but did not look over forty. They placed Sir Gawain to eat at a luxurious ivory table and sat down all around him. "My lord," said the head knight, "if you remember tonight what the good king told and urged you, you will have healed him."—"May God help me," said Sir Gawain. Then they brought forth roast stag and boar meat and a great profusion of other dishes. The table was set with expensive gold plates, large lidded drinking vessels, and an expensive gold chandelier in which large candles burned. But the other brightness in the room obscured their light. At that moment two maidens came forth from a chapel; one held in her two hands the most holy Grail and the other the Lance whose tip bleeds. Walking one beside the other, they entered the hall where Sir Gawain and the others were dining. There wafted from the maidens such a delightful and blessed fragrance that they forgot to eat. Sir Gawain looked at the Grail and thought he saw a chalice within it—an object rarely seen in those days—and saw red blood from the Lance's tip falling into it. And there were two angels bearing two candelabra with burning candles. The maidens passed before Sir Gawain and went into another chapel, leaving Sir Gawain lost in thought. But his thoughts brought him such joy that he could think only of God. The knights were all downcast and disconsolate as they watched him. At that moment the two maidens came out of the chapel and passed again before my lord Gawain, and it seemed to him that he saw three angels where previously he had seen but two, and that in the middle of the Grail he saw the shape of a child. The head knight alerted Sir Gawain, and he looked up and saw three drops of blood fall upon the table. He was so astonished at seeing this that he did not speak. Then the maidens passed on and the knights were frightened and looked at one another. My lord Gawain could not take his eyes off the three drops of blood, but when he wished to kiss them they disappeared, which saddened him immensely, for he could not touch them with his hand or any other part of his body. Then he saw the maidens come back in front of the table, but it now seemed to Sir Gawain that there were three, and as he looked up the Grail seemed to be floating on air; and above it, so it seemed to him, he saw a crowned King crucified on a Cross with a Lance in his side. When my lord Gawain saw this, he was deeply saddened and he could think only of the pain that this King was suffering. The head knight again urged Sir Gawain to speak and said that if he delayed any longer he would not have another chance. Sir Gawain, who did not hear the knight, kept his eyes raised and said not a word as the maidens went back into the chapel carrying the most holy Grail and the Lance.

The knights arose from table, removed the tablecloths, and entered another room, leaving Sir Gawain all alone. He looked all about and saw that the doors were closed and locked; at the foot of the couch he saw two lit candelabra beside the chessboard, on which the pieces had been set up, the ones ivory and the others gold. Sir Gawain began play with the ivory pieces and the gold pieces played against him and checkmated him twice; during the third match, in which he had hoped to get his revenge, he saw he was losing and scattered the pieces. A maiden came forth from a room and had a squire take the board and pieces and carry them away. My lord Gawain, exhausted from riding many a day to get there, fell asleep on the couch until dawn, when he heard a horn sounding loudly. He quickly took up his arms and intended to take leave of the Fisher King, but he found the doors so tightly locked that he could not go in, though he heard a beautiful Mass being celebrated in a chapel; he was very sad that he could not assist at the service. A maiden came into the room and said: "My lord, you can hear the service and the great joy being made over the sword you presented to the good king; you would be truly joyful in your heart if you were in the chapel, but you have lost that right for speaking too little, for the door of the chapel is such a holy object because of the holy relics that are within that no priest or earthly being can enter from Saturday noon until Monday after Mass; but one can hear the sweetest voices and the finest service ever sung in any chapel." Sir Gawain, ashamed, spoke not a word, and the maiden continued: "My lord, may God watch over you, no matter what you've done, for it seems to me that all you lacked was the desire to say the word that would have brought joy back to this castle." Thereupon the maiden left and Sir Gawain heard the horn sound again and a loud voice calling: "Anyone who does not belong within must leave, whoever he may be. The door is open, the drawbridge is lowered, and the lion is in his den! Afterwards the bridge must be raised against the King of Deadly Castle who is besieging this castle, and it will be the death of him" (354).

[Attention shifts now to the adventures of Lancelot as he heads toward the Grail Castle. First he helps the brother of a slain knight regain his castle; next he defeats the keepers of Beard Castle, who attempt to kill him for his beard; finally, he kills another knight in a cemetery, before arriving at the deserted city of the next selection, which begins on page 388.]

Then Lancelot left the hermitage and rode until he came out of the forest and found a waste land and a wide and large country where there were neither beasts nor birds, for the land was so dry and poor that they could find no food. Lancelot looked ahead and perceived a city in the distance. He rode rapidly in that direction and saw that the city was so large it seemed to take in a whole country. He saw the walls crumbling all around and the gates falling with age. He passed through them and found the city completely devoid of people, and saw the large palaces crumbled and laid waste and the large cemeteries full of sarcophagi, and the large churches all laid waste; he found the markets and exchanges empty. He rode through the main streets and came to a palace that seemed to him in better shape and more inhabited than the others. He stopped in front of it and heard knights and ladies grieving and saying to a knight: "Ah, God, what a great sorrow and pity it is that you are going to die in this way, and that your death cannot be delayed. We are right to hate the one who has condemned you to this fate!" The knights and ladies all fainted before him as he was leaving. Lancelot heard all this and was confused, but he could see no one. Then he saw the knight coming from the great hall, dressed in a short vermilion robe. He wore an expensive gold belt, an opulent broach studded with jewels at his neck, and a gold garland on his head. He was holding a large axe in both hands. He was young and exceedingly handsome. Lancelot admired him as he approached, for he appeared quite fit. The knight said to him, "Dismount, fair sir!"—"Gladly," replied Lancelot. He dismounted and tied his horse to a silver ring that was on the mounting block; he removed his shield from his neck and put down his lance. "What is your pleasure?" he asked the knight.—"My lord, you must behead me with this axe, for I am doomed to die by it, or else I must cut off your head."—"Wait, sir knight! What did you say?"—"Just what you heard, sir," replied the knight. "You must do it since you have entered this city."—"My lord," said Lancelot, "one would be a fool in this game not to choose the more advantageous side! But I'd be blamed if I were to kill you without cause."—"Indeed," said the knight, "you have no other choice!"—"Fair sir, you are so noble and so fit. Why do you go so graciously to your death? You know that I would rather kill you than have you kill me, since that is the choice!"—"I am well aware of all that," answered the knight, "but you must swear to me before I die that you will return to this city at the end of a year and expose your own head, without argument, in the same manner as mine is about to be."—"By my head," said Lancelot, "there is no way you could persuade me to die now rather than put it off. But I am perplexed to see you so splendidly arrayed for dying."—"My lord," he replied, "one should dress the best one can to meet the Savior of the world. Through confession I have expunged all the wicked and evil things I have ever done and am truly repentant; I wish to die in this state." Then he handed Lancelot the axe, which he saw to be sharp and cutting. "Stretch your hand out toward that church you see in the distance," he ordered.—"Willingly," said Lancelot.—"Now you will swear to me upon the relics in that church that one year from today at the very hour you slay me, or before, you will return to this spot and will expose your own head in the same manner as mine will be, without protection."—"I do swear and affirm this," said Lancelot. Thereupon the knight knelt and stretched out his neck as far as he could. Lancelot took the axe with both hands, saying, "Sir knight, for God's sake, take pity on yourself!"—"Gladly, my lord," replied the knight. "Now let yourself cut off my head, otherwise I cannot obtain mercy."—"I'd rather spare you such mercy!" said Lancelot. Then he raised the axe and swung so hard that the head flew seven feet from the body. The knight slumped to the ground when his head was cut off. Lancelot threw down the axe and thought it would be bad to remain here, and against his own interests. He came to his horse, took up his arms, and mounted. When he looked behind him, he did not see the knight's body, nor his head, and did not know what had become of them, except that there was a great lamentation and loud weeping of knights and ladies in the city; they felt sorrow for a good knight and said that he would be avenged, God willing, at the agreed upon time, or before. Lancelot left the city and heard everything that the knights and ladies said (394; this episode is continued in Branch IX).

[Branch VII. Having spent a long while atoning for his failure to ask the Grail question, the "Good Knight" Perlesvaus finally makes his appearance. First he wounds Lancelot, whom he failed to recognize. While Lancelot is left with the Hermit King Pelles to recover from his wounds, Perlesvaus wins back a castle by killing Cahot the Red, who had stolen it from Perlesvaus's mother. Cahot turns out to have been the brother of the Red Knight that Perceval had killed with his javelin in Chrétien's *Story of the Grail*, and the uncle of Clamados, with whom Perlesvaus now meets up. But when Clamados is wounded in combat with another knight, Perlesvaus is free to return to find Lancelot.]

[Branch VIII. Lancelot has healed meanwhile, left the hermitage, and easily defended an aged knight's castle from his enemy. (We take up the story again on p. 448.)]

The tale says that Lancelot went seeking adventure through unknown forests and rode until he reached a plain outside a large city that appeared to be very strong. As he was riding across the plain he saw a great company of people coming forth from the city along the road he was taking; they were accompanied by the sounds of bagpipes, flutes, viols and other instruments. When the first group arrived they stopped, more joyful than ever, and said: "Welcome, my lord!"—"My lords," replied Lancelot, "whom are you going to greet with so much happiness?"—"Our masters, who are following behind, will tell you." Then the priests and lords of the city approached Lancelot and said: "My lord, this city is overcome with joy on your account, and all these instruments are playing in honor of your arrival."—"And why for me?" asked Lancelot.—"We shall tell you: one of the corners of this city began to burn as soon as our king died. The fire cannot go out until we have had a king to rule for one year over this city and all the lands that depend on it; after one year he must leap into the fire and then it will go out. Before that it cannot weaken or go out. We have come to meet you in order to give you the kingdom, because we have heard that you are a good knight."—"My lords," replied Lancelot, I don't need such a kingdom; may God save me from it!"—"Because you have entered this land, you cannot keep from receiving it, and it would be a great shame if a city as beautiful as the one you see here were to be destroyed just to save the life of one man. It's a most powerful city and would bring you great honor. When you have come to the end of the year in which you were crowned, you will save this city and all its many people, which will redound to your fame." Lancelot was astonished by what they told him. They surrounded him on all sides and led him into the city. The ladies and maidens climbed up to look out the stone-arched windows, and said to one another amidst great joy: "This is the new king they are bringing! The fire will go out at the end of the year!"—"Oh God," said many people, "it's a shame that such a fine knight will end in this way."—"Silence!" said the others. "To the contrary, it is a happy thing that such a good city as this will be saved by his death, and we will have prayers said for his soul throughout the kingdom until the end of time." They led Lancelot into the palace amidst great joy and said that they would crown him. He found the palace strewn with flowers and draped with expensive silk curtains; all the lords of the city were prepared to offer him homage, but he stiffly refused and said that in no way would he become their king or lord.

At this moment a dwarf leading one of the most beautiful maidens in the kingdom entered the city and asked what all the joyful festivities were for. They told him all about the fire and how they intended to make a knight their king, but that he refused. The dwarf and the maiden dismounted before the palace and went up its stairs. The dwarf spoke to the most powerful lords of the city: "My lords, since this knight doesn't wish to be king, I'll gladly accept the crown and will rule the city at your pleasure and do everything you've told me about."—"In faith," they said, "since the knight refuses this honor and you want it, we'll gladly let you have it. Let him be on his way, for we release him of all his obligations." Then they put the crown on the dwarf's head. Lancelot was delighted and took his leave, as they all commended him to God. He mounted his horse and rode back through the city fully armed; the ladies and maidens said he did not want to be king and have to die so soon (452).

He was glad to leave the city. He reentered the forest and rode until nightfall, when he saw a newly founded hermitage, because the hut and chapel had been freshly built. He rode over to it and dismounted. The hermit, who was a beardless young man, came out of the chapel and said to Lancelot: "Welcome, my lord!"—"And good fortune to you, sir," replied Lancelot. "I've never seen anyone as young as you living as a hermit."—"The only thing I regret, my lord, is not having become one sooner." Then he had Lancelot's horse stabled and led him into his hermitage, where he had him disarmed and saw to his comfort. "My lord," the hermit asked, "can you tell me any news of a knight who lay a long while sick at the home of a hermit king?"—"I saw him not long ago."—"Where?"—"I saw him at the home of the good Hermit King, who sheltered me and gently nursed a wound the knight gave me."—"And is the knight healed?" asked the hermit.—"Yes," said Lancelot, "and that is happy news. Why are you asking?"—"I must ask," said the hermit, "because my father King Pelles is his uncle and his mother is my father's first cousin."—"Ah! so the Hermit King is your father, sir?"—"Indeed, yes, my lord."—"Then I love you the better," said Lancelot, "for I've never found anyone who treated me as well as he did. And what is your name?"—"I am called Joseus, my lord; and you?"—"I am called Lancelot of the Lake."—"My lord," said the hermit, "you and I are close relatives."—"By my head, my heart rejoices to hear this." Lancelot looked and saw a shield, lance, sword, hauberk and some javelins in the hermit's hut. He asked: "My lord, what do you do with these arms?"—"This forest is vast and this hermitage is far from people; only my servant and I live here, and when robbers and wicked people come to attack us, we defend ourselves."—"I didn't think," said Lancelot, "that hermits were permitted to wound or kill people."—"May God keep me from ever wounding or killing anyone!" exclaimed the hermit.—"Then how do you defend yourself?" asked Lancelot.—"I will tell you, my lord: when robbers attack, we arm ourselves. If I can get my hands on one, he cannot escape; then our brave servant kills him or gives him a blow that puts him out of commission."—"By my head," declared Lancelot, "I can see that if you weren't a hermit you'd behave quite differently!"—"That is very true, my lord," said the servant, "I don't believe there is anyone stronger or braver in all the kingdom of Logres!"

That night the hermit lodged Lancelot as best he could. Just after they had all fallen asleep, four robber knights from the forest, who knew a knight had been given shelter there, came to steal his horse and arms. The hermit, who was in the chapel, was the first to see them; he woke up his servant and had him bring his armor very quietly, which he put on and had his servant arm himself. "My lord, should I awaken the knight?" asked his servant.—"No, not until we know what's up." He had the chapel door opened and, taking a long length of cord, went out with his servant and saw the robbers in the stable where Lancelot's horse was. The hermit shouted at them and the servant rushed up and struck one with his sword. The hermit grabbed him and tied him so tightly to a tree near the chapel that he was unable to move. The other three wanted to defend themselves and rescue their companion. Lancelot was startled on hearing the noise; he leapt up and put on his armor as quickly as he could. But he was not quick enough, because the hermit had already captured the other three and tied them up with their companion; some of them were badly wounded. "My lord," the hermit said to Lancelot, "I'm sorry that you've been awakened."—"You were wrong not to have warned me before!"—"We often experience such attacks." The four robbers pleaded pathetically with Lancelot to ask the hermit to take pity on them, but Lancelot told them that God would never again help him if he had pity on thieves. As soon as day broke, Lancelot and the servant led them into the forest with their hands tied behind their backs and hanged them in a remote spot far from the hermitage. Lancelot returned and took leave of the young hermit Joseus, saying it was a loss to this world that he was not a knight. "On the contrary," said the servant, "it's a good thing, because many men would otherwise pay dearly!" Lancelot mounted and Joseus commended him to God. He urged him to greet his father and his nephew for him when he sees them, and also my lord Gawain whom he had met in the forest when he came weeping into the hermitage (456).

Lancelot continued his way and rode through vast forests and found many hermitages and strongholds, but the tale does not record all the places where he lodged. He rode so long that he came out of the forest and found a most beautiful flower-covered prairie, with a mighty river, very deep and clear, running through the middle. There were forests to either side, but the prairie was wide between the river and the forest. Lancelot looked before him and saw a man navigating a large boat; in the boat were three old white-haired knights and a maiden who, it seemed to Lancelot, was supporting on her lap the head of a knight who was lying on a straw quilt and was covered by an ermine coverlet. A second maiden was seated at his feet. In the middle of the boat was a knight fishing with a golden rod and hook, and he was catching many fish. The large boat was followed by a small one, into which he put the fish he was catching. Lancelot approached the river as closely as he could, greeted the knights and maidens, and they responded most graciously. "My lords," he inquired, "is there a castle or stronghold nearby?"—"Yes, sir, over this mountain. It is strong and well-provisioned; this large river flows around it."—"Whose castle is it, my lords?"—"It belongs to the Fisher King, and the good knights lodge there when they come into this land. But some knights have lodged there that the lord of the castle has a right to complain of." The knights continued down the river, and Lancelot rode until he reached the foot of a mountain and found a hermitage beside a spring. He thought that since he must go to such a mighty and well-provisioned castle as that where the Grail appears, he would confess to the good hermit. He dismounted and acknowledged all his sins and confessed to the good man, saying he repented of all but one. The hermit asked him which sin it was he did not want to repent of. "Good sir," said Lancelot, "it seems to me to be the most pleasant and best sin I ever committed."—"My lord," replied the hermit, "sins are pleasant to commit, but the punishment is very bitter, and no sin is good or noble: each sin is worse than the next!"—"I can confess this sin with my tongue but can never regret it in my heart: I desire my lady the queen more than anyone alive, though she is married to one of the best kings in the world. This desire seems so high-minded and so noble that I cannot abandon it, and it is so rooted in my heart that it can never go away. All my great valor comes to me from this desire."—"Oh mortal sinner," remarked the hermit, "what have you said? No valor can come from such lust without being paid for dearly! You are a traitor to your earthly lord and mortally wound your Savior. Of the seven deadly sins, you have taken on one of the deadliest; its pleasure is most false and you will pay dearly for it unless you repent at once!"—"Good sir," said Lancelot, "I have never before wished to confess it to anyone on this earth."—"All the worse!" exclaimed the hermit. "You should have confessed it long ago and repented, for as long as you continue in it you will be an enemy of the Savior."—"Oh, good sir, there is so much beauty, worth, wisdom and courtesy in the queen that anyone whom she deigned to love should never forget her!"—"Because there is so much beauty and worth in her, she is the more to blame, and you as well, because the harm is not so great from a thing of little value as from a thing that should be of great value: and here is an anointed and crowned queen, dedicated from her coronation to God, who has given herself to the devil for love of you, and you for her! Good dear friend, abandon this cruel folly you have undertaken and repent this sin, and I shall pray to the Savior every day for you, asking him to pardon this sin which you have long maintained, if you are sorry and make a true confession, just as He pardoned the one who struck him the mortal blow in his side. I will take the penance for it upon myself."—"Good sir, mercy, for God's sake!" said Lancelot. "I have no desire to abandon this sin, and I don't wish to tell you something my heart does not agree to. I am willing to do the penance assigned for such a sin, because I wish to serve my lady the queen as long as it pleases her for me to be her lover. I love her so much that I trust I'll never desire not to love her, and God is so sweet and forgiving, as good men of religion testify, that He will have mercy on us, for I have never been unfaithful to her, nor she to me."—"Ah, good dear friend," said the hermit, "nothing I can say will ever help you. May God give her, and you too, the desire to do the Savior's bidding and save your souls! But this much I can assure you: if you take lodging with the Fisher King, you will not see the Grail because of this sin that is fixed in your heart."—"May the Lord God and his sweet Mother help me as they please and desire."—"May they indeed," said the hermit, "it is my fervent wish!" (464).

Lancelot took his leave, remounted, and left the hermitage. As vespers approached he saw that it was time to seek lodging. Before him he saw the castle of the rich Fisher King. The bridges appeared wide and large, not at all the way they were for Sir Gawain. He looked at the splendid entryway, where God was depicted on the Cross, and saw two lions guarding the door. Lancelot considered that Sir Gawain had passed between the lions, and so would he. He rode toward the door and the lions, which were chained, pricked up their ears and looked at him; Lancelot passed right between them without fear: neither of them intended him any harm. He dismounted in front of the main palace and mounted the stairs fully armed. Two old knights came to meet him. They welcomed him with great joy and had him sit down on a couch in the middle of the room. They had two squires disarm him, and two maidens brought him a costly robe, which they had him don. Lancelot beheld the opulence of the hall, whose walls were covered with portraits of saints, both male and female. The hall was hung here and there with silk cloths. The two knights led Lancelot into a room where the rich Fisher King was lying in splendor. He found the king lying on a bed that was more splendid and opulent than anyone had ever seen; he had a maiden at his head and another at his feet. Lancelot greeted them most nobly and the king replied in a most gracious manner. There was such a brightness in the room that it seemed the sun was shining from every side, but it was deep night and Lancelot could not see a single candle lit. "My lord," said the Fisher King, "can you tell me news of the son of my sister, also son of Julain the Fat of the Vales of Camelot, who is called Perlesvaus?"—"I saw him not long ago, sir, at the house of his uncle the Hermit King."—"I have been told that he is a most excellent knight."—"He is the best in the world," said Lancelot. "I myself have experienced his goodness and his valor, because he wounded me seriously before I recognized him, nor he me."—"And what is your name?" inquired the king.—"My lord, I am called Lancelot of the Lake and am son of King Ban of Benoic."—"Ah," said the king, "you are closely related to us; by rights you must be a good knight! And you are, so I've heard tell. Lancelot, there is the chapel that contains the most Holy Grail, which appeared to two knights who have been here. I don't know the name of the first, but I never saw one so calm and so quiet, nor who seemed a better knight; because of him I have fallen into this languor. The second was my lord Gawain."—"Sir, the first was your nephew Perlesvaus!"—"Ah," said the king, "be sure that you're telling the truth!"—"I am, my lord, and I should know him well."—"Oh, God! Why didn't I realize it then? Because of him I have fallen into this languor, but if I had known it was he, I would now be completely well in my body and limbs. I pray you earnestly to tell him, when you see him, to come to me before I die, and also go to help and succor his mother whose men and lands are all being besieged, and who cannot regain them except through him. His sister has come through all the kingdoms in search of him."—"My lord," said Lancelot, "I shall gladly tell him if ever I find him anywhere, but it is not easy to find him, because he disguises himself in many ways and hides his name in many places" (468).

The Fisher King was very happy to hear the news about his nephew and had Lancelot treated with much respect. The knights led him into the hall and sat down at an ivory table to eat. After they had washed, the table was set with expensive vessels of gold and silver. They were served many elaborate courses and cuts of stag and boar. But the tale testifies and states that the Grail did not appear at this meal. If it did not appear, it was not because Lancelot was not one of the three best knights in the world, but rather on account of his unrepented sin of loving the queen, because he thought of nothing so much as her and could not wean his heart from her. After they had eaten, they rose from table and two maidens helped prepare Lancelot for bed. He lay down upon an opulent couch and they did not leave him until he had fallen asleep. As soon as dawn came, he arose and went to hear Mass, then took leave of the Fisher King and the knights and maidens, and departed the castle between the two lions, praying to God to let him see the queen soon, for it was his greatest desire. He rode until he was some distance from the castle and entered the forest. He was eager to meet up with Perlesvaus, but he would not have news of him for a long time (470).

[Branch VIII (continues)

[Lancelot returns to Arthur's castle of Pennevoiseuse, to the company of Arthur, Guinevere, and Gawain. The tale returns to Perlesvaus, who chases off his evil uncle, the King of Deadly Castle, who has been besieging the castle of the Queen of Maidens. He comes secretly by boat one night to Pennevoiseuse and exchanges his shield for the one left by the Bald Maiden in Branch II, then disappears just as secretly. His sister Dandrane, Gawain, and Lancelot all set off to seek him. Gawain fails to recognize him on three occasions, because he is in disguise. (The third time is at the tournament in the Red Land, alluded to in the following selection.) Lancelot, meanwhile, is besieged by kinsmen of the brigands he hanged in the forest earlier in this Branch. Gawain finally catches up with Perlesvaus, and the two of them rescue Lancelot. Perlesvaus then finds his sister, Dandrane, and they go to Camaalot, just in time to rescue their mother and her castle from the wicked designs of the Lord of the Fens. He punishes the latter in a particularly gruesome manner, suspending him head downward until he drowns in a vat filled with the blood of his own slain men.

[Branch IX. The following selection provides a good example of the gore, marvelous elements, militant Christianity, and allegorical adventures that characterize the Perlesvaus. (Beginning on p. 622.)]

Here begins one of the most important branches of the Grail, in the name of the Father and of the Son and of the Holy Spirit. Perlesvaus had stayed as long as he wanted with his mother. He left with her accord and that of his sister, saying he would return to that land as quickly as he could. He entered the vast lonely forest and rode for many days until he came around noon one day to a most beautiful clearing, where he saw a cross that was completely red. At the head of the clearing he saw a strikingly handsome knight dressed in white and holding a golden cup in his hand, sitting in the shade of the forest; he looked next toward the opposite side of the clearing and saw an exceptionally lovely maiden, just as young and fair, dressed in white silk speckled with gold, sitting and holding in her hand a most beautiful golden cup.

Josephus tells us in his inspired writings that a beast as white as the fallen snow, larger than a hare but smaller than a fox, came out of the forest. The beast was frightened as she entered the clearing, for she carried twelve pups in her belly, yapping within her like hounds, and she was fleeing across the glade for fear of the barking she heard from inside her. Perlesvaus was leaning on the butt-end of his lance and observing the mystery of this beast, for which he felt great pity, since she appeared very gentle and was quite beautiful, and it seemed that her eyes were two emeralds. She ran all frightened toward the knight, then after a moment ran to the maiden, because the pups tormented her again, but could not remain there either, because she was terrified by the incessant barking of the hounds inside her. Seeing Perlesvaus, she approached him for help. She tried to leap upon the neck of his horse and he reached out his hands to keep her from hurting herself; the hounds were still barking. The knight yelled to Perlesvaus: "Sir knight, let the beast go! It's not for you or anyone else to hold her—leave her to her fate!" The beast, seeing she would have no protection, ran toward the cross. The pups could no longer remain within her and came out like full-grown dogs. They were not gentle or noble like her; she cowered submissively among them and acted as though she were asking them for mercy. She stayed as close to the cross as she could. The dogs surrounded her and attacked her from all sides, ripping at her with their jaws, but they were unable to eat of her flesh or drag her away from the cross (624).

After the dogs had killed the beast, they raced madly into the woods. The knight and the maiden came to where the beast was lying torn apart beside the cross; they both took a part of her and put it in their golden cups, then they took the blood just as they had the flesh; they kissed the spot and worshipped the cross, then went back into the forest. Perlesvaus dismounted and knelt before the cross; he kissed and worshipped the cross as well as the spot where the beast was killed, just as he had seen the knight and maiden do. A sweet fragrance, unlike any other, came from the cross and the spot where she had died. He looked up and saw two priests coming out of the forest on foot, and the first shouted: "Sir knight, get away from the cross and let us approach it!" Perlesvaus moved away and the first priest knelt before the cross, bowed down and worshiped it, and kissed it more than twenty times, overflowing with joy; the second priest then approached, carrying a switch, and he pulled the other priest away and began whipping the cross all over with the switch, weeping piteously. Perlesvaus looked at him in amazement, saying: "You look like a priest to me, sir—why are you behaving so wickedly?"—"What we are doing, sir, is none of your business, and you'll never learn anything about it from us!" Had the man not been a priest, Perlesvaus would have been very angry with him; but he did not want to do him any harm, so he turned away at once, mounted his horse, and rode off fully armed into the forest.

He had gone but a short distance when he met the Cowardly Knight, who shouted to him as soon as he caught sight of him, "In God's name, sir, do I have any reason to fear you?"—"Who are you, then?" asked Perlesvaus.—"I am called the Cowardly Knight and am in the service of the Cart Maiden. I beg you in God's name and on your valor not to touch me, for it is of little value to hit a man who doesn't dare strike back!" Perlesvaus looked at him and, seeing that he was tall, handsome, well-proportioned and fully armed on his horse, asked: "If you are so cowardly, then why are you armed?"—"Because of the wickedness of some knights I'm afraid of, who might kill me if they found me unarmed."—"Are you then as cowardly as you say?" asked Perlesvaus.—"Yes, my lord, and even more!"—"By my head," said Perlesvaus, "I'll give you some courage! Come along with me, for it's a great shame that such a handsome knight is so full of cowardice. I want your name to be changed at once, because yours is too wicked for a knight to have!"—"Ah, my lord, for God's sake!" said he. "Now I know that you want to kill me. I don't want to change either my manner or my name."—"Then, by my head," said Perlesvaus, "you'll die shortly!" Perlesvaus made him ride ahead whether he wanted to or not, and the knight was most reluctant (628).

After only a few paces the knight heard off in the forest two maidens lamenting most piteously and praying Almighty God to send them help quickly. Perlesvaus and the knight whom he was driving on ahead of him rode in that direction; they saw a massive fully armed knight carrying off the two disheveled maidens, striking them time and again with a long switch so that blood was streaming down their faces. "Hey there!" shouted Perceval, "What do you want from these maidens you are treating so maliciously?"—"My lord, they have deprived me of a lodging I have here in this forest, and which Sir Gawain gave them."—"For God's sake, take pity on us, sir!" the maidens implored Perlesvaus. "He's a robber knight, the last one left in this forest! My lord Gawain, Lancelot, and another knight who came with them killed all the other robber knights. Because of our want and the great poverty they witnessed in our brother's house, the night they stayed in the Waste Castle, Lancelot and Sir Gawain gave us the lodging and all the treasure they had won from the robber knights. That is why he is carrrying us off to destroy and kill us, and he would do the same to you if he could, and to all other knights who pass through the forest."—"Sir knight," said Perlesvaus, "release the maidens! I know they are telling the truth, because I was there when they were given the lodging."—"Then you helped destroy my lineage," said the knight, "and therefore I challenge you!"—"Ah, my lord," said the Cowardly Knight to Perlesvaus, "Don't pay any attention to what he says! Don't get angry, but go your way and I'll go mine."—"No," said Perlesvaus, "you'll help me protect the honor of these maidens."—"Oh, my lord," said the Cowardly Knight, "I could never defend their honor!" Perlesvaus backed away and said: "Sir knight, here is my second, whom I offer in my stead." The robber knight headed for the Cowardly Knight and struck him such a mighty blow on his shield that he broke his lance, but he could not shake him and he sat unmoved between his saddlebows. He looked at the other knight, who had drawn his sword; the Cowardly Knight looked from one side to the other and would gladly have fled if he dared, but Perlesvaus shouted to him: "My knight, strive to save my honor, your life, and the honor of these two maidens!" The robber knight gave him a mighty blow with his sword and nearly knocked him out, but the Cowardly Knight still did not move. Perlesvaus watched him in amazement and thought that he had chosen too cowardly a knight to second him. Now for the first time he realized that the other had told him the truth. The robber knight attacked him on all sides and gave him so many blows that the Cowardly Knight saw he was bleeding. "By my head, you've wounded me," he exclaimed, "but you'll pay for it! I never thought you'd want to kill me!" He fewtered his sturdy lance, hotly spurred his horse, and struck the robber knight such a powerful blow to the chest that the lance's iron tip passed through his body and carried him to the ground beneath his horse. He dismounted, unlaced his adversary's ventail and lowered his coif, then struck off his head and presented it to Perlesvaus, saying: "I offer you this from my first joust."—"By my head," said Perlesvaus, "I am most grateful for this gift. Take care now never again to sink into cowardice as you did, for it is a great shame for a knight."—"I won't. I never thought it was so easy to be brave or I would have done it long ago, and I would have had prowess and honor, because many knights who held me in dishonor and spite would have honored me."—"Truly it is right to honor good knights more than the others," said Perlesvaus. "I commend to you these two maidens to watch over and escort safely to their lodging, where you will be at their beck and call. And tell everyone that you are called the Brave Knight, because this name is nobler than the other!"—"You speak truly, and I love this name coming from you." The maidens thanked Perlesvaus profusely, took their leave and rode on, grateful to the knight who was accompanying them for having slain the other. They called him the Brave Knight (632).

Perlesvaus left the place where the knight lay dead and rode until he neared Carduel, where King Arthur was. He found the land round about in great fear and consternation, and wondered why. He asked the peasants why they were so fearful: "Is King Arthur no longer alive?"—"Yes, my lord," several of them answered. "He is here in this castle, but he has never been so pressed and afraid as he is now, because he is being attacked by a knight whom no knight in the world can better." Perlesvaus rode until he reached the main hall, where he dismounted at the block. Lancelot and my lord Gawain came out joyfully to greet him, as did the king and queen and all the court. They had him disarmed and dressed in an expensive robe; those who had never seen him admired him for his valor and the greatness of his deeds. The court, which had been sad, was somewhat gladdened to see him.

One day while the king sat at table, four armed knights burst into the hall, each carrying before him a dead knight whose feet and arms had been cut off, but whose bodies were still armed in halberks as black as if struck by lightening. They tossed the knights into the middle of the room, saying to the king: "My lord, once again you see the shame that is done to you, and which is not made right. The Dragon Knight is destroying your lands and killing your men and coming as near to you as he can, boasting that he'll not find a knight at your court brave enough to face him or attack him." The king was greatly shamed by these words, as were Lancelot and Sir Gawain, who were sad in their hearts that the king would not let them go there. The four knights turned back, leaving the dead knights in the middle of the hall; the king had them carried off and buried with the others. Loud murmurings arose in the hall among the knights, with many saying that they had never heard of anyone who killed knights as cruelly as did this man, but Sir Gawain and Lancelot were not to blame for not going to face him, because no knight in the world could defeat such a man without a miracle by God Almighty, since he threw fire and flames from his shield whenever he wanted (636).

While the knights' murmurings were filling the hall, there appeared the maiden who had long been escorting the body of a dead knight in a litter. She came before the king, saying: "Sire, I pray and request you to give me justice at your court. You see before you your nephew Sir Gawain who participated in the tournament in the Red Meadow, where there were many knights, including the son of the Widow Lady, whom I see sitting beside you. He and my lord Gawain won the most glory at the tournament; he wore white armor and those at the tourney said that he had done better than Sir Gawain because he was the first to enter the battles. Before the tournament I was promised that the victor would avenge this knight. My lord, I have long sought him and have now found him here at your court; therefore I beg and request you to pray and order him to act in such a manner as not to be blamed, for Sir Gawain well knows that I am telling the truth. But this knight left the tournament so quickly that I didn't know what had become of him, and my lord Gawain too was very sad that he'd left, for he sought him, though he didn't know who he was."—"Dear maiden," said Sir Gawain, "it is indeed true that he was the victor at the tournament, and for the rest he must find satisfaction with you, if it please God."—"My lord Gawain," countered Perlesvaus, "it seems to me that you did better than all the others!"—"Upon my word," said Sir Gawain, "your fine protestations do you honor, but in spite of what I and the others did, it was to you that the knights adjudged the prize. Of that I can bear witness to the maiden."—"Thank you, my lord!" said the maiden. "He must not refuse what I ask of him, because the knight whose corpse I have been escorting for a long time in its litter was the son of his uncle Elynant of Escavalon."—"Be careful that you are telling the truth!" said Perlesvaus. "I am well aware that Elynant of Escavalon was my uncle on my father's side, but I have never heard of his son."—"His valor, my lord, makes him worth hearing of: he was killed because of his bravery, and was named Alain of Escavalon. The Lady of the Golden Circle loved him with all her being, because he was the handsomest knight she had seen in her whole life. And he would have been the best, had he lived longer. Because of her great love for him, she had his body embalmed after he was slain by the Dragon Knight, who is so cruel that he lays waste to all lands and all islands. He defied the Lady of the Golden Circle and has already killed many of her knights. She is locked into her castle and doesn't dare come out, but she wants me to tell every knight I meet that the one who will avenge this knight will have the Golden Circle from which she has never before agreed to be separated; it will be the greatest honor a knight can attain. My lord (she said, addressing Perlesvaus), you must strive to avenge the son of your uncle and win the Golden Circle, because if you slay the knight, you will have assured protection of King Arthur's lands, which the Dragon Knight has threatened to destroy, as well as that of all the lands adjoining Arthur's, for he hates no king more than Arthur, because of the joy he manifested when the giant's head was brought to his court."—"Fair maiden," asked Perlesvaus, "where is the Dragon Knight?"—"He is on Elephant Island, which was once the most beautiful and opulent land in all the world; but now he's completely laid waste to it, they say, so no one dares live there. And the island where he lives sits just below the castle of the Queen of the Golden Circle, and every day she can see him bring fully armed knights out of the forest, then kill and dismember them, which moves her to great pity" (640).

Perlesvaus heard what the maiden said and was much amazed; he thought to himself that since he was responsible for the vengeance he would be greatly blamed if he did not take it. He took leave of the king and queen and left court. My lord Gawain and Lancelot went with him, saying they would accompany him to this piece of land if it was possible. Perlesvaus was very pleased with their company. King Arthur and the queen were greatly frightened for Perlesvaus and everyone said that no knight had ever set off to face such peril, and it would be a great shame for everyone if he died. The king sent messages to all the priests and hermits in the forest of Carduel, asking them to pray God to protect Perlesvaus from the devil knight against whom he was going to do combat. Lancelot and Sir Gawain accompanied him through the unknown forests and the islands, and they found the forests to be deserted and the lands ruined and laid waste on every side. The maiden followed him with the dead knight's corpse. When they finally came to the plain beyond the forest, they saw before them a castle situated on the plain in the middle of the prairie, surrounded by swiftly flowing rivers and a wall. Within were large windowed halls. As they approached the castle, they saw that it was spinning around faster than any wind blew and that there were copper automatons in the battlements shooting arrows with such force that no armor in the world could protect one from them. With them were living men blowing trumpets and sounding horns so loudly that the earth seemed to be shaking. Below the entry were chained lions and bears roaring so fiercely that the forest and the valley echoed with their growls. The knights stopped and looked at this marvel, and the maiden said: "My lords, you see before you the Impregnable Castle! My lord Gawain and you, Lancelot, turn back now; don't go any nearer the archers or you will die! And you, my lord," she said to Perlesvaus, "if you wish to enter the castle, give me your lance and your shield and I'll carry them ahead to protect you. You must follow after me, comporting yourself like a good knight, and you will pass through the castle; but your companions should withdraw, for it is not their time to pass. Only the one who wishes to win the Golden Circle and the Grail by defeating the devil knight and the false religion of the castle with the copper bull may pass" (644).

Perlesvaus was much saddened when he heard the maiden say that Sir Gawain and Lancelot would not accompany him, and yet they are the best knights in the world. He took sad leave of them and they left most unwillingly, but they gently urged him, if God let him escape alive from where he was going, to find some occasion where they could finally see him without disguise. They stopped to watch the Good Knight, who had given his lance and shield to the maiden, pass through; she placed her dead knight on his litter in front, then showed those in the castle the Good Knight's shield, quite unmistakably indicating that it belonged to the knight who had pulled up behind her. Perlesvaus was sitting in his saddle without a shield, but with his sword drawn. He rose so powerfully in his stirrups that they cracked and his horse's spine sagged. He then looked at Lancelot and Sir Gawain, and said: "My lords, I commend you to the Savior of the world!"—"May He who was crucified watch over your body and your life!" they replied. He spurred his horse and it raced full speed beneath him to the Spinning Castle. He struck so hard with his sword at the gate that he drove it three fingers deep into the marble pillar. The chained lions and bears that guarded the gate retreated to their cages. The castle stopped turning all at once and the archers ceased shooting. There were three drawbridges in front of the castle that lifted as soon as he crossed. Lancelot and Sir Gawain witnessed this marvel and wanted to approach the castle when they saw it stop, but a knight shouted to them from the battlements: "My lords, if you come forward, the archers will shoot, the castle will spin, and the bridges will lower; you'll be trapped!" They drew back at once, but could hear sounds of great joy within and many people saying that the one was come who would save them in two ways—save their lives and save their souls—if God let him defeat the knight possessed by a devil's spirit.

Lancelot and Sir Gawain turned back, disconsolate and depressed that they could not pass through the castle, for they saw no other entry than that one. They rode until they neared the Waste City where Lancelot had killed the knight. "Ah," said he to Sir Gawain, "the time is near when I must go to die in this Waste City, unless God helps me!" And he told Sir Gawain the whole adventure that had happened to him there. Just as Lancelot was about to take leave of Sir Gawain, the poor knight of the Waste Castle rode out to Lancelot and said: "My lord, I have gotten you a reprieve in this city for the knight you killed, until forty days after the winning of the Grail. Never before have I left the castle where you stayed, and would not now have come had you not arrived to keep your promise, nor will I come out again until the hour of your return, on the day I've said. I thank Sir Gawain and you for the horses you sent us, which were very helpful to us, and for the lodging and treasure you gave to my sisters who were in great want. But I cannot overcome the poverty I suffer until the hour of your return, on the date that I was able, with great difficulty, to get postponed by your enemies, because of the many good things you have done for me. I pray you not to forget, so your loyalty may be intact."—"By my head, I'll not forget!" said Lancelot. "And many thanks for getting me the reprieve." He left the knight and rode back with Sir Gawain to Carduel, where King Arthur was staying (648).

Here the story leaves Lancelot and Sir Gawain and says that Perlesvaus is in the Spinning Castle, about which Josephus tells us the truth when he says that Virgil created it by the art of his intelligence when philosophers went in search of earthly paradise. And it was prophesied that the castle would not stop spinning until the hour when the knight who had a golden head, the gaze of a lion, a heart of steel, the navel of a spotless virgin, virtues without wickedness, the valor of a man, and faith and belief in God, came; and this knight would carry the shield of the good soldier who took down the Savior of the world from the Cross. It was also prophesied that all the people in this castle and in all other castles that depended on it would follow the Old Law until the hour that the Good Knight came, and therefore those in the castle said, as soon as he had arrived, that the one had come who would save their souls and postpone their deaths, for as soon as he came they all rushed to be baptized and believed firmly in the Trinity and kept the New Law. This was why there was great rejoicing in the castle, that death had been overcome as well as fear of the devil knight—that is, fear that they might die—and the sin of the false religion, that they might be damned for it.

Perlesvaus was very happy to see the inhabitants of the castle converted to the holy faith of the Savior, and the maiden said to him: "You have done well, my lord! Now you need only do the rest: the people will never be able to leave the castle as long as the Dragon Knight is alive. You must delay no more, for the longer you delay the more he will destroy the lands and kill the people." Perlesvaus took leave of the castle's inhabitants, who were all rejoicing for him, but who also were fearful for him because he had to go to fight the knight; they said that if Perlesvaus defeated him, no knight had ever had a finer adventure. He heard Mass before he left and they offered rich gifts for him in honor of the Savior and his sweet mother. The maiden, who knew where the evil knight was, preceded him.

They rode until they came to Elephant Island. The knight had dismounted beneath an olive tree, where he had immediately slain four knights who belonged to the household of the Queen of the Golden Circle. She was standing by the windows of her palace and witnessed the deaths of her knights, which greatly tormented her: "Oh God!" she said. "Will I ever see the day when some man can avenge me on this evil-doer who lays waste to my lands and kills my men in this way?" She looked and saw Perlesvaus and the maiden coming; she shouted to him: "Sir knight, unless you are stronger and more powerful than other knights, do not approach this devil! But if you feel in your heart that you can do battle with him and defeat him, I will give you the Golden Circle that is here in this castle and I will believe in the New Law that has recently been established. I can clearly see from your shield that you are a Christian, and if you can defeat him, then I must acknowledge that your religion is better than ours, and that God was born of woman" (652).

Perlesvaus was elated at what he had heard her say. He blessed and crossed himself and commended himself to God and his sweet mother, then became ferocious and bold like a lion. He beheld the Dragon Knight on his horse and was astonished to see how huge he was; never before had he seen a man so large. At his neck he saw his large, black and hideous shield, in the middle of which was the dragon's head that spewed fire and flames violently, so ugly and horrible that all the land about stunk. Leaving the dead knight upon his litter in the field, the maiden went toward the castle and said: "In this plain, my lord, your uncle's son was slain, and here I leave him, because I've already escorted him enough; avenge him now as best you can. I turn him over to your care, for I've done enough already for him that I should not be blamed." With that she left.

The Dragon Knight saw Perlesvaus approaching all alone and held him in utter contempt. He did not even deign take up his lance, but approached him with drawn sword, which was huge and as red as burning coal. Perlesvaus saw him approaching and rode toward him with his lance lowered, as fast as his horse would go, intending to strike him in the breast with his lance; but the knight raised his shield and the flame that came from the dragon's mouth burned his lance right up to his fist. The knight meant to strike the top of his head with his sword, but Perlesvaus covered himself with his trusty shield and the knight's sword could not harm him. (Josephus tells us that Joseph of Arimathia had had some of Our Lord's blood and a fragment of his clothing encased in its boss.) When his adversary saw that he had not harmed Perlesvaus or his shield, he was sorely shamed, because never before had he struck a knight without killing him. He turned his shield with its dragon's head toward Perlesvaus's shield, thinking to set it afire and burn it, but the flame coming from the dragon's mouth was turned back, as if by the wind, and could not touch it. The knight became enraged. He rode past Perlesvaus and came to the dead knight's litter; he turned his shield with its dragon's head toward the litter and burned the knight's corpse and the litter's horses to ashes. "You won't have to bury this knight!" he boasted to Perlesvaus.—"I am indeed saddened," Perlesvaus responded, "but I shall make it good, if it pleases God." The maiden who had escorted the dead knight was standing in the palace window beside the queen; she shouted to Perlesvaus: "My lord, if you don't make it good, the shame is greater and the wrong increased!"

Perlesvaus was sorrowful to see his nephew reduced to ashes, but he realized the knight had the devil's strength with him and did not know how he could avenge him. With sword drawn he came forward and struck him a mighty blow upon the shield that split it up to the middle where the dragon's head was, and the flame leapt to his sword, turning it as red and enflamed as his adversary's sword. The maiden shouted: "By my head, sir, now your sword is as strong as his! Now we'll see what you can do. I have been told—and it is true–that the knight can only be killed by a single blow to a single spot; but I'm sorry that I cannot tell you how." Perlesvaus looked at his sword, which was aflame with the devil's fire, and was greatly amazed. He struck the knight such a powerful blow that he forced his head down to the saddle horn, but the knight straightened back up and was enraged that he could not do him in: he struck Perlesvaus such a mighty blow with his sword that it pierced the hauberk at his right shoulder, opening the flesh and burning him to the bone. As he was withdrawing his blade, Perlesvaus struck him such a fierce blow that he cut off his sword hand. The queen and all the people in the palace heard his shriek and were very heartened. Yet the knight gave no sign of defeat and rushed upon Perlesvaus, again directing the flame against his shield, but it was to no avail because he was unable to do him any harm. Perlesvaus beheld the dragon's head, which was huge, broad, and terrifying. He took aim at it with his sword, striking inside its mouth as directly as possible, and the dragon's head let out a cry that echoed through the fields and forest for two Welsh leagues. The dragon's head turned angrily toward its lord and burned him to ashes before departing like lightening toward the heavens.

The queen was overjoyed; she and all her knights approached Perlesvaus. He saw that he was sorely wounded in his right shoulder, and the maiden told him he would not be healed unless he dabbed it with ashes from the dead knight. They led him up to the castle amidst much rejoicing, had his armor removed, washed out his wound, and dabbed it with ashes from the dead knight in order to heal it. The queen sent for all the knights of her land and said: "My lords, this is the knight who protected my land for me and saved your lives and mine. You well know that it was prophesied that the knight with the golden locks would come and save us. See him here now, come among us! The prophecy cannot be wrong; I want you to obey his command." They said that they would gladly do so. Then she took him to where the Golden Circle was and placed it herself upon his head; afterwards she brought him his sword and presented it to him, the one with which he had slain the devil and the knight who carried him upon his shield. "My lord," she told him, "may all those who refuse to be baptized and believe in the New Law be killed by your sword! I present it to you." She herself was the first to be raised over the font and baptized, then all the others after her. Josephus tells us that she was given the baptismal name Eliza and that she led a good and holy life and died a virgin. Her body still lies in the kingdom of Ireland, where it is much honored (660).

Perlesvaus remained in the castle until he was healed. News spread throughout the lands that the Knight with the Golden Circle had slain the Dragon Knight, and there was great rejoicing everywhere. It was heard at King Arthur's court, where everyone was greatly amazed to learn that the Knight with the Golden Circle had vanquished him, for they could not know who the Knight with the Golden Circle was.

When Perlesvaus was healed, he left the Queen of the Golden Circle's castle. All the land was under her command and the queen told him that she would keep the Golden Circle for him as long as he liked, and he left it with her because he did not want to take it with him, not knowing where he was headed.

The story tells us that he rode until he came one day to the Castle of the Copper Bull. Inside were many people who worshipped the copper bull and did not believe in another god. The Copper Bull was in the middle of the castle on four copper columns and bellowed loudly at all hours of the day, such that it could be heard a good league round about; inside it was an evil spirit that gave them answers to whatever they wanted to hear. At the entry door were two automatons in human form with two iron hammers, which beat and hit so mightily that nothing in the whole world could pass between them without being struck down; and the castle was so locked down elsewhere that nothing alive could enter.

Perlesvaus looked in amazement at the castle's fortifications and its dangerous gateway. He crossed a bridge that led to the gate and approached the guards. A voice from above the gate began to cry out that he should advance confidently and that he should not fear the copper automatons or their blows, because they were powerless to harm a knight as good as he. He was much comforted by what the voice told him. He approached the copper knaves and they held their blows; immediately the iron hammers ceased striking and he passed through into the castle, where there were many non-believers. In the middle of the castle he beheld the tall and horrific Copper Bull surrounded by people, all worshipping it. The bull was bellowing so loudly that it was difficult to hear anything else within the castle. Those inside were amazed to see Perlesvaus and wondered how he had gotten in. But no one spoke to him because they believed so strongly in this false religion and faith that if anyone tried to kill them while they were worshipping, they would let them and believe that they were saved. No one else in all the world shared this faith. They were not used to bearing arms within the castle, because the gate and fortifications were so strong that no one could enter against their will, unless it was Almighty God's pleasure, and the devil in whom they believed gave them such abundance that nothing in the world was lacking to them (664).

When Perlesvaus saw that they were not speaking to him, he moved toward a large hall and called them to him; many came, but a few refused to come. The voice cried out to Perlesvaus to make them all cross through the entryway with the copper knaves; that way he could well tell who wanted to believe in God and who did not. The Good Knight drew his sword and herded them together, forcing them to move forward whether they wanted to or not, and those who refused to go willingly were assured of death. He made them pass through the entryway where the automatons struck mighty blows with their iron hammers; of one thousand five hundred, only thirteen were saved from being killed and having their brains knocked out by the iron hammers; but these thirteen believed firmly in Our Lord and had no reason to fear. The evil spirit in the Copper Bull shot from it like lightening and the Copper Bull fell in a heap: nothing was left. The thirteen remaining men summoned a hermit who lived in the forest and had themselves baptized; afterwards they took the bodies of the unbelievers and had them thrown into a river called the river of hell. This river flows into the sea, say many who have seen it, and where it flows out the sea is most filthy, horrible and dangerous, for a ship can scarcely sail through there without being lost.

Josephus tells us that the hermit who baptized these thirteen was named Denis and that the castle was called Trial Castle. They remained there until the New Law was established and followed throughout all the kingdoms, and they led a very good and holy life, and anyone who entered where they were and did not believe firmly in God was beheaded and killed. Once the inhabitants of all the islands were converted, the thirteen left the castle and spread through the unknown forests, building hermitages and chapels, and flagellating their bodies in atonement for the false religion they had followed and to win the love of the Savior of the world (666).

Perlesvaus, as you have heard, was a soldier of Our Lord, and God clearly showed him that He loved his deeds, because the Good Knight suffered much and had many travails, but that pleased him greatly. One day he came to the castle of his uncle the Hermit King, who was very eager to see him and greeted his nephew joyfully when he saw him. Perlesvaus told him of the most important adventures he had had since he left, and the Hermit King was amazed by many of them. "Uncle," said Perlesvaus, "I was particularly amazed by a small white beast I found in a clearing in a forest, which had twelve pups in her belly that were yelping and barking inside her; in the end they came out and killed her at the foot of the cross, but didn't eat her flesh. A knight and a maiden took her flesh and blood and put it into two golden vessels, and the dogs to which she'd given birth fled into the forest."—"Fair nephew," said the Hermit King, "I am sure that God loves you, to let you behold such things because of your valor and the chastity of your body. The sweet, pure and good beast with the twelve barking dogs inside represents Our Lord, and the twelve dogs represent the Jews of the Old Law, whom God created and made in His likeness. When He had made and created them, He wanted to test how much they loved Him; He put them in a desert for forty years; their clothing did not rot and he sent them delicious nourishment from heaven, as much as they wished to eat and drink. They remained there with no pain, no suffering, no torments, and had all the happiness and pleasure they could desire. One day they met in council and their leaders said that if God grew angry and took this manna from them, they would have nothing to eat—and this manna could not last forever, because God sent it in such great abundance. They proposed that they bury a large heap of it and, when God became angry, they would distribute it and could live off it a good while. They all agreed to this plan. Afterwards they did as they had decided. God, who sees and knows everything, knew their thoughts: He took from them the manna from heaven. They went to the caves, thinking they would find what they had put aside to live on, but by God's will it had been changed into lizards, snakes, and vermin. When they saw that they had erred, they scattered into foreign lands. Fair nephew, the twelve dogs who barked at the beast were the Jews whom God nourished and who were born into the Law He established. They refused to believe in and love him, and instead they crucified him and defiled his body as vilely as they could, but they could not destroy his flesh. The knight and the maiden who placed the beast's flesh into the golden vessels represent the divinity of the Father, who could not suffer his Son's flesh to be destroyed. The dogs who fled into the forest and became wild after they had defiled the beast are the Jews who will be wild and subject henceforth to the followers of the New Law."—"Dear uncle," said Perlesvaus, "it is only right that they be punished, since they crucified and killed the one who created and made them, and who deigned to be born into their religion! But two priests came afterwards; one of them kissed and worshiped the cross, rejoicing in it, while the other whipped it with a large switch, weeping and showing signs of the greatest grief in the world. I would have been very angry with this latter had he not seemed to me to be a priest."—"Fair nephew," said the hermit, "the one who whipped the cross believed in God as much as the one who worshiped it; the first priest worshiped it because it bore the flesh of the Savior of the world, who freely accepted his death; he laughed and showed great joy because He rescued his friends from death and the pains of hell, who otherwise would have remained there forever. And his greatest joy came from his knowledge through faith that He was both God and man eternally; whoever does not believe and remember this will never have true faith. Fair nephew, the other priest whipped the cross and wept for the immense anguish, pain and torment that the Lord God suffered upon it, for the anguish was so great that the rock split, and no human mouth can tell you the pain He felt on the cross. And so he whipped and cursed it because He was crucified upon it, just as I would hate a lance or sword that killed you. He did it for no other reason: every time he thinks of the pain that God suffered, he comes to the cross just as you witnessed. They are both hermits and live in the forest; the one who kisses and worships the cross is named Jonas, and the one who whips and curses it is called Alexis" (672).

Perlesvaus was glad to hear and understand what his uncle told him. Next he recounted how he fought the devil knight who had a burning dragon's head upon his shield, which spit fire and flames, and how the dragon burned up its master in the end. "Fair nephew," spoke the hermit, "I am very happy to learn this news you relate, because I had been led to understand that the Knight of the Golden Circle had defeated him."—"It might well be, sir," responded Perlesvaus, "but I have never seen such a huge and fearsome knight!"—"Fair nephew, only a Good Knight could defeat him, because all good men must fight the devil, and no one can become a good man unless he does; and just as the devil on the shield burned and killed his master, each devil torments and harms the next in the other world. The devil knight could do you no greater harm than to burn the body of your uncle's son whom he had slain, as I have heard; he had power over the body, but the soul had nothing to fear, as it pleased God."

"Dear uncle, I went to a spinning castle where there were copper archers shooting, and bears and lions chained at the entry to the gate; as soon as I approached and struck with my sword, the castle stopped turning."—"Fair nephew, this was the only protection that the devil had; it was the entry to his fortress, and those within would never have been converted but for you."—"I am very sad that Lancelot and my lord Gawain were unable to enter with me, for I would have liked their company very much and they would have been of help to me."—"Fair nephew, if they were as chaste as yourself, they too could have entered there because of their fine deeds, for they are the two best knights in the world, were they not lustful. Fair nephew, through your own good deeds you have promoted the Savior's Law, for you have destroyed the falsest belief in the world: the religion of those who believed in the devil in the Copper Bull. Had these people lived and your mission failed, they would not have been destroyed before the end of the world. Do not be amazed if you suffer in the service of God; accept it gladly, for no good man ever won honor without pain.

"But now you have another duty to perform: all the inhabitants of the land that belonged to your uncle the Fisher King have abandoned the new religion and reverted to the one prohibited by God; but most of them were forced to do so more from fear of the king who seized the land—he is my brother and your uncle—than for any other reason. You must restore order here, for this can only be accomplished by you; the castle and the land must rightly be yours, because it is a great sadness when someone descended from such a holy and noble lineage is a traitor to God and disloyal on earth. Fair nephew," he continued, "the castle is strongly fortified, guarded by nine newly constructed bridges, each defended by three tall, strong and hardy knights—a mighty defense! Your uncle is within, guarding the castle, and since then none of the Fisher King's knights or priests have been seen there, and no one knows what has become of them. The chapel where the Holy Grail appears is completely empty of its holy relics; the hermits who live in the forest await your arrival, for they no longer see any knights passing by who believe in God. Once you have accomplished this deed, God will be most grateful to you."—"Dear uncle," said Perlesvaus, "since you urge me, I shall truly go there. It is not right that my uncle who entered this castle remain there: my mother, who is first born after the Fisher King (whose death I mourn), has more right to it!"—"Fair nephew, you are correct, for he fell ill because of you, and had you returned there, it is commonly thought that he would have been healed; I don't know that for certain, but I believe that the Lord God desired his languor and death, for had He so wished, you would have asked the question—but He didn't wish it. Therefore we should worship him and give thanks for all He gives us, for He has granted to each one what is his due. I have here a white mule that is very old. You shall take her with you, fair nephew, and she will follow you most willingly; you shall also carry a banner, because God's strength and power are much greater than your own. Twenty-seven elite knights, all of proven bravery, guard the nine bridges, and no one should think that any knight could defeat so many except by a miracle of Our Lord and the aid of his power. I urge and pray you always to remember God and his sweet mother, and when you are wearied or wounded from your efforts, mount the mule and take up the banner, and your enemies will lose some of their force, for nothing confounds your enemy more quickly than the strength and power of God. It is well known that you are the best knight in the world, but don't put faith in your own force and valor against so many men, for you will not last."

Perlesvaus gladly heeded all his uncle's advice, for he had great faith in his good words. "Fair nephew," said the hermit, "there are two lions at the entry to the gate, one red and the other white. Put your faith in the white one, for it is sent by God; look at it each time your strength fades, and it will look at you, too, and you will know its thoughts immediately, through the will and pleasure of Our Lord. Do what you see it indicate, for all its thoughts will be to help you, and without its help you cannot conquer the nine bridges guarded by the knights. May God grant you a victory that will save your life and advance the cause of Our Lord's faith, which your uncle has opposed as much as he could!" (678).

Perlesvaus left the hermitage, carrying the banner as his uncle advised, and the white mule followed him. He went in the direction of the land that once belonged to the Fisher King and came upon a hermit who had left his hermitage and was hurrying through the forest. He stopped as soon as he saw the cross on Perlesvaus's shield, and said: "My lord, I can clearly tell that you are a Christian, of which I've not seen any in a long while. The King of Deadly Castle, who has renounced God and his sweet mother, drives us all from this forest and we dare not remain here against his command."—"You shall, by my head," replied Perlesvaus. "God will lead you and I shall follow behind. Are there more hermits in this forest?"—"Yes, my lord, there are twelve waiting for me by a cross up ahead; we are all planning to go into exile in the kingdom of Logres for love of God, abandoning our buildings and chapels in this forest for fear of the wicked king who has seized the land, for he doesn't want anyone who believes in God to remain here."

Perlesvaus came with the hermit to the cross where the good men were gathered. There he was delighted to find Joseus, the young hermit who was the son of King Pelles. He had the hermits turn back with him and said that he would defend them with God's help and protect them in the kingdom. He gently urged them to pray for him to Our Lord that He might grant him to reconquer what was rightly his.

He came out of the forest, accompanied by the hermits, and approached the castle with its mighty defenses before the gate. Most of the knights knew that Perlesvaus would win the castle, because it had long been prophesied that the bearer of such a shield would win back the Grail from the one who denied God. The knights watched Perlesvaus approaching with the company of hermits and were amazed at the beauty of the sight. On the bridge at two bowshots' distance was a chapel built like the one at Camaalot. There was a sarcophagus and no one knew who was inside. Perlesvaus and his company stopped; he rested his lance and shield against the chapel, then halted his horse and mule. He looked at the magnificent sarcophagus and it immediately unlocked and opened, with the stone on top lifting to reveal a knight lying within, from whom arose such a sweet and pleasant fragrance that the good hermits who beheld him thought he must be embalmed. They found a plaque that indicated that the knight's name was Joseph. As soon as the hermits saw the open sarcophagus, they said to Perlesvaus: "My lord, we now know that you are the most holy and most chaste Good Knight." The knights guarding the bridges knew that the sarcophagus had opened for Perlesvaus. They were immediately thrown into confusion, realizing that this was the one who had come first to the Grail castle. The news reached the king occupying the castle; he told his knights not to be afraid before a single knight, because he would not have the strength to overpower them all, and never had a single knight defeated so many (682).

Perlesvaus was fully armed upon his horse; the hermits made the sign of the cross over him, blessed him, and commended him to God. With his lance in hand, he rode toward the three knights who guarded the first bridge. They rushed upon him all together and broke their lances against his shield. Perlesvaus struck one of them with such force that he was upended into the river that flows beneath the bridge; he was not troubled again by him or his horse, for the river was wide, deep, and raging. The other two fought long against him with swords, but he defeated and beheaded them and threw their bodies into the river. The men guarding the second bridge advanced toward him and offered him stiff opposition and a fierce battle, for they were all good knights. Joseus, who was his uncle's son, said to the other hermits that he would gladly go to help if they did not consider it a sin, and they replied that he need not worry about such a sin, because it was a great penance to destroy God's enemies. He removed his gray cape from over his robe, then took hold of one of the men fighting Perlesvaus, lifted him over his shoulder, and tossed him fully armed into the river, while Perlesvaus killed the two others, who likewise fell into the water. After he had captured the two bridges, he felt very exhausted and overcome. Remembering the lion that his uncle had told him about, he looked towards the entry to the gate and saw the white lion standing up on its rear paws in an effort to make him out. Perlesvaus gazed at him between the eyes and, through the will of God, knew what the lion thought: that the knights at the third bridge were so bold and strong that they could never be defeated by any knight except with God's help, and that he should fetch the mule and carry the banner with him if he wanted to defeat them. Perlesvaus understood the lion's thoughts. He and Joseus both withdrew. When they had gone some distance from the bridges, they looked back and saw that the first bridge had been raised. Perlesvaus came to the mule, which was starred with a red cross upon its forehead. He mounted, taking the banner and his drawn sword. As soon as the white lion saw him returning, it pulled loose from its chain and ran amongst the men who had raised the bridge, and lowered it at once. The King of Deadly Castle, who was standing on the parapets, shouted to those guarding the bridges: "You are all elite knights, the bravest in my land, but you don't act bravely when you raise the bridges because of a single knight whom you don't dare fight man to man! But the lion, which lowered the bridge, is braver than any of you; if I had placed it at the first bridge, it would have guarded the entry better than those men who let themselves be killed!" At that moment Perlesvaus came up on the white mule with his sword drawn; he attacked the men guarding the third bridge and struck one so hard that he tumbled him into the water. The hermit Joseus advanced and was about to seize the other two when they begged mercy of him and Perlesvaus, saying they would do anything he wanted, would believe in God and his sweet mother, and would abandon their evil lord. The knights at the fourth bridge said the same. He let them live on the same conditions, following Joseus's advice, and they laid down their arms and crossed the bridges. Perlesvaus thought to himself that God's power was great, but that a knight who possessed strength and boldness should test his own might for God's sake and the good of his heart, for God would reward him for whatever he does in his name. If everyone in the world were opposed to God and to his will, He could defeat them all in an hour, yet He wishes us to suffer for him just as He suffered for humanity. Perlesvaus turned around and got off the mule; he gave the banner to Joseus, then mounted his horse and returned to face the knights at the fifth bridge. And they, like the brave knights they were, defended it mightily and gave Perlesvaus a good fight. The hermit Joseus came and attacked them vigorously. Had the Lord God not protected him, they would have crippled and killed him, but he carried the banner and when he could reach them he held them so fast that they could not escape, and Perlesvaus felled and killed them and threw them into the river that flowed rapidly beneath the bridges. When the defenders of the sixth bridge saw that the first five had been captured, they begged mercy of Perlesvaus, surrendering to him and offering him their swords, and the defenders of the seventh bridge did likewise (686).

When the red lion saw that the seven bridges had been conquered and that the knights of the last two had surrendered to Perlesvaus, it leapt up in anger and stretched its chain. It came to one of the knights and killed and devoured him; the white lion became enraged and rushed upon the other, ripping it to pieces with its teeth and claws. Immediately afterwards it rose upon its back paws and looked at Perlesvaus, who returned its gaze. Perlesvaus understood that the lion was thinking that the knights defending the last two bridges were more difficult to defeat than the others, and had they not been destroyed by the will of God with the lion's help, they would never have been defeated; that he must never befriend them no matter what they promise him, because they are traitors; and that he should remount his white mule, for it is a creature sent by God, and Joseus should carry the banner, and all the hermits should come forward, who are good men leading good lives, to frighten the traitor king, for his end and the capture of his castle will be at hand. Perlesvaus had great faith in the lion's thoughts. He dismounted from his horse and got up on the white mule; Joseus held the banner, and the beautiful and most holy company of twelve hermits approached the castle. The knights who were at the last bridges saw Perlesvaus and Joseus holding the banner coming toward them, whom they had seen pressing and destroying their other companions. The might of Our Lord, the worthiness of the banner, the goodness of the white mule sent by God, and the holiness of the good hermits praying to Our Lord, so foiled the knights' force that they were powerless. But treachery could not leave their hearts, and they were much aggrieved at having seen their companions slain in front of them. They thought that if they could escape by imploring Perlesvaus's mercy, they would not stop until they had killed him. So they came to Perlesvaus, pretending to beg his mercy in all sincerity and saying they would submit to his will, if only he would let them leave alive. Perlesvaus looked to the lion to see what he should do; he saw that the lion thought they were disloyal traitors and that if they were destroyed and killed, then the king in the castle would have lost his power, and that the lion would help kill them if he attacked. So Perlesvaus told the knights that he would never have mercy on them: he rushed upon them with sword drawn and was so displeased to see that they did not defend themselves that he nearly stopped from killing them, since he did not see any resistance. But the lion did not hesitate; it rushed upon them, killing and devouring them, and tossing their limbs and corpses into the river. Perlesvaus let the lion be, very pleased at what he saw it doing, never before having seen a beast so worthy of his love. The King of Deadly Castle, who was at the parapets, saw his knights were dead and that the lion was helping kill the last ones. He went to the highest spot on the walls, lifted aside the bottom of his hauberk, and drew his razor-sharp sword. He plunged it through his body and fell down over the walls into the deep and rushing waters, so that Perlesvaus and all the good hermits could see him and marvel at this king killing himself in this manner; and they said that the Scriptures declared that an evil man's end must be evil itself, as was the end of this king of whom I've spoken. Josephus tells us that we should not be surprised if there is one bad brother among three or four good ones; and it is a great wonder, he says, if this one bad one does not spoil the good ones! For evil is sharp and bitter and aggressive, whereas goodness is gentle, humble, and naïve. Cain and Abel were two brothers, and Cain killed his brother: flesh of the same flesh deceived and killed his own. And it is a great sadness, Josephus tells us, when flesh, which should be one, draw apart through evil to do ill to one another. Josephus tells us this because of this evil, deceitful, and wicked king: he was of the lineage of the good soldier Joseph of Arimathea, and Joseph was his uncle. And this evil king was the brother of the Fisher King; the brother of good King Pelles, who renounced his inheritance to serve God in a hermitage; and the brother of the Widow Lady, Perlesvaus's mother, the most loyal woman in all of Great Britain. This entire lineage was always in the service of Our Lord, from the beginning to the end, except for this evil king who died so wickedly, as you have heard (692).

You have heard the manner in which the king who seized the castle that had belonged to the Fisher King was killed and all his knights defeated. Perlesvaus and the good hermits entered the castle, and when they were in the main hall it seemed to them they heard *Gloria in excelsis Deo* being sung in an inner chapel and Our Lord being devoutly praised. They found the rooms to be very beautiful, very costly, and very finely ornamented. They found the chapel open, where the holy relics used to be. The holy hermits offered their prayers there, begging the Savior of the world to show them promptly the most Holy Grail and the holy relics that used to be there, which comforted them.

Perlesvaus loved the company of the hermits who were in the castle with him. Josephus bears witness that the knights who made up the Fisher King's court, the priests, and the maidens all left when the king who was killed seized the castle, because they did not wish to be in his power; the Lord God protected them from him and sent them to a place where they were safe. The Savior of the world knew well that the Good Knight, by his strength and goodness, had recaptured the castle that was rightly his. He sent back all those who had served the Fisher King. Perlesvaus was overjoyed to see them and they him. They clearly seemed to be people who had come from a place where the Lord God and His commandments were obeyed (694).

This high history affirms that when the castle was recaptured, the Savior of the world rejoiced and was pleased. The Holy Grail reappeared in the castle chapel, along with the lance whose tip bled and the sword with which John the Baptist had been beheaded—which my lord Gawain had won—as well as many other holy relics, which were there in abundance because the Lord God dearly loved this place. The hermits returned to their hermitages throughout the forests and served Our Lord as they had before.

Joseus remained with Perlesvaus in the castle as long as he wished, but the Good Knight sought out the places in the land where the New Law was slow to be established. He took the lives of all those who refused to believe. The land was maintained and guarded by him, and the religion of Our Lord was exalted by his strength and valor. His uncle's priests and knights who had returned to the castle loved Perlesvaus dearly, for they never saw his goodness fade; rather, his valor and faith in God grew and multiplied constantly. They showed him his uncle the Fisher King's tomb in the chapel before the altar. The sarcophagus was magnificent, all inset with precious stones, and the priests and knights testified that as soon as the body had been placed in the tomb and they had left, when they returned they found the sarcophagus as splendid as he now saw it, and could not discover who had installed it, unless it were the command of Our Lord. And they told him that every night there was a great light, as bright as many candles, and they did not know its source, unless it was God.

Perlesvaus had captured the castle by the will of God. The Grail and the other relics reappeared in the holy chapel, as you have heard. The false religion was driven from the kingdom and everyone believed firmly in the New Law thanks to the valor of the Good Knight (696).

[Perceval's quest, for which he was predestined, is now completed with the capture of the Castle of the Fisher King. At this point, somewhat over half way through the work, the *Perlesvaus* turns its attention to the problems of Arthur's kingdom, threatened by internal intrigues and external enemies. Two plot lines dominate: Gawain and Lancelot's combats to protect the kingdom's frontiers, and Perlesvaus's campaign to spread Christianity. We pick up the story briefly, still in Branch IX, at page 734 in order to conclude Lancelot's adventure at the Waste City.]

King Arthur rode along, accompanied by Sir Gawain and Lancelot. They crossed many an unknown land and entered a vast forest. It was a bright, clear day and the sun's rays beamed from time to time on their shields as they passed among the trees of the forest. Lancelot remembered the knight he had slain in the Waste City where he had promised to return, and he knew that the day of his return was approaching. He told King Arthur about this and said that if he did not go, he would be untrue to his oath. They rode along until they came to a cross, where the roads forked and went through the forest. "My lord," said Lancelot, "I must go and keep my promise, though it is dangerous and life-threatening; I don't know whether I'll ever see you again, for I killed a knight, which I very much regret, and I had to promise before slaying him that I would return to risk my own head just as he was risking his. Now the day is come that I must return. I would be greatly to blame if I were to break my oath. But if God permits me to escape alive, I shall quickly follow you into the land where you must go." The king and Sir Gawain embraced and kissed him before he left, praying that God spare his life so that they might see him again soon. Lancelot would gladly have sent greetings to the queen, had he dared, for she was more present in his heart than anything else; but he chose not to, lest the king or Sir Gawain should think it suggested love and feel ill-will toward him. Love was so rooted in his heart, in whatever danger he entered upon, that he could not overcome it, but prayed fervently to God every day to protect her and to save him from this danger so that he might see her again. Lancelot rode until he came around noon into the Waste City and found it as empty as the first time he was there.

In this city Lancelot had entered there were many churches laid waste and many splendid palaces crumbled and many a great hall standing empty. Scarcely had he entered the city when he heard a loud cry and a weeping of ladies and maidens, though he could not tell from where. They all were saying, "Oh God! how the knight who killed the knight here has betrayed us by not returning! The day has come to keep his oath: never more should we believe a knight, when he doesn't return! All the others before him betrayed us, and this one will too, for fear of dying because he cut off the head of the handsomest and best knight there ever was in this kingdom. And his head, too, should have been cut off, but he has done all he could to avoid it!" Thus spoke the maidens. Lancelot heard them clearly, but wondered where they were since he could not see any of them. He came before the palace where he had killed the knight. He dismounted and tied his horse to a silver ring that was on a mounting block; scarcely had he gotten there when a tall, handsome, strong, and carefree knight came down from the palace. He was wearing a very short silk tunic and holding the scythe in his hand with which Lancelot had beheaded the other knight; he was sharpening it on a whetstone to cut better. Seeing him approach, Lancelot asked: "What will you do with this scythe, fair sir?"—"By my head," replied the knight, "if I can do anything about it, you will learn what it's for just as my brother, whose head you chopped off, learned."—"What? You are going to kill me, then?" said Lancelot.—"You will learn that before you leave here," said the knight. "Did you not swear to risk your own head just as the knight you killed risked his? Otherwise you cannot leave here. Step forward, now, kneel down and stretch out your neck, and I'll cut off your head. If you don't want to do it of your own accord, you'll find plenty of people here to force you, even if you had the strength of twenty knights! But I know that the only reason you came back was to respect your oath and that you'll offer no resistance." Lancelot thought he was about to die and wanted to respect without fail what he had promised: he lay down upon the ground, spread his arms like a cross, and prayed for God's mercy. He remembered the queen: "Ah, my lady! I'll never see you again! Had I been able to see you one last time before dying, it would have been a great comfort, and my soul would have departed happier. But never seeing you again distresses me more than death: when one has lived this long it is time to die, but I swear to you that my love will never cease, and that my soul will love you as much in the other world as my body has in this, if it is able." Then tears flowed from his eyes, and the story tells us that this and one other occasion were the only times when he wept for grief or suffering. He took three sprigs of grass in communion, blessed and crossed himself, then rose and knelt down and stretched out his neck. The knight raised the scythe. Lancelot heard the blow coming; he lowered his head and the scythe missed. "Sir knight, my brother you killed didn't do that: he held his head and neck still, and you must too!" Two exceptionally beautiful maidens appeared in the palace windows and recognized Lancelot. Just as the knight was preparing a second blow, one of the maidens shouted to him: "If you want to have my love forever, throw down the scythe and forgive this knight; if not, you will never win my love!" The knight immediately threw down the scythe and fell at Lancelot's feet, begging his mercy, as of the most loyal knight in the world. "Rather it is for you to have mercy on me," said Lancelot, "by not killing me."—"And I will not," replied the knight, "but will help you against the whole world, even though you killed my brother." The maidens came down from the palace to Lancelot, saying: "We should love you more than anyone in the world, because we are the two sisters you found so destitute in the Waste Castle, when you lodged with our brother; you and Sir Gawain and another knight gave us the treasure and protection from the robbers you killed. And this Waste City and our brother's Waste Castle would never be repopulated, and we would never again reclaim our lands, unless a knight as loyal as you came here. A good twenty knights had come here just as you did, and each of them killed a brother or uncle or first cousin, just as you beheaded the knight; and each of them swore to return on the day assigned, but they all broke their oaths, for none dared return; and if you had failed to come back like the others, we would have lost this city forever and the castles that are its dependencies."

The knights and maidens led Lancelot into the palace and had his armor removed. In many places in the forests that surrounded the city he heard manifestations of great happiness. "My lord," said the maidens, "you can hear the joy your coming has brought: those are the townspeople and residents of this city who have already heard the news." Lancelot rested at the windows of the hall and saw the city repopulated with the finest people in the world, and the great halls and large palaces filling, and clerics and priests in procession praising and adoring God that they could come back to their churches, and blessing the knight who gave them the ability to return. Lancelot was shown every honor in the city; the two maidens strove to serve him (744).

[In the final forty percent or so of the *Perlesvaus* threats, treason, massacres, rapes, false accusations, and the death of Guinevere all contribute to an increasingly somber tone.]

Notes

1. *Le Haut Livre du Graal (Perlesvaus)*, ed. William A. Nitze and T. Atkinson Jenkins, 2 vols., Chicago: University of Chicago Press, 1932; and *Le Haut Livre du Graal (Perlesvaus)*, ed. and trans. Armand Strubel (Lettres gothiques) Paris: Le Livre de Poche, 2007.

2. Missing except for the last few pages in BN fr. 1428, most of this Branch has been translated from the Nitze-Jenkins edition, based on the Oxford manuscript.

La Queste del Saint Graal (The Quest of the Holy Grail): Selections

Translated by R. BARTON PALMER

Chrétien's *Conte du Graal*, and its various continuations, constituted one source of inspiration for what was to prove the most massive and comprehensive treatment of Arthurian material in the Middle Ages, the so-called Vulgate Cycle, which includes five lengthy prose works, of which the *Queste del Saint Graal* is perhaps the most notable one. The others, all composed in the first decades of the thirteenth century, are: *Estoire del Saint Graal*, *Estoire de Merlin*, *Estoire de Lancelot*, and the *Mort le Roi Artu*. An earlier model for such a global approach to the legend of Arthur was offered by Robert de Boron (fl. 1210), who composed a prose trilogy devoted to the history of the Grail vessel (*Joseph d'Arimathie*), its transference to Britain and connection to Merlin (*Merlin*), and the quest of Arthur's knights to regain it, along with the eventual destruction of Arthur's kingdom (*Perceval*). The Vulgate Cycle utilizes these materials but is even more inclusive, offering, among other changes, a full version of the love affair between Lancelot and Guinevere, which is connected to the outcome of the quest for the Grail, whose hero has become Lancelot's son Galahad. The Vulgate Cycle served in the fifteenth-century as the principal source for Thomas Malory's *Le Morte d'Arthur*. Through Malory and his imitators (including Edmund Spenser and Alfred Tennyson), the Vulgate Cycle version has come to exert the greatest influence on modern versions of the Arthurian legend such as T.H. White's novel *The Once and Future King*, which was in turn the source for the long-running musical by Alan J. Lerner and Frederick Loewe, *Camelot*.

There is a tradition, accepted by some scholars, that the Norman churchman Walter Map (1140–c. 1210), who in a rich and varied career spent considerable time at the court of Henry II and Eleanor of Aquitaine, initiated this encyclopedic prose retelling of the story of Arthur. Even if this is true, the Vulgate Cycle was a collective effort, a profusion of text-making by authors who did not sign their work and thus have remained anonymous. The Vulgate Cycle included and summarized, while also adding to, materials that were ultimately of Celtic origin (but not included in Geoffrey's *Historia*); these were either drawn from Chrétien's romances, especially the central characters of Perceval and Lancelot, or were later inventions, notably Lancelot's son Galahad. If Merlin continues to play a decisive role and Mordred remains the villain of the piece, bringing about the demise of Arthur's kingdom, as they do in Geoffrey, the Vulgate Cycle essentially offers a version of Arthur's life and accomplishments that constitutes a powerful alternative to that presented in the *Historia*, one first inspired by Chrétien's Arthurian romances but which soon became inclusive of other materials (such as the various legends associated with Merlin). Throughout the various "books" of the whole, sometimes significantly referred to as "histories," reference is made to authors (Robert de Boron in addition to Walter Map), but these seem hardly plausible for the most part. It is possible, as some have argued, that an architect figure planned the whole of the cycle to which others, in their turn and over a period of years, then contributed, but the composition of the cycle was more likely the result of successive acts of imitation and continuation driven by a desire to sketch the entire story, exactly the kind of unplanned but productive collective effort that "finished" Chrétien's *Perceval*. And yet it may be some such shared notion of the entire story that prompts the frequent reference to "the story" (*li contes*); such a "text" is even given an imagined source in the clerks who are imagined at the end of the *Queste* as recording the narratives furnished them by the returning knights, Bors and Perceval.

The Christianization of the Grail story, which seems to have begun with Robert de Boron, reaches its apotheosis in the Vulgate Cycle's version of the quest, as success in the venture is determined by the knight's moral nature. Lancelot, victimized by his adulterous liaison with Arthur's queen, finds himself debarred from success at a quite early stage, even as he is forced to face up to his sinfulness by the holy men who seem the endless forest's most numerous inhabitants. Perceval, because he remains a virgin (even if sorely tried at one point), is permitted a vision of the Grail and its mysteries, along with Bors, who has sincerely repented and done penance for a single lapse. The tale's main character, however, is Galahad, who, though born as a result of one of Lancelot's sexual adventures, is a type of Christ, whose virginity remains perfect and whose otherworldliness finds expression in the narrative goal, as Galahad dies soon—and fulfilled—after being granted a full view of the mysteries of the Grail. The *Queste* offers a powerful melding of pagan and Christian symbols: the Grail, a Celtic fertility symbol, becomes the cup Jesus drank from at the Last Supper; the Bleeding Lance and Broken Sword, found in earlier versions of the story, become the spear of Longinus and the sword of King David. The story features several elaborate dreams whose spiritual significance is explained by hermits or monks, commentators who are easily persuaded to assign a higher meaning to the various events in the story as well.

Characters and motifs are transparently allegorical at times, increasing the sense of a mystery gradually penetrated, which is the poem's main concern. Secular chivalry, of which Lancelot is the exemplar, is shown throughout to be inferior to the spiritual knighthood embodied in his son and most tellingly thematized by Galahad's absolute refusal of carnality. Arthur's court, and the knights who in the romance tradition have come to populate it, becomes the setting for what is essentially a spiritual drama. Stylistically, however, what is most notable about the *Queste* is its clear, supple prose style, adapted from the historical chronicles then coming into fashion. In an imagined landscape far removed from the real world, human actions unfold in carefully calculated time and space, with such mundane actions as going to bed and eating a dinner sharing space with the deliberately anti-realistic (Perceval borne off at supernatural speed by a horse that turns out to be a devil; Perceval seduced by a beautiful woman who turns out to be once more a disguised demon). The narrative is leisurely paced, enlivened by dialogues that feature interesting revelations of character (such as the conversation between Perceval and a recluse who turns out to be his aunt). A plain verbal style, reminiscent of the *sermo humilis* or humble style that medieval commentators found in the New Testament, is only rarely abandoned for a learned theological term or concept. Absent as well is the language of courtly love and the emotional self-examination that had become standard within that tradition by this time and so deeply marks Chrétien's romances. Aside from their delight in martial combat (which is occasionally evoked in some detail reminiscent of earlier Arthurian epic) there is little to distinguish the knights of the *Queste* from other Christians who seek a perfected form of living and an initiation into the mysteries of the faith.

The passage from the *Queste* that here follows begins about one-third of the way through the text after Galahad has appeared at Arthur's court to be knighted and to succeed at various tests that prove he is a knight destined for greatness. The quest for the Holy Grail then commences and the knights go their separate ways, sometimes accompanying each other, as Lancelot and Perceval do for a time. Because the focus of this part of the anthology is on Perceval, sections in which Lancelot or another knight becomes the character have been omitted. Translation based on Albert Pauphilet, *La Queste del Saint Graal* (Paris: Champion, 1923)

Perceval's Journey

The story now tells how when Perceval separated from Lancelot he returned to the recluse, and from her he expected to learn something about the knight who had escaped from them. And as he made his way back, it happened that he could find no true path that might lead him to that place. Even so, he kept going in the proper direction, as best as he could determine what this might be. And when he arrived at the chapel, he knocked at the recluse's little window, and she opened immediately, as if she were not in the least asleep. She stuck her head out as far as she could and asked who he was. And he answered that he was of Arthur's household and that his name was Perceval the Galois. And hearing his name, she was greatly cheered, for she loved him dearly, and so she should, for he was her nephew. So she summoned her servants from within, ordering them to open the door to the knight who was then outside, and they were to give him food if he had need of any, serving him in whatever way they could, for he was the man she loved most in all the world.

And those within did as she commanded, making their way to the door and opening it, receiving the knight, whose arms they removed, and giving him food. And he asked if it were possible for him to speak further to the recluse this day. "My lord," they replied, "not at all, but after mass in the morning we think it will then be possible for you to speak to her." And he accepted this at once, taking his rest in a bed that those within made up for him. And that night he slept the sleep of a man who is tired and wearied by his labors.

The next day, as soon as day broke clear, Perceval arose and heard mass, which the priest of the household celebrated. And after he armed himself, he went up to the recluse and said this to her: "My lady, for the sake of God tell me what you know about the knight who passed this way yesterday, the man you said you had good reason to know well. For I am eager to learn who he is." And when the lady heard this news, she asked why Perceval was seeking him. "The reason is simple," he said, "I can never be at ease until, finding him, I have fought against him. He has so grievously wronged me that I cannot let the matter rest without being shamed."

"Hold on, Perceval," she said, "What are you saying? You intend to do battle against him? Are you eager to die the same death your brothers did, who were killed and lie dead because of their arrogance? And, of this there is no doubt, if you die in this same fashion, it will cause great harm, bringing your family low. And do you realize that you will be defeated if you do combat against this knight? Listen to what I say. It is true enough that the high Quest of the Holy Grail has begun, and this is an adventure you share, so I think, and it will be brought soon to its conclusion if God is so pleased. And thus you are seeking an honor much greater than you believe it to be if you persist in fighting this knight by yourself. For what is well known by us in this land and by others in different places is that three worthy knights will share the honor and glory of this Quest above all others who seek it. And two of these will be virgins, the third a chaste man. And these two virgins will be yourself and the knight you seek, while the third will be Bors de Gaunes. The Quest will be brought to its end by these three. And since God has determined that you are to achieve this honor, it would be a great mishap if in the meantime you were to seek out your own death. And you will indeed hasten toward this should you do combat with the man you are seeking since—and of this there is no doubt—he is a greater knight than you are, greater indeed than any man could be aware."

"My lady," said Perceval, "it seems from what you have said concerning my brothers that you know well who I am." "I do indeed," she rejoined, "and this is something I should know well, for I am your aunt and you are my nephew. Do not doubt this in the least even though I live in such wretched surroundings; instead, you should know well that I am the woman who in times past was called the queen of the Wasteland. And if you see me now transformed from what I once was, in days gone by I was one of the richest ladies in the world. Nevertheless, such wealth never pleased me as much as the poverty that is now my lot."

Hearing these words, Perceval began to weep out of the pity he then felt; and his memory was wakened enough so that he recognized her as his aunt. Then he sat down before her to ask for news about his mother and the rest of his family. "Is it true," she asked, "fair nephew, that you know no news of your mother?" "To be sure," he said, "Nothing at all. I do not know if she is dead or still living. And yet many times she has appeared to me in dreams and told me that she has more cause to blame than to praise me, for I have come close to treating her badly." And hearing these words, the lady answered in a manner both thoughtful and sad: "Surely," she said, "You cannot but have failed to lay eyes upon your mother except in your dreams; for she died when you set out to Arthur's court." "My lady," he asked, "How could this be?" "In faith," she said, "Your mother felt such sorrow at your departure that as soon as she made her confession, she died on that very day." "May God now have mercy on her soul," he said, "for surely this weighs heavily upon me; yet since this is what has happened, I must come to accept it since we all come to the same end. But truly I never heard these tidings before. Yet concerning this knight whom I seek, for God's sake do you know where he is now, and if he is the one who came to the court bearing red arms?" "Yes," she answered, "I swear to you that he is the one who came there. And I will explain what significance this has."

"You know well that since the coming of Jesus Christ there have been three principal tables in this world. The first was the Table of Jesus Christ, at which the apostles took their meals many times. This was the table that sustained them in body and soul with heavenly nourishment. At this table sat the brothers who were at one in their hearts and souls, and of this the prophet David spoke in his book words that were truly remarkable. 'It is a very great thing,' he wrote, 'when brothers, sharing one will and work, live together.' There was peace and good will among the brothers who shared this table, and good works of all kinds were made manifest in them. And this table was established by the spotless Lamb who was sacrificed in order to redeem us."

"Later, another quite similar table was established in remembrance of this first one. This second was the Table of the Holy Grail, and there great miracles unfolded in this country at the time of Joseph of Arimathea, after Christianity was brought into this land, and such things came to pass so that all good people and all those who did not then believe might from that day forward keep the memory of those miracles. It happened then that Joseph of Arimathea made his way into this land, along with a host of four thousand, and these were all poor men. And arriving in this country, there were greatly troubled because they did not then have food sufficient for such a multitude. One day, they were wandering through a forest where they found nothing to eat and came upon not a single soul. And this greatly dismayed them, for they had not thought it would be so. That day they endured as best they could, and on the next they searched high and low, at last finding an old woman, who brought them twelve loaves from her oven. And they bought them.

And when they were about to divide the loaves, there was much anger and discontent, for not one among them would agree to what any other there wished to do. News of what was happening was brought to Joseph, and he became quite angry when he was told. He asked for the bread to be brought to him. And those who had bought the bread did as he asked. And then he learned from their very mouths that they all disagreed with one another. And he asked them all to sit, just as they did when commemorating the Last Supper. And he broke the bread into pieces, which he placed here and there on the Table of the Holy Grail, and after being put there, the twelve loaves multiplied in such a fashion that the people, of whom there were fully four thousand, were fed and made full in a miraculous fashion. And witnessing this, the people offered grace and thanks to Our Lord, Who in such an evident fashion had sustained them."

"At this table was a seat where Josephus, who was the son of Joseph of Arimathea, was appointed to sit. And this seat was established as the place where their master and pastor should take his seat, and no other was granted this privilege. And it had been sanctified and blessed by the very hand of Our Lord, just as the history tells us, and it embodied the pastoral care Josephus was to provide the Christian people. And at this seat Our Lord himself had sat; and for this reason, there was no man audacious enough to dare take his seat there. And this seat had been made in the likeness of the one upon which Our Lord sat on the day of the Last Supper, when it was as master and pastor that he was among his apostles. And just as he was lord and master over all his apostles, so Josephus was to conduct himself among all those who took their seats at the Table of the Holy Grail. He too was to be master and lord over them. But it happened, after they came into this country, wandering great distances through strange lands, that two brothers, who were of the kin of Josephus, were envious that Our Lord had elevated him higher than them, choosing Josephus as the greatest of that company. And they spoke of this privately, saying that they would not suffer him to be their master since they were of a lineage as high as his, and so they would not consider themselves his disciples in the least, nor would they call him lord. And the next day, after they had mounted a huge trestle and placed the table upon it, with the intention of seating Josephus in the place of honor, his two brothers rose in opposition, and one of them, as all witnessed, took his seat there. And at once there was a great miracle as the earth swallowed upon the man sitting at this place. And all in the country learned of this wonder, and the seat was afterward called the Siege Perilous. And henceforth no man was foolhardy enough to sit there, save the one so designated by Our Lord."

"After the time of this table, the Round Table was established, as Merlin then counseled, and this event was not without great importance. For in regard to this Round Table, its circular shape should be understood as signifying the roundness of the world, the spherical nature of the planets and the other elements in the firmament; and the circular paths that, as one sees, characterize the stars and other heavenly bodies. And so one could say that by the Round Table, the universe itself is truly signified. For you can see that from every land where chivalry exists, whether Christian or pagan, knights make their way to the Round Table. And when God gives them the grace to become one of the companions here, these men consider this the greatest boon they might gain in this world. And, as you see, they abandon for its sake their fathers and mothers, their wives and their children. You have witnessed this in your own person. For ever since you left your mother and were made a companion of the Round Table, you have felt no desire to return whence you came, but have been instead surprised by the sweetness of that fraternity that is meant to exist among those who are its companions."

"After Merlin established the Round table, he proclaimed that it would be through those who were its companions that the truth of the Holy Grail would be known, for no sign of it could be seen in Merlin's time. And he was asked how those who were the worthiest might be recognized. And this was his answer: 'there will be three who succeed at this quest: two of them virgins, and the third living in chastity. One of them will prove superior to his father just as the lion surpasses the leopard in strength and fierceness. This man is destined to be considered lord and pastor over all the others. And the companions of the Round Table will continually fail in their quest for the Holy Grail until Our Lord dispatches him among them with such swiftness it seems a miracle.' And, hearing these words, they then said: 'Now Merlin, since such a man of worthiness as you describe will come to be, you should construct a seat meant for him, and on which no one save him will sit, and it should be so big in comparison to the others than it would be so recognized.' 'This is what I will do,' said Merlin.

And then he had made a seat larger and more marvelous than any of the others. And having made it, he began to kiss it, saying he did so out of love for the Good Knight who would take his rest there. And then they said this to him: "Merlin, when will he whose seat this is appear?" "Surely," he responded, "many a miracle will come to pass before that time, for now no man may sit there who is not maimed or killed as a result until the True Knight takes his seat there." "In God's name," they said, "then does the man who sits there put himself in great peril?" "It is in peril that he puts himself," said Merlin. And because of the perils that will come to pass, it will bear this name: the Siege Perilous."

"Fair nephew," said the lady, "now I have explained to you the reason why the Round Table was established, and for whom the Siege Perilous was made, and there many a knight has met his death, for those who sat there were not worthy. Now I will tell you how the Knight came to the court in red arms. You know well that Jesus Christ was lord and pastor over his disciples at the table of the Last Supper. And Josephus bore this title at the Table of the Holy Grail, and this knight for the Round Table. Our Lord promised his apostles before his passion that he would come to visit and see them. And, sad and dismayed, they awaited the fulfillment of this promise. And so he did come, on Pentecost, when they were all in one house, where the doors had been closed. And the Holy Spirit descended on them in the form of fire, assuring them and giving them comfort about what made them afraid. And then he had them depart, sending them out to bear witness to the world and teach the Gospel. This is what happened to the apostles on the day of Pentecost, when Our Lord came to visit and comfort them.

And I think that this was exactly the form in which the Knight whom you are to take as your lord and pastor came to you. For just as Our Lord appeared in the semblance of fire, so the Knight appeared in arms of red, which is the color of fire. And just as the doors were closed during the advent of Our Lord, so were the doors of the palace shut when the Knight arrived. And it happened that he came so suddenly to you that there was none among you wise enough to recognize whence he had come. And on this same day the Quest of the Holy Grail was undertaken, which will not be abandoned until its truth has been revealed, and the truth of the Lance as well, and an explanation given of why so much has happened in this land. I have now told you the truth about the Knight so that you will not move to do battle against him. For you know well this is something you should not do, because you are also a companion of the Round Table and because you cannot last against him since he is a better knight than you."

"My lady," he said, "what you have said has cooled my desire to meet him in battle. But for the sake of God teach me what I might do to find him. For if he were my companion, I would never leave his side as long as mine was the power to follow him." "I will offer you advice in this matter," she said, "as best I can. But at the moment I cannot tell you where he is, though I can readily point out the path along which you soon find him; and when you have found him, you can keep him company as long as you prove able. You should go from here to a castle that is called Got, where resides one of his close cousins, and it is there for the sake of the love she bears him that he took his lodging the night before yesterday. And if she is able to tell you what way he went, then you should pursue him with all the speed you can muster. And if she is able to tell you nothing, then you should make your way directly to the castle of Corbenyc, which is the residence of the Maimed King. And of this I am certain, you will hear reliable news of him if it happens you don't find him there."

This is what the recluse and Perceval had to say about the Knight, talking until the hour came to noon. And then she said to Perceval: "Fair nephew, tonight you will stay with me, for this will put me more at ease. It has been a long time since I've laid eyes on you, and your departure will be quite painful for me." "My Lady," he replied, "there is so much I must do I can hardly spend the day in this place; so I ask you, for the sake of God, to let me go my way." "Be certain," she said, "that you will not have my leave to depart this day. But tomorrow, as soon as you have heard mass, I willingly grant you leave to go." And he said that in this case he would spend the night there. So he had his arms taken off at once. And those in the household set the table, and they all ate what the lady had prepared.

Perceval spent the night there with his aunt. And they spoke about the Knight and about other matters as well until she said these words: "Fair nephew, you have kept yourself pure until this time, and your virginity has not been violated or impaired, nor have you ever learned the truth about the flesh and intercourse in it. And this has served you very well. For if it had happened that your body had been marred by the corruption of sin, you would have failed to become one of the companions of the Quest, just as has happened to Lancelot of the Lake, who has forfeited through the passions of the flesh and a destructive lusting any possibility of his completing this quest, and this now pains all the others. And this is why I beg you to keep your body as pure as when Our Lord enrolled you as a knight so that you can approach, in purity and virginity, the Holy Grail, and with no taint of lust. And surely this would be one of the most magnificent forms of prowess ever achieved by any knight, for among all those of the Round Table, there are none whose virginity has not been tainted, save for you and Galahad, who is the Knight I have been telling you about." And he replied that he would keep himself as pure as need be, should God be pleased.

Perceval remained within the entire day, and his aunt forcefully exhorted and admonished him to do well. But above all else she begged him to keep his body as pure as he was obligated to do, and he agreed that this is what he would do. And after there was much talk about the Knight and the court of King Arthur, Perceval asked her how it came about that she was sent to such a wild place after losing her own land. "By God," she said, "it was the fear of death that moved me to flee to this place. For you knew well, when you made your way to the court, that my lord the king was engaged in a war against King Libran; and so it happened, as soon as my lord was killed, that I, a vulnerable woman, feared that he would kill me were I to become his prisoner. So I took with me a great part of my possessions and fled to this wilderness in order not to be found. And I had built this hermitage and house just as you now see, and installed myself there, along with my chaplain and household, entering into this place of seclusion in such a condition that, if God be pleased, I will not abandon as long as I live, but instead will die in the service of Our Lord, spending the rest of my life so doing." "By my faith," said Perceval, "this is indeed a strange turn of events. But now tell me what became of your son Dyabiaus, for I am very eager to know what he is doing." "Surely!" she said, "He went to serve King Pelles, who is of your kin, in order to obtain arms; and later I heard he had been made a knight. But it has been two years since I have laid eyes upon him; he went to seek out tournaments in Britain Major. So I think you will find him at Corbenyc should you travel there." "Certainly," he replied, "I would not go there except to see him, if I go at all, for I very much want to be his companion." "By God," she said, "I have been quite eager for my part that he should encounter you, for I should have felt at ease were you two companions."

In this fashion, Perceval spent the day with his aunt; and on the next day, as soon as he heard mass and armed himself, he left there and rode all day long through the forest, which was a wondrous place, with the result that he came upon no man or woman. And after vespers it happened that he heard to his right a bell ring. And he turned in that direction, for he knew well this was some hermitage or religious foundation. And after he had gone some way, he could see well it was an abbey, enclosed by walls and a deep ditch all around. And he made for the place, calling out when he came to the gate until it was opened to him. And when those within saw he was armed, they thought he was a knight errant; they took his arms from him and greeted him in a friendly fashion. They took his horse to their stable where they generously fed it hay and oats. And one of the brothers led him to a room where he could sleep. And that night he was lodged in the best fashion that the brothers could manage. And in the morning it happened he did not awake before the hour of prime, proceeding then into the abbey to hear mass by himself.

And entering the church, he saw to his right an iron grill that one of the brothers had decorated with the arms of Our Lord, and this man wanted to begin celebrating mass. He walked that way, like someone eager to hear the service, and came up to the grill, thinking to go inside; but he could not do so, as it seemed to him, finding no point of entrance. And seeing this, he held himself back and kneeled down outside. And, looking behind the priest, he spied a bed nicely made up with silk cloth and other things; there was nothing on it that was not pure white. Perceval gazed at the bed and began to realize that someone was lying in it, a man or a woman, which he could not tell, for the face was covered completely with fine, white cloth, so that he could not see it clearly. And when he saw that such musings were in vain, he looked away and gave his attention to the service, which the good man had begun. And when the time came for the priest to elevate the body of Our Lord, the person lying in the bed sat up and uncovered his face. And he was a very old man, with grey hair, and a crown of gold on his head, with his shoulders bare and his torso as well, down to his umbilicus. And as Perceval looked at him, he saw that his body was full of hurt and wounds, his palms, arms, and face as well. And when the priest displayed openly the body of Jesus Christ, this man reached his hands out toward him and began to exclaim: "Sweet merciful father, do not forget what I am due!" Nor would he afterward lie back down, but uttered prayers and called upon God, his hands reaching out toward his creator and the crown of gold always on his head. Perceval gazed upon this man on his bed for a long time, for he seemed quite discomfited by the wounds from which he suffered; and it seemed to him that the man was so aged he might be three hundred years old, or even older. And he looked at him without stopping, thinking this was a great miracle. And after the mass had been sung to its end, he saw the priest take in his hands the Corpus Domini and bring it to the man lying on the bed, giving it to him to take. And receiving it, he removed the crown from his head and placed it above the altar. And the man then lay back in his bed, just as he had done before, covering himself so that no part remained visible. And then the priest removed his garments, as someone does who has finished saying mass.

After Perceval witnessed these things, he left the church and returned to the room where he had passed the night, summoning one of the brothers from within and saying to him: "Good sir, for God's sake, give me an answer to what I now ask; for I am quite certain you know the truth of the matter." "Sir knight," he responded, "tell me what this is, and I will tell you what I know, in so far as I am able or obligated to do so." "In faith," he responded, "I will tell you what it is. I was just in the church and heard the service; and there I saw inside a grill in front of the altar a bed in which a man of very great age was lying, a crown of gold on his head. And when he sat up in the bed, I saw he was covered with wounds, from one part of his body to the next. And after the mass had been sung, the priest gave this man the Corpus Domini for his use. And after he had received it, he lay back down and removed the crown from his head. Fair sir, this seems something of great import, and I would like very much to know what that might be, so I beg you please tell me." "Certainly," responded the good man, "and willingly."

"It is true, and you have heard this said by many, that Joseph of Arimathea, that good man, that true knight, was first sent by the High Master into this land to plant the seed of Christianity and edify it for the sake of his Creator. And when he came here, he suffered greatly from persecution and hard treatment at the hands of those who are enemies to the Law, who at that time there were only Saracens in this country. And in this land there was a king named Crudel, and he was the most evil and the cruelest in the world, a man without pity or humility. He heard tell that Christians had come into his territory, bringing with them a precious vessel, a thing so miraculous that the grace that flowed from it gave life to almost all, and he considered all this a lie. And he was offered more and more proof, and he was told that this was indeed the truth. And he said he would find out in his own good time. So he took prisoner Josephus the son of Joseph, along with two of his nephews and nearly one hundred of those that man had chosen to be masters and pastors throughout Christendom. And when he seized and imprisoned them, they had with them the Holy Vessel, which, they did not doubt, provided everything necessary for the sustaining of the body. And the king kept them forty days in prison, sending them neither food nor drink, and he proclaimed that no one should be bold enough to have anything to do with them until this term had passed.

And the news of this went out through all the lands where Josephus had been, namely that King Crudel was holding him in prison along with a great number of Christians, and eventually it came to the notice of King Mordrain, who held the city of Sarraz not far from Jerusalem and had been converted by the preaching of Josephus and by the words he had spoken to him. And this grieved him mightily, for it was by the counsel of Josephus that he had recovered the lands Tholomers had intended to take from him, and these would have been seized had it not been for the advice Josephus had given and for the assistance provided by his brother-in-law named Seraphe. When King Mordrain learned that Josephus was in prison, he proclaimed he would do all in his power to set him free. So he hastily summoned whatever armies he had and set out by sea, supplied with arms and with horses, and he managed to come to this country by ship. And when, along with all his men, he arrived, he sent word to King Crudel that if he did not surrender Josephus to him, he would seize his lands and disinherit him. But Crudel paid this little mind, taking his army out instead to meet him. And the two hosts drew up opposing one another. And it so happened by the will of Our Lord that the Christians gained the victory, while King Crudel, along with his men, was slaughtered. And king Mordrain, who took the name Evalach when he became a Christian, had been so successful in the battle that everyone held it to be a miracle. For when he was disarmed, it was discovered that he had on his body more wounds than those who had been killed in the fight. And the question was asked, how could this be? And he answered that he felt neither pain nor hurt on their account. So he took Josephus from the prison, and, looking upon him, that man was very joyful, for he loved him with an intense love. And Josephus asked him who had led him to these parts, and he answered that he had come in order to deliver him.

"And on the next day it happened that the Christians made their way to the Table of the Holy Grail, where they said their prayers. And when Josephus, who was master there, had arrayed himself to make his way to the Holy Grail and was in the midst of conducting the service for it, king Mordrain, who had always greatly desired to see the Holy Grail as close up as he might manage, drew nearer to it than he should have done. And a voice came down from above them that spoke these words: 'King, advance no further, for this you should not do!' And he had already moved closer than mortal tongue could tell or earthly creature imagine, and so desirous was he to gaze upon it that he stepped ever closer and closer. And just then a cloud descended from above before him, and it stole the sight from his eyes and the strength from his body, so that he could see nothing and do little if anything on his own. And when he saw that Our Lord had taken such a great vengeance on him (for he had broken his commandment), this is what he said so that all might hear: 'Sweet Lord God Jesus Christ, who with this has demonstrated the madness of transgressing your commandment, truly the scourge you have sent pleases me, and I suffer it willingly; please grant me as a reward for serving you that I will not die until that very hour when the Good Knight, the ninth of my line, the one who is destined to gaze openly upon the miracles of the Holy Grail, should come to visit me, so that I can embrace and kiss him.' After the king made this request to the Lord God, the voice spoke these words: 'King, do not be dismayed: Our Lord has heard your prayer. What you wish will come to pass, for you will not die until that same hour the Knight you are seeking comes to see you, and the moment he appears, the light in your eyes will be returned to you so that you can see him clearly; and then your wounds shall heal, those which until then have never closed.'"

"This is what the voice said to the king, telling him that he would witness the coming of the Knight he had so much desired. And it seems to us that all of these things have proven true. For four hundred years have passed since the unfolding of this adventure, and he does not see at all, nor are his wounds healed, nor does his possess the strength to walk. And now the Knight is in this land, just as it was said to be, the one who is destined to bring this adventure to its conclusion. And by the signs we now have seen of this, we think very much that he will regain his sight as well as power over his limbs; but after this happens he will not live long.

"And what happened to king Mordrain is just what I have told you; so you should know for truth that this is the man you have seen this very day. And he has lived four hundred years in so saintly and religious a fashion that he has never tasted of earthly nourishment save for what the priest shows us in the sacrifice of the mass, and this is the body of Jesus Christ. And this you were able to witness this very day; for as soon as the priest finished singing the mass, he brought him the Corpus Domini and had him receive it. And this is the fashion in which the king has waited from the time of Josephus to the hour when the knight he has so much desired should arrive. Just as aged Simeon did, who waited so long for the advent of Our Lord that he has brought to the temple, and there he received, the old man, taking him in his arms, happy and joyful as he was that the promise had been fulfilled. For the Holy Spirit revealed to him he would not die until he had laid eyes upon Jesus Christ. And, seeing him, he sang the sweet song David has memorialized. And just as Simeon waited with great desire for Jesus Christ, the son of God, the high Prophet, the sovereign Pastor, so this king awaits the advent of Galahad, the Good Knight, the perfect one.

"Now I have related to you the truth of the matter you have asked me about, just as it occurred; so I ask you to tell me who you are." And he said that he was of the household of king Arthur, and a companion of the Round Table, and his name was Perceval the Galois. And when the good man heard this name, he was very pleased for he had heard him spoken of many times. And the man begged Perceval to remain there longer, for they would pay him honor and celebrate with him since this was something they were quite obligated to do. But Perceval replied that he had so much to accomplish there was no way he could stay with him, and for that reason he must depart the place. So he asked for his arms, and they were brought to him. And when he had armed himself, he mounted his horse and took leave, parting from those within and riding through the forest until the hour of noon.

At noon his path took him into a valley. And there he met up with twenty armed men conducting a bier in which lay a man but recently slain. And when these men spied Perceval, they asked where he was from. And he said he was from the household of king Arthur, and with one voice they cried out: "At him!" Seeing this, Perceval prepared to defend himself as best he could, riding toward the one who first approached him. And he struck this man so fiercely that he brought the horse down onto the man's body. And when he thought to finish him off with his spear point, he could not manage it; for seven of them struck at his shield, and the others killed his horse, and this brought him to the ground. And his thought was to get back up, like a man of great prowess, so he drew his sword and prepared to defend himself. But the others charged at him with such fury that defense was pointless, and they struck his sword and his helmet, giving him so many blows he could not regain his feet, but fell back down, striking the earth with one of his knees. And they continued to strike and harass him, bringing him to the point where he should have been killed, for they had struck off the helmet from his head, wounding him, had not the Knight with the red arms made his way to this spot by chance. And when this man saw him all alone and on foot, surrounded by so many enemies intending to kill him, he rode there as fast as his horse would take him, crying out to them: "Leave this knight be!" And he rained blows upon them with his lance, striking the first so fiercely he brought him to the ground. He drew out his sword after breaking the point of his lance. And he rode here and there delivering blows against one and all so marvelously that every man he struck was forced to the ground. And he accomplished so much in a short time with the great blows he delivered, and with the quickness that filled him, that no man there was hardy enough to stand up under his attack. Instead, one and all took flight, fanning out through the forest, which was thick, so that only three of them could now be seen: one whom Perceval had unhorsed and wounded, as well as the two who had been similarly served by the Knight. And when he saw that they had all departed and that Perceval had nothing more to fear from them, he returned himself to the forest, just where it was most dense, like a man who wished that no one should follow him.

And when Perceval saw him depart with such haste, he cried out to him as loud as he could with these words: "Hold there, sir knight, for the sake of God stay your course a while, until you speak to me!" The Good Knight made no sign that he had heard Perceval, but rather made off at great speed, like a man with no desire to retrace his steps. And Perceval, who had no horse, for those men had killed his, followed after him as quickly as he could on foot. And, so doing, he met up with a squire riding a pack horse that was strong, if slight, and rather speedy, and the man was leading by his right hand a huge black charger. Seeing him, Perceval did not know what to do. For he was quite eager to have the charger so that he might pursue the knight, and he was willing to do the squire harm if he could not obtain the horse by some agreement, and yet he did not wish to take the horse by force unless great need compelled him since he did not want to be thought a base fellow. So he greeted the squire as soon as he drew near, saying, "God bless you!" "Fair friend," said Perceval, "in the name of all forms of service and reward, and because I will be your knight in whatever circumstance arises that you call on me, lend me your horse at once for I have great need of help to overtake that knight who there goes his way." "Lord," answered the squire, "that I will do under no circumstance. For it belongs to a man who would do my body shame if I do not return it to him." "Fair friend," Perceval then said, "do as I ask. Certainly, I have heard of no sorrow as great as that which will come upon me if I lose that knight for the lack of a horse." "Upon my faith," said the man, "I will do nothing else about this. You will never have the horse willingly from me as long as it is in my keeping. You can take it by force." And as he said this, Perceval was so filled with sorrow it seemed he would go out of his mind. For he did not wish to do the squire any harm. He would not wrong the squire; and yet if in this fashion he lost the Knight, who was then riding away, no joy would ever again be his. These two things brought such anger to his heart that he could not remain on his feet, but fell down by a tree as his heart failed him. And he turned pale and bloodless just as if he had lost all power over his body. And his sorrow was so great he wished at that moment to die.

Then he took off his helmet, and seizing his sword said this to the squire: "Fair friend, since you will not save me from the sorrow that is so great I cannot escape it save through death, I beg you to take my sword and kill me now with it. In this way, my suffering will find an end. And then if the Good Knight, whom I travel in search of, hears tell that I died of sorrow on his account, he will never be so evil-minded not to pray Our Lord to have mercy on my soul." "In God's name," said the squire, "may God never be pleased that I take your life, for this you have not deserved." And he took off at great speed, and Perceval remained there so filled with pain he thought he should die from this chagrin. And when he saw the squire no longer, or anyone else, he began to give voice to this too great sorrow, calling himself wretched and neglectful, saying these words: "Alas, unfortunate man, now you have failed at what you have been seeking because it has fled from you. Never again will you have such a good chance of finding it as you do now!"

While Perceval gave vent to his sorrow in such fashion, he heard and listened to the noise of horses that were approaching; and he opened his eyes and saw a knight in arms who was riding along the widest path through the forest on the horse that the squire had previously been leading. Perceval readily recognized the horse, but he did not think that he who possessed it had gotten it by force. And when he could no longer see it, he began to lament once more, never stopping until he saw the squire come toward him on his pack horse. He was very troubled. And the man spied Perceval where he was and spoke these words to him: "Greetings, sir. Have you seen pass this way a knight in arms riding the horse you saw me leading earlier?" "In truth, yes," said Perceval, "why do you mention it?" "Because," he replied, "the man had it from me by force. So doing, he has wronged me and delivered me to death, for my lord will kill me as soon as he meets up with me." "And so," said Perceval, "what would you like me to do about it? I cannot give it back to you because I am on foot. But if I had a horse, I think I might be able to return him to you in due time." "Lord," said the squire, "get up on my pack horse, and if you defeat this man, it will be yours." "And concerning your pack horse," said Perceval, "how will you get it back if I manage to gain the victory over him?" "Sir," he replied, "I will follow you on foot, and if you can defeat the knight, I will take back my pack horse, and the charger will be yours." And Perceval said he could ask for no better.

Then Perceval laced his helmet back on and mounted on the pack horse and took up his shield, and made off as fast as he could manage after the knight. And he proceeded a goodly distance and then came upon a tiny clearing, of which there were many in this forest. And there he saw before him the knight who had made off at a gallop on the charger. And, seeing him, he called out to him from some distance: "Sir knight, come back, and return to the squire the horse which you have wrongly taken from him!" And when that man heard what had been screamed at him, he rode at him with his lance lowered; and Perceval drew his sword, like a man who knows well that a battle is coming. But the knight, eager to get rid of him at once, came at him as fast as the horse could carry him and struck the pack horse in the chest with such force that it was knocked end over end. And it fell to the earth, mortally wounded, and Perceval flew off over its neck. Seeing the blow he gave, the knight spurred on his horse and rode across the clearing, striking out into the forest in the place he knew it to be the thickest. And when Perceval saw what had happened, he was so distressed that he did not know what to say or do. So he shouted out to the man in flight: "You of the weak body and coward's heart, come back and do combat with me, who am on foot, and you are mounted on a horse!" And that man responded to nothing that he said, for he had little to fear from him. Instead he raced through the woods along the very path he had come down. And when Perceval could see him no longer, he felt such anguish that he threw to the ground his shield and sword, ripping the helmet from his head, and then began again to lament as before. And he wept and cried out in a loud voice, calling himself an unfortunate wretch, the unluckiest of knights, and he spoke these words: "I have now failed to achieve everything I thought to achieve."

Percival remained in great sorrow and distress the entire day, as no one came who might comfort him. And when night began to fall, he found himself so weak and tired that there was no strength left in his limbs, or so he thought. And feeling a desire to sleep, he did fall asleep, not waking before midnight. And when he did awaken, he looked around him and saw a woman who, in her terror, asked him: "Percival, what are you doing here?" And he answered that he was doing no good, but no evil either, and that if he had a horse he would quickly depart. "If you would," she replied, "pledge to do what I wish when I ask it, I will provide you with a good and useful horse immediately, one that will carry you wherever you wish." And when he heard this, Percival was more joyful than any man could be, like someone who paid no attention to who it was who was speaking to him. And he believed without question that this was a woman who addressed him, but that was not the case, as it was instead the enemy, who was intent on deceiving him and making sure that his soul would be forfeit forever. And hearing the promise that she made regarding the thing he most desired in the world, he answered that he was prepared to do whatever she might request. Provided she gave him a horse that was good and useful, he would do all in his power to accomplish her wish. "Do you," she asked, "pledge me this as a faithful knight?" "Yes, truly," was his answer. "Now wait here," she then said, "and I will soon return." And then she made her way back into the forest, quickly returning with a horse that was large and of exceptional appearance, and it was so black that it was a wonder to look upon it.

When Percival saw the horse, he gazed upon him and felt a shudder of apprehension. Yet nonetheless he was brave enough to mount it, like someone unaware of the enemy's tricks. And after mounting the horse, he took up his shield and his lance. The woman standing before him then asked: "Percival, where are you going? Do remember you owe me recompense?" And he replied that he did remember. Then he went off at a gallop, heading through the forest, while the moon shone clear. But the horse carried him at such speed that he moved through the forest in a short time and had soon traveled three days distance. And he rode on until he saw before him a valley through which flowed a river broad and swift. And the horse headed in that direction, being eager to cross it. But when Percival saw how broad and deep it was, he was fearful about crossing, for night had fallen and he spied no bridge or planks. So he raised his hand and made the sign of the cross on his forehead. When the enemy felt the burden of the cross placed upon him, which he found heavy and troublesome, he shook himself and dislodged Percival, striking out into the water howling and screaming and greatly troubled. And at that moment flames shot out of the water in several places, and it seemed to Percival that the river itself was catching on fire.

Witnessing these things, Percival realized at once that it was the enemy who had brought him to this place in order to deceive him, bringing about the destruction of both body and soul. And then he made the sign of the cross, commending himself to God and praying Our Lord to not let him fall into temptation, which might make him forfeit the company of heavenly knights. So he reached out his hands toward the heavens, thanking Our Lord with all his heart for aiding him so well in this time of need. For when the enemy was in the water, he certainly could have let him fall in as well, and thus he would have been drowned and lost, forfeiting both body and soul. And he stepped back a bit from the riverbank, for he still feared an attack from the enemy, and he kneeled in the direction of the east and said his prayers and orisons, just as he had learned to do. Now he was very eager for day to break so that he might learn what country he was in, for he was quite certain that the enemy had carried him quite far from the abbey where he had seen king Mordrain.

Perceval passed the time until dawn in his prayers and orisons, waiting for the sun to complete its circuit in the firmament and appear once again to those on earth. And when the sun had risen clear and beautiful, drying out the dew, Perceval looked all around him and saw he was atop a mountain high and wondrous, and quite savage as well, which was close by a sea that surrounded it, and this was of such great extent he could see land only at considerable distance. And he realized he had been brought to some island, but which island, this he did not know. And he was eager to find out, but did not know how this might come about, for nearby there was no castle or fortress or building or house in which there might be people living, at least this is what he thought. And nonetheless he was by no means alone, for around him, as he soon saw, there were savage beasts—bears and lions and leopards—as well as serpents coursing through the air. And seeing himself in such a place, he hardly felt at ease, afraid as he was of the savage beasts, who would not leave him in peace, as he knew well, but would kill him if he could not put up some defense. Nonetheless, if He who saved Jonah from the belly of the fish and rescued Daniel from the den of lions intended to be his shield and defense, he need feel no concern on account of any creature he saw there. And he put his trust firmly in the aid and help He would provide, more than he did in his sword, for he fully realized that earthly chivalry would not effect his escape if Our Lord did not provide guidance. And he looked around him and noticed, there in the middle of the island, a cliff, high, and of unusual appearance, and he believed he need fear none of these wild animals if he could make his way there. And so he set out in that direction armed as he was. And when he had come to that place, he looked around and spied a serpent carrying a small lion, which he was holding by the neck with its teeth. At the top of the cliff, the serpent coiled up. And a lion was hot in its pursuit, loudly roaring and raising such a clamor that to Perceval it seemed that the beast was sorrowing for the lion cub that the serpent had carried off.

When Perceval witnessed these events, he ran at full speed to the top of the cliff. But the lion, which was much faster, passed him and began to struggle against the serpent the moment it reached the summit. As it turned out, as soon as Perceval came to the top and could see the two beasts, he determined to assist the lion, which was a more natural beast and of a more refined nature than the serpent. And then he drew out his sword, raised the shield to protect his face because of the fire that might do him harm, and stepped to encounter the serpent, dealing him a heavy blow between the ears. And the serpent spit out flame and fire, burning up his shield and the front of his mailshirt; and he would have done more damage if he could have managed it. But Perceval was agile and quick, and was scorched by the base of the flames, not being hit squarely by them, and so the fire proved less harmful. And seeing this, he was quite concerned, for he was afraid that the fire was laced with venom. Nonetheless he renewed his attack on the serpent, dealing it deadly blows wherever he could reach it. And it happened that he struck him again on the same place he had struck him at the outset. And the sword was light and well-forged, and he cut through his head quite easily, for its skin had already been split and the bones were thin there. The serpent fell dead on the spot.

When the lion saw that he had been saved by the assistance the knight provided, he did not make as if he wished to fight him, but rather approached the man, with his head lowered, and treated the man with as much friendliness as he could muster. In this way, Perceval saw clearly that it wished him no harm. So he returned his sword to its scabbard, letting fall his shield, which was burned all over, and removed the helmet from his head so that he could feel the wind, for the serpent had terribly scorched him. And the lion followed after him, its tail swishing with the great joy it felt. And when Perceval saw his, he began to stroke the beast's neck, head, and shoulders, saying that Our Lord had sent him this beast as a companion; so he considered this a fine bit of luck. And the lion fawned on Perceval as much as any animal might do, remaining by his side until the hour of noon. But as soon as noon passed, he made his way down to his den, taking the cub with him by the neck. When he saw that he was all alone on this wondrous cliff, which was desolate, no need to ask if he felt desperate. And he would have been desperate enough, had it not been for the firm hope he had in his Creator, for he was one of the knights in this world who possessed a perfect belief in Our Lord. And yet this was contrary to the custom of this country. For at this time, men were so perverse and lacking in moderation throughout the entire kingdom of Wales that if some son found his father lying sick in his bed, he would have dragged him by the head or arms and killed him without hesitation. For he would have lost his honor had his father died in bed. But when it happened that a son killed his father, or some father his son, and all the family should die of such violence, then their countrymen would say that such people were of high lineage.

Perceval passed that whole day on the cliff, looking at the far-off sea to discover if there were some ship passing by the island. But as it happened, as he looked this way and that, he saw nothing. Since this was how things stood, he summoned up his courage and sought consolation from Our Lord, praying that He would prevent him falling into temptation or into some trap laid by the devil, even something that might spring from his own mind; but God, he prayed, should protect him as the father protects the son, offering him safety and nourishment. And he raised his hands up toward heaven and spoke these words:

"Gracious Lord God, You who permitted me to ascend to that eminence that is the order of chivalry, who chose me as your servant, though I am completely unworthy of it, Lord, in your pity do not let it happen that I leave your service, but let me ever be like the good and reliable champion, who ably defends the quarrel of his lord against that man who accuses him unjustly. Lord gracious and fair, just the same, give me the chance to defend my soul (the quarrel is yours just as my soul is your true heritage) against that man who wrongly wants to take it away. Lord gracious and fair, You Who have said yourself in your gospel: "I am the good shepherd, and the good shepherd lays down his life for his sheep, but the man who has been hired to guard them does not do so, but leaves the sheep unguarded until the wolf seizes them by the throat and devours them at the moment he comes upon them."[1] Lord, you are my guide, my shepherd, and my protector, and so I am one of your sheep. And if it happened, Gracious Lord God, that I became the hundredth sheep, wayward and foolish, who strays from the other ninety-nine and makes his way aimlessly in the desert, Lord, have mercy on me and do not abandon me in that wilderness, but lead me back to your presence, which is Holy Church and holy faith, the place where the good sheep are and where true men, good Christians, find their residence, so that the enemy, who desires nothing of me but the substance, which is the soul, might not find me unprotected."

After Perceval said this, he saw approach him the lion for whose sake he had done combat with the serpent, but the lion gave no indication that he intended to do him harm, but drew near in a quite friendly way. And when Perceval saw this, he called out and went over to him to pet his neck and head. And the lion lay down before him in the manner of the tamest of animals. And he in turn lay down next to the lion and rested his head on the beast's shoulder; and they remained in this fashion until night fell, black and obscure. And straightaway he fell asleep beside the lion. No desire to eat troubled him, for he was thinking deeply about other things.

After Perceval fell asleep, an amazing adventure befell him. For it seemed, as he slept, that two ladies were making their way to him, one of whom was quite aged and old, and the other not very old at all, but very beautiful. The two ladies were not traveling on foot, but were mounted on two quite different beasts, a lion and a serpent. And he gazed at the two ladies, wondering how they could manage riding such two beasts as these. And the younger approached Perceval and spoke these words: "Perceval, my lord sends greetings to you and asks you to make ready with all the speed you can muster; for in the morning you are bound to do combat against the champion who in this world does the most to make himself feared. And if you are defeated, you will not find yourself quit with only the loss of a limb, but rather such ill will be visited upon you that your shame will endure forever." Hearing this, Perceval responded: "My lady, who is your lord?" "To be sure," she rejoined, "he is the world's richest man. Now take care that you are worthy and resolute enough to be able to win some honor in this combat." And then she departed with such suddenness and speed that Perceval did not know what had become of her.

Then the other lady came forward, the one who was mounted on the serpent, and she said this to Perceval: "Perceval, I have a serious complaint to lodge against you. For you have disrespected me and mine, and this I have not deserved." And hearing this, Perceval responded with embarrassment: "My lady, I am certain that I have never done wrong to you or to any other woman in this world. And I ask you to explain to me how I have wronged you, and I will readily do my best to make such amends as you require." "I will certainly tell you," she rejoined, "How you have injured me. For some time I have nourished in my castle a beast that is called serpent, which has served me more than you can imagine. And by chance, this beast made its way to this hillside, finding there a lion cub, which it carried to the top of that cliff. And you followed after it, running with your sword, and you killed it even though it did not attack you. Now tell me why you killed the serpent. Have I done anything against you that you should bring about its death? Was the lion yours or under your care so that you were obligated to fight on its behalf? Are the beasts of the air so abandoned to their own fate that you should kill them without reason?"

After Perceval heard the words that the lady had spoken to him, this was his answer: "My Lady, you have not wronged me in any way that I know of, nor does the lion belong to me, nor are the beasts of the air free for me to do with them as I would. But because the lion is of a more gracious nature than the serpent, and of much higher rank, and because I saw that the lion was less in the wrong than the serpent, I rushed to attack the serpent and kill it." And hearing these reasons, the lady said: "Perceval, have you nothing more to offer me?" "My lady," Perceval responded, "what is it that you would like me to do for you?" "I wish," she said, "that in order to make amends for my serpent you became my man." And he answered that this was something he would not do. "No?" she said, "This is what you once were; before you were bound to your lord you belonged to me. And because you were mine before you were anyone else's, I do not regard that claim as voided; rather I assure you that if I come upon you any time you are not on your guard, I will possession of you again, for you were someone who once belonged to me."

With these words, the lady departed. And Perceval remained asleep, though much troubled by this vision. And he slept so soundly all night long that nothing wakened him. And in the morning, when day broke clear and the sun rose up, its rays warm and fiery upon his head, Perceval opened his eyes and saw that day had come. And then he sat up and made the sign of the cross, praying that Our Lord would counsel him to the profit of his soul since he no longer cared as much for the body as he once had, believing that he might never find his way down from the cliff where he now was. And he looked all around, but saw nothing, neither the lion that for a time had been his companion, nor the serpent he had killed. And he wondered very much what had become of them.

Lost in such thoughts, Perceval happened to glance far out to see and he spied a ship with its sail raised that was making right for the spot where Perceval was waiting to learn if God might grant him some fortunate adventure. And the ship was moving at great speed, running before the wind that was hastening it on; and its course took it directly toward him until it arrived at the foot of the cliff. And when Perceval, who was on the crest, saw this, he felt great joy, for he was certain that the boat would be filled with men. And so he stood up and armed himself. And, now armed, he made his way down the cliff like someone eager to discover who exactly was in this boat. Approaching it, he saw that the deck was curtained off with white silk cloth, so that his eye saw whiteness, nothing more. And coming on board, he saw a man wearing a surplice and alb, just as priests do, and on his head was a crown of white silk, with a width of two fingers on which were written the holy and sanctified names of Our Lord. Seeing this, Perceval was filled with wonder. He drew near the man, greeted him, and spoke these words: "My lord, you are welcome here! God brought you to this place!" "Fair friend," he replied, "Who are you?" "I am," Perceval replied, "of the house of King Arthur." "And what adventure," the man rejoined, "has brought you to this place?" "Sir," Perceval said, "I don't know how or in what manner I came here." "And what do you wish?" said the good man. "Sir," he replied, "if it should please Our Lord, I would very much like to depart from this place and join my brothers on the Quest of the Holy Grail; it was for no other reason that I departed from the court of my lord the king." "When it pleases God," answered the man, "You shall leave this place behind. You will be quickly dispatched when it is His pleasure to do so. If He thinks of you as his servant and sees that you might better deploy your worthiness in some other place, know that He would effect your departure from here at once. But here is where He is now testing you so that He might learn if you are indeed His faithful servant and a loyal knight, just as the order of chivalry demands. Since you have been raised to such high estate, your heart should not falter on account of any earthly fears or perils. For the heart of a knight must be so resolute and determined in the encounter with the enemy that nothing can weaken it. And if that heart succumbs to fear, it is not the heart of a true knight or true champion, for men such as these would accept dying on the field of battle rather than failing to uphold the cause of their lord."

Perceval then asked this man who he was and where he was from; and he answered that he had come from a far-off land. "And what adventure," Perceval inquired, "Led you to this strange place, which seems quite savage to me?" "Truly," said the good man, "I have come here to see and comfort you, and so that you yourself could tell me how you are doing. For if there is anything that you need to be counseled about, just tell me, and I will offer you the best advice I can." "I am amazed," said Perceval, "that you say you have come here to counsel me. For I do not see how this could be so, for no one, save God and myself, knows that I am now on this cliff. And even if you had known I was here, I do not believe in the least you might know my name, for in so far as I am aware you have never before laid eyes upon me. And so I am bewildered by what you have just said."

"Indeed, Perceval," the good man replied, "I know you much better than you think. For some time you have done nothing that I do not have deeper knowledge of than you do yourself." And hearing the man call him by name, Perceval was astonished. And he regretted what he had previously said. He asked the man to forgive him, saying: "Truly, sir, do forgive me in God's name for the words I spoke to you. For I thought you were not acquainted with me in the least, but now I see quite well that you know me better than I know you. And I consider myself a fool and you a man of considerable wisdom."

Then Perceval rested his elbows on the ship's rail and spoke with the good man about different things. And in everything they discussed, Perceval found him so wise that he greatly wondered who he might be. And his company pleased Perceval so much that during all the hours he spent with him he found himself neither hungry nor thirsty, so sweet and pleasant were the man's words. And after they had spoken a long time, this is what Perceval said to him: "My lord, please share your wisdom with me about a vision I experienced while sleeping, for it seems so strange to me that I will not be at ease until I know the truth of it." "Tell me about it," said the good man, "And I will explain it so that you see clearly what it means." "And I will do as you ask," said Perceval, "It happened last night as I was sleeping that before me there were two women, one mounted on a lion and the other on a serpent. And the one mounted on the lion was a young woman, and the other on the serpent was old, and it was the young woman who first spoke to me." And at this point, he undertook to report all he had heard them say to him while he slept, and this was so true to what they had in fact said, that nothing was omitted. And after he had recounted his dream, he asked the good man to explain its meaning to him. And he said he would willingly undertake to do this. And this is how he began.

"Perceval," he said, "of these two ladies that you saw so differently mounted in that one was riding a lion and the other a serpent, the meaning is quite marvelous, and I will explain it to you. The one mounted on the lion stands for the New Law, which is set on the lion who is Jesus Christ; it has its foot and foundation in him and by him was raised up and exalted in the view and sight of all Christianity.

And for this reason it is to serve as a true mirror and light for all who lift up their hearts to the Trinity. And this lady sits on the lion, that is to say Jesus Christ, and this lady then is Faith and Hope and belief and baptism. This lady is the stone hard and firm on which Jesus Christ said that he would establish Holy Church, in the passage where he said: "On this rock I will build my church."[2] And this same lady who is mounted o the lion should be understood as the New Law, which Our Law maintains in force and power just as a father does for his child. And that she seems younger in appearance than the other is no wonder, for she is not as old, not the same in age. This woman was born in the Passion of Jesus Christ and in the Resurrection, and the other held sway on earth long before. This one went to speak to you as to her own son, for all good Christians are her sons, and she showed herself to be your mother, for she has such power over you because she came to you before this blow to announce what would happen to you. She came to tell you this on behalf of her lord, who is Jesus Christ, that a fight is in your future. By the faith that I owe you, if she did not love you, she would not have come to tell you this, for she would not have cared if you were defeated. And she hastened to inform you so that you would be better prepared before this fight. And against whom will you fight? Against the most feared champion of the world, on whose account Enoch and Elijah, brave men both, were lifted up from the earth and brought to heaven, not to return before the Day of Judgment in order to do battle against the man who is so mightily feared. This champion, he is the enemy who constantly works and labors to lead men into mortal sin and lead then thence into hell. This is the champion against whom you must fight, and if you are defeated, as the woman told you, you will not get away with the loss of only a single limb, but instead be dishonored from that day forward. And you can certainly see the truth of that for yourself. For if the enemy gains the upper hand, he will place you in jeopardy of losing both body and soul, and from this place he will take you into the house of shadows, which is Hell itself, where you will suffer shame and misery and torment as long as the power of Jesus Christ endures.

"Now I have explained to you the significance of the lady whom you saw in your dream, the one who was riding upon the lion. And in so doing I have told you enough so that you can figure out who the other woman is, and what her significance might be." "Sir," said Perceval, "concerning the young woman you have explained enough so that I understand well her significance. But now say something more about the other who was riding on the serpent, whose significance I will not clearly understand if you do not explain it to me." "Very well, I will explain further," said the good man, "Listen to me. The woman you saw riding on the serpent, she is the Synagogue, the First Law, which was displaced as soon as Jesus Christ brought the New Law to us. And the serpent who bears her, that's Scripture badly understood and misinterpreted, for it is hypocrisy and heresy and iniquity and mortal sin, in other words the enemy himself; that's the serpent who for his pride was driven out of Paradise; that's the serpent who said to Adam and to his woman: 'If you eat of this fruit, then you will be as God.'[3] And through these words, an evil desire made its way into them. For they were eager then to be of higher estate than they were and so, believing what the enemy counseled, they fell into sin, for which they were expelled from Paradise and sent into exile. All their heirs share in this sin, and daily pay the price. And when this lady came to you, she complained that you had murdered her serpent. And do you know what serpent she was complaining about? She was not complaining about the one you slew yesterday, but the one she still is riding, which is to say the enemy. And do you know when you did her this hurt? At the moment when the enemy was carrying you and taking you onto this cliff; for right then you made the sign of the cross. Because you crossed yourself, he could go no further, for he felt such fear he thought he would die. So he fled at great speed, like someone who could no longer endure being your companion. And thus you killed him, robbing and destroying the power he has been wont to enjoy and by which he hoped to enjoy a victory over you; this is the grievance your mistress holds against you. And when you answered her request in the best way you knew how, she demanded that you make amends for what she had done against you by becoming her man. And you told her that you would not do. And she said that some time ago you had been her man before making homage to your lord. And this gave you cause for much thought, and yet you should have known very well what she meant. For without doubt before you received baptism and Christianity, you endured subjection to the enemy. But as soon as you received the seal of Jesus Christ, that is the holy oil with which you were anointed, you renounced the enemy and passed beyond his control, for in this way you offered homage to your Creator. Now I have explained the significance of the two ladies; and I must depart, for there is much that I am obligated to do. But remain here and remember well the battle you are to fight; for if you are vanquished, you will have nothing beyond what has been promised to you."

"Fair sir," said Perceval, "Why are you making such haste to leave? Surely your words and your companionship please me so much that I would never wish for you to depart. And for God's sake, if it is possible, remain here with me; for beyond a doubt I think I would benefit on every day of my life from what you have to say to me." "I must go my way," said the good man, "for many men expect me, but you are to remain here. So take care not to be unprepared for the one against whom you must do battle. If he finds you unready, things might quickly go badly for you."

With these words, the man departed; and the wind filled his sail with such power that the ship was borne off at such speed Perceval could scarcely register it with his eyes. And it had gone so far in just a short time that it was lost from his view completely. And after he could no longer see it, he climbed back up the cliff, armed as he was. And, reaching the top, he found the lion that had been his companion the day before. And he began to pet it because the beast seemed so happy to see him. And afterward he remained there until after noon when, looking out to sea, he saw a ship making for him as if all the winds in the world were driving it onward, cleaving the waves. And before it was a whirlwind that roiled the sea, making the waves rise up like towers. Seeing this, Perceval wondered what this could be, for the whirlwind made it impossible for him to see the ship. But then it got close enough for him to see truly that this was a ship, and it was covered completely with black cloth, whether silk or linen, this I do not know. And when it got nearer, he descended the cliff, wishing to learn what it might be. And, as he climbed down, he very much hoped this might be the good man he had spoken to earlier. And it was good fortune that it happened, either by the strength of God or something else, that there was no beast so fierce on that mountain that it was moved to approach or attack him. And he moved down the high ground and came to the ship as fast as he could manage. And when he stood at the entrance of the tent that had been erected on deck, he saw sitting within a woman of very great beauty who was dressed more richly than any other might be.

Spying Perceval, the woman rose to meet him and with no formal greeting said these words to him: "Perceval, what are you doing here? Who brought you to this mountain, which is so desolate that you will never be rescued from it except by some lucky chance and have nothing to eat here so will die of hunger and discomfort before you find anything to pay attention to your condition?" "Damsel," he replied, "if I die from hunger, then I am no loyal servant, and this would be the proof. For no man serves another of such high rank as the one I serve, providing he does so faithfully and with a good heart, and asks for something that he does not receive. And he himself has said that his door is closed to no one who comes there; for if he knocks, he will enter, and if asks, then he will receive. And if any one seeks him, he will not hide himself, but rather allows himself to be found easily."[4] And when the woman heard that he made mention of the Gospel, she did not respond to these words, instead broaching another matter, saying: "Perceval, do you know whence I come?" "Who is it, damsel," said Perceval, "that told you my name? "I know it quite well," she rejoined, "And I know you better than you think I do." "And whence have you come to this place?" said Perceval. "Upon my faith," she said, "I come from the Waste Forest, where I witnessed the most remarkable adventure in the world, and it involved the Good Knight." "Now damsel," he said, "tell me about the Good Knight, by the faith that you owe the thing in the world you most love!" "I will not," she answered, "tell you what I know of this in any way if you do not swear on the order of chivalry of which you are a member that you will do whatever I wish at whatever hour I summon you to do so." And he answered that he would do so if he were so able." "You have said enough," she said, "I will now tell you the truth of the matter. Truly, not long ago I was right in the middle of the Waste Forest, the part where flows the great river called Marcoise. There I saw that the Good Knight riding along, chasing before him two other knights whom he intended to kill. And these two plunged into the water, afraid as they were for their lives, and as it happened, they were able to cross the river. But this other man fared much worse; for his horse was drowned, as he should have been as well if he hadn't managed to climb out immediately, for it was because he turned back that he was saved. So you have now heard tell, as you have requested, the story of the Knight. And now I want you to tell me how you came to this desolate island, where you are as good as lost if you don't make your escape. For you see well that no one comes here who might aid you, and you must leave this place if you are not to die. And so, unless death is what you want, that you must plead that someone rescue you. And I am the only one who can accomplish this. Therefore you must satisfy me so that I effect your rescue, that is, if you are wise enough to do so, for I know no greater stupidity than for someone who can help himself and yet does nothing."

"Damsel, if I thought," said Perceval, "Our Lord would be pleased for me to depart this place, I would in fact depart were I able. Otherwise, I would not want to leave. I never would have done anything had I not believed it would please Him, for my entrance into chivalry should have been a great misfortune if I took up arms against Him."

"Let's forget this," she advised, "Tell me if you have eaten today." "To be sure," Perceval replied, "I have eaten no earthly food this day. But not long ago a good man came here to comfort me, and the many good words he spoke nourished and fed me so completely I have since felt no hunger or thirst providing I remember him." "Do you know," she said, "who that man is? He is an enchanter, a multiplier of words who turns one of these into a hundred more, and he could not speak the truth to you even if he could manage it. And, if you believe him, you will be dishonored, for you will never depart from this cliff, but die here of hunger, and these wild beasts will feast on your body. As you can readily see, the truth of this is already apparent. For you have been here for two days and two nights, and during the passing of this present day. And that man of whom you speak has brought you nothing to eat, but has abandoned you and will abandon you, for he will never rescue you. And it will be a great shame and misfortune should you die here. For you are such a young man and so worthy a knight you could do much of value to me and others were you to depart this place. And this I tell you: that I will take you away from here if that is your wish."

After Perceval heard what she offered, he said this to her: "Who are you, damsel, who would willingly take me from here if I so wished?" "I am," she replied, "a damsel who has lost her inheritance, who formerly was the richest woman in this world, and would still be had I not been expelled from my heritage." "Disinherited, damsel?" said he, "Tell me now who took your heritage, for I am at this moment more taken with pity for you than I was before." "I will tell you who," she answered. "The truth is that in days gone by a rich man put me in his dwelling to serve him, and this rich man was the richest king known to anyone. And I was so beautiful and attractive there was no man who did not marvel at me, for I was more beautiful than any other creature. And because of this beauty I grew somewhat arrogant, more than I had before, and said things that did not please him. And when I did so, he became so angry with me he would no longer suffer me in his company, but sent me away, impoverished and disinherited, nor did he ever feel pity for me or for anyone who was of my party. And this was how the rich man chased off my household and myself, exiling me to the wasteland. And he considered that I was terribly punished, and so I should have been had I not had the great sense to launch a war against him at once.

And it happens that this has well advanced my cause. For I have taken a great many of his men, who, abandoning him, have come over to my side because of the great host they see I lead against them. For they ask nothing from me I do not give them, and even more. And so I wage war night and day against the one who has disinherited me. I have assembled knights and sergeants and men of all degrees; and so there is no knight in the world, I say to you, no man of worthiness known to me whom I would not offer honorable payment to join my company. And because I know you are a good knight and a worthy man I have come here so that you can aid me in this endeavor. And you certainly should because you are a companion of the Round Table; for no man who is a companion of this band should fail to aid a disinherited damsel asking for his help. And you know well this is the truth, for when you took your seat at this table, King Arthur put this oath to you, and when you swore to it it was the first oath you made, namely that you would not fail to help any damsel who should make such a request of you." And he said that he had sworn such an oath beyond any doubt; and he would help the lady since she had asked him. And she thanked him very much.

They spoke for so long that midday came and went, and the hour of noon approached. And then the sun was hot and burning. The damsel spoke these words to Perceval: "Perceval, in this boat is a tent of the richest silk you have ever laid eyes upon. If you please, I will have it brought ashore and set up there so that you are not harmed by the sun's heat." And he answered that he did indeed so wish. And she stepped onto the boat and had her two servants pitch the tent on the shore. And after it had been set up as best they could manage, the damsel spoke these words to Perceval: "Come take your rest herein, and sit until night falls, coming in out of the sun, for I think you have been overheated by it." And he went inside the tent and fell asleep at once. But before this happened, she had relieved him of his helmet, hauberk, and sword. And after he had been stripped in this fashion, she let him go to sleep.

After sleeping a quite long time, he awoke and asked for something to eat. And she ordered the table to be set, and this was done. And he saw that it was then so filled to overflowing it seemed miraculous. And they ate this meal, just the two of them. And when he asked for drink, it was given to him. And he found that the drink was wine, the finest and strongest he had ever drunk. And he wondered very much where it had come from. For at this time there was no wine in Great Britain except in the houses of the very rich, for they commonly drank beer and other beverages they made themselves. And he drank so much of the wine he got drunker than he should have. And his gaze fell upon the damsel, who seemed so beautiful to him that, so he thought, he had never laid eyes on any other who could equal her in beauty. And she pleased him so much, and he found her so appealing because of the clothes she was wearing as he looked at them, and because of the soothing words she had spoken to him, that she aroused him more than was proper. Then he spoke to her of many things, until in the end he asked for her love, begging to be hers just as she should be his. And she deflected his advances as best she could, for it was her intention that he should become even more filled with ardor and desire for her. And he did not stop pushing himself on her. And when she saw that his desire had peaked, she spoke these words: "Perceval, know this much, that I will not in the least do those things that would please you if you do not first swear from this time forward to be my man, assisting me against all others and doing nothing I do not first command." And he said he would be willing to swear to this. "So swear it," she demanded, "as a faithful knight." "Yes," he said, "and it will satisfy me to do what pleases you. And know it as the truth that you have not desired to possess me anymore than I have desired to possess you. For you are one of the knights in this world I am most impassioned to possess."

And then she asked her servants to make up the most beautiful and attractive bed that they could and have it placed in the middle of the tent; and the servants said that they would as much. And they made up the bed, removing the shoes from the damsel and they lay together on it, Perceval beside her. And after he got in bed with the damsel and saw that he was under the covers, it happened by chance that he spied his sword, which they had taken from him, lying on the ground. And he reached out his hand to take it. And when he went to lean it against the bed, he noticed a red cross engraved on the hilt. And, spying this, he came to his senses. He immediately made the sign of the cross on his forehead, and at once witnessed the tent collapsing, as he was engulfed by smoke and a cloud, and this was so thick he could see nothing, while a horrible stench arose from every side, making him think that he was now in Hell itself. And he shouted out these words: "Fair sweet father Jesus Christ, do not let me perish in this place, but rescue me through your grace, for otherwise I am lost!" And after he said all this, he opened his eyes, but he saw nothing of the tent in which he had previously gone to bed. And looking toward the shore, he saw the same boat he had seen before, and the damsel spoke these words to him: "Perceval, you have betrayed me!" And at that moment, the ship embarked onto the sea, and Perceval saw that so great storm followed closely behind it that he thought the ship would be driven off its course, and the sea was filled with flames, in so marvelous a fashion that he thought the entire earth was being consumed by fire, and the ship went faster than any wind could have sped it on its way.

When Perceval saw this turn of events, he became so filled with sorrow it seemed likely he would die of grief. He looked at the ship as long as it remained in view, wishing misfortune and destruction might overtake it. And when he lost sight of it, he said: "Alas, I am dead!" And he was so grief-stricken he indeed wished to be dead. And he drew out his sword and struck himself with such fury on his left thigh that blood spurted everywhere. And, seeing this, he said: "Sweet Lord God, this is an amending of the wrong I committed against you." Then he looked at himself and saw that he was naked except for his underclothes, noticing that his clothes were in one place and his arms in another, and he called out: "Alas, miserable one! You are so vile and sinful, being led so quickly to the point of losing what can never be recovered, which is virginity, which can never be restored after it is one time forfeited!" He withdrew the blade of the sword from the wound and put it back into its scabbard. And he was quite despondent because he thought God would be angry that he had turned his sword on himself. He put on his shirt and robe, fixing himself as best he could, then lying down on the cliff side; he prayed Our Lord to send him such counsel as might enable him to earn ity and mercy for himself. For he felt that he had sinned so grievously against him, and was guilty, that his grace alone would be able to restore his peace of mind. And in this fashion rceval passed the entire day by the shore, like someone who could go neither forward nor :k because of the wound he had. So he asked Our Lord to aid him by sending such counsel is soul that might profit his soul, for nothing else did he seek. "And never, my Lord," he "Would I seek to leave this place, were it a matter of either life or death, if it were not will."

In this fashion, Perceval passed the day on this cliff side, and he lost a lot of blood from ound that he had. But when he saw night begin to fall and darkness moving over the earth, he moved closer to his hauberk and rested his head upon it, making the sign of the true cross on his forehead and praying Our Lord to protect him through His sweet mercy so that the devil, who was the enemy, would not gain power over him and lead him into temptation. Finishing his prayer, he stood up, then cut off the end of his shirt and used it to bandage his wound so it would no longer bleed. Then he began saying his prayers and orisons, and of these he knew several, passing the time in this way until day came. And when it pleased Our Lord to send out the light of day throughout the earth, and the rays of the sun fell where Perceval was lying, he looked around him and saw on one side the sea and on the other the cliff. And when he remembered that the day before the enemy had embraced him in the form of a maiden, for he thought surely that this is what must have happened, he commenced to grieve terribly and beyond measure, saying that truly he was dead if the grace of the Holy Spirit did not afford him consolation.

And while he was talking to himself in this way, he looked far out to see toward the east and saw coming toward him the ship he had seen the other day, the one covered with white samite in which a good man dressed as a priest had been. And when he recognized it, he was very assured by the fine words that the good man had spoken to him several times and which he had found filled with much wisdom. When the ship came to shore and he saw that the good man was on board, he sat up where he was as best he could manage, and said he was welcome. And the good man got off the boat and approached him, sitting down on the cliff. He spoke these words to Perceval: "How has it been for you?" "Sire, not very good; for a damsel nearly led me into mortal sin." And then he told him the story of what had happened. "Did you recognize her?" asked the good man. "Sir," he said, "Not in the least. But I know for sure that the enemy sent her to shame and deceive me. And I would have been dishonored had it not been for the sign of the holy cross, for this brought me back to my senses and to a true remembrance of who I am. As soon as I made the sign of the cross, the damsel hastened away, and I never caught sight of her again. And I ask that, for the sake of God, you advise what I should now do, for I have never had more need of good counsel than I do now." "Now Perceval," said the good man, "You have always been simple in your thinking! Did you not recognize the damsel, who had led you to the point of committing a mortal sin, when the sign of the cross caused her to flee?" "To be sure," Perceval said, "I did not recognize her very well. So I beg you tell me who she is and what country she is from, and who the rich man might be who disinherited her, against whom she asked me to provide assistance." "I will certainly tell you this," said the good man, "And you will know all there is to know. Now listen carefully:

"The damsel to whom you spoke is the enemy, the lord of Hell, the one who has power over all others. And it is true that he was formerly of the company of angels in the heavens, and so beautiful and splendid that because of this great beauty he grew filled with pride and wished to be the equal of the Trinity, saying: 'I will ascend on high and be like the Fair Lord.' But as soon as he said this, Our Lord, who did not want His dwelling soiled by the poison of pride, threw him down from the high seat in which he had once installed him, making him travel to the house of shadows that is called Hell. When he saw himself dismissed from the high place and the exalted rank that he was accustomed to enjoy and exiled into eternal darkness, he decided to make war with all his might against the one who had done this to him. But he could not easily think of what means to use. In the end he made the acquaintance of Adam's wife, the first woman in the human lineage. He used his guile and tricks to entice her into the same mortal sin that had brought about his fall from the great glory of the heavens, which is covetousness. He enticed her into acting out his own faithless designs by picking the fatal fruit from the tree that had been prohibited her by the very words of the Creator. When she did pick it, she ate of it and gave Adam her lord to eat of it, and the result has been that all their heirs feel this mortal pain. The enemy that urged this course on her was the serpent you saw the old woman riding the other day, and he was the damsel who came to you the other day. And concerning what she said about her travelling day and night, that was true enough, and you yourself know it as such. For there is no hour when she does not lay snares for the knights of Jesus Christ, and the good men, freed and in bondage, in whom the Holy Spirit is lodged.

When she had made peace with you through her false words and with her deceptions, she had her tent pitched for you, saying: 'Perceval, come rest and lie here until night falls, and get out of the sun, for it seems to me that you are too much heated by it.' The words she said to you are not without great significance. But she intended something other than what you understood. The tent, which is round in the manner of the circumference of the earth, manifestly stands for the world, which will never be without sin; and because sin is there always, she did not want you to take shelter outside the tent. And this is why she had it readied for you. And when she called you, she did so with these words: 'Perceval, come here to take your rest, and stay here until night falls.' And by saying that you should sit and take your rest, she meant that you should be lazy and nourish your body in gluttony with earthly food. She does not advise that you work in this world and sow such a seed as good men might then harvest, which will be the Day of Judgment. And she advised that you rest until night falls, that is, until you are overtaken by death, which is rightly called night at all times when she surprises men unawares in mortal sin. She called out to you because she feared that the sun was overheating you. And it is no wonder that she feared this. For when the sun, by whom we understand Jesus Christ, the true light, warms the sinner with the fire of the Holy Spirit, then the chill and ice of the enemy can do little to harm him, for he has fixed his heart on the high sun. Now I have told you enough about that lady so that you know who she is and that she came to you for her benefit and to your detriment."

"Sir," said Perceval, "you have told me enough about this lady that I know well that this is the champion I must fight." "Upon my faith," said the good man, "You speak the truth. Now consider how you did in this combat against him." "Sire," he said, "Not very well, so I think. For I should have been vanquished had it not been for the grace of the Holy Spirit, which did not let me perish, and for this I give thanks!" "No matter what happened to you in the past," answered the good man, "from this point on you must be on your guard. For it you slip a second time, you will not find yourself saved as quickly as happened before."

The good man spoke to Perceval for a long time, admonishing him forcefully to do what was right. And he said God would not forget him, but would send him assistance quite soon. Then he asked him about his wound. "Upon my faith," Perceval said, "Since your arrival I have felt no pain or misery from it, nor more than if I had never had a wound; nor since you have been speaking to me have I felt anything, but from your words and look I have felt a sweetness and assuagement so comforting throughout all my members that I think you are no earthly man, but a spiritual one. And this I know as the truth: that were you to spend every day with me, I would never feel hunger or thirst. And if I dared, I would say that you are the living Bread that descends from the heavens, of which all who worthily partake live eternally."

As soon as she said this, the good man disappeared in such a fashion that Perceval did not know what had become of him. Then a voice spoke to him: "Perceval, you are vanquished and healed. Embark on this boat and go where chance leads you. And let nothing you witness dismay you, for wherever you go God will be your guide. It has gone well enough with you that in due time you will lay eyes on your companions Bors and Galahad, the ones you are most eager for." Hearing these words, he felt a greater joy than any man could feel, and he reached out his hands toward the sky and thanked Our Lord for this happy turn of events. He took up his arms and, now armed, embarked on the boat, which set out on the ocean and distanced itself from the cliff as soon as wind struck the sail.

Now at this point the story ceases speaking of Perceval and returns to Lancelot, who had remained with the good man, the one who had so ably explained to him the significance of the three words the voice had spoken to him in the chapel.

* * *

Now the story tells how Galahad and Perceval spent the whole night together in the chapel, where they prayed God to keep Bors safe and look after him wherever he might go. In the morning, when day broke bright and clear; and as the storm cleared and the weather grew calm, they mounted on their horses and set out for the castle to see how those within had fared. Coming up to the gate, they found everything had burned and that the walls had all been thrown down. They went inside, and, having entered, they were more bewildered than before, for there was no man or woman therein who was not dead. And they searched the place from one end to the other, saying that such a great loss of life was a terrible shame. And when they came to the main palace, they found the walls destroyed as well as the ramparts, which had fallen in, and the knights dead, one and all, as if Our Lord had loosed thunder and lightning on them because of the sinfulness they had indulged in. When the companions saw all this, they proclaimed it a heavenly vengeance. "And this would not have happened," they maintained, "except that the anger of the Creator of this world needed repayment." And just as they were discussing the matter, they heard a voice that spoke these words to them: "This is the vengeance for the blood of the virtuous maidens, which here was spilled for the worldly profit of a faithless woman sinner." And hearing these words, they proclaimed how wondrous was the vengeance taken by Our Lord, calling that man a fool who sets himself against His will, whether to save his life or prevent his death.

When the two companions had searched up and down the castle to look upon the host of the dead, they found in front of a chapel a cemetery thickly planted with small trees, their leaves as green as the surrounding grass, and full of attractive tombs. And there were, perhaps, more than sixty of these. And all was there so beautiful that it seemed no storm had passed that way. Nor had it done so, for therein lay the bodies of the maidens who out of love for the lady had suffered death. Entering the cemetery on horseback, they came upon the tombs, and above each one they found the name of her who lay beneath. And they went along reading these letters until discovering that twelve damsels were buried there, all daughters of kings and of the highest lineage. And seeing this, they railed against the villainous and evil custom that had been maintained in the castle, for the people in that land had suffered much too long since many a high-born family had been brought low, even destroyed because these maidens had been put to death.

The two companions remained there until the hour of prime, and by then they had seen enough. They then departed, wandering until they came upon a forest. And as they approached the path leading in, Perceval said this to Galahad: "Sir, this is the day when we must separate, and each of us is to follow his own path. So I commend you to Our Lord, who will grant, I hope, that we come upon each other again before too long. For I have never met any man whose company I found as pleasing and valuable as your own. And so I dread this parting more than you can imagine. But it must be so, for it pleases Our Lord. Then he removed his helmet, as did Galahad, and they kissed each other as they parted company, for they loved each other with a great affection. And so this was apparent at the times of their deaths, for the one lived only a short time after the death of the other. And so the companions went their different ways at the entrance to this forest, which those in this land called Aube, and each set out on his own path. The story leaves off speaking of them at this point and returns to Lancelot, for it has been too long silent about him.

* * *

Now the story relates that when Galahad parted from Lancelot he rode on for many days as adventure led him, one hour forward and the next back, until he arrived at an abbey where king Mordain then was. And when he heard the news that the king was waiting for the Good Knight, he thought he would go to see him. That next day, as soon as he had heard mass, he went to where the king was. And when Galahad went inside, the king, who had lost his sight and the power over his limbs by the will of Our Lord, saw clearly again as soon as Galahad drew near. And he quickly sat up on the spot and spoke these words to Galahad: "Galahad, servant of God, true knight whose coming I have long awaited, kiss me and let me lay my head on your chest, so that I might die in your embrace, for you are pure and virginal beyond all other knights just as the lily, which symbolizes virginity, is whiter than all other flowers. You are the lily in your virginity, you are the true rose, the proper flower of real virtue with the color of fire, for the fire of the Holy Spirit burns and blazes so much that my body, which had been decayed and withered, is completely rejuvenated and regains the strength it once had."

When Galahad heard these words, he sat down by the king's head, embraced him and laid him by his side, for the king then wanted to rest. And the king leaned toward him, put his arms around him, holding him close as he said: "Sweet father Jesus Christ, now I possess what I have desired! I pray that you come to take me just as I now am, for I could not pass on in a state of more ease and well-being than what I enjoy at present. For in this great joyfulness that I much longed for is nothing but roses and lilies." As soon as he made this request to Our Lord, there was immediate proof that Our Lord listened to this prayer, for the king was given at once to Him whom he had served for so very long. He breathed his last in Galahad's arms. And when those in the household knew that this had happened, they came for the body and discovered that the wounds from which he had so long suffered were now healed; and they found this a great miracle. Then they gave the body all the honor due that of a king, later burying him inside the abbey.

Galahad remained there two years. On the third, he departed, riding ahead for some days until he came to the Forest Perilous, where he found the fountain, and there the water was roiled by huge waves, as was related earlier in this story. And as soon as he put his hand in the water, it was no longer steamy or roiling, for in him that was no ardor that comes from lustful living. And the people of this country, when they learned about it, considered a great miracle that the water had cooled. Then it lost the name it bore previously, thereafter to be called Galahad's Fountain.

When he had completed this adventure, his chance wandering bore him into the land of Gorre, and there he rode on until arriving at the abbey where Lancelot had been before, which was the place where he had found the tomb of Galahad, the king of Hoselice, the son of Joseph of Arimathea, as well as the tomb of Symeon, and it was the place where Lancelot had suffered failure. And when he entered the place, he looked into the crypt beneath the church. And when he saw the tomb that was so wondrously aflame, he asked the brothers who this was. "Sir," they said, "this is a marvelous adventure that cannot be brought to a conclusion, except by that man who will surpass in goodness and chivalry all the companions of the Round Table." "I would like, if you please," he said, "for you to show me a door through which I might enter this place." And they said they would be happy to do so. And he was led to the entrance of the crypt, there to descend by stairs. And as soon as he approached the tomb, the fire died out and the flames were quenched, though they had burned this way for many a day, because the man was now in the place who suffered not at all from the fever of lust. Coming to the tomb, he lifted up the stone and gazed therein at the body of Symeon, who had died; and as soon as the heat dissipated, he heard a voice that said: "Galahad, Galahad, you must give many thanks to Our Lord, who has granted you such a favor; for by the virtuous life you have led, you are able to reclaim souls from earthly suffering and deliver them to the joys of paradise. I am Symeon, your ancestor, who in the great heat you witnessed here have remained three hundred and fifty four years in order to expunge the sin that I committed long ago against Joseph of Arimathea. And along with the pain I have suffered I would have been lost and damned but for the grace of the Holy Spirit, more powerful in you than earthly chivalry, looked with pity upon me because of the great humility that is yours. And, thanks be to him, for he has transported me from earthly suffering to the joys of heaven solely through the grace of your coming. "Those within the chapel, who had come forward as soon as the flame died down, heard what was said; and they considered it a great wonder and miracle. And Galahad took up the corpse and removed it from the tomb where it had lain for so long and carried it into the church. And after he did so, those within took it from him and buried it near the main altar, just as a knight should be buried, for he had been a knight. And having done this, they approached Galahad, according him as much honor as they could, and they asked him where he was from and from what nation. And he told them the truth of the matter.

The next day, after Galahad heard mass, he left that place, commending the brothers to God, and he set out on his path and rode on for five years before he arrived at the house of the Maimed King. And for those five years Perceval was his companion everywhere he went. And during that time, they endured and succeeded at the adventures of the kingdom of Logres, which are such things as are no longer seen in our day, unless it be some miracle Our Lord performs. And it was never the case that in whatever country they traveled, no matter how filled with people, that they were defeated, or made to feel dismay or fear.

One day it happened that they left behind a forest that was thick and wondrous. And just then they met up with Bors, who was riding along all by himself. And when they recognized him, do not ask if they were happy and joyous, for they had been a long time without his company and were very eager to lay eyes upon him. And they celebrated with him, doing him honor and wishing him well, and he did the same to them. Then they asked how he had been; and he told them the truth about what success he had enjoyed. And he said that in five years he had spent just four nights in a dwelling with other people, staying instead in wild forests and far-off mountains more than one hundred times. And more than one hundred times he would have died had it not been for the grace of the Holy Spirit, who comforted and sustained him in all his times of distress. "And did you find after all this what we had gone off in search of?" said Perceval. "To be sure, not at all," he said, "But I believe that we will not quit until we have brought to a conclusion the quest upon which we have embarked." "God grant that we may do so!" answered Galahad, "For, as God is my help, I know nothing that might make me as happy as your coming here, for I have long desired this and it pleases me very much."

And so chance brought together again the three companions whom chance had separated. And so they rode on together for a long time until it happened that one day they came to the castle of Corbenic. And when they entered and the king recognized them, the joy they felt was wondrously great, for all within realized that the coming of those three signaled the end of the adventures of the castle, which had long endured. And the news spread here and there until all those in the castle came out to see what had happened. And king Pellés wept over Galahad, who was his nephew, as did the others there, who had not seen him since he was a child.

After they removed their arms, Elyezer, the son of King Pellés, conveyed them before the Broken Sword, mentioned earlier in this tale; this is the sword with which Joseph had been wounded in the thigh. And after it was taken out of the sheath and he told them how it came to be broken, Bors picked it up to see if it could be repaired. But this could not be. When he saw that he must fail to accomplish this, he gave the sword to Perceval and said: "Sir, see if you can succeed at this adventure." "Gladly," he said. So he took up the sword just as it was and brought the two pieces together; but he could not rejoin them in any way. And when he saw this, he said to Galahad: "Sir, we have failed at this adventure. Now it is up to you to attempt it, and if you fail too, I believe that no man is capable of bringing it to a conclusion." Then Galahad seized the two pieces of the sword, brought them together, and at once they were joined together so perfectly that no man could tell where it was that the break had been, nor—in fact—that the sword had ever been broken. When the companions saw this, they said that this was a fair beginning, as God had demonstrated to them, and that they believed very much that they would easily succeed at the other adventures since this one had been completed in such a fashion. And when those in the castle saw that the adventure of the sword had been concluded, they celebrated with enthusiasm. And they gave the sword to Bors, saying that it could be put to no better purpose, for he was a knight of exceptional worthiness and virtue.

When the hour of vespers approached, the weather began to change and darken, and a wind great and marvelous arose that roared throughout the palace. And it was so hot that many within thought they would be burned up, while several passed out from the great fear they felt. And just then they heard a voice that spoke these words: "Let those who are not to sit at the table of Jesus Christ go their way, for now is the time that true knights are to be nourished by heavenly food." When they heard these words, they all departed from the place without delay, save for king Pellés, who was a very worthy man and had lived a saintly life, Elyezer his son, and a young girl, the king's niece, who at that time was the most saintly and blessed being known anywhere. And with these three remained the three companions to see what sign Our Lord would make manifest to them. And after waiting a while, they saw coming through the door nine armed knights, who removed their helmets and their arms and then came up to Galahad, bowed toward him and spoke these words: "Sir, we have made great haste to be with you at the table where the exalted meal shall be served." And he said that they had come in good time, for they too had only just arrived. And they all took their seats within the palace, and Galahad asked from whence they had come. And three said they were from Gaul, three others from Ireland, and the last three that they were from Denmark.

And while they were speaking, they saw issuing from one of the rooms within a bed made of wood that four damsels were carrying. And on this bed was lying a worthy man who seemed terribly stricken, and there was a crown of gold on his head. And when they entered the palace, they put him down and departed. And that man lifted up his head and said to Galahad: "Sir, you are quite welcome here! I have been very eager to see you and have waited a long time for your coming, in such pain and misery that no other man could suffer this as long as I have. But, as God be pleased, the time has now come when this pain will be alleviated, for I will now pass out of this world just as it has been long promised to me."

And while they were exchanging these words, they heard a voice that said: "Let him who has not been a companion on the Quest of the Holy Grail make his way from here, for it is not right that he remain here any longer." And as soon as these words were spoken, king Pellés, Elyezer his son, and the maiden went out. And when the palace was empty, save for those who considered themselves companions of the Quest of the Holy Grail, it then seemed to those remaining within that from the direction heaven came toward them a man dressed as if he were a bishop, with a cross in his hand and a mitre on his head. And four angels were bearing him in a richly adorned chair, and they seated him close to the table where the Holy Grail had been put. The man who seemed a bishop as he was borne forward had inscribed on his forehead letters that read: "See here Josephus, the first Christian bishop, the same man that Our Lord consecrated in the spiritual palace of the city of Sarraz." And the knights who looked upon this understood the writing, but they marveled greatly that such a thing might be, for this Josephus of whom the message spoke had passed away more than three hundred years before. And right away he spoke to him, saying: "Now you knights of the Lord God, servants of Jesus Christ, do not be dismayed that you look upon me here before you just as you look upon this holy vessel. For just as I served it on earth, so I continue to serve it in spirit."

After saying this, he walked toward the table made of silver and sunk down to his elbows and knees before the altar. And after remaining there in this fashion for a long time, he heard the door of the room open and slam shut with great force. And he looked in that direction, as did the others as well; and through it they saw come through that door the angels who had brought Josephus to that place. Two of them were carrying a pair of candles, and the third a towel of red samite cloth, and the fourth a lance that bled so swiftly that drops from it trickled down into a container he held with his other hand. And the two put their candles on the table, and the third angel held the lance directly above the Holy Vessel, so that the blood that flowed down the shaft should run into it. And as soon as these things had been done, Josephus got up, lifted the lance up somewhat from the Holy Vessel, and covered it with the towel.

Then Josephus acted as if he were about to begin the sacrifice of the mass. And, pausing a bit before the vessel, he took from it a wafer that had the appearance of bread. And as he elevated it, he caused to descend from the heavens a figure in the guise of a child, whose face was as red and inflamed as fire. And this child entered into the bread; all those in the palace saw clearly that the bread took on the form of a human being. And after Josephus had held it for some time, he put the bread back into the vessel.

After Josephus did all these things, which a priest does during the service of the mass, he went over to Galahad and kissed him, saying that he should kiss his companions in the same fashion. And this is what he did. And when he, then Josephus spokes these words to them: "Servants of Jesus Christ, you who have labored in your journey to look upon some of the mysteries of the Holy Grail, seat yourselves now at this table, and you will be nourished by the most exalted food and the very best that knights have ever tasted, and it is from the hands of your Savior himself. And you can certainly say that you have labored as men should, for you will today receive the most sublime reward that knights have ever received." After speaking these words, Josephus vanished from their midst so mysteriously t they did not know where he had gone. And they then took their places at the table. Their fear was great, and they wept so tenderly their faces were soon wet with tears.

Then the companions looked at the Vessel and saw emerging from it a man who seemed completely naked, and his hands and feet were bleeding, as was his body. And he said to them: "My knights, my servants, and my faithful sons, who in this earthly life have become spiritual in your nature, who have sought me with such diligence I can no longer conceal myself from you, it is just and right that you now witness this part of my mysteries and secrets, for your accomplishments have earned you places at my table, at which no knight has eaten since the time of Joseph of Arimathea. Others have partaken of what is fitting for servants to have. By this I mean to say that the knights of this place and many others have been nourished by the grace of his Holy Vessel. But they have not experienced what you will now. Now take and receive the exalted nourishment you have so long desired, and for which you have labored for so long on your journeys."

Then he took up the Holy Vessel and went over to Galahad, who knelt down as he gave his Savior to him. And this he received with joy, his hands joined prayerfully. And each one of the others did the same, and to all it seemed as if he placed a host made of bread in his mouth. After they all received this exalted nourishment, it seemed so incredibly sweet that they thought deep in their hearts that every kind of sweetness had entered into their bodies. The one who had nourished them in this fashion said this to Galahad: "Son, you who are as pure and free from the stain of sin as any earthly man might be, do you know what it is that I am holding in my hands?" "Not at all," he replied, "If you do not tell me." "This is," he said, "the platter on which Jesus Christ was served the paschal lamb along with his disciples. It is the platter that has served as they wished all those I have found in my service. It is the platter that greatly troubles those unbelievers who look upon it. And because it has to their satisfaction served everyone, it is rightly called the Holy Grail. Now you have seen what you have so fervently wished to see, and which you have desired. But you have still not seen as clearly as you will. And do you know where this will be? In the city of Sarraz, in the spiritual palace, and for this reason you must go there and accompany the Holy Vessel, for it must depart tonight from the kingdom of Logres, where it will never again be seen, nor will the adventures it gave rise to ever again take place. And do you know why it must depart? Because it is not served or honored properly by those of this land. For they have sought out an inferior way of life, and a more worldly one, even though they had once been nourished by the grace of the Holy Vessel. And because they have paid it so little honor in return, I am divesting them of the grace that was previously shown them. And for this reason it is my wish that you travel in the morning as far as the ocean, and there you will come upon the boat in which you took the sword with the strange belt. And I do not wish you to go alone. Instead, you should take Perceval and Bors with you. Furthermore, because I do not want you to leave this land without taking along what will cure the Maimed King, you should take with you some of the blood from this lance, with which you should anoint his limbs.

For this is the only thing that can bring about his cure—nothing else can make it happen." "But my lord," said Galahad, "why do you not allow me to bring the others with me?" "Here is the reason," he said, "that it is not my wish. This should be done as a figure of what occurred with my apostles. For just as they ate with me on the day of the Last Supper, so you ate with me this day at the table of the Holy Grail. And you will be twelve, just as there were twelve apostles. And I am the thirteenth placed above you as your master and shepherd. And just as I dispatched them all to journey throughout the world and preach the holy law, so I send you too, some one way, others on another path. And all will die on this quest, save one." And then he gave them his blessing, vanishing so mysteriously they did not know what became of him, save that he ascended toward the heavens, for this they saw.

And Galahad went to the lance that was lying on the table and touched the blood with his fingers, afterward going over to the Maimed King and anointing him on his wounded legs. And the king put on his clothes at once, jumping out of the bed hale and hearty. And he gave thanks to Our Lord for having looked upon him with such kindness. And he lived a long time after this, but not in a worldly fashion, for quite soon he entered a monastery of white monks. And Our Lord performed many a miracle for his sake, but the story does not deal with these matters, which are not pertinent to its themes.

Around midnight, after they had prayed a long time to Our Lord to protect and guard their souls in whatever region they traveled through, a voice suddenly spoke to them, saying: "My sons, and not only those who are so by nature, my friends and not only my warriors, you are to leave this place behind and go wherever you believe you can do best, and just as adventure moves you." Hearing this, they responded with a single voice: "Father of the heavens, blessed be You Who deigns to keep watch over your sons and those dear to you! Now we will see clearly that we have not spent our time in vain."

Soon afterward they left the palace and walked down into the courtyard where they found arms and horses. They put on their armor and mounted their horses at once. And they made their way from the castle on horseback. And they talked among themselves, both to get better acquainted but also the better to know exactly where they now were. And they soon discovered that of the three from Gaul, one was Claudins, the son of king Claudas, and the other two, from different parts of that country, were men of similarly noble lineage. When the time came for them to part company, they kissed one another as do brothers, weeping quite tenderly. All spoke to Galahad: "Lord, know it for the truth that we have never felt such joy as we did at that hour when we became your companions, nor have we ever felt such sadness as at this departure, which has come upon us so quickly and will take us from you. But we see clearly that this separation is what pleases Our Lord; and for that reason we must do this without too much sorrow." "My good lords," said Galahad, "if you found friendship in my company, I did just the same in yours. But you see clearly that we may no longer journey together. And so I commend you to God, and I beg you, should you come to the court of King Arthur, that you greet on my behalf Lancelot my father and the others of the Round Table." And they said that if they journeyed there they would not forget to do so.

Soon afterward they parted company. And Galahad, along with his two companions, rode on until all three of them came to the sea, and this journey lasted a bit less than four days. They would have arrived even sooner, but they did not take the most direct path, being strangers who did not know all the roads. Arriving at the ocean, they found the ship on the shore, the one in which the Sword of the Strange Belt had previously been found, and they found the inscription on the ship's rail that said no man should embark thereon who did not firmly believe in Jesus Christ. And, moving closer, they looked around and saw that the silver table which had been with the Maimed King was now standing in the middle of a bed that had been placed amidships. And the Holy Grail was standing atop it, covered with red samite, fashioned like the veil that covers a chalice. The companions marveled at this wondrous turn of events, and moved forward to point it out to one another, saying that this was good fortune indeed for the object they loved and desired the most to journey with them to the place where they were to remain. They each made the sign of the cross, commending themselves to Our Lord, and embarking onto the ship. And as soon as they were all aboard, the wind, which had before been quiet and breezy, struck the sail with such terrifying force that it pushed the ship quickly from the shore and onto the high seas. And then the power of the wind increased, driving the ship along ever faster.

They traversed the water in this fashion for a long time, not knowing which way God was conveying them. Whenever Galahad took his rest or awakened from sleep he prayed to Our Lord that that He would allow him to pass from this life, right then, as he was making this request. And Galahad offered up this prayer morning and night, so often that a heavenly voice at last spoke to him: "Do not be dismayed, Galahad, for Our Lord will do what you wish, just as you are asking; at that time you ask for the death of the body, this prayer will be granted, and you will receive the life of the soul and a joy that endures forever." Now Perceval heard Galahad making this request many times, and he wondered why he did so. And he asked, as his companion and on the bond of faith that joined them, why he should pray God for this. "I will readily explain," said Galahad. "The other day, when we looked upon some of the mysteries of the Holy Grail that Our Savior out of his holy pity made manifest to us, as I saw revealed secrets that were not revealed to everyone, but only to those who minister to Jesus Christ, at that moment when I saw such things earthly men cannot imagine in their hearts or put into words, such an immense sweetness overcame my heart and I was filled with such great joy that had I passed at that very moment out of the world, I know no man had ever died in more blessedness than I felt at that time. For before me there was such a great company of angels and spiritual beings, I should have been transported from the earthly into the spiritual realm, into the joy possessed by the glorious martyrs and those beloved of Our Lord. And because I believe that I will experience again the sight of such great bliss, or perhaps even greater bliss, I say this prayer you have heard me utter. And so I believe I will leave this world behind, according to the will of Our Lord, when I look upon the mysteries of the Holy Grail."

This was how Galahad made known to Perceval his coming death, just as the answering voice from heaven had instructed him. And so too, just as I described it for you earlier, did those of the kingdom of Logres forfeit by their sinfulness the Holy Grail, which many times had nourished and sustained them. And just as Our Lord sent the Grail to Galahad and Joseph and its other inheritors because of their goodness, so he deprived evildoers of it because he found them wicked. And in this way you can clearly see that evil-minded descendants forfeited through their wickedness all that those of virtue acquired by moral living.

The companions spent a long time at sea, until one day they finally said to Galahad: "In this bed that was prepared for you (as indicated by what was written about it), you have never taken your rest. And you should do so, for the letter states that you are to repose yourself thereon." And he said he would take his rest there. And he lay down there and slept for a long time. And awakening, he looked around and spied the city of Sarraz. Then a voice came to them that said: "Make your way from the ship, knights of Jesus Christ, and when you enter the city take with you this table of silver just as it is, never putting it down until you go inside the spiritual palace, where Our Lord consecrated Josephus as the first bishop."

Just as they were making to remove the table where it had been placed, they looked over the water and saw coming toward them the ship into which they had long ago embarked the sister of Perceval. Seeing it, they said to each other: "In God's name, this damsel has kept well the agreement she made with us, following us to this place." Then they lifted up the table of silver and took it out of the ship, with Bors and Perceval holding it in front and Galahad behind, and in this fashion they moved off toward the city. But when they came to the gate, Galahad felt himself quite tired out because of the weight of the table, which was quite heavy. And he spied a man on crutches slumped by the gate in hopes of receiving alms from passers-by, who often did so out of love for Jesus Christ. When Galahad neared him, he called out to the man, saying: "My good man, come over here and help me so that we might carry this table over there into the palace." "Good sir," he replied, "What are you saying? For ten years now I have been unable to even walk without someone helping me." "Don't worry about it," said Galahad, "but just get to your feet. Have you fear because you have been healed." And as soon as Galahad had uttered these words, the man tried to see if he could stand; and when he did try, he discovered that he was indeed as hale and hearty as he had ever been at any time in his life. Then he walked quickly to the table and took hold of the corner across from Galahad. And as he moved into the city, he proclaimed to everyone whom he met there the miracle that God had performed for his sake.

When they had made their way up to the palace, they saw the throne that Our Lord had prepared for Josephus to sit upon in years gone by. Just then crowds of people, an incredible number, rushed up from the city to see the maimed man who had just recently been made whole. After the companions did everything they had been asked to do, they returned to the waterside and embarked on the ship where the body of Perceval's sister was lying. They picked up the bed with her upon it and brought it to the palace; and there she was buried with the ceremony proper to a king's daughter.

When the king of the city, who was called Escorant, caught sight of the three companions, he asked them who they were and what exactly it was that they had brought to the palace on the table of silver. They answered all his questions as fully as they could, and as truthfully, including what they knew about the nature of the Grail and the power with which God had endowed it. And he was an untrustworthy and cruel man who reflected perfectly the evil of his pagan lineage. So he believed not one word that they said, but declared instead that they were faithless traitors of some kind. And he waited until he saw they had disarmed, and then he had them seized by his men and thrown into prison. And he kept them in that prison for an entire year, never letting them out. But in the end this turned to their advantage, for as soon as they were thrown into prison, Our Lord, who had not forgotten them, but sent them the Holy Grail, which kept them company, filling them with its grace the whole time they languished in prison.

After as year had passed, one day Galahad made his complaint to Our Lord, and he said these words: "Lord, it seems to me that I have remained long enough in this world. If you please, take me from it now." On that day it happened that king Escorant was lying ill from a disease that soon would kill him. And he summoned them before him and asked for them to forgive the wrong he had done them. And willingly they pardoned him, and he died soon afterward. And after he had been buried, those in the city were quite dismayed, for they did not know who they should now make king. And so they held a council for a long time, and while they were debating the matter, a voice spoke to them saying: "Choose the youngest of the three companions, and that man will protect you well and give you good counsel as long as he remains among you." And they did as the voice commanded, choosing Galahad to be lord over them whether he so wished or not, and they placed the crown on his head. And this weighed heavily on him. But since he saw that this is how it must be, he agreed, for otherwise they would have slain him.

After Galahad came into lordship over the land, he had installed over the table of silver a golden ark inlaid with precious stones that enclosed the holy vessel. And every morning, as soon as he arose, he and his companions made their way to the holy Vessel, where they said their prayers and oriisons.

After a year had passed, on the same day Galahad had received the crown to wear, he and his companions arose and made their way to the palace that is termed spiritual, where they looked in the direction of the Grail. And there they saw a man dressed much like a bishop, and he was kneeling before the table and recounting his sins. And around him was a multitude of angels, just as if he were Jesus Christ himself. And after he had spent a good while on his knees, he stood up and began celebrating mass in honor of the Glorious Mother of God. And when it came time for the sacrifice of the mass, as he lifted the patten off the Sacred Vessel he called out to Galahad and spoke these words to him: "Come forward, you servant of Jesus Christ, and you will see what you have desired so much to see." And he stepped ahead and looked inside the Holy Vessel. And as he made his examination, he began to tremble violently as soon as mortal flesh begins to gaze upon spiritual things. Then Galahad raised up his hands toward the heavens and said: "Lord, I worship you and give you thanks for having brought my desire to fruition, for now I see openly what no tongue can describe or heart conceive. Here I witness the well-spring of the great display of bravery and of what makes prowess possible. Here I gaze upon marvels that are beyond all other marvels! And since things have come to this pass, fair sweet Lord, namely that you have made it possible for me to see what I have always desired to see, I pray that you allow me, in the state I am now in and the great joy I feel, to pass on from this earthly life into heavenly existence."

As soon as Galahad made this request to Our Lord, the good man before the altar who was dressed as a bishop took the Corpus Domini from the table and offered it to Galahad. And this he received with all humility and with great devotion. And after he received it, the good man spoke these words to him: "Do you know," he said, "who I am?" "Lord, not in the least, unless you tell me." "Now you may come to know," he said, "that I am Josephus, the son of Joseph of Arimathea, and Our Lord has sent me to you as a companion. And do you know why he sent me rather than some other? Because you and I are similar in two ways: for you have gazed upon these marvels of the Holy Grail just as I have done; and you are a virgin, just as I am. And it is just that one virgin be a companion to another."

After he spoke these words, Galahad went up to Perceval and kissed him, doing the same to Bors. And he spoke these words: "Bors, greet my father Lancelot on my behalf as soon as you meet up with him." Then Galahad went back before the table, sinking down to his knees and elbows. And he did not remain long there before he fell face down on the floor of the palace, for the soul had fled from his body. And angels bore his soul away with great joy, blessing Our Lord all the while.

Once Galahad departed from them a great miracle occurred. A great hand appeared in the sky, but they could not see the body to which it belonged. And the hand went right to the Holy Vessel and seized it, taking up the Lance as well, and it took these things up toward the heavens, and the result has been that since that moment no other living man has laid eyes upon the Holy Grail.

When Perceval and Bors saw that Galahad was dead, they were more grief-stricken by this than by any else. And had they not been such virtuous men and of such unsullied character, they could have fallen into despair because of the great love they felt for him. And the people of that country grieved mightily for Galahad, and they were terribly distressed. The spot where he died became his tomb, and as soon as he was buried, Perceval made his way to a hermitage outside the city, and there he took the monk's habit. And Bors was with him, but he did not abandon his worldly dress because he was eager to return to the court of King Arthur. Perceval lived on for one year and three days in the hermitage, but then he passed away out of this world. And Bors had him buried by the side of his sister and Galahad in the spiritual palace.

When Bors saw that he alone remained in these far-off lands of Egypt, he departed from Sarraz dressed in his armor; coming to the sea, he embarked upon a ship. And his fortune was so good that soon enough he was borne into the land of Logres. And entering that country, he rode on for some days until he arrived at Camelot, where King Arthur then was. And at no other time had those there celebrated as they did when he arrived, for they thought for a long time that they had lost him since he had been gone for so many years out of the country.

After they ate, the king had come forward the clerks who were to put into writing the adventures of the knights from that place. And after Bors had related the adventures of the Holy Grail to which he himself had been witness, they were written down and preserved carefully in the library at Salisbury, and from these sources My Lord Walter Map composed his book of the Holy Grail out of love for his lord King Henry, who had then translated from Latin into French. And here the story falls silent, for it has nothing more to say about the adventures of the Holy Grail.

Notes

1. Based on John 10: 1–21.
2. Matthew 16:18.
3. Genesis 3:4.
4. Matthew 7:7.

La Mule sans Frein
(The Girl with the Mule)

Translated by William W. Kibler

The Girl with the Mule (*La Demoiselle à la mule*, or *La Mule sans Frein*) is one of many romances of which Gawain is the principal hero. The author, active in the early thirteenth century, names himself Paien de Maisières in line 14. Another short Gawain romance, *Le Chevalier à l'épée*, found in the same manuscript (Bern, Burgerbibliothek 354), may be by the same poet. Paien draws on numerous conventions of the genre: the contrast between the boastful but incompetent Sir Kay and the heroic Sir Gawain; the theme of the dispossessed younger sister; the beast-filled forest; the valley of serpents; the narrow bridge over treacherous waters; the whirling castle; multiple combats (against lions, knights, and dragons); the heads of defeated knights displayed on stakes; and the beheading game (also found in the *Perlesvaus* selection in this volume, as well as in the celebrated English romance, *Sir Gawain and the Green Knight*).

Whether because of deliberate ambiguity or rank incompetence, the tale is obscure in parts: for example, why does the sister need a champion to recover a bridle? why does she leave at the end without rewarding Sir Gawain as promised? what does the prologue have to do with the story? The first of these questions, at least, can be answered by reference to a German version of the same story, by Heinrich von dem Türlin: *Die Krône*. Here we learn that the bridle is key to a patrimony, seized by the one sister to the deprivation of the second, who then comes to court to demand justice. Similarly, in Chrétien de Troyes's *The Knight with the Lion (Yvain)*, the elder daughter of the Lord of White Thorn has refused to share their ancestral lands with her younger sister, who seeks redress at Arthur's court.

The edition used is that by R.C. Johnston and D.D.R. Owen, *Two Old French Gauvain Romances* (New York: Barnes & Noble, 1973).

The Girl with the Mule

    The peasant in his proverb says
that something old and put aside
can later prove most useful.
So it is sensible for each of us
5 to value what he has fully,
for worth can swiftly accrue
to something that proves useful.
The old ways are less prized
10 nowadays than new ones,
which are considered finer—
and they do appear to be better—
yet it happens so often
that the old ways are the best.
That is why Pagan of Mézières says
15 that one should always hold faster
to the old ways than the new.

La Mule sans Frein *(The Girl with the Mule)* (Kibler)

      Here begins an adventure
about a girl with a mule
who came to King Arthur's court.
20   It happened on the feast of Pentecost
that King Arthur held his court
at Carlisle, as was his custom.
There were many knights
who had come to court,
25 assembled from every land.
With the Queen were all
the ladies and maidens,
many of great beauty,
who had come to be at court.
30 The conversation was lively,
so after dinner the barons
went strolling through the hall
and into the upper rooms.
From the windows they looked
35 down over a meadow below.
Scarcely had they come there
when they saw a fair
and lovely girl swiftly
approaching the castle,
40 all alone and on a mule.
She was riding so rapidly
because her mule had
no bridle, but only a halter.
The knights puzzled among themselves
45 what this might mean:
after discussing it at length,
they decided that the Queen
would know, if she were there,
what brought the girl into this land.
50 "Kay," said Gawain, "go fetch her,
and tell the King, too,
that nothing should keep him
from coming here at once."
The seneschal went straight
55 to where the King and Queen were.
"My lord," said Kay, "come up!
Your knights are calling for you."
The King asked him straight away:
"Seneschal, what do they want of us?"
60 "Come with me," he replied,
"And I will tell you;
I'll show you something unusual
we all have seen."
      At that moment the maiden came
65 and dismounted outside the hall.
Gawain ran to greet her,
and many of the others hastened
to serve and honor her.
But from her face it was clear

70 that she had suffered much
and was in no mood to make merry.
The King sent for her and she was brought
before him; as soon as she neared
the King, she greeted him and said:
75 "My lord, you can clearly see
that I am overcome with grief.
I will always be this way,
and will never cheer up,
until my bridle, which has been wickedly
80 stolen from me, is given back;
that is why I've lost all happiness.
I know that I could get it back
if there were a knight in this castle
who would dare to promise
85 to undertake this journey.
And if he returns it to me,
I will be his alone
as soon as I have my bridle back,
undisputed and without question.
90 And for love of him I will
immediately and without any hesitation
give him my mule,
which will lead him to a beautiful castle,
strong and splendidly situated,
95 but which he won't hold peacefully."
      Upon hearing this, Sir Kay stepped forward
and said that he'd go seek the bridle,
no matter where it was.
But he wanted her to kiss him first,
100 before he set off, and then he went
at once to claim his kiss.
"Stop, my lord," she said. "Until
you have the bridle I don't want
to grant you the kiss.
105 But when the bridle is returned,
then the castle will be given you,
and the kiss, and the other."
Kay did not dare trouble her further.
Then she in turn commanded him
110 to do nothing to keep the mule
from going wherever it wanted.
Kay had no desire to remain
any longer there among them.
He went immediately to the mule
115 and mounted it by the stirrup.
He did not wish for company,
and when they saw that he was going
off alone, with no companion,
and was moreover going unarmed,

120 save only his sword,
the maiden stood there weeping,
for she saw clearly—and I agree—
that she'd never get her bridle
back this time, no matter what he,
125 who was riding off upon the mule
at breakneck speed, might say.
And the mule, which had learned
the route well, guided him well.
    Kay rode for so long
130 that he was swallowed up
in a deep and thick forest.
Scarcely had he entered it
than the beasts of the place
all gathered around: there were
135 lions and tigers and leopards.
They all came on account of
Kay, who was to cross there.
But before he could pass through,
the beasts all hastened up
140 and came to meet him.
Kay was more frightened
than he'd ever been in his life
and said that had he not already
set out upon this path, nothing in the world
145 could ever make him
enter these woods again.
But the beasts, out of consideration
for the lady and to honor
the mule when they saw it,
150 fell to their knees on the ground.
Thus in honor of the lady
they all bent their legs,
and in this way they can be assured
of having their lair and free run of the forest.
155 They could not honor her more highly.
But Kay did not wish to remain there
and left as quickly as he could.
The lions and the leopards
all returned to their dens.
160   The mule led Kay
down a narrow path
which was seldom used.
The mule knew the path well,
having taken it frequently,
165 and it led out of the forest
where Kay had suffered much.
So there he was, out of the forest.
But before he had ridden far at all
he came into a valley
170 that was uncommonly deep and wide,
and uncommonly dangerous too,
so very grim and shadowy
that no one in the world
could pass through that valley
175 and not fear for his life.
Yet he had no choice but to pass;
like it or not, he had to enter.
So he entered, having no option.
With great trepidation he entered,
180 though he was scared to death,
for he saw in its depths
huge snakes and dragons,
scorpions and other beasts,
spitting fire from their heads,
185 which frightened him immensely.
But the stench troubled him even more,
because he'd never been in such a foul-smelling
place at any time in his whole life—
he was lucky he didn't tumble into it!
190 He nearly fainted, and said to himself
that he would rather be
with the lions in the woods
where he'd been earlier.
At the very height of summer
195 or in the hottest of heat waves
it was still as cold in that valley
as if it were the very heart of winter,
for the bitterness of winter,
I believe, reigns there forever.
200 The north wind howls constantly,
bringing the deep cold with it;
the other winds blow there too,
crashing together in that valley.
There is such misery there
205 that I couldn't tell the half of it.
Yet he pushed onward
until he reached the end,
where he saw a plain
and was somewhat relieved.
210 With great effort he freed himself
from the heat and the stench;
he was afraid he'd never see the day
that he'd get out of this place.
    He dismounted in the plain
215 and unsaddled his mule.
Then he saw water in the middle
of the plain, quite close: a spring
that was very clear and wholesome.
It added to the beauty of the spot,
220 being surrounded by flowers,
pine trees and junipers.

His mule began to drink from it
at once, for she was very thirsty.
To refresh himself, Sir Kay too
225 began to drink from the fountain,
which seemed beautiful to him.
Then he resaddled his mule
and went trotting off,
for the journey seemed endless to him
230 and he was afraid he'd never find
what he was searching for.
    Kay rode on until he came
to an immense body of water;
he was astounded to see
235 how deep and wide it was,
and he couldn't find a boat or raft,
nor any bridge or crossing.
He rode along the shore
until he happened to find
240 a very narrow plank;
but it could bear their weight
if he dared get on it,
for it was all of iron.
He was a little afraid to cross
245 because the water seemed so black,
and he didn't believe he could find
any way to get across.
He decided it was better to turn back
than to risk his life there—
250 but he could have been better
    advised.
So he said to himself he would be
    damned
if he'd risk his life
for such a small and worthless thing.
The way he'd come
255 seemed very dangerous indeed,
but crossing over the plank
seemed much more risky yet.
    At that, Kay turned around
and started to retrace his route.
260 He kept carefully to the path
along which he had arrived.
He came straight to the valley
where he found the stinking reptiles.
He didn't stop until he'd ridden
265 straight through and exited;
his body was in great pain,
broken and fatigued.
He plunged into the forest
where the wild beasts are.
270 They came toward him
as soon as they saw him;
they rushed at him so ferociously

that I thought they'd eat him,
were it not for the mule
275 whom they strove to honor.
But Kay was so frightened
that he'd rather give up the gold
of ten cities, or all the wealth of Pavia,
than have to enter these woods.
280 He came out of the forest
onto the prairie before the castle.
    King Arthur, who was delighted
to see him returning,
had come to the windows,
285 along with Gawain and Gueheriet,
my lord Yvain and Girflez,
and numerous other knights
whom he had summoned.
When they saw the seneschal coming,
290 they sent for the maiden.
"Come along, miss," they said.
"You will soon have your bridle;
Sir Kay is nearly here
and he has it, you can be sure."
295 But they were mistaken,
because he didn't have it, and she
    shouted:
"Truly, if he were the one to fetch it
he wouldn't be coming back so soon."
Then she grabbed and tore at her
    hair—
300 you should have seen the torment
and suffering she endured!
"So help me God," she said, "if it
were up to me, I'd rather be dead!"
With a smile, Gawain said to her:
305 "Miss, grant me a boon."
"What boon, sir?"—"Don't cry any
    more:
cheer up and have something to eat.
You'll never be unhappy again,
because I'll help you wholeheartedly
310 and bring your bridle back to you."
—"My lord," she replied, "did you say
that I'd have my bridle without fail?"
"Yes indeed."—"Then I'll eat
and be merry, but you'll have
315 to swear it to me." My lord Gawain
swore that if ever anyone were to have
    it,
he would be the one,
no matter where it was.
Then the maiden arose
320 and walked to the end of the room
to her mule. Kay retired

to his quarters grief-stricken,
overcome with sadness and pain.
After they told the King
325 how Kay had behaved poorly,
and therefore didn't dare to come to court,
the King agreed it was a serious matter.
I don't wish to speak further of him
at this time, but you
330 will hear more of how
the girl approached the King.
   She spoke at such length
that Gawain promised her
that the bridle would be returned;
335 he said, too, that if he had leave
he would return it personally
no matter how carefully it was guarded.
The King and the Queen each said,
"I freely grant him my leave,"
340 as they granted it. The girl bowed to them
and encouraged Gawain to make haste.
But Gawain wished to embrace her
first, before he left;
it was right that he kiss her,
345 and she willingly kissed him.
Now the girl is greatly comforted,
for she knows full well that, no matter what,
she'll get it back without fail:
No need to plead her case further.
350 Gawain approached the mule
and leapt into the saddle.
The girl blessed him
more than thirty times
and everyone commended him to God.
355 Gawain didn't tarry:
he set off immediately
and didn't forget his sword.
   He entered the prairie
that led him toward the forest
360 where the beasts lurked,
and the lions and the leopards.
He hastened in that direction
and all the beasts came forth
to meet him as he passed.
365 As soon as they caught sight
of the mule and recognized it,
they fell on their knees to the ground.
They humbled themselves before the knight
out of love and recognition;
370 and here is what this means:

that he will recapture the bridle
no matter how carefully it is guarded.
When Gawain saw the beasts
he was sure that Kay
375 had taken fright as he passed by,
and that that was why he had turned back.
With a smile Gawain rode through the forest
and came to the narrow path
that led him straight to the valley
380 that was so noxious.
Gawain rode on fearlessly
without stopping, until he
came out on the other side.
He dismounted in the plain
385 where the clear spring gushed forth.
He removed the saddle from his mule,
wiped it down, and readied it again.
He did not stay there long,
for the journey seemed hard to him.
390   Gawain rode on steadily
until he reached the black waters
that were wilder than the Loire.
All I want to say about them
is that no one had ever seen such ugly,
395 horrible and fearsome waters.
I don't know what more I could tell you,
but I can tell you without lying
that this was the devil's river:
to all appearances, all you
400 can see there are devils.
And there is no way across.
He rode along the shore
until he found the plank,
no more than a palm's breadth wide,
405 but fashioned all of iron.
He wasn't at all afraid of crossing,
but he could clearly see now
that Kay didn't dare go on
and turned back at this point.
410 Gawain commended himself to God
and spurred the mule; she leapt
onto the plank, which didn't give,
but it often happened
that half of one of her hooves
415 stuck out over the edge of the plank.
It was no wonder he was afraid,
but he was even more frightened
to feel the plank swaying beneath them.
With great effort he crossed,
420 but there is no question
that had the mule not known

the way, he'd have fallen in;
this time he made it safely over.
    He hurried on.
425 He whom Fortune favored
entered upon a narrow path
that led him to a beautiful castle,
strong and splendidly situated.
The castle was so mighty
430 that it could withstand any assault,
for it was closed all around
by a large, wide, and deep moat.
And it was further enclosed
by massive, heavy, sharp stakes,
435 and on every stake—
except one where it was lacking—
was a knight's severed head.
Gawain wouldn't give up.
He couldn't see a gate or door:
440 the castle was whirling
as fast as a racing mill wheel
or like a top that had been
spun from its cord.
He needed to enter at once,
445 but he was very puzzled
and wondered to himself
what all this might mean.
He would like to understand everything,
and he is no coward.
450 So he stopped on the drawbridge
right in front of the gate
and Courage exhorted him
not to renounce his good deed.
The castle was whirling unceasingly,
455 but he said he'd stand there
until he could enter, whatever the pain.
He was really exasperated
that no sooner was the gate in front
of him, than it was gone again.
460 He chose his time carefully
and said that he would enter
when the gate was exactly opposite him,
no matter the consequences.
So as soon as he saw the gate coming,
465 he spurred his mule sharply
and she leapt forward
and raced though the gate,
but she was struck so hard
on her rump that nearly half
470 of her tail was clipped away.
    So he entered the gate
and the mule, happy to be
home again, carried him swiftly
through the streets of the town.

475 Gawain was a little sad
not to find any woman,
man or child inside.
He pulled up right under
the overhanging eave of a house,
480 but before he could dismount
a dwarf came racing down
the street and hailed him,
saying: "Welcome, Sir Gawain!"
Never slow, Gawain
485 returned his greeting at once,
saying: "Who are you, dwarf?
Who's your lady, who's your lord?"
The dwarf wouldn't deign to reply,
but only turned as if to go.
490 Gawain didn't understand what he was
    seeing
and wondered what this could mean:
The dwarf wouldn't answer him!
If he'd lower himself to confront him,
Gawain would exact an explanation;
495 but he let him go away.
    Gawain immediately leapt down.
Through an archway he saw
a cavernous cellar
dug far beneath the earth.
500 He said to himself that he wanted to
    explore
all its hidden corners before going
    inside;
he wouldn't be worth a penny
if he didn't check it out completely
    first.
Just then he saw a churl
505 with a shaggy head of hair
coming toward him up the stairs.
The sight alone made him feel
that he'd wasted his trip coming here.
The churl seemed terribly forbidding:
510 he was taller than St. Martial,
and on his shoulder he carried
a huge and heavy axe.
Sir Gawain was most taken aback
by the look of the churl:
515 he resembled a Moor from Mauritania
or one of those peasants from
    Champagne
all tanned by the sun.
He stopped in front of Gawain
and greeted him at once;
520 Gawain looked intently
at his face and appearance:
"And the best to you, too,"

said Gawain, "if you mean what you say."
—"Indeed I do, and I think you're
525 pretty brave to come in here.
But you've wasted your steps,
because the bridle you've come looking for
could not be more tightly locked up,
with strong guards all around it.
530 You'll have to fight a mighty combat,
so help me God, before you capture it."
—"Don't worry about a thing," replied Gawain,
"I'll put up a tremendous fight,
so help me God; I'll die
535 rather than leave without the bridle."
The churl didn't delay any longer
but, seeing the night approaching,
he began to assist Gawain
and took him straight to his lodgings.
540 He did his best to make him comfortable
and took care of the mule as well.
Since there were no servants in the house,
the churl brought him two basins
and a broad white towel
545 so he could wash his hands.
The table was already laid
where Gawain could sit to eat,
and so, feeling hungry, he ate.
The churl served huge quantities
550 and Sir Gawain ate his fill.
As soon as he had eaten,
the churl took down the table
and brought him water to wash up.
He prepared a tall and wide bed
555 for Gawain to sleep in,
for he wanted to make him comfortable,
as one should such a knight.
He returned at once to his side:
"Gawain," he said, "you will sleep
560 all alone tonight in this bed,
without anyone objecting to it.
But before you go to bed,
I have a friendly offer for you:
because I've heard so much about you,
565 and since I see my chance,
I have a game of choice for you;
you may take whichever you want."
So Gawain promised him
he'd make a choice, whatever it might be.
570 "Speak up," said Gawain, "for I will

choose at once, so help me God,
and I'll not be proved a liar,
for I find you to be a splendid host."
—"Cut off my head tonight,"
575 he said," with this sharp axe;
cut it off, but on condition that
I cut off yours tomorrow morning,
when I return. Make your choice,"
he said, "no one's stopping you!"
580 —"I'd be pretty stupid," said Gawain,
"if I didn't know which option to take;
so here's my choice, for better or for worse:
Tonight I'll cut off your head,
and tomorrow I'll offer mine,
585 if you want me to give it to you."
—"Cursed be anyone who'd ask for more,"
said the churl. "Come on now!"
Then he led him off. The churl
stretched out his neck on a block.
590 Gawain immediately took the axe
and, without any hesitation, cut off
the churl's head with a single blow.
The churl leapt promptly
to his feet, grabbed his head,
595 and went back into the cellar.
Gawain returned to his bed
and lay down in it at once;
he slept soundly until morning.
The next day Gawain arose
600 at dawn and donned his armor.
Shortly afterwards the churl arrived,
in good spirits and completely healed,
with his axe on his shoulder.
When he saw the head he'd cut off
605 reattached, Gawain could well
consider himself a fool,
yet he wasn't scared of him at all.
And the churl, who wasn't the least bit troubled, spoke up at once:
610 "Gawain," he said, "I've returned
to remind you of our agreement."
—"I'll not deny it in the least,
for I can clearly see it cannot be opposed
and must be honored."
615 He should have opposed it,
but he did not wish to act disloyally.
Because he had given his promise,
he said he'd keep it willingly.
"Then step forward," said the churl.
620 Gawain went outside and laid
his neck out on the block for him.

Then the churl said to him:
"Stretch it out all the way!"
—"That's all there is, by God.
625 So strike your blow if you've a mind to."
So help me God, it would be a sad
and awful thing were he to strike!
He raised his axe over his head,
but it was only to frighten Gawain,
630 as he had no intention of touching him
because he had honored
the promise he had made
and proven himself true to his word.
　　Then Gawain asked him
635 how he could win the bridle.
"You will soon find out," he said.
"Ere the hour of noon is past
you will face a mighty battle;
you won't think it a joking matter,
640 for you will have to fight
against two chained lions.
The bridle is guarded ferociously
and not easily given up.
May hell's fires burn me!
645 I know those lions are so fierce
that even if there were ten knights,
not one would escape alive
if they were allowed to fight—
but I'll be there for you!
650 But before you go into battle
you need to eat a little something
to keep up your strength
and so you won't be disheartened."
—"Eating would be a waste of time,"
655 said Gawain, "in any event.
But fetch me some armor
so I can equip myself."
—"In the castle," he said, "is a good horse
that hasn't been ridden in months,
660 and there's lots of other equipment
which I'll gladly lend you.
But before you don your armor,
I'll show you the beasts
to see whether you'll think better
665 of fighting against the lions."
—"So help me St. Jude," said Gawain,
"I don't want to see them
until it is time to fight.
Bring me my armor at once!"
670 Quickly the churl, who knew
what needed to be done, armed him
with splendid armor from head to toe,
and brought him a warhorse.
Gawain mounted by the stirrups,
675 for there was no fear in his heart.
The churl brought him seven shields,
all of which he would sorely need.
　　Then the churl went to unchain
one of the lions, which he brought
forth.
680 And the lion displayed such ferocity,
such great fury and mad rage,
that it tore at the ground with its claws
and ripped at the chain with its teeth.
When the lion realized it was outside
685 and caught sight of the knight,
the hairs bristled up on its back
and it beat its sides with its tail.
Whoever fought against him
would have to be clever with his sword,
690 to be sure, and not have the cowardly
heart of a goat or a slug.
The churl set him loose
before the castle, on a leveled terrace.
Gawain didn't flinch, but flew
695 to the attack with his sword drawn;
The lion raised its head and swiped
at Gawain, who returned the blow;
they both fought hard.
With its first blow, the lion
700 knocked loose Gawain's shield,
and then pushed it away from him.
The churl readied another
for him, and Gawain seized it.
In his rage, he struck the lion
705 on its back with his sword,
but the skin was so thick and tough
that he couldn't cut through.
The lion was furious
and turned on him like a storm,
710 striking him with his tail
on the head, knocking away
the second and the third shields,
and leaving nothing of the fourth,
either.
"Don't hold back a minute more,
715 by my beard!" shouted the churl.
My lord Gawain struck the lion
such a mighty blow that his sword
pierced through the beast's hide
and wounded it to the death.
720 "Now let the other attack me,"
he said. And the churl loosed it.
The lion roared mightily with rage
on seeing its companion dead.
It charged straight at the knight
725 and struck him with such power

that his initial blow destroyed another
  shield.
The churl readied another
and encouraged him as best he could.
The lion rushed Sir Gawain again
730 and pressed him hard;
with its claws it ripped
his chain mail down to the ventail
and knocked aside another shield.
The churl gave him another.
735 Now Gawain clearly saw
and understood that it would be
  disaster
if the lion destroyed this last one.
With his trenchant sword Sir Gawain
struck it on the top of its head,
740 splitting its skull to the teeth,
and the lion slumped to the ground.
  "This lion's war is over,"
said Gawain; "it's made its peace.
Now by the faith you owe your Father,"
745 he added, "give me the bridle at once."
—"It won't be that simple, by St. Peter,"
said the churl, "there are further trials
you can't avoid, and I'll see the sleeve
of your hauberk soaked in blood first.
750 If you'll take my advice,
remove your armor and eat
until you've regained your strength."
But nothing could delay Sir Gawain.
  So the churl, who knew all
755 the secret passages, led him
through doors and across rooms
until he came right into the chamber
where the knight who'd been wounded
through his body was lying.
760 "Welcome, my lord Gawain,"
he said as soon as he saw him;
"Lady Fortune sent you here!
Since I am already healed,
and since you are very bold,
765 you must now do battle with me."
Because it could not be otherwise
Sir Gawain consented to the combat.
The other knight stood up at once
and armed himself to his liking.
770 But I have skipped over something
that I shouldn't have omitted,
and which needs to be told:
why the wounded knight got up.
There was a custom in this land:
775 when a knight from another land
came on behalf of the girl to seek

the bridle that was in the castle,
he had to do battle against him.
And if he defeated the challenger,
780 the latter would have gained nothing
except to have his head chopped off
and stuck upon one of the stakes
that surrounded the castle.
But if the opposite occurred,
785 if the challenger should defeat him,
another stake would be prepared
until another knight should come
and defeat him in battle.
  So they both put on their armor
790 and the churl brought
each of them a good warhorse;
they leapt into their saddles
without benefit of stirrup,
and each had a shield strapped on.
795 You are about to hear of their blows!
As soon as they were mounted,
the churl readied two stout lances
and gave one to each to start the battle.
They first took some distance,
800 then charged full speed at one another;
they struck such powerful blows
that both were nearly unhorsed.
Their lances split and shattered,
their saddlebacks crumpled,
805 and their stirrups broke;
not a strap was left unbroken,
because they couldn't take the shock.
They had no choice but to dismount.
As soon as they were on their feet
810 they resumed the attack, shields at the
  ready.
They tried to strike mightily,
and rained such blows on their shields
that the sparks flew;
they damaged the shields with their
  swords
815 so much that pieces fell off.
they fought the time it would take to
  cover
two leagues, but neither could win
a single foot of ground from the other.
Gawain was most chagrined
820 that he'd been delayed so long;
he struck his enemy so hard
that he smashed through
his helmet and cut its bands.
He was so stunned
825 that he fell toward the earth;
but Gawain clutched at the vassal

and seized him with such wrath
that it seemed he was about to kill him.
The knight shouted to him at once:
830 "Gawain, don't kill me!
I was a fool to challenge you,
but even this morning I thought
that there was no knight under heaven
who'd dare measure himself against me;
835 but you've defeated me in arms
and this redounds to your great glory.
I had intended to cut off
your head and stick it on this stake
that is still empty.
840 I've chopped off all the heads
that are displayed along this palisade
from knights who'd come
in here to do what you have done.
I planned to do the same with yours,
845 but there's no knight under heaven like you."
Gawain turned away and left him;
back in the room he removed his armor.
"Churl," said Gawain, "now think
what I can do to get the bridle."
850 —"Gawain," he replied, "do you want to know
what you have to do first?
You will have to fight
two nasty, evil dragons
that spout blood from their bodies
855 and fire from their mouths.
This armor you were wearing
won't help you a bit against them.
I'm going to bring you another suit
that is stronger and more durable.
860 In this castle are over four hundred
complete sets of strong triple-meshed hauberks
that once belonged to those knights
whose decapitated heads you see."
The churl quickly brought him
865 armor of several different types.
He handed him a complete suit
of strong armor to wear.
The Gawain said, "Go fetch
the devils you told me about."
870 ...[1]
he said, "Ere the hour of noon is past,
you'll have your hands full.
There is no man under heaven,
except me, who is bold enough
875 to challenge, or even look at them."

Gawain told him, "Don't worry!"
The churl then went down to unleash
the huge, ferocious dragons,
and ushered them from their den;
880 they were truly savage beasts,
and his shield was soon on fire
all over. Gawain attacked
one of them vigorously
and gave him such a sword blow—
885 as we find written in our source—
that he lopped off its head
and killed it on the spot.
There's not much more to tell you,
because ere the hour of noon was past
890 he had so dealt with the two of them
that both were dead and cut to pieces.
His face was somewhat befouled
with their blood and filth.
The churl retrieved the armor
895 in which Gawain had done combat.
Even before he had disarmed,
the little dwarf—the same one
who had first approached him
and hailed him beneath the overhang
900 but didn't deign speak further to him
and turned away—came up to him.
"Gawain," he said, "on behalf of my lady
I offer you my services,
but on the condition
905 that you dine first with her;
afterwards you may do whatever you please
with the bridle you've come seeking,
without any opposition whatsoever."
Gawain replied that he would go to her,
910 if the churl, whom he trusted
completely, could accompany him.
Hand in hand they went off together,
and the churl escorted him well:
after passing through many rooms
915 they came right to the chamber
where the lady who had sent
the dwarf to seek my lord Gawain
was reclining in a bed.
As soon as she saw him coming,
920 she moved toward him and said,
"Gawain, you are most welcome,
even though you have caused me
very great suffering and great loss
by killing all my wild beasts
925 you found in your path.
Nevertheless you must now
dine with me straightway.

          To be sure, I've never known
          a better or braver knight than you."
930   They both sat down upon the bed.
          And the bed where the lady and Gawain
          were sitting was not, it seems to me,
          constructed of willow or aspen,
          for the four bed-posts were all
935   of pure silver, plated with gold.
          Over it was spread a silk coverlet
          with circular motifs, worked with
          precious stones and many other riches.
          If I wanted to describe them all to you
940   it would take too much time and sweat,
          but it's not necessary to do so.
          She called for water to wash up,
          and the churl immediately brought them
          the golden basins and the towel
945   to dry their hands.
          Then the lady and my lord Gawain
          sat down to eat; the dwarf
          and the churl served them,
          as there were no other servants in the castle.
950   The lady was full of joy
          and made her guest feel very welcome.
          The maiden had him sit
          right next to herself, side by side,
          and eat from a precious platter
955   that she proudly offered him.
          I have nothing to add or tell you
          about what was served,
          but as soon as they had eaten
          and the table was taken away,
960   the lady requested water,
          which the churl brought immediately.
          Gawain, who felt he'd delayed too long,
          was eager to be on his way.
          So he asked the lady for the bridle,
965   since it was right that he have it.
          "My lord," she answered, "I place
          myself and all I have at your service.
          You have undertaken a very great task
          for my sister in this adventure.
970   Yes, she is my sister and I am hers,
          so I too must honor you.
          If it pleased you to remain
          in this castle, I would take you
          as my husband and give you this whole castle,
975   for I have thirty-eight more!"
         —"My lady," he replied, "please don't take offense,
          but upon my word I'm already late
          in returning to the King's court,
          for that is what I've sworn to do.
980   So give me without further delay
          the bridle that I've come to seek.
          I've tarried too long in this land;
          this is how it is: I must be off.
          Nevertheless, I'm grateful to you
985   for all the goodness you've shown me."
         —"Gawain," said she, "take the bridle;
          see, it's hanging there on that silver nail."
          He took it immediately
          and was truly overjoyed to have it.
990   The churl brought him the mule;
          Gawain put on the bridle and saddle
          and took leave of the maiden.
          She ordered the churl to lead
          my lord Gawain out of the castle
995   with no opposition whatever,
          and to see to it that the castle
          remain peaceful until he has left.
          My lord Gawain mounted up,
          happy to be on his way at last;
1000 the churl ordered all the castle
          to stay peaceful, which it did.
          Gawain rode through in safety,
          and after he'd crossed the drawbridge
          he looked back toward the castle
1005 and saw in the streets
          great crowds of people,
          who were all dancing
          and having such a merry time
          that, had God Himself ordered it,
1010 they couldn't have been merrier;
          they were all rejoicing together.
          The churl who'd accompanied him
          through the town was above the gateway,
          so Gawain asked him what it meant
1015 that when he'd entered the town
          he hadn't seen anyone at all, poor or rich,
          whereas now he beheld such rejoicing
          that they were vying with one another
          to see who could be the happiest.
1020 "My lord," he replied, "they were hiding
          in the cellars out of fear
          of the beasts you killed,
          which raised such a commotion
          when the people chanced to come forth
1025 for some reason or another

that there was no option
but to unleash them, whatever the risk,
and in their fury and rage
they tore everyone to pieces.
1030 Now they say among themselves:
through you God has delivered them
and has illumined in every way
those who had been living in darkness.
So overjoyed are they by what they see
1035 that they could not be happier."
You must know that this answer
truly pleased my lord Gawain.
    He set off at once along the trail
that led right to the great waters
1040 where the iron plank was,
and he crossed back over safely.
Afterwards he rode along
until he came to the valley
that was infested by reptiles.
1045 He crossed safely through
and entered the forest
haunted by the wild beasts.
As soon as they saw him,
they hurried up to escort him;
1050 they knelt down on the earth
and approached him confidently;
they kissed his feet and legs,
and kissed the mule as well.
Gawain hurried along
1055 and was soon out of the forest.
Ere long he was in the prairie
that stretched out before the castle.
    King Arthur and his Queen
had left the hall and gone for a stroll
1060 through the upper rooms,
accompanied by many knights
of their household.
Gawain suddenly appeared.
The Queen saw him first
1065 and pointed him out to the knights.
Knights and maidens
all hastened out to greet him.
The girl—the one for whom the bridle
was destined—was overjoyed
1070 when she heard the news
that my lord Gawain was approaching.
    My lord Gawain drew near
and the girl went to greet him:
"My lord," said she, "May God grant
    you
1075 good fortune, and all the happiness
there is, both day and night."
    —"The best of fortune to you, too,"

he said as he placed his foot in the silver
    stirrup
and climbed down from the mule.
1080 The maiden took him in her arms
and kissed him more than a hundred
    times.
"My lord," she said, "it is right
for me to offer myself freely
and entirely to your service,
1085 for I know that no one else I could have
sent to the castle would have
gotten it back for me,
for many a knight has died
and lost his head,
1090 who couldn't get it back."
Then Gawain described for her
all the adventures he'd encountered:
the deep valley and the woods,
and the fountain in its thicket,
1095 and the black waters,
and the revolving castle,
and the two lions he slew,
and the knight he defeated,
and his promise to the churl,
1100 and the battle with the dragons,
and the dwarf who greeted him
but deigned say no more,
and how he returned afterwards,
and how he had to dine
1105 in the chamber of the girl
who was the maiden's sister,
and how the bridle was given him,
and when he'd left the castle
how he had seen everyone
1110 dancing through the streets,
and how he'd come through
without opposition or difficulty.
    After Gawain had narrated all this,
and the maiden had taken leave
1015 of the barons of the court,
Queen Guinevere hurried up to her,
and the King and his knights
all went to urge her
to stay there at court with them
1120 and to love one of
the Knights of the Round Table.
"Sire, may God confound me
if I wouldn't want to stay here,"
she replied, "if only I dared—
1125 but I couldn't do it for any price."
She asked for her mule; it was brought
    to her
and she mounted by the stirrup.

	The King himself offered to accompany her,		She took leave and departed,
	but she said she hoped it didn't offend them		urging her mule to an ambling pace.
1130	but she didn't care for any escort;	1135	Here ends the adventure of the girl with the mule,
	besides, it was getting late.		who rode off all alone.

Note

1. Lack of a rhyme word indicates a line missing at this point. Little or no content appears to be lacking.

Selected Bibliography

This bibliography includes only works written in English that are accessible to both the undergraduate and non-specialist general reader. Most are books. The journal articles cited are readily obtained. The only anthologies included are ones that include extensive contextual and introductory materials. Arthurian scholarship pertaining to authors not covered in this anthology, such as Thomas Malory, is not included. Older works whose reach and influence have not fallen out of date are included, but the emphasis is on scholarship published during the last three decades or so. A number of works that deal with the Arthurian presence in contemporary popular culture are listed.

Adams, Alison, et al., eds. *The Changing Face of Arthurian Romance: Essays on Arthurian Prose Romances in Memory of Cedric E. Pickford*. Cambridge: D.S. Brewer, 1980.

Alamichel, Marie-Françoise. "King Arthur's Dual Personality in Layamon's *Brut*." *Neophilologus* 77.2 (April 1993): 303–19.

Alcock, Leslie. *Arthur's Britain*. Harmondsworth, Middlesex: Penguin, 1971.

Arberth, John. *A Knight at the Movies: Medieval History on Film*. New York: Routledge, 2003.

Ashe, Geoffrey. "A Certain Very Ancient British Book." *Speculum* 56 (1981): 301–323.

———. "The Origins of the Arthurian Legend." *Arthuriana* 5.3 (Fall 1995): 1–24.

Barber, Richard. *Arthur of Albion, an Introduction to the Arthurian Literature and Legends of England*. London, 1971.

———. *King Arthur: Hero and Legend*. Woodbridge: Boydell and Brewer, 1986.

Barron, W.R.J. *English Medieval Romance*. London: Longman, 1987.

Baswell, Christopher, and William Sharpe, eds. *The Passing of Arthur: New Essays in Arthurian Tradition*. New York: Garland, 1988.

Bell, Kimberly. "Merlin as Historian in *Historia Regum Britanniae*." *Arthuriana* 10.1 (Spring 2000): 14–26.

Bloom, Harold, ed. *King Arthur*. Philadelphia: Chelsea House, 2003.

Braswell, Mary Flowers, and John Bugge, eds. *The Arthurian Tradition: Essays in Convergence*. Tuscaloosa: University of Alabama Press, 1988.

Bromwich, Rachel, ed. *The Arthur of the Welsh*. Cardiff: University of Wales Press, 1991.

Chambers, E.K. *Arthur of Britain*. London: October House, 1967 (1927).

Coe, John B., and Simon Young. *The Celtic Sources for the Arthurian Legend*. Felinfach: Llanerch, 1995.

Davidson, H. E. *Myths and Symbols in Pagan Europe*. Manchester: Manchester University Press, 1988.

Dean, Christopher. *Arthur of England: English Attitudes to King Arthur and the Knights of the Round Table in the Middle Ages and the Renaissance*. Toronto: University of Toronto Press, 1987.

De Looze, Laurence N. "A Story of Interpretations: The *Queste del Saint Graal* as Metaliterature." *Romanic Review* 76.2 (1985): 129–147.

Donahue, Dennis P. "The Darkly Chronicled King: An Interpretation of the Negative Side of Arthur in Lawman's *Brut* and Geoffrey of Monmouth's *Historia regum Brittannie*." *Arthuriana* 8.4 (Winter 1998):135–47.

Everett, D. "Layamon and the Earliest Middle English Alliterative Verse." In *Essays on Middle English Literature*, edited by D. Everett, 28–45. Oxford: Oxford University Press, 1955.

Falsani, Teresa Boyle. "Parke Godwin's Guenevere: An Archetypal Transformation." *Quondam et Futurus: A Journal of Arthurian Interpretations* 3.3 (1993): 55–65.

Fenster, Thelma S. *Arthurian Women: A Casebook*. New York: Garland, 1996.

Gallix, François. "T. H. White and the Legend of King Arthur: From Animal Fantasy to Political Morality." In *King Arthur: A Casebook*, edited by Edward Donald Kennedy, 281–311. New York: Garland, 1996.

Goodman, Jennifer R. *The Legend of Arthur in British and American Literature*. Boston: Twayne, 1987.

Green, M. J. *Celtic Myths*. Austin: University of Texas Press, 1993.

———. *Dictionary of Celtic Myth and Legend*. London: Thames and Hudson, 1992.
Hanning, Robert W. *The Vision of History in Early Britain from Gildas to Geoffrey of Monmouth*. New York: Columbia University Press, 1966.
Harty, Kevin J. *King Arthur on Film: New Essays on Arthurian Cinema*. Jefferson, NC: McFarland, 1999.
Higham, N J. *King Arthur: Myth-Making and History*. London: Routledge, 2002.
Jones, Gwyn. *Kings, Beasts, and Heroes*. London: Oxford University Press, 1972.
Kennedy, Edward Donald, ed. *King Arthur: A Casebook*. New York: Garland, 1996.
Lacy, Norris, and R. Thompson. *The Lancelot-Grail Reader*. New York: Routledge, 2000.
———. *The New Arthurian Encyclopedia*. New York: Garland, 1992.
Lagorio, Valerie M., and Mildred Leake Day, eds. *King Arthur Through the Ages*. 2 vols. New York: Garland, 1988.
Locke, F.W. *The Quest for the Holy Graal: A Literary Study of a Thirteenth-Century French Romance*. Stanford: Stanford University Press, 1960.
Loomis, R.S. *Arthurian Tradition and Chrétien de Troyes*. New York: Columbia University Press, 1932.
———. *The Development of Arthurian Romance*. New York: Dover, 2000 (1964).
———. "Geoffrey of Monmouth and Arthurian Origins." *Speculum* 3 (1929): 16–33.
———. *Wales and the Arthurian Legend*. Cardiff: University of Wales Press, 1956.
———, ed. *Arthurian Literature in the Middle Ages*. Oxford: Oxford University Press, 1959.
Lupack, Alan. "The Once and Future King: The Book That Grows Up." *Arthuriana* 11.3 (2001): 103–14.
———, ed. *New Directions in Arthurian Studies*. Cambridge: D.S. Brewer, 2002.
MacCana, P. *Celtic Mythology*. London: Thames and Hudson, 1968.
MacKillop, J. *Dictionary of Celtic Mythology*. Oxford: Oxford University Press, 1998.
Mahoney, Dhira B., ed. *The Grail: A Casebook*. New York: Garland, 2000.
Mancoff, Debra N. *The Arthurian Revival: Essays on Form, Tradition, and Transformation*. New York: Garland, 1992.
———. *The Return of King Arthur: The Legend Through Victorian Eyes*. New York, Abrams, 1995.
Matarasso, Pauline. *The Redemption of Chivalry*. Genève: Droz, 1979.
McCracken, Peggy. "Mothers in the Grail Quest: Desire, Pleasure, and Conception." *Arthuriana* 8.1(1998): 35–48.
———. "The Poetics of Sacrifice: Allegory and Myth in the Grail Quest." *Yale French Studies* 9 (1999): 152–68.

Moorman, Charles. "King Arthur and the English National Character." *New York Folklore Quarterly* 24 (1968): 103–112.
———, and Ruth Moorman. *An Arthurian Dictionary*. Jackson: University Press of Mississippi, 1978.
Morris, Rosemary. *The Character of King Arthur in Medieval Literature*. Cambridge: D.S. Brewer, 1982.
Nastali, Dan. "Arthur Without Fantasy: Dark Age Britain in Recent Historical Fiction." *Arthuriana* 9.1 (1999): 5–22.
Owen D.D.R. *Arthurian Romance: Seven Essays*. New York: Barnes and Noble, 1973.
Padel, O.J. *Arthur in Medieval Welsh Literature*. Cardiff: University of Wales Press, 2000.
———. "The Nature of Arthur." *Cambrian Medieval and Celtic Studies* 27 (1994): 1–31.
———. "Recent Work on the Origins of the Arthurian Legend." *Arthuriana* 5.3 (Fall 1995): 103–14.
Pearsall, Derek. *Arthurian Romance: A Short Introduction*. Oxford: Blackwell, 2003.
Piggott, S. *The Druids*. London: Thames and Hudson, 1968.
Pors, Mette, ed. *The Vitality of the Arthurian Legend: A Symposium*. Odense: Odense University Press, 1988.
Shichtmann, Martin, and James P. Carley, eds. *Culture and the King: The Social Implications of the Arthurian Legend*. Albany: State University of New York Press, 1994.
Sjoestedt, M.-L. *Gods and Heroes of the Celts*. Berkeley: University of California Press, 1982.
Sklar, Judith. "Thoroughly Modern Morgan: Morgan le Fay in Twentieth-Century Popular Arthuriana." In *Popular Arthurian Tradition*, edited by Sally K. Slocum, 24–35. Bowling Green, OH: Bowling Green State University Popular Press, 1992.
Slocum, Sally K., ed. *Popular Arthurian Traditions*. Bowling Green, OH: Bowling Green State University Popular Press, 1992.
Southern, R. W. *The Making of the Middle Ages*. New Haven: Yale University Press, 1953.
Stevens, John. *Medieval Romance: Themes and Approaches*. London: Hutchinson, 1973.
Tatlock, J.S.P. *The Legendary History of Britain: Geoffrey's Historia and its Early Vernacular Versions*. Berkeley: University of California Press, 1950.
Thompson, Raymond H. *Return from Avalon: A Study of the Arthurian Legend in Modern Science Fiction*. Westport, CT: Greenwood, 1985.
Traxler, Janina P. "Dying to Get to Sarras: Perceval's Sister and the Grail Quest." *The Grail: A Casebook*, edited by Dhira B. Mahoney, 261–78. New York: Garland, 2000.
Vinaver, Eugene. *Form and Meaning in Medieval Romance*. Leeds: Maney, 1966.
———. *The Rise of Romance*. Oxford: Clarendon, 1971.

Waite, Arthur Edward. *The Holy Grail; The Galahad Quest in Arthurian Literature.* New Hyde Park, NY: University Books, 1961.

Walters, Lori J., ed. *Lancelot and Guinevere: A Casebook.* New York: Garland, 1996.

Wheeler, Bonnie, and Fiona Tolhurst, eds. *On Arthurian Women: Essays in Memory of Maureen Fries.* Dallas: Scriptorium, 2001.

Williams, Andrea M. L. "The Enchanted Swords and the Quest for the Holy Grail: Metaphoric Structure in *La Queste del Saint Graal*." *French Studies* 48.4 (1994): 385–401.

Wilson, Anne. *The Magical Quest: The Use of Magic in Arthurian Romance.* Manchester: Manchester University Press, 1988.

Zatta, Jane. "Translating the *Historia*: The Ideological Transformation of the *Historia regum Britannie* in Twelfth-Century Vernacular Chronicles." *Arthuriana* 8.4 (1998): 148–61.

About the Contributors

Craig **Davis** teaches Old and Middle English, Old Norse, and Medieval Celtic languages and literatures at Smith College in Northampton, Massachusetts. He is the author of *"Beowulf" and the Demise of Germanic Legend in England* (Garland, 1996). He has also written on Celtic Britain and Anglo-Saxon England for the *Oxford Dictionary of the Middle Ages* as well as articles on the Anglo-Saxon royal genealogies, the Old English Battle of Maldon, Chaucer's *Canterbury Tales*, Malory's *Morte Darthur* and the Welsh origins of the Arthurian legend.

William W. **Kibler** is retired from the University of Texas at Austin, where he taught medieval French language and literature for more than 35 years. He has translated many works from medieval French into modern English and French, including *Chrétien de Troyes, Arthurian Romances* (Penguin, 1991). He has also edited many Old French texts, written an *Introduction to Old French* (MLA, 1984) and published numerous articles on medieval literature.

Douglas **McFarland** holds a Ph. D. from the University of California, Berkeley, and is a professor of English literature and classical studies at Flagler College in Saint Augustine, Florida. He has published on Spenser, Rabelais and Montaigne as well as numerous articles in film studies. He is editing a volume on the film adaptations of John Huston.

R. Barton **Palmer** is the Calhoun Lemon Professor of Literature and director of film studies at Clemson University. Among his many publications in the field of medieval literature are several anthologies designed for classroom use. He is a co-director of a collaborative project devoted to the poetry and music of the late medieval poet Guillaume de Machaut. The first of a planned thirteen volumes is scheduled to appear in 2014.

Index

Adam 183, 206, 254, 259–260
The Aeneid 1, 31
Alain of Escavalon 221
Alclud 9–10, 15
Alexander the Great 1
Allobroges 16, 18, 28
Angevin Dynasty 25, 28, 30, 45, 51
Anjou 13–14, 31, 42
The Annales Cambriae 5, 71
Ariosto, Ludovico 1
Arsley Kings 50–51
Arthur, King 1, 4–6, 13, 18, 27–28, 30, 57–60, 64, 67, 99, 102, 104, 108, 110, 113, 123, 127–128, 140–142, 150, 163, 172, 182–183, 188–190, 192, 196–204, 206, 220–221, 223, 225, 233, 242, 245, 252, 257, 267, 271, 273, 275, 283, 285–286
Asaph, St. 4
Aschil 14, 23, 25, 29, 42
Auguselus, King of Albany 11–12, 14, 17, 23, 28
Aurelianus, Ambrosius 70–71, 74
Aurelius 52, 57, 62
Autun 20, 23–24, 32, 40–41, 43

Bald Maiden 205–206, 217
Baldulf 8, 10
Ban, King of Benoic 216
Barron, W.R.J. 52, 285
Bath 9, 14, 23, 26, 42, 46, 64–67
Battle of Hastings 30
Bede, St. 51
Bedevere 13–15, 19–20, 22–23, 25, 27
Bedwyr 76, 79, 81–83, 85, 90–93, 95–96
The Black Book of Carmarthen 72
The Black Hermit 206
The Black Knight 195, 202–203
Blackbird of Cilgwri 91
Boccus 18, 25, 45–46
Bodel, Jean 1
Book of Judges 5
Book of Taliesin 72, 80
Boso of Rydychen 14, 20–23, 25
British Library 51
Brittany 4, 8, 11, 47, 52, 56–57, 61, 71, 80, 94–95, 97
Bron 194
Budicius 8

Cador 8, 10, 12, 14, 16, 22–23, 29, 38, 42, 59

Caen, City of 31
Caesar, Julius 1, 4, 16
Cahus 195, 197
Caledon Forest 9
Camblam (river) 29
Camelot 72, 195, 203, 216, 235, 271
Camelot (play) 235
Carduel 196–197, 204–205, 220–221, 223
Carolingian Era 1
Carucius, Quintus 18, 22, 25
Cassibellaunus 29
Castle of Inquiry 205–206
Catellus, Lucius 25, 38, 40
Catellus, Vulteius 22–23
The Cauldron of Diwrnach 87, 95
Cei 76, 78–79, 81–84, 90–93
Celliwig 72–73, 81–82, 93–94, 97
Chanson de geste 1, 31
La Chanson de Roland 30
Chapel of St. Augustine 195, 198, 200
Charlemagne 1, 30
Chartres 14, 18, 20–21, 23, 34, 38, 42
Cheldric 8, 10, 28
Chinon 27, 42, 49
The City of Legions 7, 9, 14, 28
Clamados 213
Claudas, King 267
Claudins, Prince 267
Cligès 99
Colgrin 7–8, 10
Constantine 17, 29, 52, 55, 57, 62
Corbenyc 241–242
Cornwall 8, 10, 14–16, 22–23, 25, 28–29, 39, 42, 52, 59, 71–73, 78 80–82, 93–94, 97
The Cowardly Knight 207, 218–219
Crudel 243–245
Culhwch 70–73, 75–77, 79, 81, 83–89, 91, 93, 95, 97–98
Cumbria 71
Custennin the Shepherd 84–85, 90, 97–98
Cyddelig the Guide 83

Dandrane 195, 217
David 15, 236, 238, 245
De Excidio Britanniae 5, 70–71
de Boron, Robert 194, 235–236
de France, Marie 31, 50
de Gaunes, Bors 238
de Maisières, Païen 272

de Mayence, Doon 1
de Sainte-Maure, Benoît 31
de Troyes, Chrétien 2, 31, 99–194, 276, 286, 289
Dillus the Bearded 88, 93
Doldavius, King 12, 14
The Dragon Knight 220–221, 223–225
Dubricius 7, 9, 14–15
Dyabiaus 242

Edward I 70
Eleanor of Aquitaine 31, 51, 235
Elyezer 264–265
Erec and Enide 99
Escorant 269
Estoire de Lancelot 235
Estoire de Merlin 235
Estoire del Saint Graat 235
Estoire des Engles 31
Evalach 244
Evander 18, 22–23, 38–40

The Faerie Queene 7
France 1, 31–34, 42, 50, 61, 80–81, 89, 95–96
Frollo 12–13

Gaimar, Geffrei 31, 52
Galahad 235–237, 242, 245, 261–262, 271, 287
Gawain 1, 6, 12, 20–21, 23, 26, 28, 32–37, 42, 46–47, 141, 144–163, 166–194, 205–211, 215–217, 219–223, 228, 232–234, 272–273, 275–283
Gay the Fat 195
Genesis, Book of 51, 71, 271
Geoffrey of Monmouth 1, 4–31, 285–286
Gerin of Chartres 14, 18, 21, 23, 25, 32, 34–35, 38, 42
Gildas 5, 70–71, 74, 80, 286
Gilmaurius 12
Gilmour 11
Glamorganshire 14
Glewlwyd 72–73, 75 78–79, 96
Gorlois 52
Gorre 263
Gotland 12, 14, 18
Grail Castle 99, 194–195, 205, 211, 229
Great Britain 1, 4–8, 12–18, 23–24, 28–29, 42, 49, 51, 58, 61, 64–65, 70–74, 81–82, 87, 91, 94–95, 97–

291

98, 194–196, 204, 231, 235, 292, 257, 285–286, 289
Guinevere 1, 5–6, 99, 285
Guitard 13–14, 22–23
Gunhpuar 12
Gurguran 205
Gwalchmei, Son of Gwyar 82–83
Gwrhyr, Interpreter of Tongues 79, 82–84, 90–92, 95

Hanning, Robert 6, 286
Harold 30
Hengest and Hora 52–55, 58, 67
Henry II 30–31, 51, 235
The Hermit King 210, 213–214, 216, 226
Hiberius, Lucius 15, 18, 20, 23–24, 27
Hibernia 11–12, 18, 28
Historia Regum Britanniae 1, 4, 31, 285, 287
The History of the English Church 51
Hoel, King 8–11, 13–15, 17–20, 23, 26, 28, 42, 46–47
Hostiensis, Lelius 25
Hyrelgas 23, 25, 45

Iglai 195
Île de France 31
Île de la Cité 31
Island of Avalon 10, 29, 65, 104, 148, 154, 196, 221, 286
Island of Jersey 30

Jerusalem 195, 244
Joseph d'Arimathie 235
Joseph of Arimathea 194–195, 231, 239, 243, 263, 266, 270
Josephus 195–196, 199, 206–207, 218, 223–226, 231–232, 239–240, 243–245, 265–266, 269–270
Julian the Fat 195, 203, 216
Julius the Martyr 14, 28

Kaerluideoit 8
Kay, Sir 13–15, 19, 23, 25, 27–28, 42, 44–45, 49, 109–112, 123, 127–129, 140–141, 143–146, 272–276
The King of Deadly Castle 195, 211, 217, 229–230
The Knight with the Golden Circle 225
Die Krone 272

Lais 50
Lancelot (The Knight of the Cart) 99
Lawman 2, 50–67, 285
Leo, Emperor of the Romans 28
Lerner, Alan J. 235
Libran, King 242
Limenich, Cador 29
Lincoln 9, 11, 61–63
Lindsey 9
Livy 5
Loch Lomond 11
Loewe, Frederick 235

Longinus 194, 236
Lord of Tides 203
Loth 11–12, 14, 23, 42, 53–54
Lucifer 206

Mabon, Son of Modron 75–76, 88, 91–92, 94, 97
The Maimed King 194, 241, 262, 266–268
Malory, Thomas 235, 285, 289
Map, Walter 235–236, 271
Margaret, St. 31
Matter of Britain 1
Matter of France 1
Matter of Rome 1
Menw, Son of Teirgwaedd 80, 83, 85, 94, 97
Merlin 4, 52–53, 235–236, 240, 283
Merlin (book) 235
Mirabilia Britanniae 71
Moray 10–12, 14, 65
Mordrain, King 244–245, 249
Mordred 5, 6, 12, 18, 28–29, 71, 235
Mort le Roi Artu 235
Le Morte d'Arthur 235
Morvid 23, 27, 41, 49
La Mule sans Frein (The Girl with the Mule) 2, 272–283
Muteus, Marcellus 21

The Needle Bridge 208
Nennius 5, 71
Neustria 13, 25, 39
Nicholas, St. 31
Normandy 13–14, 30–32, 49, 64, 95
Norway 12, 24, 42, 126, 166, 171

Odbrict, King of Norway 29
Old English Alliterative Poetry 50, 285
Olwen 71–73, 76–77, 79, 83–85, 98
The Once and Future King 235, 286
Orkneys 12, 14, 18
Orlando Furioso 1
Oxford 4, 14, 20–21, 23, 28, 32, 37, 194, 234, 285–287, 289

Pa Gwr yw y Porthawr? (What Man Guards the Gate?) 72, 75
Pandrasus 18, 25
Pauphilet, Albert 237
Pelles, King of the Lowly People 195, 213–214, 229, 231, 242, 264–265
Pendragon: Sword of His Father (2008) 1
Perceval (The Story of the Grail) 1–2, 94–195, 213, 219, 232, 235–238, 241–243, 245–264, 266, 268–271, 286
Perilous Siege 240
Perlesvaus 2, 99, 194–234, 272
Petreius 21–22, 36–38
Phillip of Flanders 99
Picts 8–11, 13, 28–29, 52, 58
Piramus 11

Politetes 18, 25, 27
Pontius Pilate 195
Preiddeu Annwn (The Spoils of Annwn) 72, 74
Prophecies of Merlin 4

Queen of Maidens 217
Queen of the Golden Circle 221, 223, 225
Queen of the Wasteland 238
Le Queste del Saint Graal (Quest of the Holy Grail) 2, 235–271, 285, 287

The Red Book of Hergest 72
The Red Knight 109–112, 126, 140–141, 204, 213
Renaissance Era 1, 30, 285
Rhymhi 82, 88, 92
Rich Fisher 165, 194, 216
Riculf, King 12
Roman de Brut 2, 30–51
Roman de Rou 30
Roman de Troie 31
The Round Table 1, 99, 182, 196, 204, 240–242, 245, 257, 263, 267, 283, 285

Sabrina Sea 11, 14
Salisbury 14, 26, 271
Sarraz 244, 265–266, 268, 271
Scotland 8–12, 14, 25, 28–29, 42, 54–55, 58, 60–61, 65, 71
Serses 18, 25
Sertorius 18, 22, 25, 27, 45, 48
Shakespeare, William 6
Silchester 7, 15, 57
Silvanus, Mauricius 25
Simeon 245, 263
Sir Gawain and the Green Knight 272
Snowdonia 52
Southern, R.W. 7, 286
Spenser, Edmund 7, 235, 289
Statius 1
Subuculus, Sulpicius 25
Sulpicius, Pope 12, 25

Tennyson, Alfred 235
Teucer 18, 25
Thanet 10
Thebaid 1
Tholomers 244
Tintagel 23, 39, 47, 52–53, 149
Trojan Brutus 4

Urian 11–12, 14, 28
Usk (river) 14
Uther, King 7, 52–58, 61–63, 65, 201
Utherpendragon 5, 7, 104, 188

Venedotia 15, 70
Virgil 1, 31, 223
von dem Turlin, Heinrich 272
Vortigern, King 4, 28, 52, 71
Vulgate Cycle 235–236

Wace, Robert 2, 30–52

Wales 4, 11, 46, 70–97, 104, 127, 142, 196, 250, 285–260
Walter of Oxford 28
Weinberg, S.C. 52
Weiss, Judith 32
Westminster Abbey 30
White, T.H. 235, 285

White Book of Rhydderch 72
Winchester 28–29, 55
Worcester 14, 50
Wrnach the Giant 89–91

Ygerne 52–53
York 8, 11, 14, 28, 53, 58–60

Ysbaddaden, Chief of Giants 72–73, 77, 79, 84–86, 93–94, 98
Yvain (The Knight with the Lion) 99
Ywain, Son of Urian 23